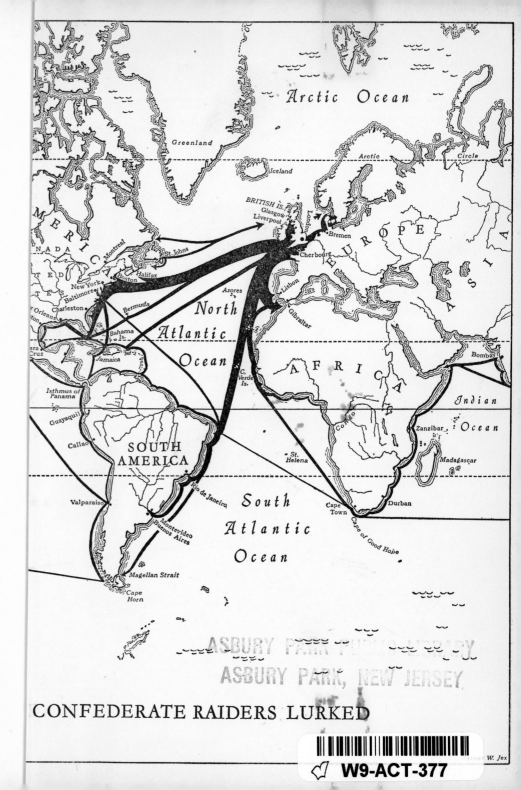

CONFEDERATE RAIDERS LURKED

W. Jex

W9-ACT-377

★ THE CIVIL WAR AT SE

★ *Volume III*

THE CIVIL WAR
AT SEA

JULY 1863 ★ NOVEMBER 1865

★ THE FINAL EFFORT

by Virgil Carrington Jones

FOREWORD BY ADMIRAL E. M. ELLER
DIRECTOR OF NAVAL HISTORY

illustrated with maps and photographs

HOLT ★ RINEHART ★ WINSTON
New York   Chicago   San Francisco

FIRST EDITION

Library of Congress Catalog Card Number: 60–14457

84728–0512
Printed in the United States of America

★ *Foreword*

No book could start more graphically than Pat Jones's concluding volume of the ceaseless and overwhelming influence of sea-based power in the Civil War. The heroic attack on and defense of Fort Wagner is one of the most bitterly fought combined operations of history. In many respects, Fort Wagner reminds one of Tarawa and Iwo Jima of World War II—each a desperately defended island that required the utmost effort of each element of strength the United States possessed in its military power.

This effective use of total power in combined operations is fundamental in the true concept of seapower's meaning to a nation. While strength afloat can achieve many useful things of itself, a mighty virtue indeed is the added capability it gives of concentrating a nation's total power at the point of decision.

Dahlgren had a strong fleet, including ironclads that could take an incredible amount of punishment and in turn deliver knockout punches from guns that fired some of the largest projectiles in the history of modern gunnery. Yet even these paladin, well led and well fought, could not have overcome this fort without the army—the artillery, the engineers, the quartermasters, and above all the brave infantrymen who time after time stormed gallantly defended Wagner.

On the other hand, the stay of the army on Morris Island under Fort Wagner would have been brief indeed without the Navy. The troops needed the big guns to create havoc in the fort in continuous fire support that shocked and destroyed the Confederates. They needed its boats, its control of the water that insured the flow of the tide of supplies and reinforcements fighting men must have. They needed these mobile forts coursing the waters to prevent Confederate flanking attack and to cut off reinforcements and supplies to the courageous defenders of Wagner. They needed all of this strength, added to their own courage and resolution, to overcome one of the most ably defended forts in the history of man's eternal struggles.

This gripping and stirring chapter in a sense is the climax of the final years of the war. Pat Jones follows this fine chapter with many other well-told events in which the South fought with remarkable ingenuity, skill, and fortitude, afloat and ashore. Interesting chapters cover both the pilot waters of Dixie and range afar to such unlikely regions as the Great Lakes and the remote Arctic Seas.

Yet despite the great outpouring of strength from the minds and hearts of Southerners, the North's effective use of total power, ably directed and courageously executed, assured victory. Given similar leadership, skill, and courage, superiority in numbers and resources inevitably weighs the balance. Indeed, just as the battles of Fort Wagner and Fort Fisher (likewise brilliantly recounted) have counterparts in World War II, so has this wise use of total power continued to this day as the key to victory.

America has vast potentials of strength in the soul, in the mind, in the machine, in the fruitful land and in her blessed heritage of the sea. When she effectively combines these with integrity and purpose, she is invincible.

May Pat Jones's stirring trilogy of *The Civil War at Sea* help to make Americans aware of the incalculable benefits the sea has brought to this nation's history. May it cause them to realize that only by combining strength at sea with other strength, and remaining true to her charge of liberty, can she achieve the grand goal of leading mankind into freedom.

—E. M. Eller
Rear Admiral, USN (Ret.)
Director of Naval History

★ *Preface*

After six years of research and writing, here is my story of the naval side of the Civil War. It is no encyclopedia. I set out to prepare a good, readable account, one that is accurate and yet not loaded down with statistics and smaller details of interest only to the student or expert. I have written with the average reader in mind as my audience.

Haunting me throughout my labor have been the so-called "professionals." I have found as I worked that these individuals make up an element that gives no quarter, grants no mercy. With this occasional digging by the "overlords" as a backdrop, I have written, openly encouraged by the "legitimate" naval authorities who have ridden herd on every word of my manuscript.

The Navy's part in the Civil War has been ignored, the so-called "professional" writers on the subject to the contrary notwithstanding. I have tried to tell it without bias, and in language not too heavily dipped in the brine of the sea.

The most common fault with naval literature, I found as I went about my research, is that it is caged in terms that are too naval. These, to the Navy student, are a part of the catechism, to be rolled on the tongue and loved, and to be injected into everyday conversation. To the average reader, the man who takes the Navy as the complement of the Army and who gets seasick at the roll of an R, they are objectionable. He gets the feeling that the Navy has a chip on its shoulder, that it is trying to sell itself to the public and striving to get credit for the job it is doing. This very definitely should not be the case.

'Tis true the man on the ship did not slog through the mud and briefly pause at the homesteads on the beaten paths followed by the Civil War buffs a century later. That was not his good fortune, and by circumstance it could not have been. His assignment was of a different nature. The call made upon him took him elsewhere, denied him the intimacies of social intercourse.

Whereas on land the warrior faced an enemy, he of the sea faced two enemies—the foe of a different conviction and the foe generally identified as Boredom. There is no grasp of the hand, no bewitching eye, no inviting smile on the crest of a wave. Fate has made it that way. The soldier fought his battles and between times looked to the countryside—to the fair damsels and the everyday entertainment—for diversion. The seaman fought, and then whiled away his time wondering how soon he would be able to get back on land.

There are myriads of people, virtual strangers as well as friends, I should thank for the help they have given me in the preparation of this trilogy. I wish it were possible for me to grasp each of them by the hand and to express anew the thanks which surge up from my heart. At least that, or to put their names on every village green. But the impossible is impossible, and the human being can be extended only so far.

A few, however, I must mention. Rear Admiral E. M. Eller, Director of Naval History, has been a constant influence and has watched over me like a father. So has Rear Admiral John D. Hayes, USN (Ret.), of Annapolis, Maryland, a gentleman other naval experts say carries more knowledge of the Navy's history in his head than anyone else alive. And so has William Henry Davis, of Jackson Heights, New York, an attorney whose avocation has made of him an authority on the Confederate Navy. These gentlemen have gone beyond the call of duty in their efforts to help me make the telling worth while. I am grateful also to Mrs. Irene McKay, of Cleveland, Ohio, who spent her Saturdays and Sundays copying journals in longhand, to make sure I got a better account of the Johnson's Island expeditions.

I do thank these I have named, as well as all the others, and I hope the trilogy in itself may be of such a nature that they will gain personal satisfaction from the realization that it is actually in existence and that they had a part in bringing it about.

Finally, my hat is off to the Navies of both sides. Their individual efforts can only be praised. No Navy with the facilities it had at hand ever fought more gallantly than did the skeleton force under Secretary Mallory. It was a Navy that seldom, if ever, had need to use the terms fleet and squadron and armada. History gives no better example of individual bravery than that set by its heroes. And no Navy ever did a more thorough job than did Gideon Welles's gunboats as they beat their way up the sluggish Southern rivers, or patrolled day and night the important waterways, tightening a blockade that could not help but choke the life out of a Confederacy with virtually no navy.

The story these two vastly different naval powers left could not fail to draw the interest and admiration of even a landlubber like me. I know I have broadened my education since I started work on this trilogy, for the great amount of research alone was enough to make me absorb the Navy's side of the picture. In view of what I have learned, I say without reservation that until the sea activity has been studied, the follower of the Civil War cannot understand this great conflict in its entirety.

—V.C.J.

Centreville, Virginia

CONTENTS

CONTENTS

Dramatis Personae

ABLES, JAMES—Confederate seaman assigned to the David.

ALDEN, JAMES—Commander of the U.S.S. *Brooklyn.*

ALEXANDER, WILLIAM A.—Confederate surgeon who aided in constructing the submarine *H. L. Hunley.*

AMMEN, DANIEL—Commander of the U.S.S. *Mohican.*

ARCHER, J. J.—Confederate general.

BAILEY, JOSEPH—Union Army officer who directed building of the Red River dam.

BAILEY, THEODORUS—Union commander of the East Gulf Blockading Squadron (EGBS).

BALCH, GEORGE B.—Commander of the U.S.S. *Pawnee.*

BALL, W. B.—Confederate officer on the Johnson's Island expedition.

BANKS, NATHANIEL P.—Union general commanding the Department of the Gulf.

BARNEY, JOSEPH NICHOLSON—Confederate naval officer.

BARRETT, G. W.—Commander of the U.S.S. *Whitehead.*

BARRON, SAMUEL—Senior Confederate naval officer in the European theater.

BEALL, JOHN YATES—Confederate soldier, guerrilla leader, and acting master in the Navy.

BEAUREGARD, PIERRE G. T.—Confederate general.

BEHM, CHARLES F. W.—Commander of the U.S.S. *Southfield.*

BELL, HENRY H.—Union commander of the West Gulf Blockading Squadron (WGBS).

BIRTWISTLE, JAMES—Acting ensign on the U.S.S. *Minnesota.*

BOYD, BELLE—Confederate spy.

xv

BRADFORD, OTEY—Confederate officer on the Johnson's Island expedition.

BRAGG, BRAXTON—Confederate general.

BUCHANAN, FRANKLIN—Confederate naval officer.

BUCK, CHARLES W.—Executive officer of the U.S.S. *Water Witch*.

BULLOCH, JAMES DUNWODY—Confederate purchasing agent in Europe.

BUTLER, BENJAMIN FRANKLIN—Union general.

BUTT, WALTER—Confederate naval officer.

CANBY, EDWARD—Union general.

CANNON, WALKER—Assistant pilot of the C.S.S. *Palmetto State*.

CARLIN, JAMES—British naval officer fighting for the Confederacy.

CASE, A. LUDLOW—Captain of the U.S.S. *Iroquois*.

CHATFIELD, JOHN L.—Union colonel.

CHEVES, LANGDON—Confederate engineer officer.

CHEW, FRANCIS T.—Lieutenant on board the C.S.S. *Shenandoah*.

CILLEY, GREENLEAF—Officer on board the U.S.S. *Catskill*.

CLAY, CLEMENT CLAIBORNE—Confederate agent in Canada.

COLE, CHARLES H.—Former Confederate cavalryman aiding with the Johnson's Island expedition.

COLLINS, JOHN—Pilot of the U.S.S. *Tecumseh*.

COLLINS, NAPOLEON—Commander of the U.S.S. *Wachusett*.

CONRAD, DANIEL B.—Surgeon of Admiral Farragut's fleet.

COOKE, JAMES W.—Confederate naval officer assigned to superintend construction of the C.S.S. *Albemarle*.

COOPER, SAMUEL—Confederate Adjutant General.

CRAVEN, TUNIS AUGUSTUS M.—Commander of the U.S.S. *Tecumseh*.

CROCKER, FREDERICK—Captain of the U.S.S. *Clifton*.

CROSBY, J. K.—Acting master on board the U.S.S. *Housatonic*.

CUSHING, WILLIAM B.—Union naval officer who engineered the sinking of the C.S.S. *Albemarle*.

DAHLGREN, JOHN A.—Union naval officer and armament expert.

DAVENPORT, H. K.—Union naval officer commanding the U.S.S. *Hetzel*.

DAVIDSON, HUNTER—Naval officer and mine expert for the Confederacy.

DAVIS, JEFFERSON—President of the Confederate States of America.

DE CAMP, JOHN—Commander of the U.S.S. *Wabash*.

DELEON, P. M.—Confederate officer on the Johnson's Island expedition.

DIXON, GEORGE E.—Confederate engineer who aided in constructing the *H. L. Hunley.*

DOWLING, RICHARD W.—Confederate leader of the Davis Guards at Sabine Pass.

DRAYTON, PERCIVAL—Commander of the U.S.S. *Hartford.*

DU PONT, SAMUEL FRANCIS—Union commander of the South Atlantic Blockading Squadron (SABS).

EBAUGH, DAVID C.—Niter plant operator who aided in developing the David.

ELLIOTT, GILBERT—Confederate engineer who directed construction of the C.S.S. *Albemarle.*

EVANS, ROBLEY D.—Acting ensign on the U.S.S. *Powhatan.*

FARRAGUT, DAVID GLASGOW—Union naval officer.

FAUCON, E. H.—Commander of the U.S.S. *Montgomery.*

FINNEY, WILLIAM—Confederate officer on the Johnson's Island expedition.

FLUSSER, CHARLES W.—Union naval officer.

FOOTE, ANDREW HULL—Union naval officer.

FOSTER, JOHN G.—Union general.

FRANKLIN, WILLIAM B.—Union general.

FREEMAN, MARTIN—Pilot of the U.S.S. *Hartford.*

GANSEVOORT, GUERT—Union captain.

GARDNER, J. M.—Confederate officer on the Johnson's Island expedition.

GIFT, GEORGE W.—Confederate officer on the Johnson's Island expedition.

GILLIS, JAMES H.—Senior Union naval officer at Yorktown.

GILLIS, JOHN P.—Union captain and senior officer on duty off Galveston, Texas.

GILLMORE, QUINCY A.—Union general.

GLASSELL, W. T.—Confederate naval officer assigned to the David.

GOODWIN, M. P.—Confederate officer on the Johnson's Island expedition.

GORMLEY, CRAWFORD H.—Confederate gunner on the Johnson's Island expedition.

GRANT, ULYSSES S.—Union general and commander in chief.

GRAY, M. M.—Confederate officer in charge of the submarine defenses at Charleston.

GREEN, THOMAS—Confederate general.

GREENHOW, ROSE O'NEAL—Confederate spy.

HAGOOD, JOHNSON—Confederate general assigned to Battery Wagner.

HASKELL, CHARLES T., JR.—Confederate officer.

HAWLEY, S. C.—U.S. consul at Nassau.

HEBERT, LOUIS—Confederate general.

HOKE, ROBERT F.—Confederate general.

HOLLINS, GEORGE N.—Confederate naval officer and fleet commander.

HORLBECK, HENRY B.—Confederate surgeon.

HOWARD, C. W.—Acting ensign on board the U.S.S. *New Ironsides.*

HOWELL, J. C.—Commander of the U.S.S. *Nereus.*

HUDGINS, A. G.—Confederate officer on the Johnson's Island expedition.

HUNLEY, HORACE L.—Confederate submarine inventor.

HUNTER, DAVID—Union general.

HUNTER, T. T., JUNIOR—Acting master on the C.S.S. *Florida.*

HUSE, SAMUEL—Commander of the U.S.S. *Britannia.*

JACK, CHARLES E.—Acting master on board the U.S.S. *Iroquois.*

JACKSON, M. M.—U.S. consul at Halifax, Nova Scotia.

JENKINS, THORNTON A.—Senior Union officer in the Mobile area.

JOHNSTON, AMOS—Commander of the U.S.S. *Sachem.*

JOHNSTON, JAMES D.—Commander of the C.S.S. *Tennessee.*

JOHNSTON, JOSEPH E.—Confederate general.

JONES, CATESBY AP R.—Confederate naval officer.

JORDAN, THOMAS—Confederate general and chief of staff to Beauregard.

JOURDAN, JAMES—Union officer commanding at Beaufort, North Carolina.

KEITT, LAWRENCE M.—Confederate colonel assigned to Battery Wagner.

KELL, JOHN MCINTOSH—First officer of the C.S.S. *Alabama.*

KINNEY, JOHN C.—Signal officer of the U.S.S. *Hartford.*

LAMB, WILLIAM—Confederate colonel commanding at Fort Fisher, North Carolina.

LAMSON, C. W.—Acting master of the U.S.S. *Granite City.*

LANCASTER, JOHN—Owner of the English yacht *Deerhound.*

LATCH, EDWARD B.—Seaman on board the U.S.S. *Hartford.*

LEE, FRANCIS D.—Confederate engineer.

LEE, ROBERT E.—Confederate general and commander of the Army of Northern Virginia.

LEE, SAMUEL PHILLIPS—Commander of the North Atlantic Blockading Squadron (NABS).

LINCOLN, ABRAHAM—Union President during the Civil War.

LOCKWOOD, HENRY H.—Union general.

LOYALL, B. P.—Confederate officer on the Johnson's Island expedition.

LYNCH, WILLIAM F.—Confederate naval officer.

MCCARRICK, PATRICK—Confederate officer on the Johnson's Island expedition.

MCCLINTOCK, JAMES—Confederate submarine inventor.

MCKERNAN, MICHAEL—Confederate gunner at Sabine Pass.

MCKINLEY, ALEXANDER—Secretary to Admiral Farragut.

MACOMB, W. H.—Commander of Union fleet off North Carolina.

MADISON, JOHN—Commander of the U.S.S. *Owasco*.

MAFFITT, JOHN—Confederate naval officer and blockade-runner.

MAGRUDER, JOHN B.—Confederate general.

MARCHAND, J. B.—Union naval officer.

MAURY, DABNEY H.—Confederate general.

MAURY, MATTHEW FONTAINE—Noted hydrographer and developer of mines for the Confederacy.

MINOR, ROBERT D.—Confederate naval officer.

MITCHELL, JOHN K.—Confederate flag officer.

MORRIS, CHARLES MANIGAULT—Commander of the C.S.S. *Florida*.

MURDAUGH, WILLIAM H.—Confederate naval officer and originator of the Johnson's Island expedition.

NESTELL, D. D. T.—Acting assistant surgeon of the U.S.S. *Clifton*.

OULD, ROBERT—Confederate Agent of Exchange.

PAGE, RICHARD L.—Confederate commander of Fort Morgan in Mobile Bay.

PAGE, THOMAS JEFFERSON—Commander of the C.S.S. *Stonewall*.

PARKER, WILLIAM A.—Union naval officer.

PATTERSON, R. O.—Acting master of the U.S.S. *Memphis*.

PAYNE, JOHN A.—Commander of the Confederate submarine *H. L. Hunley*.

PECK, JOHN J.—Union general.

PENDERGRAST, AUSTIN—Commander of the U.S.S. *Water Witch*.

PERRIN, H. W.—Confederate officer on the Johnson's Island expedition.

PHELPS, S. LEDYARD—Union naval officer.

PHINNEY, ALVIN—Acting master of the Union schooner *Racer*.

PICKETT, GEORGE E.—Confederate general.

PINCKNEY, ROBERT F.—Confederate flag officer.

PORTER, DAVID DIXON—Commander of the Union fleet in the Red River campaign.

PORTER, JOHN L.—Confederate marine architect and engineer.

PORTER, N. J.—Ensign assigned to the U.S.S. *New Ironsides*.

PORTER, THOMAS K.—First lieutenant of the C.S.S. *Florida*.

PRESTON, SAMUEL W.—Flag lieutenant to Admiral David Porter.

PUTNAM, HALDIMAND S.—Union colonel.

RAVENEL, ST. JULIEN—Charleston physician and scientist who helped in building the David.

RAWLINS, JOHN A.—Union general.

READ, CHARLES W.—Confederate naval officer.

RHIND, ALEXANDER C.—Union naval officer.

RHODES, ROBERT—Executive officer of the U.S.S. *Clifton*.

ROBY, F. M.—Confederate officer on the Johnson's Island expedition.

RODGERS, GEORGE W.—Union naval officer and Dahlgren's chief of staff.

ROE, FRANCIS A.—Union naval officer.

ROSS, FITZGERALD—British war correspondent.

SCEMPS, CHARLES—Confederate seaman assigned to the David.

SCHENCK, JAMES FINDLAY—Commander of the U.S.S. *Powhatan*.

SCHENCK, ROBERT C.—Union general commanding at Baltimore.

SCHROEDER, J. CHARLES—Confederate officer on the Johnson's Island expedition.

SEDDON, JAMES A.—Confederate Secretary of War.

SELFRIDGE, THOMAS O.—Union naval officer.

SEMMES, RAPHAEL—Commander of the C.S.S. *Alabama*.

SEWARD, WILLIAM H.—Union Secretary of State.

SHAW, ROBERT G.—Union colonel.

SHEPPARDSON, WILLIAM—Confederate officer on the Johnson's Island expedition.

SHERMAN, WILLIAM TECUMSEH—Union general.

SINCLAIR, ARTHUR—Master of the C.S.S. *Alabama*.

SMITH, A. J. (WHISKEY)—Union general.

SMITH, KILBY—Union general.

SMITH, KIRBY—Confederate general.

SMITH, LEON—Confederate naval officer.

SMITH, MELANCTON—Union naval officer.

SMITH, PETER EVANS—Mechanic who aided in constructing the C.S.S. *Albemarle.*

STANTON, EDWARD MCMASTERS—Union Secretary of War.

STEELE, FREDERICK—Union general.

STONEY, THEODORE D.—Charleston resident who helped in developing the David.

STRONG, GEORGE C.—Union general.

SULLIVAN, JAMES—Fireman on board the C.S.S. *Chicora.*

TABB, JOHN B.—Confederate officer on the Johnson's Island expedition.

TALIAFERRO, WILLIAM B.—Confederate general assigned to Battery Wagner.

TERRY, ALFRED H.—Union general commanding troops in the attack on Fort Fisher.

THOMPSON, JACOB—Confederate agent in Canada.

TIBBITTS, HOWARD—Acting master of the U.S.S. *Arizona.*

TOMB, JAMES H.—Confederate engineer assigned to the David.

TUCKER, JOHN R.—Confederate naval officer.

TUCKER, JOHN T.—Confederate officer on the Johnson's Island expedition.

VAN BOSKIRK, JAMES—Acting master of the mortar schooner *Adolph Hugel.*

WADDELL, JAMES IREDELL—Commander of the C.S.S. *Shenandoah.*

WAMPLER, J. M.—Confederate engineer assigned to Battery Wagner.

WARLEY, ALEXANDER F.—Commander of the C.S.S. *Albemarle.*

WATERS, JOHN—Confederate gunner on the Johnson's Island expedition.

WATMOUGH, PENDLETON G.—Commander of the U.S.S. *Kansas.*

WATSON, BAXTER—Confederate submarine inventor.

WATSON, JOHN CRITTENDEN—Flag lieutenant on board the U.S.S. *Hartford.*

WEEKS, B. S.—Acting master on board the U.S.S. *Clifton.*

WEITZEL, GODFREY—Union general.

WELLES, GIDEON—Union Secretary of the Navy.

WELLES, W. N.—Acting master on board the U.S.S. *Miami.*

WESSELS, HENRY W.—Union general commanding at Plymouth, North Carolina.

WHITING, W. H. C.—Confederate general.

WHITING, WILLIAM D.—Naval officer assigned to the U.S.S. *Ottawa.*

WILKES, CHARLES—Union naval officer.

WILKINSON, HENRY—Confederate officer on the Johnson's Island expedition.

WILKINSON, JOHN—Confederate naval officer and blockade runner.

WILSON, THOMAS F.—U.S. consul in Brazil.

WINSLOW, JOHN ANCRUM—Commander of the U.S.S. *Kearsarge*.

WISTAR, ISAAC J.—Union general.

WOOD, JOHN TAYLOR—Grandson of former President Zachary Taylor and former U.S. Naval Academy instructor fighting for the Confederacy.

WOODBURN, J. G.—Union paymaster.

WOODMAN, JOHN—Acting master's mate on board the U.S.S. *Commodore Hull*.

WRIGHT, H. X.—Confederate officer on the Johnson's Island expedition.

★ THE CIVIL WAR AT SEA

★ *1*

Parapets from the dead

JULY-SEPTEMBER 1863

Connecticut troops, bent on saving the Union, pushed raggedly along the moonlit beach of Morris Island, the same Morris Island from which two years earlier the first shot of the war had come. Up front, a few managed to get past the salient of Battery Wagner, the outpost of Fort Sumter in Charleston Harbor, lying near an impenetrable South Carolina swamp.

Inside the fort, Georgia and South Carolina soldiers stood shoulder to shoulder. They had waited throughout the night, expecting an attack. At the sleepy hour of 4:00 A.M., the sound of footsteps on the soft sand reached the ears of the pickets. In a matter of seconds, the quiet of the island, until then broken only by the monotonous sound of waves rolling in along the shore, was replaced by a din so terrible it brought tremors to the fort.

Out in the harbor, where they had been anchored with the sights of their guns set, the Union fleet of ironclads and gunboats suddenly joined in with a fierce barrage, their mortars and

3

rifles sending a roar across the water that drowned out the noise from the smaller weapons on land.

Lieutenant Robert C. Gilchrist of the Gist Guards, battling in the fort, stood with the lanyard of the thirty-two-pounder in his hand. He saw the silhouette of a lone Connecticut soldier rise atop the parapet, dimly outlined against the sky, and shouted a challenge. Like lightning, a bullet creased Gilchrist's hair, and powder blinded his eyes. He ducked in panic, automatically tightening the lanyard; and grape belched forth in a deafening reply, cutting the hazy figure in two.

This tragic moment was among many in the North's desperate drive to storm into the heart of Secessionland. It was part of an all-out campaign to silence Fort Sumter and take Charleston, an interminable drive, it would seem, characterized by joint Army-Navy action of the first order. This particular phase of it, in which Connecticut troops bore the brunt, would have no parallel. Never had there been a better example of determination on either side.

From the very start, the Union was dead set on taking Charleston. Earlier efforts to capture the city by way of James Island had failed, and now the push was following a new route. Morris Island, within easy gunfire of Sumter, would be taken first, and then, as the strategists saw it, Charleston would be virtually won.[1] Guns placed on the island should be able to demolish Sumter, opening the way for the fleet to remove obstructions in the harbor channel, run by the batteries of Sullivan's and James Islands, and compel the city to surrender.[2] But strategy does not always materialize.

Charleston lay at the head of the harbor, on the tip of a peninsula between the Ashley and Cooper rivers, seven miles from the bar at the outer entrance formed by Sullivan's Island on the north and Morris Island on the south. These islands, traversed by numerous streams, were low, narrow, sandy, and separated from the mainland by soft, impassable marshes, some of them submerged at times by the tides. The harbor was bounded by the mainland on the north and by James Island on the south.

Five approaches to the city presented themselves to the Federals. Three of these were by way of the islands. The other two, by land to the north and south, were considered impracticable because Army and Navy operations would be too far apart to co-ordinate.

Morris Island was nearly four miles long, a narrow outcropping of fine white quartz sand. The island varied in width from twenty-five to one thousand yards. At its narrowest point it was bordered on the west by a swamp, fed by Vincent's Creek. It was there the Southerners built Battery Wagner, the principal advanced work of Fort Sumter, an enclosed earthwork measuring six hundred thirty by two hundred seventy-four feet.[3] Three-quarters of a mile to the north, at the end of the island, was a smaller fortification called Battery Gregg, designed to protect Sumter from fire out of the main ship channel and from the creeks between Morris and James Islands. In the other direction, two thousand yards or so from Wagner, began a range of sand hills that stretched all the way to Oyster Point, at the southern end.[4]

South of Morris, and separated from it by Lighthouse Inlet, a stream four hundred to five hundred yards wide, was Folly Island, another narrow outcropping of sand, much of it covered with an impenetrable undergrowth. Near the north end of the island, for two thousand yards or more, the ground was barren and so low that spring tides frequently inundated it. The northern tip, sometimes referred to as Little Folly, was covered with sand ridges and a verdant growth, ideal for concealing batteries. The Federals planned to use this strategic foothold as a steppingstone to reach Morris and, eventually, Fort Sumter. It was one of the few prizes the Union forces had been able to hold onto in Charleston Harbor by bringing ships into nearby Stono Inlet.

Behind the new attempt to take the Southern stronghold from

the sea lay divided opinions. Warnings of the plan's futility had come chiefly from Admiral Samuel F. du Pont, the veteran naval officer who for many long months had been head of the South Atlantic Blockading Squadron and who early became convinced that Charleston would fall only when foot soldiers, co-operating with the Navy, pushed in from the land. Failure of a naval attack, made without the help of the Army as late as April 7, strengthened his conviction, and it also persuaded the Union high command in Washington to make some changes in leadership in the department entrusted with the silencing of South Carolina.

General David Hunter, commanding Army troops in the area, brought matters to a head. The day after the April attack, he urged Du Pont to co-operate in a new offensive. But the Admiral was in no mood to waste lives in an effort he was certain would end in failure. He replied that he "would not fire another shot." [5] This angered Hunter, who reacted by writing a long letter to his friend, Abraham Lincoln, charging that Du Pont was settling down to a period of inactivity.[6]

For naval leadership, Lincoln now turned to a man known to be universally popular—Andrew Hull Foote, hero of Forts Henry and Donelson, Island No. 10, and other campaigns already a part of history. But the action came too late, for that officer's death occurred before he could report for duty at Charleston. Next choice was John A. Dahlgren, son of the Swedish consul at Philadelphia, and a White House confidante who long had desired to try his talents with the South Atlantic Blockading Squadron. Here was an aspirant who already had gained world renown as an armament expert, having among his inventions a ship's cannon that bore his name. He was selfish and conceited, and he wore an expression on his face like that of a spoiled child who thinks he has been wronged. Fifty-four years old, unapproachable, severe, slim, and better than six feet tall, he made a part of his uniform an old-fashioned black stock that caused him to look more like a minister of the gospel than a naval celebrity. Since February, he had been a rear admiral, enjoying a rank conferred upon him for his services as chief of the Bureau of Ordnance, largely through the influence of Lincoln. This was done despite Dahlgren's lack of experience at sea during the war.[7]

The Army assignment went to Brigadier General Quincy A. Gillmore, West Point graduate and chief engineer on the Port Royal expedition in the fall of '61. Since then, he had commanded a division of the Army fighting in Kentucky and Ohio and had taken a leading role in the capture of Fort Pulaski. His choice in the Charleston campaign was influenced by his engineering skill, for the Army recognized that the reduction of Batteries Wagner and Gregg would call for proficiency in this particular science.

The first consultation to map the Charleston campaign was held in Washington in May. Out of it grew a plan of attack that involved four stages:

1. Capture of the south end of Morris Island, known to be occupied by the Confederates.

2. Reduction of Battery Wagner, followed by the consequent fall of Battery Gregg on Cumming's Point at the northern end of the island.

3. Demolition of Fort Sumter by means of combined fire from the fleet and from land batteries which then could be placed on Morris Island.

4. Removal of channel obstructions in the harbor and the final advance on the city by water.

Dahlgren took over his new command July 6, amid rumor that he had come down for only a few months to take Charleston.[8] Gillmore was there ahead of him, having arrived far enough in advance to get preliminary details of the offensive so well under way that Federal pickets were staring out from the undergrowth along the north end of Folly Island, within musket range of the Southerners on the other side of Lighthouse Inlet.[9]

The attack on Morris Island was meant to be a surprise. While Dahlgren was at the entrance to the bar, getting his fleet in condition, Gillmore was directing troops in the establishment of batteries behind the sand hills at the north end of Folly. Forty-seven guns, ranging from rifled three-inch fieldpieces to thirty-pounder Parrotts, were placed in position, each with two hundred rounds of ammunition, suitable epaulements, splinter-proof shelters, and magazines. Quietly, during the period from the middle of June to early July, ordnance and stores were accumulated there. Most of the work was done under cover of darkness. Men labored through the night hours and then, as day dawned, carefully concealed their enterprise and lay down to sleep.

In this period, an incident occurred which the Federals employed to divert the attention of the enemy. One night the blockade runner *Ruby* was chased ashore near the entrance to Lighthouse Inlet, within easy range of the guns on Folly. A few Union fieldpieces were run out from the undergrowth in a threat to blow the ship to pieces, but the moment the Southerners opened on them, they were withdrawn, giving the impression that they had no support. They did not appear again, and the Confederates proceeded to strip the ship in peace, working night and day and apparently unaware that only a few yards away were enough cannon to blow them to smithereens.[10]

Whether they knew what was going on or not, the Confederates as early as June 12 began firing on Folly Island from eight guns and three mortars they had placed on the southern tip of Morris. They bombarded by day the very area in which the Federals worked by night.[11]

Batteries on Folly Island were completed July 6, the day Dahlgren took over his command. The Confederates that night organized an expedition to cross the inlet and ascertain the nature of these works, but unsuitable weather and the nature of the boats at hand prevented the reconnaissance.[12] Two nights later, the last of six thousand five hundred additional troops gathered there under cover of darkness, bringing Gillmore's total strength to about eleven thousand. In the afternoon preceding this activity, Union troops moved up Stono River and confronted the Southerners on James Island, drawing atten-

served: "The whole island smoked like a furnace and trembled
as from an earthquake." [25] As the tide rose during the afternoon,
the vessels pushed closer to land, the *Montauk* finally winding
up only three hundred yards from the water's edge. Toward
the end of the attack there was no answering fire from Wagner.

Near sunset an aide brought Dahlgren a note from Gillmore.
In answer to the message, the Admiral gave the signal to cease
fire, and a great calm seemed now to settle over Morris Island.
But suddenly, blue-clad soldiers came pouring out of the first
parallel, storming toward the fort. They ran to within five hundred yards of the battery before they met a blizzard of Confederate gunfire—shot, shell, grape, shrapnel, canister, and musket
balls. The guns in Battery Gregg, Fort Sumter, and on James
and Sullivan's Islands also opened up on the attacking army.
The severity of the bombardment during the late afternoon
made it clear to the Confederates that an assault was coming,
and they had manned their ramparts.[26]

Leading the Federals was the Fifty-fourth Massachusetts,
made up of Negro troops under command of a white officer,
Colonel Robert G. Shaw, a neat man of medium height, whose
short jacket and long, light hair falling to his shoulders gave
him the appearance of a boy. One thousand strong, they
bounded over the ditch surrounding the fort, mounted the ramparts, and planted their flag upon the parapet. At this moment
of the attack, Shaw was killed, and the Fifty-fourth seemed to
go to pieces. One eyewitness related that its members were
"seized with a furious panic and acted like wild beasts let loose
from a menagerie." [27] Turning, they rushed back, coming down
first on the Ninth Maine and then on the Seventy-sixth Pennsylvania, cutting the units in two. Portions of these regiments
mingled with the fugitives and could not be rallied. "They ran
away like deer, some crawling on their hands and knees," another witness recounted.[28]

This demoralization of troops broke the force of the attack,
and the fighting soon faded away and died out. The Sixth Con-

necticut had taken the southeast salient, but it had failed to get support and was forced to wait there until surrounded and captured.

Four thousand men had been dashed against Wagner. In addition to Shaw, many were killed, among them Brigadier General George C. Strong and Colonels John L. Chatfield and Haldimand S. Putnam.[29] It was a fierce assault, hot and deadly, and set at a fast pace; and by 9:30 A.M. it was a thing of the past. Then, after a sweltering day, came the long hours of night, hours that would burn their tortured moments into the minds of the men who endured them. Throughout the period, quiet lay over the fort, broken only by the moans and cries of the wounded and dying.

Dawn ushered in a peaceful Sabbath and bared a scene that was dreadful to look upon. "Blood, mud, water, brains, and human hair, matted together," remembered one of those who was there. "Men lying in every possible attitude, with every conceivable expression on their countenances; their limbs bent into unnatural shapes by the fall of twenty or more feet; the fingers rigid and outstretched, as if they had clutched at the earth to save themselves; pale, beseeching faces, looking out from among the ghastly corpses, with moans and cries for help and water, and dying gasps and death struggles." In the salient and on the ramparts they lay, heaped in some places three deep. Up on the parapet, near the flag he had so valiantly planted, sprawled the body of the youthful Colonel Shaw.[30]

"Praise be to God," Beauregard wired Confederate General Joseph E. Johnston that morning. "The anniversary of Bull Run has been gloriously celebrated. . . ." [31]

The total Union loss was one thousand five hundred fifteen. Ten regiments had participated. Of these, the Fifty-fourth Massachusetts, Forty-eighth New York, Seventh New Hampshire, and One Hundredth New York had suffered the most, their totals in killed, wounded, and missing reaching nine hundred five.[32]

These losses reflected a determination on the part of the Southerners to hold Morris Island at any cost. A telegram to that effect had been sent by Beauregard to the commander of the island at 1:00 A.M., and reinforcements were thrown in before daylight.[33]

There was no firing on the 19th. Dahlgren's fleet, standing by for further action, had mute evidence during the day of the Union defeat. Bodies of Negro soldiers floated past the ships and went on out to sea with the tide.

"So we passed a quiet Sunday," Dahlgren recorded, "for it was impossible to fire while our wounded men were lying about."

There were other incidents in the war the night of the 19th. A British blockade-runner, taking advantage of the horror around Morris Island, attempted to run into Charleston, was chased, and grounded on a shoal, where her crew set her afire. But several runners waiting at the city's wharf managed to elude the blockade, and put out to sea before dawn.[34]

At this stage, Gillmore was worried by the heavy toll from battle casualties and from sickness. He estimated that a third of his force had been lost due to these causes.[35]

The combined bombardment of Wagner was resumed on the 20th. During the day, long-range rifles opened on Sumter from Morris Island, the first fire to come from the batteries erected by the Federals since their landing. The Southerners in the fort proceeded with their work, filling up the officers' quarters on the gorge with wet cotton bales laid in sand, building a new wharf, and cutting a new sally port on the western front.

During a lull on the 21st, a flag of truce was carried from the Union side with a communication from General Gillmore asking for a conference with the commander of Wagner. An officer from the fort was sent out to meet the emissary. But Dahlgren's fleet, uninformed of what was happening, quickly put an end to any such peaceful arrangement. It began dropping shells around Wagner while the men still stood in the open under the truce flag. The interview quickly ended.[36]

On July 23, Dahlgren issued an order: "The batteries of the Army are to be advanced tonight to close range of Wagner, and at daylight the ironclads must be in position to keep down the fire of Wagner, the gunboats assisting." At dawn on the 24th, the fleet moved up and opened fire, the Army in the meantime proceeding with its program of arming the batteries and other works that had been constructed during the night. Once, during the morning, a steamer came down from Charleston under flag of truce to exchange prisoners, and a halt in the firing was ordered. During the lull, the Confederates could be seen repairing Wagner.

On the night of the 26th, the command of Battery Wagner changed. Brigadier General Johnson Hagood, lawyer, planter, and Citadel graduate, a leader who had seen much action, including the firing on Fort Sumter and the first battle of Manassas, succeeded Brigadier General William B. Taliaferro, Harvard law student and Mexican War veteran who had taken part in much fighting in Virginia before coming to South Carolina. There had been talk of evacuating the fort, but the final decision was to maintain it as long as possible. This would afford the opportunity for other defenses in the Charleston area to be strengthened, some of them with guns taken from Fort Sumter, now accepted as expendable in view of the pounding it might take from batteries the Union could locate on Morris Island. In the first sixteen days of the assault, the Confederates had lost eighty-five dead, three hundred twelve wounded, and one hundred thirty-two captured.[37]

From this date, Morris Island was a symbol of endurance. Night and day, with few intermissions, it was shelled from sea and land. On one particular day, Beauregard recorded five hundred ninety-nine shots fired by the Federals during a period of two and a half hours.[38]

"The burning sun of a Southern summer, its heat intensified by the reflection of the white sand," wrote one of the men shut up in Battery Wagner, "scorched and blistered the unprotected garrison, or the more welcome rain and storm wet them to the skin. An intolerable stench from the unearthed dead of the previous conflict, the carcasses of cavalry horses lying where they fell in the rear, and barrels of putrid meat thrown out on the beach, sickened the defenders. A large and brilliantly colored fly, attracted by the feast and unseen before, inflicted wounds more painful though less dangerous than the shot of the enemy. Water was scarcer than whiskey. The food, often in transit from the wharf in Charleston over forty-eight hours, was unfit to eat. The unventilated bombproofs, filled with smoke of lamps and smell of blood, were intolerable, so that one endured the risk of shot and shell rather than seek its shelter." [39]

The garrison fought valiantly. Time and again the Confederate flag waving from the ramparts was shot away. Each time, some brave Southerners rushed to remount it until Hagood at last issued orders forbidding them to.

The Federals learned by experience that the mines used by the Confederates worked as well on water as they did on land. One of the charges exploded at midnight under the stern of the *Pawnee,* destroying its launch; and another, at 4:00 A.M., went off within thirty yards of the ship. The *C. P. Williams* picked up two mines, and a little later a boat was captured that had a platform for ten. They were ingenious devices, rigged up around the stock of a musket, its trigger set to explode a charge of sixty pounds of powder. Floating, they had the appearance of innocent tin cans drifting in the water. "They may be one of the means that the enemy has thought fit to use in the desperate attempt to burn the shipping in Stono, and for which, I learn, volunteers were asked in a late Savannah paper," the *Pawnee*'s skipper, Commander George B. Balch, advised Dahlgren. "I trust all their other attempts may prove no more successful, though I regret much the loss of my launch." [40] But this experience had thoroughly alarmed Dahlgren. Before many more nights passed, some of his seamen were stretching a net, buoyed by fifteen barrels, across Lighthouse Inlet to stop the floating mines.[41]

The days lengthened into weeks and the weeks into a month. By the end of July, a second parallel was completed. Opening these trenches was grilling work for the engineers, who were forced to shovel on their knees, as noiselessly as possible. The men, spaced six feet apart, grasped the rope with their left hands and held a short-handled shovel in their right. In the lead was the officer in charge. They marched forward in stooping position. At a signal the rope was dropped, and the men dug pits where they stood, throwing the earth over the rope. The digging continued until the openings were connected and deep enough to provide cover.

On August 9, the third parallel was established, with the most advanced point within five hundred yards of Wagner. After that date, the trench work was greatly impeded by Confederate sharpshooters, who fired from the vantage point of a ridge near the fort. The little Minié balls of the sharpshooters were especially annoying. From dawn to dark, these marksmen sat in their nests, formed out of sandbags, and watched for some target—a hat, a head, a hand. Their Whitworth rifles had telescopic sights and were fatal at fifteen hundred yards. The heavy charge of powder used in them caused such a recoil that the faces of the men often were bruised. A black ring around the eye was recognized as a badge of distinction.

Similarly, artillerists on both sides were given so much practice that their aim became almost perfect. An eight-inch rifle ball struck the muzzle of a siege howitzer on the land face of Wagner. The captain of the squad serving the howitzer said it was a chance shot and told his men to run the weapon in battery again. They did, and another ball tore into its muzzle and shattered the piece. The huge shells from the monitors were fired at a low elevation, causing them to ricochet across the water, strike the edge of the beach, and bound over the parapet into the fort.

The evening of the 16th, Gillmore informed Dahlgren: "I shall open on Sumter at daybreak. Can you open on Wagner as early as that?" The Admiral replied that the monitors would begin to move at 6:00 A.M. and would open soon afterward.

As indicated by this exchange, the 17th was another day of bombardment. While Gillmore pounded Sumter, Dahlgren threw shells at Wagner, bringing into action a fleet of fourteen ships, including seven wooden gunboats. The latter fort was silenced at 9:20 A.M., after which the Admiral shifted his flag from the *Weehawken* to the *Patapsco* and steamed up to within two thousand yards of Sumter. Battery Gregg alone returned a deliberate fire, aiming its projectiles at the *Passaic* and *Patapsco*.

This day was the last for Captain J. M. Wampler, chief engineer at Wagner. While he sat writing a letter home in a chair just vacated by Surgeon Henry B. Horlbeck, a fifteen-inch shell ricocheted across the water and struck him in the back, killing him instantly. It also was the last day for Dahlgren's chief of staff, Captain George W. Rodgers, a deeply religious man and the officer who at the start of the war had had the distinction of towing the historic old frigate *Constitution* from Annapolis, Maryland, to Newport, Rhode Island. Three times that morning he asked Dahlgren if he should go in the flagship as usual or resume command of his own vessel, the *Catskill*. Each time the Admiral replied, "Do as you choose." Rodgers finally said, "Well, I will go in the *Catskill*, and the next time with you."

Dahlgren's journal recorded this development of the battle: "Wagner now firing very rapidly, and using every conceivable form of projectile imaginable, from a Minié ball to a solid ten-inch shot. . . . At 9:15 *Catskill* moved down the harbor with a signal flying, which, on account of the smoke, could not be seen. On asking the *Patapsco* what it was, she replied, 'Captain of *Catskill* is disabled.' . . . Learned when within hail of the *Catskill* that early in the fight a shot from Wagner had struck her on the top of the pilothouse, had broken the plates, which were forced into the pilothouse, instantly killing Captain G. W. Rodgers and Paymaster J. G. Woodburn and wounding two other men in the pilothouse." [42]

During the attack, twelve batteries of the heaviest caliber were opened on Sumter at a distance of a little less than four thousand yards. It was the beginning of a bombardment that would continue for a week, entirely destroying the barbette battery in the fort, ruining its gorge and sea walls, and so disabling its armament that but one gun would remain in serviceable condition.[43]

That day the Federals received further education in the art of underwater explosives. In Lighthouse Creek they found a mine made of three metallic cases, on the upper side of which were delicately arranged hammers, connected with cords designed to catch on a passing vessel and set off the charge by means of percussion caps under the hammers. Another style found was called "devil fish" because it was about four feet long, slender, and shaped like a fish.[44]

The Confederates at this date had nine hundred and twenty-two men on Morris Island. These included six hundred sixty-three infantry, two hundred forty-eight artillery, and eleven cavalry. Because of enemy pickets stationed on the water at night and the strong calcium lights used by the Federals, reinforcements and supplies had to be stealthily transported to the island by small boat.

The night of August 18 the Federals began working on a fourth parallel, laboring in two feet of water in trenches within three hundred yards of Wagner. The nearer they got to the fort, the more deadly became the fire of the Confederate sharpshooters, especially on nights lighted by a harvest moon. The sickening part of the work in the trenches involved the removal of bodies. At first these were buried out of the line of approach, but, as the engineering operations expanded, all space not covered by marsh was employed. This meant disturbing again and again the graves of the dead, until at last all attempt to rebury them beyond reach was abandoned, and they were thrown along with earth into the parapets and left there.[45]

The developments of the 20th were watched from Charleston by a distinguished observer from England, FitzGerald Ross, then making a tour of the South.[46] "In the evening especially," he wrote, "it is very interesting to watch the contest, as all the guns use hollow shot, with time fuses, which go blazing through the air like meteors. The mortar shells are the prettiest, going high up into the air, and then slowly descending." He was told by

Colonel Alfred Rhett, commanding at Sumter, that all this bombing had its effects upon the cuisine; things shook so badly that yeast could not make dough rise, and thus everyone was eating flat bread. He was also informed that the Federals had to expend seventy thousand pounds of iron to kill or wound one Confederate soldier.

Until ten-thirty at night, the Union guns continued to hurl shells at the forts. The Confederate fire had not been as continuous, but it had been destructive. When the fleet withdrew, the smokestack of the *Patapsco* "looked like the top of a pepper box." [47]

Four and a half hours later, Colonel Lawrence M. Keitt, commanding Fort Wagner, reported: "3 A.M.—All Quiet; garrison very much exhausted; repairing damages." But things were not to remain quiet long. Before 5:00 A.M., the *Ironsides* and two monitors steamed up again and began shelling Wagner. The bombardment continued throughout the morning, silencing a rifled gun in the fort. At 12:30 P.M., the wind rising, all three vessels withdrew.

While taking part in the daily action, the *New Ironsides* was slowly providing a demonstration that would advise against any more ships of her design. She was found to be powerful but impracticable. Her size made her a large target. Her draft prevented her close approach to the forts, and her ports allowed such limited elevation that her guns were almost ineffective. But worst of all, her ends were not armored, keeping her always vulnerable whenever she moved into the orbit encompassed by Forts Sumter and Moultrie and Battery Wagner.

Ensign N. J. Porter was officer of the deck on the *Ironsides* the morning of August 21. "At 1:00 A.M.," he reported, "I saw a strange vessel, sitting very low in the water and having the appearance of being a large boat, coming up astern very fast. I hailed the stranger twice, receiving for an answer to the first hail, 'Aye, aye,' and to the second, 'I am the *Live Yankee,* from Port Royal.' Beat to quarters immediately and threw up rocket. In the meantime the stranger ran rapidly past our broadside and fell athwart our bows, where we could bring no guns to bear upon her. She remained there a few minutes and then started off rapidly in the direction of Fort Moultrie. Meanwhile our chain had been slipped, and backing astern, the bow guns were fired at her, but at what effect I cannot say." [48]

The Confederacy got a much more detailed account of the incident from the man in charge of the "strange vessel" sighted from the deck of the *Ironsides*. He was Captain James Carlin, an Englishman fighting on the side of the South.[49] he volunteered to attempt the sinking of the Union ship with a torpedo ram, armed it with a guard of eleven men commanded by Lieutenant Eldred S. Fickling of the regulars on duty at Fort Sumter, and headed for his target; but, as he revealed, he was unsuccessful:

At 11:30 P.M. I passed the obstructions, and at 12:00 sighted the *Ironsides* lying at anchor in the channel off Morris Island, with five monitors moored immediately in a S.S.W. direction from her, and about three hundred yards distant. When I came within quarter of a mile of the *Ironsides* I lowered the torpedoes and proceeded directly for the ship, feeling at the same time fully confident of striking her in the right place. At this time she was lying across the channel and heading for Morris Island. I steered up, keeping the object on our port bow, and when within forty yards from the ship I stopped the engine and ordered the helm put hard astarboard.

I attribute my failure to the want of proper execution of this order. I noticed the slow obedience of the ship to her helm, and again gave the order, repeating it three times. It was a moment of great anxiety and expectation, and not doubting but I would strike her, I was obliged to attend to the proper command of the officers and men and restrain any undue excitement. In this I was ably assisted by the cool, courageous bearing of Lieutenant Fickling, who commanded the force stationed for defense. I discovered as we ranged up alongside that in consequence of the *Ironsides* being in the act of swinging to the ebb we must miss with our torpedoes, but feared that her chain cable would either ignite them or detain us alongside. In either case we must have been captured. A kind Providence, however, intervened and saved our little band from such disaster. When about fifty yards distant we were hailed, "Ship ahoy!" After deliberating whether I should not give him some warning, I felt so sure of striking him, I finally answered, "Hello," and in an official and stern tone as possible. Another hail, "What ship is that?" I answered almost immediately, "The steamer *Live Yankee.*"

We were still moving slowly past the bow. I gave the order to go ahead with the engine, and was informed at the same time that the enemy was boarding us. Without looking to see whether such was the case, I gave the order to defend the ship and get my arms ready in time to prevent the firing upon some sailors that were looking at us from the ports. I saw they were not boarding and I immediately ordered the men to hold and not fire. Just at this time he hailed again, "Where are you from?" Answered, "Port Royal." I found that we had ranged just clear of his bow and out of danger of being boarded except by launches. I then went to the engine room to see what was the matter, as fully two minutes had elapsed since the order had been given to go ahead. I found that the engine had caught upon the center and notwithstanding a continued effort for at least four or five minutes, they failed to get started ahead. I was again hailed, "What ship is that?" Answered, "The United States steamer *Yankee.*"

I again went to the engine room, and by encouragement to the engineers, found her in the act of starting. Another hail and another called me to the deck, and as none of my officers heard the question, I surmised it to be an order to come to anchor or surrender. I answered, "Aye, aye, sir; I'll come on board." I found we were moving ahead slowly, and in two minutes must have passed out of his sight, as he commenced firing in the opposite direction. He afterwards fired, sweeping the horizon, two shots passing on either side about twenty feet off.[50]

Carlin received high commendation from Beauregard. "I know no one to whose skill and experience I would sooner trust the boat on so bold and gallant an undertaking." [51]

The 21st was another day of heavy bombardment, most of it aimed at Fort Sumter. During the day, four hundred sixty-five shot and shell struck outside the fortification, two hundred fifty-nine inside, and two hundred nineteen passed over.[52] The effect was to batter the eastern face and to wound seven men, three dangerously.

But some of the attack during the day was against Battery Wagner, especially on the rifle pits directly in front. That night, at a quarter to eleven, a flag of truce was carried to Wagner with a communication for Beauregard. It was from Gillmore and demanded the surrender of Fort Sumter and Morris Island, under threat of bombardment of Charleston within four hours in case of noncompliance. Without being read, it was sent by messenger to Beauregard's headquarters.[53] There it was found to have no signature, so at 2:30 A.M. it was sent back to Morris Island. At about 1:30 A.M. shells began falling on the city from one of the most notorious guns on either side during the war. It was a ten-inch, three-hundred-pounder Parrott, part of a new battery erected in the marsh a little to the west of Thomas Island.[54] Officially it was identified as the Marsh Battery, but the men firing it called it the "Swamp Angel." It was situated on a platform in the marsh mud, midway between Morris and James Islands, and was aimed at the steeple of St. Michael's Church, near the Mills House Hotel, a distance of nine thousand yards. The gun caused the destruction of some medical stores and the battering of one or two walls.

The firing on Sumter was resumed at 6:00 A.M. on the 22nd. The east face was further damaged, several guns were disabled, and the arches of the northwest face were demolished. Later in the morning, monitors opened on Wagner and continued to shell until 2:00 P.M., when they all withdrew. As soon as they were out of range, Confederate sharpshooters on Morris Island went back to their posts, sniping busily at the Federals, who were extending their trenches.

Night came on with a heavy haze. Vessels lying toward the bar tightened their guard, listening for ships trying to steal through the blockade. At ten minutes to midnight, men on the gunboat *Ottawa,* anchored at the west end of Rattlesnake Shoal, heard the wheels of a steamer. "I slipped the cable and was ready to chase," reported her captain, Lieutenant Commander William D. Whiting, "but nothing could be seen; I chased in direction of the sound, also hearing distinctly the command given to the helmsman, 'Starboard,' 'Port,' etc. I was standing to the northward and eastward to cut him off; at one time caught sight of the wake of her wheels in the water and fired the bow pivot, but saw nothing more after chasing out toward the point of the shoal; and hearing or seeing nothing more, returned to an anchorage."

Five monitors continued to bombard Sumter before dawn. Both fog and darkness hindered operations, but the gunners were able to aim by the stars. When daylight came, it could be seen that the walls were further damaged and the gorge completely destroyed. During the morning, the *Ironsides* opened on Wagner and received nine shots from Battery Gregg, one of which cut away a small four-oared boat that the Confederates secured as it floated near them.

The daily bombardment of Sumter during this period was conducted at a terrific pace. From August 18 to 23, a total of five thousand six hundred forty-three shots, varying in weight from thirty to three hundred pounds, were fired at the fort. Of these, two thousand six hundred forty-three struck inside, one thousand six hundred ninety-nine outside, and one thousand three hundred one missed.[55] With an average weight of one hundred fifty pounds per shot, this meant a weight of nearly three hundred eighty-five tons thrown against the walls of Sumter within a period of six days. The effect was to convert the gorge wall and the northwest face into a mass of debris and rubbish.

On August 24, when the Federals attacked Battery Gregg, a surprise awaited them, for the Confederates were able to learn in advance what was coming, and they repulsed the assault within five minutes after it started.

At this stage of the siege, *The New York Times* correspondent was losing his patience. "We may remain here for ages," he wrote, "and if the ironclads remain where they now are, it does not seem very probable that any further results in the successful progress of the siege will be attained. . . . Yesterday morning the monitors did go to within a very short distance of Sumter, but as soon as the fog which enveloped them commenced rising, away they went, after firing three rounds, to their old positions among the remainder of the fleet. The excuse on former occasions has been that the Navy feared Sumter, and now Sumter is off the program, it is rather difficult to determine what new obstacle has presented itself. This sort of foolery is not going to do the work for us. If the ironclads have the virtue they claim, now is the time to display it and turn it to a glorious account. It remains with the Navy to place us in possession of Charleston." [56]

Life for the Confederates on Morris Island at this stage of the siege was one of horror and struggle. Much of the water supply was obtained from barrels sunk in the sand. Dead bodies lay in all directions, and the water, salty from the sea, smelled and tasted putrid.

One morning a heavy shell struck a big timber over a bombproof used by the Confederates as a hospital, trapping inside a number of men, and threatening them with suffocation. A detail of Georgians began digging frantically, one man at a time, for the passageway they were opening was so narrow they could not work otherwise. A short, thickset captain stood by with watch in hand and changed shifts every five minutes. Shells were still bursting and fragments were flying. A six-footer dressed in parts of Federal uniform was called on to dig. He fumbled at his coat. The captain barked, and the man answered, "Yes, Captain, soon as I get off this coat." The officer stared at him, finally jeering: "Damn, I believe you're afraid." The fellow jerked off the coat, threw it on the ground, and made a dash for the passage. He had thrown out only a few spades of sand when a shell burst overhead. When the smoke cleared, there he lay, his head in the sand, his backbone severed by a fragment. The captain dragged the body away and went to work with the shovel himself. [57]

Despite the heat and the mosquitoes and the sickness and the fading patience of some of the besiegers, the attack continued. On the 25th, the bombardment of Sumter commenced about 9:30 A.M. and was kept up throughout the day. Until about three in the afternoon, all was quiet around Wagner, but at that hour the Federals began an incessant mortar fire upon the fort and the space between it and the rifle pits. Toward night, observers watching from elevations in Charleston noticed that Union troops were accumulating for an attack, and orders were sent to batteries within range, including those of Fort Moultrie, to open upon them. The advance upon the Confederate rifle pits began soon after dark; but it was quickly checked by the combined force of the Fifty-fourth Georgia and the Sixty-first North Carolina, which had arrived to relieve the Fifty-fourth. That night, under cover of all the excitement on Morris Island, twelve thousand pounds of powder and a large quantity of ammunition and material were removed from Sumter.

An all-out assault was made the night of August 26 on the "ridge" from which the sharpshooters fired. The Confederates finally were overpowered, and they abandoned the vantage point, enabling the Federals to open the fifth and final parallel.

"The Federals were now two hundred and fifty yards from the sally port of Wagner," wrote Lieutenant Gilchrist, commanding at Battery Gregg. "An ingenious system of torpedo mines to be exploded by the tread of persons walking over them had been established in this area by the Confederates. . . . The bright moon impeded work by night almost as well as the sun by day, and the casualties of the sappers were on the increase. It was therefore determined to keep Wagner quiet with an overpowering curved fire from siege and coehorn mortars, and if possible to breach the bombproof shelter with rifled guns. Accordingly, all the light mortars were moved to the front and placed in battery; the rifled guns were trained upon Wagner and prepared for prolonged action; a large magazine was constructed to furnish ample supplies of ammunition, and the co-operation of the *New Ironsides* during the day was secured."

Gillmore was prepared at this date to throw greater illumination on the waters between Cumming's Point and Sumter as a means of preventing Confederate reinforcements from reaching Morris Island by small boat, but a project that Dahlgren was planning delayed the action. The Admiral had chosen that night for an attempt to remove the obstructions from the main channel so he could take his fleet into Charleston Harbor. These obstructions consisted of ropes with mines attached, strung between Forts Sumter and Moultrie, as well as three old boilers, each

containing one thousand pounds of powder, connected with a
battery on Sullivan's Island. Standing by to clear them away was
a tug covered by gunboats and equipped with "tackles, straps,
fishhooks, saws, augers, cold chisels, hammers, and smart seamen." But the setting in of a strong flood tide, in addition to an
outburst of stormy weather, caused postponement.

More exchange of correspondence regarding the lights took
place on the 27th, and this time, Dahlgren caused postponement
until it was too late to employ them. During the day, only four
shots were fired at the flag waving over Sumter. The Confederates, laboring throughout the night, threw three guns over the
walls of the fort and began transporting them to the city, carrying
out their program of partially disarming the works. At Wagner,
where there had been some action during the day, especially
from the sharpshooters, the Union sappers after dark extended
an unfinished trench to within one hundred yards of the works.[58]
Eight mines were uncovered by them and each deactivated by
boring a hole in it and filling it with water. An attempt was made
to explode them by firing at their plungers, but this failed.

For the next several days a strange quietness lay over the
Federal lines and extended even out to the Union fleet. There
was an occasional outburst of firing, but the fierce pace of the
last few weeks was missing. This lull in the attack was caused by
a gale that came on in the late afternoon of the 28th and by a
change of strategy on the part of the Federals.

"The dark and gloomy days of the siege were now upon us,"
reported Gillmore. "Our daily hopes were on the increase,
while our progress became discouragingly slow and even fear-
fully uncertain. The converging fire from Wagner alone almost
enveloped the head of the trench, subtending, as it did, an angle
of nearly ninety degrees, while the flank fire from the James Island batteries increased in power and accuracy. To push forward the trench, in the narrow strip of shallow, shifting sand by
day, was impossible, while the brightness of the prevailing harvest moon rendered the operation almost as hazardous by night.
Matters, indeed, seemed at a standstill, and a feeling of de-

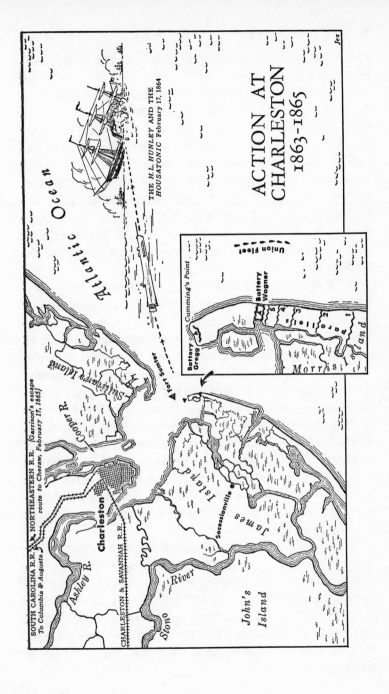

ACTION AT CHARLESTON 1863-1865

THE H.L. HUNLEY AND THE HOUSATONIC February 17, 1864

Atlantic Ocean

Battery Gregg
Battery Cumming's Point
Battery Wagner
Parallels
5 4 3 2 1
Morris Island
Union Fleet

SOUTH CAROLINA R.R. To Columbia & Augusta
NORTHEASTERN R.R. (Garrison's escape route to Cheraw, February 17, 1865)
Cooper R.
Sullivan's Island
Fort Sumter
Charleston
Ashley R.
CHARLESTON & SAVANNAH R.R.
Stono River
James Island
Secessionville
John's Island

Jex

spondency began to pervade the rank and file of the command." [59]

In this emergency the offensive was designed along two distinct methods of attack: First, to keep Wagner silent with an overpowering curved fire, so that the engineers would have only the distant shelling from James Island and other points to disturb them; second, to breach the bombproof with rifled guns and thus deprive the Confederates of their only shelter in the fort. So, days were spent in moving light mortars to the front, enlarging the capacity of the fifth parallel, training rifled guns upon the fort, and arranging powerful calcium lights to aid the night work of cannoneers and sharpshooters, as well as to blind the Confederates.

Not a shot was fired at Sumter on the 29th; but before daylight on the 30th, guns opened on the fort and pounded away until five in the afternoon, firing a total of six hundred thirty-four shots. At nightfall a brisk mortar practice was commenced on Batteries Wagner and Gregg, to cut off supplies and reinforcements. These were brought down in the steamer *Sumter,* a vessel under British register that had been waiting at Charleston since July for a chance to get to sea again. When she was ready to start the return, with the Twentieth South Carolina and Thirty-third Georgia on board, headed for a rest in the city, it was found that the tide had fallen so low as to make it necessary to go by the main channel. But this unexpected circumstance had not been provided for by establishing signal with Fort Moultrie, and when the ship passed, the guns of that fortification sank her, drowning eight men.

On the night of the 31st, a squad of Southerners landed near Battery Gregg in a rowboat, ready to do courier duty. The men they were to relieve were waiting on the beach. Two of them recognized each other. "Good God!" said Burgess Gordon. "You here?" John Harleston, walking up the sandy slope, replied without cheer in his voice, "Yes, I am." Burgess shook his head. "I thank God I am getting away from this place. I tell you it is hell, hell." [60]

Harleston soon had reason to understand what his friend was talking about. The dispatches brought from Charleston had to be taken to Wagner, and he was chosen for the assignment. He was told to take a horse from the stable in the corner of the earthwork, lead it down to the beach, keeping close to the battery until he came to the water, then to mount and let the animal go its own way. He was further advised to ride a little "flea-bitten grey," whose tail had been cut off by a shell, leaving a short stump that was still raw and bloody.

"Straight up the beach we went until I could see Battery Wagner looming up in the darkness," Harleston related years afterward. "The grey made a swerve to the right, and in a minute stopped short under the walls of Wagner to the right of the sally port."

In the days ahead, the courier learned he had been given wise advice on choice of animals. "The little grey was the best," he wrote. "He was never scared by shot or shell. I have seen them bursting all around him until he was nearly hidden by the smoke; have seen a fifteen-inch shell from a monitor strike the beach . . . ten or a dozen yards in front of him, yet he never slackened his pace, but swerved to the right or left to avoid the pits."

It was the custom for a courier to remain at Wagner a day or night until another came from Gregg. If dispatches were especially important, two couriers were sent within ten minutes of each other, so that if one was killed, the other might get through.

"You could see the big fifteen-inch shells as they left the guns on the monitors come swaying along, striking the beach and exploding, throwing up a cloud of sand twenty or thirty feet high, and making a hole where they struck big enough to put a horse and cart in," Harleston remembered. "We feared the shells from the *Ironsides* more than all. She would let off a broadside at a time and her shells you never could tell anything about until they struck, and if in their range nothing could save you. The couriers were in plain view of these vessels when riding in daytime, and we used to swear they fired at us."

For nearly a week, as August closed, action was routine. The

Federals continued their preparations for the new strategy, and at night the Confederates dropped more guns over the parapets of Sumter and transported them to other points. Mortar fire was opened occasionally on scattered targets. At periods each day, Dahlgren brought up monitors and gunboats and shelled the forts. During opportune moments, especially at night, the trenches were pushed closer to Wagner, but this had to be done with greater care than ever, for the Rebel sharpshooters were constantly looking across the sand dunes for evidence of movement.

The scene around Wagner became more and more one of horror. Just before sunset on September 4, Captain T. A. Huguenin, chief of artillery in the fort, took a careful look at the entire works. "The parade," he later described, "was strewn with parts of broken guns, carriages, and chassis, lumber and splinters, and last, but not least, thousands of fragments of shell and shot of every description which had been thrown into the fort. One eight-inch howitzer was broken in half and thrown thirty feet from its original position. The men lay in groups close under the parapet, eating raw bacon and biscuit, tired, dirty, and sleepy, for there was no rest for them day or night. While the last rays of the sun began to disappear behind the woods on James Island the infantry were marched out from the bombproof, and took their places along the parapet to guard against assault." [61]

The new strategy of the Federals was ready to be inaugurated on September 5. "For forty-two consecutive hours," reported Gillmore, "the spectacle presented was of surpassing sublimity and grandeur. Seventeen siege and coehorn mortars unceasingly dropped their shells into the work over the heads of our sappers and the guards of the advanced trenches; nine rifled guns in the left batteries pounded away at the southwest angle of the bombproof, while during the daytime the *New Ironsides,* with astonishing regularity and precision, kept a constant stream of shells from her eight-inch broadside ricocheting over the water against the parapet of Wagner, whence, rebounding upward, they dropped nearly vertically, exploding in or over the work and searching every part of it. The calcium lights turned night into day, throwing our own men into impenetrable obscurity, while they brilliantly illuminated every object in front and brought the minutest detail of the fort in sharp relief. In a short time the fort became silent, exhibiting but little sign of life." [62]

Inside the fort, passages, corners, and entrances usually considered safe were like slaughter pens. About noon a traverse, which had been protecting the entrance to one of the magazines and the hospital, was cut away and the passage obstructed by large quantities of sand. A detail of men was sent to shovel it away, and within a matter of minutes all were dead or wounded.

Conditions of the men behind the walls of the fort were desperate. Some of them had been on duty for eight days and nights. No supplies had come from Charleston for days. Commissary stores had been destroyed during the bombardment. The garrison had only a little biscuit and raw bacon. The water supply was exhausted, at a time when men were made thirstier than ever by a diet of salt meat. Their throats rasping, they dug small holes in the sand, only to find that the water springing up in them was so strong with the decay of bodies as to be undrinkable.

During the day, the Confederates observed indications that an attack would be made on Cumming's Point that night by boat. At dark they prepared for it, sending strong parties to support Battery Gregg and to take positions behind the sand hills between the Point and Wagner. Shortly after dusk, two monitors appeared and began a bombardment of Gregg that kept up until one in the morning. Immediately after this shelling stopped, the attacking party made its appearance in fifteen to twenty barges, coming from the junction of Vincent and Schooner creeks. The defenders opened up on them with ten-inch grape, evidently catching the Federals by surprise, for their officers were heard calling out for the fire to be stopped, that they were friends. But the Southerners were not to be fooled. They continued their resistance, aided by both Fort Moultrie and Battery

Bee on Sullivan's Island, and the attackers were driven off in confusion.

A North Carolinian lay among the defenders behind the sand dunes after the boats had been beaten back, and in a moment of reflection, looked off toward Wagner and said to other men lying at his side: "I have heard the preachers talk about hell, a great big hole full of fire and brimstone, where a bad fellow was dropped in, and I will allow it used to worry me at times, but, gentlemen, hell can't be worse than Battery Wagner. I have got out of that, and the other place ain't going to worry me any more." [63] One out of every nine men who had been in the fort at the start of the siege was now a casualty.[64]

At dawn the fire on the forts was reopened at a furious pace and continued throughout the day. The *New Ironsides* took part, lying just off Wagner and over a mine with enough powder in it to have torn her in two. On shore, frantic efforts were made to set off the explosion, but nothing happened. It was later found that wagons hauling sand during the night to reinforce the parapet had rubbed off the insulation of the wires running from a battery to the mine.[65]

That night the sappers crowned the crest of the counterscarp on the east front of Wagner, masking all the guns of the work. At a late hour an order went out: "Fort Wagner will be assaulted at 9:00 A.M. tomorrow. . . ." Shortly afterward, Gillmore was informed that the Confederates were evacuating Morris Island, and out along the darkened waters, forty-six men were captured trying to escape.[66] Federal troops were quickly landed on the north end of the island, but they were too late. Wagner was empty except for eighteen pieces of ordnance, of various calibers, all of them damaged.

The evacuation had begun at nine on the night of September 6. Wounded and sick, about three hundred in all, were embarked first. Then the various units followed one after another. Behind at Wagner, to bring up the extreme rear, were left thirty-five men and seven officers under Captain Huguenin. These were distributed all along the length of the fort and ordered to keep up a continual fire with small arms in the hope of making the Federals believe that the entire garrison was still there.

For more than three hours, small boats moved back and forth from the island, each filled to the last foot of space. Around 1:00 A.M., sensing that the rear guard soon would be told by courier to leave the fort, Huguenin made a final inspection to make sure no one had been overlooked. "As I walked through the darkness, lighted by a lantern, and felt the change from a crowded work where a few hours before hundreds of men had been closely packed," he recorded, "my search was interrupted by stumbling over two dead bodies, horribly mangled and left unburied in the haste of departure. A moment's pause in the dark solitude was the most impressive of my life—with the silent dead at my feet, the subdued roar of the bombardment heard from without, and the stillness within, broken only by the slow, distinct drip, dripping of the dampness overhead upon the plank floor beneath."

By 1:30 A.M. the last boat was shoved away from shore. One of the final acts of the Confederates before leaving the island was to light the fuses to the magazines in Wagner and Gregg, but these were defective and no explosion occurred. It was 2:00 A.M. before the Federals became aware of what had taken place and began throwing up rockets and shelling the area between the two forts.

Gillmore arrived after daylight for an inspection. "Fort Wagner," he said in his official report, "was found to be a work of the most formidable character; far more so, indeed, than the most exaggerated statements of prisoners and deserters had led us to expect. Its bombproof shelter, capable of containing from fifteen hundred to sixteen hundred men, remained practically intact after the most severe bombardment to which any earthwork was ever exposed.[67] The history of sieges furnishes no parallel case." [68]

Early that morning, Dahlgren sent by flag of truce a demand for the surrender of Sumter, signaling to Gillmore, meanwhile, that if it were not complied with he would move up with all his ironclads and engage it. The demand was refused, even though the fort presented a sad appearance. As Beauregard described it, "The northeast and northwest terrepleins had fallen in, and the western wall had a crack entirely through, from parapet to berme. The greater portion of the southern wall was down, the upper east magazine penetrated, and the lower east magazine wall cracked, the eastern wall itself nearly shot away and large portions down, ramparts gone, and nearly every casemate breached. The casements on the eastern face were still filled with sand, and gave some protection to the garrison from shells. Not a single gun remained *en barbette,* and but a single smoothbore thirty-two-pounder in the west face that could be fired." [69]

The Southern leader's reply to the surrender demand was a single sentence: "Inform Admiral Dahlgren that he may have Fort Sumter when he can take and hold it."

The matter of silencing Sumter was not without its complications. Dahlgren had failed in all attempts to remove the obstructions, because of a combination of factors working against him. First was the matter of tide, which had to be considered carefully before he took his heavy ships too far up the channel, and this also dictated when he could make the approach and how long he could remain in the vicinity of the obstructions. Another hindrance was a cross fire maintained between Fort Sumter on the left and Fort Moultrie on the right. He and Gillmore had conflicting intelligence regarding whether or not Sumter was quiet. The General said it was, but the Admiral had first-hand information that at least two shots were fired recently from a gun on the eastern angle. In the face of this doubt, he decided to make an attack on the fort with men in small boats.

A terrific bombardment was laid down on both Sumter and Moultrie on the 8th. Eyewitnesses looked upon it as "the severest action hitherto between armored vessels and fortifications." [70] While it was in progress, Dahlgren was busy organizing parties for an attack that night. Five divisions of four hundred fifty men, among them one hundred Marines, were to participate. "Great care was taken in organizing the column of attack," the Admiral reported. "There were no better men on hand, and they were led by officers whose standing fully justified their selection."

Late in the day, Dahlgren sent men to borrow boats from Gillmore. They returned with the surprising information that Gillmore also was planning a similar party for an attack that night, and later he confirmed it by note of warning: "I deem it of vital importance that no two distinct parties should approach Sumter at the same time, for fear of accident. I will display a red light from the fort when taken; I ask you to do the same if your party mounts first. Our countersign is 'Detroit.' Let us use it in challenging on the water." [71]

Night came on uncommonly dark. Dahlgren ordered the boats to assemble by 10:00 P.M. alongside the tug *Daffodil* that would tow them to within eight hundred yards of the fort. But, owing to signaling difficulties, it was nearly midnight before all of them reached the station, and then they were cast off in some disorder and confusion. It was understood that one division would create a diversion by moving around to the northwestern front while the others attacked from the southeast. This was not executed as planned. In approaching Sumter, the *Daffodil* swept around a buoy and fouled the boats, casting them off in such a manner that they proceeded in some disorder.[72]

Inside the fort the Southerners were waiting. They expected a night assault and, in readiness for it, had that day brought a supply of hand grenades and fireballs from Charleston. An hour after midnight, someone detected the line of boats advancing from two different directions. Men were placed along the ruined parapet of the sea face and along the crest of the gorge. As the Federals in the leading boats began to land, a galling outburst of fire from rifles and grenades was poured down upon them.

The outer boats returned the fire briefly and then rowed out of danger. Sailors who landed, fired a few times from their revolvers, but for the most part they sought shelter in the embrasures and breaches or under the large masses of debris at the base of the wall, there to be pounded by grenades and fireballs and even fragments of masonry thrown down from the parapet. Suddenly, batteries on James and Sullivan's Islands and on the ironclad gunboat C.S.S. *Chicora,* stationed north of the fort, joined in the defense, guided by the fringe of fire at the fort and by ranges they had established during the daytime. Shot, grape, canister, and shell were ricocheted along the water against the base of Sumter on three fronts. Dahlgren looked on from a small boat a quarter of a mile away. "Moultrie fired like a devil," he wrote in his diary, "the shells breaking around me and screaming in chorus." [73] In twenty minutes the attack was over. Not once had a red light been seen or the countersign "Detroit" been heard from Gillmore's party, which never put in its appearance. Low tide held it in Lighthouse Creek west of Morris Island. [74]

The Federals lost one hundred twenty-four men. Prisoners said they had expected no resistance, that they had thought the breaches in the walls of the fort would be easy of access. But what had appeared to the fleet to be openings were found to be twenty-foot thicknesses of white sand.

Among the captures was an old garrison flag, weatherworn, stained, tattered. Someone said it was the same banner that had been lowered to the Confederates when Fort Sumter surrendered on April 13, 1861. Beauregard presented it to South Carolina.

"The appearance of this flag and the circumstances under which it was found," he wrote Governor M. L. Bonham, "satisfy me that really it is the same one that Major Robert Anderson was permitted to remove, and which our adversary hoped to replace above the shattered walls of that fortress as a dramatic surcease to his humiliation. With the sanction of the War Department, I have the honor to present it, through your excellency, to the State of South Carolina as the fitting custodian of a flag that was designed to mark and make memorable the discomfiture of your people, in the face of your wives, children, and servants." [75]

★ 2

Texan valor: a theme

SEPTEMBER 1863

Admiral David Glasgow Farragut's pet vessel, the U.S.S. *Hartford,* lay at dead anchor near the mouth of the Red River. She had been there for weeks, ever since the close of the Vicksburg campaign, quietly waiting, her guns the only indication her business was warlike. One crewman, Edward B. Latch, wrote: "She seems like a thing of peace." [1] Bees swarmed on her rigging, and up among her spars, birds twitted happily, greeting each dawn with an outpouring of notes strange to the routine of the decks below.

But the serenity that surrounded the *Hartford* was not general over the Southland, especially that part of it around the mouth of the Sabine River. This river, separating Louisiana from Texas, and flowing into the Gulf of Mexico through Sabine Pass, was of great strategic importance because it afforded a short cut for operations against the interior of Texas. Moreover, it was a blockade point, more appreciated perhaps by the South than by the North, for the Federals never seemed to be able to determine how many runners stole into it laden with much-needed supplies and left it with rich cargoes of cotton.

Action that came at Sabine Pass in the opening days of September, '63, making up some of the initial operations in the push along the Texas coast, was planned well in advance and bore Farragut's approval. It was originally intended to be shrouded in secrecy. When the Admiral wrote about it on July 30, he did so in guarded language: "Captain Crocker has a little project on hand which I think well of, and will inform Commodore Bell of it and let him say when they can go down there." [2]

The "project" that Frederick Crocker, captain of the U.S.S. *Clifton,* had in mind called for a surprise attack on the Confederate forces stationed in an unfinished earthwork in Sabine Pass, known as Fort Griffin. In August, Farragut set out for New York on a leave of absence, the final decision regarding the Sabine offensive, as he had promised, left to Commodore Henry H. Bell, commanding the West Gulf Blockading Squadron, a man reputed to be one of the severest diciplinarians in the Navy, and yet one of its most honored and beloved officers. [3]

Bell, on September 2, notified Lieutenant Commander John Madison, commanding the U.S.S. *Owasco,* stationed on blockade duty off Sabine Pass, that the Army planned to effect a landing there in the course of a week. To maintain secrecy, one of the blockading vessels was to form a rendezvous with the *Clifton,* an ex-Staten Island ferryboat that had seen service in the battle of New Orleans. This was to be done out of sight of land, where a pilot could be taken on board, and the ship then anchored off the bar in such a position as to lead the attack.

But the Confederates soon got on to what was happening. Somewhere along the line, leakage occurred, and Union Captain John P. Gillis, senior officer on duty off Galveston, Texas, relayed word that the Southerners had announced the raid in their newspapers. [4] As further evidence that the plans were known, Confederate General John B. Magruder, commanding the District of Texas, issued orders to have the Pass and its approaches fortified without delay. And yet, despite the advance knowledge, nothing was done about it by the Rebels, possibly because of lack of time and scarcity of troops.

The Federals meanwhile were trying to acquire as much information as possible on what they would encounter when they pushed into the Pass. According to their best intelligence, assembled there were two thirty-two-pounders *en barbette,* a battery of fieldpieces, and two bay boats converted into rams.

Plans for the attack were laid out in New Orleans. There Bell and Crocker met with Major General William B. Franklin, commanding the land forces; and it was the consequent assemblage of ships and troops that tipped off the Confederates to impending action, although they were uninformed as to where it would come. Galveston and Matagorda were considered the most likely objectives.

The Federals planned the expedition to arrive off Sabine Pass during the night of September 6, ready to start in over the bar at early daylight next morning, catching whatever anchored Confederate ships were on duty and unable to escape. It was a well-devised plan, but its outcome was largely dependent on the element of surprise.

As details began unfolding, the side-wheel steamer U.S.S. *Granite City,* armed with six howitzers and a twelve-pounder rifle, headed for Sabine Pass a day in advance. James G. Taylor, considered one of the best pilots in the area, was on board. Her captain, Acting Master C. W. Lamson, had instructions to communicate with the blockaders on arriving at his destination, to anchor the vessel exactly at the mouth of the channel, and at night to show a light from the seaboard side that would give the fleet some guide by which to reach safe anchorage.

On the morning of the 6th, the first division of land forces under Brigadier General Godfrey Weitzel, all from Franklin's Ninteenth Corps, began gathering in transports in Atchafalaya Bay, a short run away on the coast of Louisiana. Standing by with them were the U.S. steamers *Arizona, Clifton,* and *Sachem,* all of low draft, all with light armor, all with thin boilers and unprotected machinery, and all with weak frames and badly out of repair. Sharpshooters were detailed to each gunboat, after which the entire force started out, four thousand men strong, regulating its speed so as to arrive at Sabine Pass during the night.

It was well after dark when the fleet closed in with the land and moved down the coast in not more than four fathoms of water. The object was to fall in with the *Granite City* and her signal light. Steadily it steamed along until reckoning and the trending of the coast convinced Crocker that he had passed the sought-for point. Back he came, along the same course, until he was certain the *Granite City* was not at her post, and neither were the blockaders. In this emergency, he moved the line of ships to the eastward and anchored far enough offshore to be concealed from land when daylight came.

But before Crocker could withdraw, his movements were observed. At two o'clock that morning, the Confederate sentinel at Fort Griffin reported enemy ships were signaling off the coast. When dawn came, two steamers could be seen at the bar, apparently sounding for the channel to Sabine Pass.

Shortly after sunrise, the *Granite City* appeared and ran up close to the fleet. Soon her captain was rowed across in a boat to report to Crocker. He said that on arriving off the Pass the day prior, he had found no blockaders but, instead, a lead-colored man-of-war, which his imagination quickly transformed into the South's dreaded raider, *Alabama,* the vessel, three times the size of the *Granite City,* in which the clever Raphael Semmes was ridding the seas of Union commerce. This caused him much alarm. So, without waiting further, he steamed away to the mouth of the Calcasieu River. There, further upsetting secrecy, he sent in a boat in an unsuccessful attempt to get information about Sabine Pass.

When he heard of these developments, Crocker knew the first attempt at surprise had failed. He also realized there was danger that the enemy had learned of their intentions through the boat sent ashore from the *Granite City,* and for this reason he proposed that the attack be made at once. But Weitzel balked. He was still in favor of attempting a surprise and suggested waiting until the following night. Under the circumstances, Crocker, whose orders specifically directed him to co-operate with the Army, consented.[5]

Once more the *Granite City* was sent to anchor off the Pass and show a light. Meanwhile the other steamers spread out in a line across the route the divisions of the Nineteenth Corps was expected to follow. There they waited in the hope of intercepting and aiding the other vessels. One division under General Franklin, it was learned during the day, already had passed unseen and was at anchor off the Pass.

That night the fleet moved in and stopped near the channel. Waiting there was the U.S.S. *Cayuga,* from which came an explanation as to why no blockaders had been found off Sabine by the *Granite City.* Only one ship, the *Owasco,* was assigned to the post, and on Sunday this vessel had been forced to go to Galveston for a supply of coal, sending back in its place the *Cayuga,* which had arrived too late to be sighted by the expedition.

Before dark, Confederates watching from Fort Griffin counted twenty-two vessels standing off the bar. The sight was sobering, for only forty-four men (members of the Davis Guard, a company of Irishmen from Houston) were on hand to put up a defense; and only five guns, a forty-four-pounder smoothbore and four thirty-two-pounder Parrotts, were ready for service. A sixth gun, a brass twenty-four-pounder, could not be used because ammunition was unavailable.

Out in the flat in the late afternoon, Crocker and Franklin met for a conference. The next morning they decided that the *Clifton* should steam in over the bar on a reconnaissance and, if conditions seemed suitable, signal the other gunboats to follow.

Night settled down over Sabine Pass, dense and dark, broken only by a sprinkling of Western stars. There was a strange quietness everywhere—around the ships gathered together like a nesting of ducks, up the river along the sand strip where once had stood the old battery, higher up on the elevation crowned by the threatening parapets of Fort Griffin, and two miles farther away in the little settlement with the hopeful name of Sabine City, a village populated largely by the families of the men in the fort. People waited, stirred by an undercurrent of excitement, for the manner in which the Union ships had closed in on the bar indicated that an attack was imminent.

E. P. Alsbury, one of the Irishmen on duty in the fort, watched as daylight broke. "The morning of the 8th of September, 1863, dawned brightly," he recorded, "and the golden glow from the east was reflected by the white sails of the Federal fleet which were making for a berth as near the shallow bar as possible. Some of the sailing transports were being towed by the steamers and four of the latter, as the sequel proved, were gunboats. Their movements were watched with thrilling interest by the people from the town and fort, and but few of the former anticipated any other result in the coming battle than disaster to the Confederates." [6]

As agreed, the *Clifton* crossed the bar and moved up the Pass, its captain soon learning that Federal intelligence was faulty. The Confederates were prepared. Frowning down from the Texas side of the river was the fort, opposite a point where the stream was divided by an island of sand; and higher up could be seen a small cotton-clad steamer. But few troops were in evidence anywhere.

Crocker steamed up within easy range of the fort and, during the next hour, fired a number of shells at it, hoping to draw answering fire that would give some indication of the Confederate strength. Met with only silence, he assumed the guns he could see in the embrasures of the fort were dummies, and he signaled for the other ships to cross the bar. By 10:00 A.M. all the gunboats and a number of the transports were inside at anchor. Vessels drawing more than six feet had to fight their way in through mud.

At eleven o'clock the little cotton-clad seen up the river, the

Uncle Ben, armed only with a twelve-pounder mountain howitzer, ran down near the fort and made a feint, as though she
was prepared to come charging against the fleet. She was greeted
with three shots, all of which passed harmlessly overhead.

As soon as General Franklin arrived, Crocker boarded his
steamer to discuss the next move. The fort, it was decided, was
too formidable to attack by the gunboats alone, so plans were
made for the Army to assist. Before proceeding with the assault,
Crocker, Franklin, and Weitzel were rowed ashore in a small
boat to reconnoiter, but they found it difficult to land because
of shoal water and mud. They returned, after determining that
troops could be put ashore near Old Battery Point, about a
thousand yards below Fort Griffin, at a spot where the banks
were nearly perpendicular and the water of sufficient depth to
allow steamers to run directly alongside.

In planning the attack, the officers took note that the Confederate guns appeared to be elevated and pointed to command one particular place in the channel next to the Texas
shore. If the gunboats steamed into the range of this concentrated fire, they would almost certainly be disabled. To avoid
such a possibility, it was decided that the *Sachem,* followed by
the *Arizona,* should steam up the Louisiana channel while the
Clifton advanced slowly up the Texas channel, ready to advance
upon the fort the moment its guns were turned upon the other
vessels. The *Granite City* would follow the *Clifton* and take
position just above the old battery, where it could cover the
troops when they began landing immediately after the gunboat
attack began.

This strategy was altogether different from that recommended by Commodore Bell.[7] Before the expedition left New
Orleans, it was agreed that the troops should land first to
create a diversion, after which the armed vessels should proceed up the channel. When the plan was changed during the
discussion at Sabine, Crocker protested, but Franklin said he
would take the responsibility.[8]

As the officers prepared to separate at the close of their

meeting, Crocker voiced an alarming thought: If he grounded near the fort, as was possible, he would be entirely destroyed should the troops happen not to land. Franklin scoffed at the idea.[9]

By noon the naval forces were ready for the attack, but Franklin delayed, hoping more transports would arrive. Inside the fort, the leader of the Davis Guards, young Lieutenant Richard W. Dowling, confident an assault was near, kept his men in the bombproofs and stood in position to fire the first gun himself. His reinforcements at the moment consisted of only three Confederate officers who had arrived from upstream, bringing his total strength to forty-seven. But they were welcome additions. During the impending battle, one of them, Leon Smith of the Ordnance Department, would stand upon the ramparts with flag in hand and stimulate the men around him to greater action.[10]

At 4:00 P.M. Franklin sent word he was ready. Crocker began moving up the Texas channel, rapidly throwing shells from the *Clifton*'s forward nine-inch gun. Across in the Louisiana channel, the *Sachem* also proceeded slowly upstream, followed, after considerable floundering, by the *Arizona*. These latter vessels had orders to pass the fort, if possible, and to capture the cotton-clad steamer and two river steamers that now could be seen at the wharf at Sabine City.

As the Federals had hoped, the Confederates changed the direction of their guns and began firing at the *Sachem*. Several shells were sent, before one of them, aimed by capable gunner Michael McKernan, totally disabled the vessel.[11] Her commander, Acting Volunteer Lieutenant Amos Johnston, dropped anchor to prevent grounding, and then sent a message to Acting Master Howard Tibbitts of the *Arizona* to come up and take him in tow. A number of men on the stricken ship jumped overboard and swam toward the *Arizona,* and some of them drowned. Thirty-two were killed or wounded by the shot that struck the *Sachem*.

The *Clifton,* in the meantime, as soon as it was seen that the direction of the guns had been changed, put on speed and dashed up the Texas channel. She was more than halfway toward the fort before her approach was noticed, and then every gun was brought to bear on her. For minutes the shells splashed around her, most of them harmlessly, until one of them shot her wheel ropes away, causing her to swing about and ground. She stopped in such a position that only three of her guns could be used, but these were employed with effect for a brief period before her steam drum was punctured, and steam and hot water drove the sharpshooters and crew off her upper deck.

Along with Crocker's other troubles, he was having difficulty with command. His executive officer, Acting Master Robert Rhodes, lay dead from a shell. Rhodes's duties were assigned to Acting Master B. S. Weeks, next in rank, who was in command of the after pivot gun, at the moment not in use.

"I don't see anything to do," Weeks said when given the assignment.[12]

Events were rushing forward. The vessel caught fire, and Crocker directed Weeks to extinguish the blaze.

"Do you expect me to do it by myself?" grumbled Weeks. "I don't know where the buckets are and I can't control the men."

Crocker turned in desperation to Senior Engineer James A. Fox, standing near, and the fire was promptly extinguished.

"In the meantime the enemy's fire was becoming hot and deadly," reported Crocker, "and men were falling fast. A shot struck the muzzle of one of the forward guns, partially disabling it and wounding many of the crew. While placing new men at the gun I learned that the lock of the nine-inch pivot forward (my main dependence) was broken, but the crew were manfully fighting it and exploding the primer with a hatchet.

"In this way the fight continued about half an hour, and yet the *Granite City* or the army transports had made not the slightest movement toward taking their positions, but lay drifting with the tide. The *Sachem* had become entirely silent, the

Arizona making only a few ineffectual shots, and the enemy's fire becoming more and more accurate and deadly."

While Crocker was directing the fire at the forward gun, Weeks approached him and urged that he surrender and prevent a useless sacrifice of lives, adding that he already had hauled down the flag. Crocker looked about. There was no sign that help was on its way. The *Sachem* was silenced, the *Arizona* retreating, and his men jumping overboard. Then he, too, turned away and went to destroy all signal books and ship papers.

The *Arizona* ran straight out across the bar. In passing the transports, Weitzel hailed her and pointed to refugees from the *Clifton* who had swum ashore. "Look at your men coming down the beach there!" he shouted. There was no answer from the *Arizona,* no change in her course. A little later she was hailed by Franklin. "Aren't you going to stop and protect the transports? he called. From her deck a lone voice replied: "The enemy's field artillery will be down upon you in five minutes!" [13] Shortly afterward she ran aground and remained caught until night.

Within twenty minutes after surrender flags appeared on the *Clifton* and the *Sachem,* the Confederates had the two vessels in tow. A tone of desperation marked the retreat. The transport *Crescent* grounded, and two hundred thousand rations were thrown overboard to lighten her. The steamer *Laurel Hill* foundered after losing her smokestacks, and someone ordered— without proper authority[14]—two hundred mules driven over her sides. Behind were left nearly three hundred officers and men, including killed, wounded, and captured.

A scene had taken place on board the *Clifton* during the battle that would be exposed prominently in official records. It involved Acting Assistant Surgeon D. D. T. Nestell, who was charged with running away from his post. When questioned by the Navy Department many months after the engagement at Sabine Pass, he frankly reported his behavior:

During the engagement referred to I was at my post in the sick bay, on the berth deck aft, attended by my steward, where I remained till within a very few minutes of its termination—until the following scene occurred: All the hands stationed there and in the fire room came rushing through my sick bay to the ladders leading to the main deck, shouting in the most frantic manner: "The boiler has bursted! We all will be scalded, and everybody for himself!" and I, not knowing to the contrary, was seized with the irresistible desire to save my life as well. I was panic-stricken—rather rushing into than from danger—as the following facts will show. Almost carried by a now demoralized crowd toward the stern of the vessel, where all was alike confusion worse confounded, the men retreated behind their guns for protection from the fearful missiles which seemed to whirl to within two feet of our heads; the conviction that, should the enemy depress their pieces, they must inevitably destroy us; many jumping overboard, and the screams that "We had surrendered, and still they are firing at us," I did climb over the stern of the rudder chain. I had remained there not longer than one moment, when I heard some voice from the hurricane deck saying: "Take him to the doctor." Instantly my senses returned and I went to the sick bay, where I received the first wounded, the executive officer and men, whom I discovered at a glance were fatally injured—already in a state of collapse—and was in the act of administering stimuli when a Rebel officer, covered with gold lace (whom I afterwards found to be a surgeon), sprang beside me and brutally ordered me to "leave things alone, generally"; to "get out of that"; who, on my remonstrance that I must attend to my wounded, beckoned to one Major Leon Smith, saying: "Major, clear all those Yanks out of this"; then telling me that my instruments and sick things belonged to the Confederate Navy; that they were just what he had been looking for; that he prayed for them; whereupon I was hustled onto the main deck, where I found a guard with fixed bayonets to enforce obedience.

Going to my stateroom, which was knocked into pi, the Rebel surgeon followed, denied me my clothes and money, and demanded the key to the dispensary, which I would not give him. Here he was joined by Major Smith, who ordered me to get on the Rebel vessel then moored alongside the *Clifton*. Going on board, I found Captain Crocker and others, officers and men, more fortunate than myself, with their trunks and other luggage, when a fearful cry arose that "the ship was on fire near the magazine," with excited appeals that everybody shove off, when Captain Crocker suggested that I should get out the wounded. Immediately, with that intention, I returned to the berth deck gangway of the *Clifton,* where I was again ordered back by Major Smith, this time furiously drawing his sword, who swore at the guard and told them to "shoot any damned Yankee going below," thus forcing me to Captain Crocker's side, to whom I related the event, and who must have witnessed and heard all that transpired. In a very few minutes, however, I was permitted, without leaving the Rebel vessel, to receive the *Clifton*'s wounded, and soon after we were conveyed to Beaumont.[15]

In his report of the affair, General Magruder took particular delight in pointing out that the two vessels captured "were among those which disgracefully fled under a flag of truce from the scene of triumph of Texan valor at Galveston in January last."[16] On them he found a full supply of ordnance stores, eighteen heavy guns, and other items, including ammunition and medical stores. Prisoners he placed at two hundred, and killed and wounded at fifty. Not a man on the Confederate side had been hurt.

By resolution the Confederate Congress extended its thanks to the Davis Guards, citing the defense of Sabine Pass as "one of the most brilliant and heroic achievements in the history of this war."

As a part of the aftermath, the Union tried to figure out what had happened. That it was another defeat similar to that of Galveston Bay was generally agreed. "It is my unpleasant duty to inform the Navy Department that the expedition to Sabine Pass . . . has totally failed," reported Commodore Bell. The blame appeared to rest with the Army. "The reason why the Army failed so utterly to co-operate, after having promised so fairly," Crocker informed Secretary Welles, "I have been unable to learn; but it has been since proved to me that if a single movement toward landing troops had been made, the enemy would have evacuated Sabine Pass and the expedition would have proved a success." Union General Nathaniel P. Banks, commanding the Department of the Gulf, partially agreed. "In my judgment the Army should not have returned," he wrote Abraham Lincoln, "but should have continued to the point indicated for landing upon the coast, as contemplated in the instructions." But he added that this would have been done had the *Granite City* and the *Arizona* not withdrawn.

History would make only modest note of this incident in which a little band of forty-odd Irishmen drove off a fleet of ships and an army numbering thousands. Proper acclaim, one of their own number suspected, would come with the years. "The heroism displayed at Sabine Pass," later wrote E. P. Alsbury, "has never been excelled. . . . The young hero, Dick Dowling, has passed away from earth, but his memory will remain green among those who were his fellow soldiers, and still will live in song and story, when Texan valor will be the theme as heroic deeds are recounted." [17]

Little boat with an
explosive nose

SEPTEMBER-OCTOBER 1863

The order directed to Lieutenant W. T. Glassell of the Confederate Navy on September 6 was perhaps one of the most evasive on record. It stated simply: "Sixty men, with three officers, Dr. Griggs, Midshipman Clayton, and Midshipman Hogue, are placed under your command. You will proceed to Charleston with them without any delay and report yourself and command to Flag Officer John R. Tucker for duty." [1] Nothing about it indicated that therein was represented one of the initial steps necessary to bring about an attack by a torpedo boat.

The Confederates called it a "David." [2] It was a small boat, forty-eight and a half feet long, and five and a half to six feet wide.[3] The boiler was forward, the engine aft, and between them was a cuddy, or small cabin, just big enough for the crew of five or six men to stand in and attend to their individual duties. The torpedo, made of copper and equipped with a tube of fulminate of mercury as a fuse, was carried on a ten-foot spar that protruded from the bow and could be raised or lowered by a line. In action, the boat was so well submerged that nothing was visible except her tiny smokestack, the hatch coaming, and the stanchion over which the torpedo line was brought aft.

This odd craft had been under construction quietly at Charleston for a long time, largely at the insistence of General Beauregard, who thoroughly approved of the device. But the zealot who had worked hardest for its adoption as a part of the Confederate defense was Captain Francis D. Lee of the Provisional Engineers, an officer considered more or less an expert on torpedoes. Early in '62 he visited Richmond in an attempt to get support for such a craft from the Navy Department, but the officials with whom he talked showed no interest. Then, at a conference held in September of that year to discuss the Charleston defenses, he presented the idea again, this time with more success.

Beauregard was so impressed he wrote Governor Francis Pickens of South Carolina that one torpedo boat would be worth several gunboats. "I fear not to put on record now," he added, "that half a dozen of these 'torpedo rams,' of small comparative cost, would keep this harbor clear of four times the number of the enemy's ironclad gunboats." [4]

The following month he sent Lee to the War Department in Richmond to present plans for a torpedo boat. He also forwarded a letter to Adjutant General Samuel Cooper, informing him that South Carolina had placed at his disposal fifty thousand dollars for the construction of such a craft, but due to the uncertainties of estimating the cost, he wanted the support of the Confederate Government. This he got in sufficient degree to start the project. Soon, engineers were at work. A crew of sixty officers and men, under Captain M. M. Gray, in charge of the submarine defenses of Charleston, drew the assignment. Final plans were prepared by Dr. St. Julien Ravenel. [5] Standing by, helping in every way possible, even offering to finance the boat from his personal funds, was Theodore D. Stoney, citizen of means and of great sympathy for the Confederate cause. [6]

The project was based at Stoney Landing, a plantation thirty-five miles north of Charleston on the Santee Canal.[7] Also at the Landing was a sawmill and government niter plant operated by David C. Ebaugh, of Maryland.[8] Ebaugh agreed to help with whatever facilities he could make available.[9] As the boat developed, others lent a hand and made so many offers of contributions that in the end Stoney was relieved of the financial responsibility he had assumed.

By April 1863, when the first major attack on Charleston was made by the fleet under Du Pont, Lee was instructed by Beauregard to make all the necessary arrangements to insure the complete destruction of the torpedo boat at a moment's warning.[10] But this direful necessity was avoided, and the work on the craft continued, even while the fearful attack against Battery Wagner was in progress.

The idea of sinking with torpedoes some of the ships standing guard off Charleston became a subject of general discussion. It created a gleam in the eyes of many Southerners stationed in the area. They looked admiringly at Captain Lee's "submarine repeating spar torpedo," a device of his own development. The problem concerned how best to explode one or more of them against the side of some vessel.

Lieutenant Glassell, a Virginian, and James H. Tomb, a Georgian, both assigned to the C.S.S. *Chicora* standing by in Charleston Harbor, had been experimenting for some time in an attempt to blow up the monitors off Morris Island with a torpedo on a spar attached to the bow of the first and second cutters of that ship. But every effort failed. They would pass out by Fort Sumter in fine shape on the last of the ebb tide, but soon they lost their headway as they bucked the first of the flood tide. Finally they reported to their fleet captain, Flag Officer Tucker, that they would have to have other means of propelling the boats. It was then decided that they should be assigned to the new David, now complete and painted bluish gray above the water line.

Soon they were running the craft about the harbor at night,

giving it its first tests.[11] Some study was made of the depth at which the torpedo should be carried. After trial, they finally settled on six and a half feet. When steaming under good conditions, the boat could make seven knots.

On September 18, it was announced in special orders that Lieutenant Glassell, having volunteered for special service against the fleet of the United States off the harbor, was to report for the duty and to be assisted by Captain Stoney as first officer, Tomb as engineer, and Charles Scemps and James Ables as assistants. Four days later, Glassell received more specific instructions from Flag Officer Tucker: "You will assume command of the torpedo steamer 'David,' and when ready will proceed to operate against the enemy's fleet off Charleston Harbor, with a view of destroying as many of the enemy's vessels as possible, reporting the results to me." [12]

Glassell was an ideal choice to captain such a venture. He had been active in the war only a few months, but those months had been marked by great energy. On his return from duty with the United States Navy in China in '62, he was placed in prison for refusing to take the oath of allegiance; and the moment he was exchanged, he joined the Confederate Navy.

The night of October 5 was chosen for the attack. The water was calm, a slight north wind was blowing, and up in the heavens, stars twinkled above a slight haze blanketing the harbor. It was fully dark when a quiet little group gathered on the wharf at Charleston. Four men separated from it and descended to the level of the water where the David waited. Glassell was among them, and so was Tomb, but Stoney, Scemps, and Ables for some reason were missing. In their place were only two men —Walker Cannon, assistant pilot on the ironclad *Palmetto State,* and James Sullivan, fireman on the *Chicora.*

At 7:30 P.M. the little craft moved off and nosed toward the main ship channel, her lone propeller barely audible above the grind of her steam engine aft. Between Fort Sumter and Sullivan's Island, Pilot Cannon steered toward the shore and found a tiny gap in the rope obstructions, now more formidable than ever. Then he headed toward the Union fleet, lying over a wide area. But the position of the ships was no problem to him. Much of that day he had spent staring with glasses at a single object, the *New Ironsides,* a formidable mass of might, rocking gently in the distance toward the bar. After clearing the ropes, he set his course and maintained a steady rudder.

Glassell stood with his arms resting on the rim of the cuddy, his eyes keenly studying the enemy ships as they took shape against the campfires on Morris Island. "Perhaps I was mistaken," he later reminisced, "but it did occur to me that if we had then, instead of only one, just ten or twelve torpedoes to make a simultaneous attack on all the ironclads, and this quickly followed by the egress of our rams, not only might the grand fleet have been destroyed, but the twenty-odd thousand troops on Morris Island been left at our mercy."

It was eight-thirty when the David arrived in the vicinity of the *Ironsides,* anchored in the main ship channel off Morris Island, and got close enough to be able to make out the great hulk against the background of stars. There, a matter of yards away, Glassell ordered the torpedo boat to stand off and await the flood tide. The propeller was stopped and an anchor was dropped.

Half an hour later the nine o'clock gun sounded, and immediately the noise of the camps quieted, and lights blinked out one by one. The four men standing elbow to elbow in the cuddy agreed that the time to attack had come. Without further ado, Engineer Tomb opened the throttle of the engine, and the propeller again started whirling, nosing the tiny craft through the water directly toward the *Ironsides* amidships.

Fifty yards from her side, a voice hailed from the rail of the vessel. Three times the hail was repeated, and then rifle fire blazed from the deck of the ship. Glassell raised a double-barreled shotgun and fired.[13] There was no further hail, but a clamor of excited voices came to the Southerners across the water. Seconds later the torpedo on the spar collided with the ship under her starboard quarter, fifteen feet from her sternpost.

Immediately there was a terrific explosion, and a column of water shot up into the air and came down upon the David in a deluge, flooding her hold and extinguishing the fire under her boiler. Tomb tried to back the craft, but the vessel had been shaken so violently that some of the iron ballast on board had shifted to such a position as to keep the engine from working. Suddenly, rifle fire sounded again from the deck of the *Ironsides,* and bullets began to ping against the side of the torpedo boat. Glassell, Tomb, and Sullivan, thinking the craft was doomed, leaped into the water and began swimming away.

But Tomb recovered from his desire to flee. The farther he swam toward Morris Island, the more his clothing seemed to impede him. Looking back, he saw the David still afloat, and he decided, rather than to swim farther into the darkness, to make a new effort to save her. As he approached her side, he found Walker Cannon hanging to the life lines.

"You still here?" observed Tomb in surprise.

"Yeah," said the pilot, "I can't swim a stroke."

They got back on board, and in the darkness of the hold, Tomb knelt and worked patiently to get a fire started under the boiler. An occasional rifle ball still pinged against the side of the vessel, but the men kept their heads down and continued with their efforts. At last a blaze began growing, and soon steam was building up in the pressure gauge.

When the boat was once more ready to move, Cannon took the wheel and steered out into the channel. From the *Ironsides,* as the David steamed away, came two eleven-inch shells and an outburst of rifle fire, but no damage was done. On through the fleet the tiny craft moved, at one point passing within three feet of a monitor.

On board the *Ironsides* there was considerable confusion. The shotgun blast from Glassell had severely wounded Acting Ensign C. W. Howard. Several men suffered wounds from the torpedo explosion. The damage to the ship could not be estimated.

Only brief mention of the incident was recorded in the log of the *New Ironsides:* "Hailed her rapidly four times, and she making no reply, fired into her with musketry; she returned fire. . . . Almost at the same time the steamer struck us near No. 6 port, starboard side. . . . The steamer then dropped astern; continued firing at her with musketry as long as she was in sight. . . . The explosion of the torpedo knocked down armory bulkhead and store rooms in wake of the explosion. William L. Knox, ordinary seaman, leg broken; Thomas Little, master at arms, several severe contusions from the shock of the explosion." [14]

Admiral Dahlgren, commanding the Union's Charleston fleet, heard the disturbance from his flagship anchored in a creek, but the tide was so low he could not get out until later in the night. When he could, he steamed to the *Ironsides* to investigate.

As dawn broke, sailors on the Federal vessel saw a man hanging to her rudder chains. Quickly they swarmed on him. Later he was taken before Dahlgren, who described him in his diary as "a frightened wretch." It was Sullivan. When questioned, he gave a full description of the torpedo boat and its torpedo, even to the number of nipples on the fuse.

Sometime later, Glassell, who had hailed a schooner after floundering about in the harbor for an hour or so, was brought in a prisoner. But Dahlgren did not bother to talk to him. Papers found in his pockets were taken to the Admiral and revealed that the attack had been "regularly concocted." [15]

"How far the enemy may seem encouraged, I do not know," Dahlgren wrote the Secretary of the Navy, "but I think it will be well to be prepared against a considerable issue of these small craft. It is certainly the best form of the torpedo which has come to my notice, and a large quantity may as well be exploded as sixty pounds."

Damage to the *New Ironsides* was brushed aside as unimportant at first, but later, after a carpenter had had time to make a thorough investigation, the story was changed. "In my opinion this ship ought to be docked as soon as she can possibly be spared from this harbor," Dahlgren informed Welles. It would be more than a year before the vessel would see action again.

On October 10, Dahlgren made an entry in his diary: "About sunset poor Howard died of the one little buckshot which struck him from the torpedo. I had made him a master the next day, but a Higher Power has given him a better promotion. (It savors to me of murder.)"

Back at the Charleston wharf, the little David lay where Tomb and Cannon had anchored her. In the future she would be a greater curiosity than ever, for her presence in the harbor had announced to the enemy that a new threat was at hand. The effect of her attack against the *New Ironsides* touched off panic among the Federals. Only hours passed before Dahlgren was on his way to Port Royal to see what could be done there to guard ships against such machines. He had in mind that they should be protected by outriggers and that the harbor should be strewn with a similar class of craft.

He sent off a confidential dispatch to Welles: "Among the many inventions with which I have been familiar, I have seen none which have acted so perfectly at first trial. The secrecy, rapidity of movement, control of direction, and precise explosion indicate, I think, the introduction of the torpedo element as a means of certain warfare. It can be ignored no longer. If sixty pounds of powder, why not six hundred pounds? . . . The mysterious part is that after the explosion it was thought that two monitors saw and fired at the vessel. The captain affects to believe it went down, but of the precise fact nothing is actually known. . . . By all means let us have a quantity of these torpedoes, and thus turn them against the enemy. We can make them faster than they can."

Not again would Union vessels on duty off Southern ports spend nights in peace. High steam would be carried at all hours by all of them, to make sure they could move on the instant, and around them, through the darkness, picket boats and tugs would move on constant guard. Some would have around them hawsers held in place by projecting poles. The Southerners had come up with another innovation in an attempt to offset the superior power of the Federal Navy.

★ 4

That ram up the Roanoke!

OCTOBER 1863

James Van Boskirk, acting master of the mortar schooner *Adolph Hugel,* was a man with a strong sense of duty. This he demonstrated one morning while examining the cargo of the sutler schooner *Mail* at Alexandria, Virginia, across the Potomac from Washington. This vessel had been duly inspected and cleared by the customhouse at Georgetown, only a few miles up the river. But Van Boskirk, acting for the Potomac Flotilla, was not so quick to give it clearance, having observed on board four hundred twenty-eight dozen cans of a product labeled "milk drink." To him this looked suspicious. He noticed that instead of being soldered in the usual manner, the tops and bottoms of the cans were sealed with some resinous substance. In addition, the ends could be bent over in a way that easily converted them into drinking cups. He tried them. They worked. Then he took a sip of the contents of one of the cans, and his eyes opened wide, for the liquid was a drink strongly resembling eggnog. The consignees, he learned, were from a state "celebrated for its liquor law"—Maine—and the product itself had been prepared by Numsen, Carroll and Company, 18 Light Street, Baltimore, Maryland. The *Mail,* clearing for Belle Plain, Virginia, site of Army camps, was promptly seized, and notice was sent out that sutlers were committing fraud—selling intoxicants disguised as milk and smuggled in cans.[1]

Such an attempt to sneak eggnog to Federal troops by ship was only one of the developments bothering Union Navy Secretary Gideon Welles as the war advanced. There were worries galore, some seriously concerned with happenings up the shallow rivers of North Carolina, where the Southerners were said to be building a number of ironclad ships, at least one of them a ram on the fashion of the *Merrimack.* The Union vessels along the sounds in that area were of too deep draft to reach them, so their destruction at the moment appeared to be a problem that rested with the Army.

The Union Navy's responsibility in the matter was entrusted to one of its best young officers—Charles W. Flusser, Annapolis born, but appointed to the Naval Academy from Kentucky. He had remained true to the old service, even though two of his brothers joined the South. Nothing would shake him in his determination to stay with the Union. When his old friend, George Hollins, resigned to go with the Confederacy and later wrote him that a high command awaited him in the Rebel Navy, he replied:

"Dear Cap: I shall never do it. What! Be one of the very first to fire on the flag? Not I. I have no appetite for argument tonight; my heart is sick. Is it not enough to drive an honest man out of his senses to find thieves making a great nation destroy itself? Where are your wits, man? How can this business end? In 'peace' and 'slavery.' The end may bring the death of both, forever, and worse, inaugurate an era of blood nonparalleled. Will the South be whipped by the North? Not while one Southerner lives. Will the North be whipped by the South? Not while the Alleghenies rise above level land. Just look, then, at the prospect. Blood, rapine, desolation, war. Hollins, thou canst not shake thou gory locks at me and say I did it. Yours in Union." [2]

Flusser's thirtieth birthday was still ahead of him when he moved on board the U.S.S. *Miami,* the first of a class of double-ender, side-wheel steamers designed especially for river service. She was fitted with steering gear and rudder in bow and stern, and was so erratic in her behavior that members of her crew called her "Miasma." [3] Flusser's reputation in the service was established long before he came to the *Miami*. There were laudatory stories about his behavior on board his former command, the *Commodore Perry,* one story being that he had run straight at the Rebel flagship in the action at Roanoke Island. These stimulated the imagination, for he was such an unwarlike sort. A little under medium height, of spare build, with light complexion, he wore a long tan mustache that he sometimes pulled while talking. He dressed in a blue jacket open to the breeze, without waistcoat, and his cap was usually perched jauntily to one side. Whenever he went ashore he treated himself to a spell of horseback riding, usually at full speed. His men noticed that he moved quickly, whether on deck or land. His chief station was Plymouth, a small town that lay along the Roanoke River, not far above its mouth where it emptied into Albemarle Sound. It was from there that he soon began sending information regarding the ironclads the Southerners were building, not knowing that in less than a year one of them would be an agent to his death.

An early message from Flusser relayed word that a ram and a floating battery were under construction up the Roanoke River near Edwards Ferry, and that the man who had designed the battery said it would not be completed during the year. But another informant reported that he had seen heavy guns on their way from Weldon, that both the battery and the ram were being plated, and that they were nearly complete. Flusser wrote that he was rather inclined to trust the latter report.[4]

In late July, Flusser dispatched an urgent message to Commander H. K. Davenport, stationed in the U.S.S. *Hetzel* off New Bern, North Carolina: "The floating battery and steamer up the river at Edwards Ferry are having iron put on. They could be destroyed by five hundred cavalry landing at Winton and marching on them with some combustibles. I should like to go with a party. If they are not destroyed they will give us trouble yet."

The reply Flusser received to this message came from Acting Rear Admiral Samuel P. Lee, commanding the North Atlantic Blockading Squadron. It said that the Army had in view an expedition that was to take place immediately, and that Flusser should "co-operate within the limits of your sound discretion." [5] But the Army did not have the same project in mind that Flusser had written about. Union cavalry went to Winton, followed by three gunboats which halted there while the horsemen dashed off to destroy a railroad bridge at Weldon. Flusser tried to get a small party detached to destroy the ship building at Edwards Ferry, but his efforts went for naught, for he never succeeded in impressing the commanding officer with the importance of such a move.

Nearly a month passed before a stir to destroy the ironclads again arose. This time it was encouraged by "a naturalized citizen of Irish birth" named Michael Cohen. At the start of the war, Cohen was running a distillery at Tarboro. To take advantage of the military exemption for millers, he quickly turned his establishment into a gristmill. But the personal security thus provided was of short duration. On July 30, '63, Union troops, not knowing of his allegiance, swept through the area and burned his property, leaving him liable to conscription. In desperation, he left Tarboro and followed the invaders to New Bern,[6] there exercising his faculties for avoiding the life of a soldier by getting himself assigned to the Federal Quartermaster Department as a plumber and gas fitter. In this capacity he was ready to do his bit for the cause, and he was willing to talk. One ironclad under construction back where he had come from, he told the invaders, had been destroyed by the same forces that burned his mill; but forty miles away, on the Roanoke River in Halifax County, about twenty-five miles below the town of Halifax, at a place called Smith's, both a ram gunboat like the *Merrimack* and a floating battery were under construction.

Cohen swore his information was correct. It was obtained, he said, from men who had been taken from employment at his mill to work on the gunboat. The ram had been launched about the first of the preceding July, he also revealed, and her plating had been begun around the middle of the month. He described this plating as two inches thick, in two layers, one horizontal, one vertical, with holes punched by a small engine brought from Richmond. When completed, it would be armed with a Brooke rifle. The floating battery was to be stationed at Rainbow Bluff, a fortified point just below Hamilton.

Cohen's statement gave Admiral Lee grave concern. "I hear that the ironclad on the Roanoke at Edwards Ferry, above Rainbow Bluff, is nearly completed," he wrote Major General John J. Peck, commanding the Union Army's District of North Carolina. "If not destroyed she may attack your fortified towns on the water side. We have only wooden vessels to oppose her. I respectfully suggest to you the propriety of an expedition to destroy it at once." [7] Other messages followed, in all of which he pointed out that whatever action was taken would have to be limited to land expeditions, due to the fortifications at Rainbow Bluff and the depth of the Roanoke.

More information came in, all of it in praise of Southern energy. Acting Volunteer Lieutenant Charles F. W. Behm, commanding the double-ender *Southfield,* one day ran up toward Hyman's Ferry. There he talked with Hyman, the ferryman, and with a Mr. Bell, both of whom had been supplying Flusser with Southern newspapers. He was told that between four and five hundred men were at work on the battery and the ram, and that the guns for both already were on hand. They were expected to be ready in a month or six weeks, at which time the Southerners would make an attack on Plymouth, both by land and by water.

Behm was alarmed. "If the ironclad ram is really as formidable as people say it is," he wrote Admiral Lee, "there is no gunboat in the sounds which could, except by chance, injure the ram, and as regards the obstructions about Plymouth, they do not amount to anything and could not stop a wooden propeller. The only thing would be a number of effective torpedoes or a light-draft ironclad, not to draw more than eight feet." [8]

Lee also felt some alarm, and he accepted the suggestion about the torpedoes. J. L. Lay, an engineer on duty in the sounds of North Carolina and an experimenter with a torpedo of his own invention, was sent to Washington to confer with the Navy Department. Lee wrote the Navy Department that if Lay's torpedo was approved, a number of them should be made at once and taken to Plymouth; if rejected, then some other type should be sent to North Carolina. "I have never been satisfied with a defensive policy," he added, "but this must now be resorted to unless the Rebel ironclads on the Roanoke are destroyed at once, and they can only be reached by the Army, or unless one or two of our lightest draft monitors can be floated by camels, etc., over the bulkhead at Hatteras and the shallow water of Croatan Sound, at each of which places there are on high tides but about eight and a half or nine feet of water." [9]

Toward the end of August, Flusser had an interview with General Peck at Plymouth, and when it ended, the Army leader had almost concluded that a force should be sent to destroy the ram and battery. The Navy officer informed him that failure to do this at the time of the raid in the direction of Weldon had caused the Southerners to place a guard of five hundred men at Edwards Ferry. The General suggested that he might send one thousand cavalry by a little-used road, hoping to surprise the Confederates, but he pointed out that the success of this venture would depend upon complete secrecy.

More time passed. Lee wrote Welles, and Welles wrote Union Secretary of War Stanton under date of September 17, presenting for his consideration "a subject of great importance connected with the maintaining possession of the sounds of North Carolina." He told of the Navy's helpless situation, brought about by the deep draft of its vessels and the Roanoke River's shallow water. This left the matter squarely up to the Army. Stanton replied within two days that Welles's letter had been referred to Major General John G. Foster, commanding the Department of North Carolina, with directions to take such action "as may, in his judgment, be best suited to meet the emergency thus presented." [10]

Further delay occurred. September passed, and the days of October slipped by one by one, with the brown leaves of autumn along the banks of the Roanoke a constant reminder that the seasons were changing. Admiral Lee, realizing the threat was daily becoming graver, instructed Flusser to report as soon as possible on the depth and width of the channels at the mouth of the Roanoke and to prepare a chart showing where obstructions, torpedoes, and an earthenwork with heavy guns could best be placed to prevent the ram from getting into the sounds or attacking Plymouth.

While the Federals wrote back and forth, trying frantically to obtain some definite clue as to what the Southerners were doing, a scene was developing in a cornfield on a bank of the Roanoke River that was reminiscent of one on the Yazoo River during earlier months of the war. It recalled Isaac Newton Brown and his dauntless *Arkansas,* the ironclad that defied Admiral David G. Farragut's fleet on the Mississippi River until circumstances brought about her destruction by her own crew. For there, rising above the stocks, was another giant dedicated to the cause of the Confederacy, a floating fortress with coat of mail capable of standing off any vessel the Union had in the North Carolina sounds. This one would be known as the *Albemarle*.

In the months following the success of the *Merrimack,* the

Confederacy considered ways to get more such craft into the water. At length, contracts were let for twenty of them, all to be finished within a year.[11] One contract went to Gilbert Elliott, a North Carolinian still in his teens. Born at Elizabeth City in an atmosphere of naval construction, he had inherited a love of mechanics. His grandfather on his mother's side, Charles Grice, had come as a shipbuilder from Philadelphia to found the town and start a new business in an area of fine timber and favorable waterways. From the banks of the Pasquotank River, he set afloat many craft, and there his daughter married a lawyer named Gilbert Elliott. Their son of the same name was to aid the Confederacy, backed by the knowledge he had gained while playing around his grandfather's shipyard. He joined the Seventeenth North Carolina Regiment, made up of men from the coastal communities, and by July of '61 was officially commissioned a first lieutenant and the regimental adjutant. This outfit took the field with the cards stacked against it. Outnumbered at Hatteras in August of that year, many of its members, including Elliott, were captured, and when they were exchanged and its ranks were refilled again, it was called to duty near Drewry's Bluff on the James River in Virginia. It was there that young Elliott's inspiration as a naval constructor began to make an impression.

While in prison, Elliott had sketched boat designs.[12] Some of these he later brought to the attention of Confederate officials in Richmond, having first grown a beard to make him look older.[13] He was able to impress them at a time when they were searching for every talent they could find to build up a navy with which to check the Federal advance. Eventually the youth was detached for special naval service, and '62 found him building, in co-operation with Colonel W. F. Martin, a client of his father, a flat-bottomed gunboat at Deep Creek, Virginia, a vessel Union successes finally forced the Southerners to destroy.[14]

But Elliott wanted to construct an ironclad fashioned after the *Merrimack*. The keel of this he proposed to lay in his home state, in water too shallow for the Federals to reach, and to bring it out in a mighty drive to clear the Carolina sounds of the enemy. This was the plan he used to obtain a contract.

The big need facing him as he set out on a goal that would have stumped an adult was iron. He began scouring the state. Far and wide he extended his search, for church bells, tire iron, and any other items which could be sent to the Tredegar Iron Works at Richmond to be melted down into plates for the sides of the ship. The most promising source was the Atlantic Railroad. This already had been investigated by the Confederate Government following Admiral Lee's campaign in behalf of North Carolina. Secretary Mallory wrote the state's Governor, Zebulon P. Vance, and soon the matter was brought to the attention of the railroad's directors.[15]

By the spring of '63 the project was ready to be started. Young Elliott was given his contract. He was informed that the plates would come to him from Richmond and that propeller shafting would be forged at nearby Charlotte, where the Confederacy had moved much of its shipbuilding machinery prior to the evacuation of Norfolk.[16] Plans and specifications would be prepared by its chief naval engineer, John L. Porter, the same who had helped in redesigning the frigate *Merrimack* into an ironclad.[17]

Elliott already had selected a site for his navy yard. It was at Edwards Ferry on the Roanoke River, five miles from Scotland Neck, in a cornfield that had been plowed for spring planting. This particular piece of ground, property of William Ruffin Smith, a prosperous farmer and large landowner, was of such a nature that a slip could be cut in the riverbank so the ship would slide off into water once the chocks were removed.

The young builder found another advantage in this particular site. There lived Peter Evans Smith, son of the owner, an honor graduate of the state university and a master mechanic. Thirty-four years old, he could play the fiddle and the flute like an artist, and he went about taking pictures with a camera of his own making. Inventions were among his accomplishments —a spark arrester for wood-burning locomotives, a self-coupler for railroad cars, a method of shrinking iron tires on buggy and wagon wheels, and a cotton planter. Others would come as the ship Elliott had in mind advanced.[18] He was made superintendent of construction.

In the cornfield was assembled as much equipment as could be found—a sawmill, a blacksmith's forge, and an assortment of tools. Soon, men were cutting massive yellow pine timbers on the farm of another Smith son, B.G., captain of the Scotland Neck Mounted Riflemen, at the time off fighting with the Army. A third, Charles S., would serve as courier for the builders until he became of age to join the Army, and then his place would be taken by a cousin, Frank J. Smith.[19]

The *Albemarle* slowly took shape. She was one hundred and fifty-two feet long, forty-five feet wide, with a depth from gun deck of eight feet two inches. Her draft when loaded would be eight feet. Two propellers, powered by two two-hundred-horsepower engines with eighteen-inch cylinders, would drive her along on steam supplied by two boilers. A screw steamer, her yellow pine timbers, each eight by ten inches, were fastened with iron and treenails. Her prow, or ram, was of solid oak. Oakum was scarce, so her framework was calked with cotton. Tar sealed her seams.[20]

Not a moment of daylight went by without labor of some sort on the ironclad. The carpentry moved rapidly, and there was not a disheartening moment until time came to fit the plating. Holes had to be drilled in each plate. These, an inch and a half in diameter, were made by a small engine and drill, requiring twenty minutes to complete each one. It was at this point that Peter Smith's inventive genius became known. He produced the first twist drill, a device that cut the iron out in shavings instead of powder, thus opening a hole every four minutes.

But these were details the Federals found safely guarded from them, no matter how thorough their espionage efforts. Flusser went to Hatteras Inlet one day and from there wrote

Davenport: "Report says they are pushing forward rapidly the construction of the ironclads up the Roanoke." [21] A few days later he added: "There is another report of the 'Roanoke sheep.' It is said she is surely coming down now in a few days. . . . I intend to sink her." [22]

The futility of Flusser's efforts to learn more exact information about what the Southerners were doing was reflected in a letter he wrote Admiral Lee on October 31. It was in answer to his instructions to report on the depth and width of river channels. "I tried to make a survey of the rivers and cutoffs about here," he reported, "but on account of the rough way in which it was done when the work was plotted, the streams intersected at points where they should have been several hundred feet apart, so I gave it up in disgust. The vessel building above can run through any of the small streams shown on the chart. There is water enough for her to pass through Middle River, by way of the Lower Thoroughfare and Eastmost River, into the Roanoke."

His survey had convinced him that it was going to be a problem to stop this ironclad from getting into the sound. Torpedos might be placed at the mouths of the Roanoke, Cashie, and Eastmost rivers, where the water was shoal and the current not too strong, but someone would have to be kept on duty there to prevent the Southerners from removing them. If planted farther up the Roanoke, they would have to be set off by hand, because the strength of the current and the large quantities of driftwood brought down by every freshet would make percussion impossible.

Of the many reports Flusser received, he scarcely knew which to believe. One day he was informed that the ironclad had sunk while it was being launched and that the Rebels were blocking up the river with stone. He passed on the information to Davenport, along with his own interpretation: "Both lies, I suspect." [23]

Flusser was determined, and never pessimistic. "I think we

will have time to put things in good order before our friend from above ventures down," he wrote Davenport a few days later.

But Flusser was working on a losing proposition. The Southerners also were determined, and the months ahead would develop for the *Albemarle* a success story similar to that of the *Arkansas*.

Ships that run in by night

NOVEMBER 1863

The schooner-rigged *Kate,* English built especially for the blockade-running business, was what seamen called a hard-luck ship. She made just one successful run before she was driven ashore on the coast of North Carolina. But to her credit it should be mentioned that she got close enough to land for her crew to escape. The Union boarding party sent to take her over found her hold filled with liquors, medicines, and cotton goods. But papers from the captain's cabin were all they took from her. The tide was falling too fast to get her off, so they damaged her engines, set her afire near four twenty-pound charges of powder, and removed the bonnets from her reservoirs so she would fill with water.

"She burned three hours and was effectually destroyed," reported Captain A. Ludlow Case of the U.S. steam sloop *Iroquois,* one of the vessels standing by off the North Carolina coast.[1]

Captain Case, after watching for a time, went away positive the *Kate* was a thing of the past. Acting Master Charles E. Jack, who headed the boarding party, thought the same. But less than three weeks later, they caught the Southerners trying to tow her off with a number of small boats and had to rush back and drive them away.

Fate was against the *Kate*. Even on her first trip, she had squeaked by narrowly. Just as she arrived on the edge of Charleston Harbor, a large paddle steamer started in, and its flapping wheels attracted the attention of the blockaders. Rockets were sent up by the Federals, causing a general uproar. In the ensuing chase, eight shots were fired at the *Kate,* but she got through untouched. For the next four weeks she had to wait for a favorable night to get out, and then she made the run through eighteen Union vessels, her hold and decks crammed with seven hundred and thirty bales of cotton. No such luck accompanied her second run. At Charleston the blockade seemed impassable, and she turned away and headed for Wilmington, there to be driven on shore at four-thirty in the morning.

In her steam log book was found an unsigned letter that immediately made the rounds of various Cabinet members in Washington, for it revealed choice information. To begin with, it related details of the original run, and it told that the vessel blew off steam under water in order to insure quiet running.[2] To Acting Rear Admiral S. P. Lee, the North Atlantic Blockading Squadron chief, that information was highly important.

The *Kate* was indeed one of the unfortunates in a business that by the fall of '63 had reached its peak. Over the months, blockade-running developed into a science, carried on by vessels built abroad especially for the purpose of slipping through the cordon of Union ships lying in watch off the Southern coast. These runners were long, low, side-wheel steamers of from five to six hundred tons, their frames sharp and narrow, and their length perhaps nine times their beam. They had feathering paddles and one or two rakish telescopic funnels, capable of being lowered close to the deck. Their hulls rose only a few feet out of the water, and were painted a light lilac color that simulated the clouds. Spars were two short lower masts with no yards. A small crow's-nest was in the foremast. Decks forward were oval, to enable the vessels to go through heavy seas. They burned a smokeless coal in their furnaces, and, when running in, all lights were out, the binnacle and fireroom hatches carefully covered, and steam released under water. In daylight they could scarcely be seen a matter of yards away.

The U.S. consul at London wrote that for some time he had been observing the movements of a steamer of this type called the *Merrimac*.[3] She was new and fast—built to run eighteen knots per hour—and was first named *Nangis*. He watched large rifled cannon and a quantity of shells as they were stored on board. "I think she has been purchased by the Confederates and will go full of munitions of war, and will be ready for sea by the first of next week," he wrote.[4] Her intention to run the blockade was a matter of public notoriety.[5] A little later the consul at Bermuda reported her arrival at that point, and soon she was running to Southern ports almost by schedule.

Under the routine she and others like her worked out, she loaded at Nassau or Bermuda or Cuba and then waited until the moon was favorable, affording her dark nights. Then she headed, sometimes along with two or three others, for one of the principal ports of the Confederacy—Beaufort, Wilmington, Charleston, Port Royal, Savannah, Mobile, or Galveston. In time, Wilmington on the Cape Fear River became the most used of these because it was reached by a stream that had two widely separated entrances, each defended by strong fortifications: Fort Fisher at New Inlet to the east, and Forts Smith and Caswell at Western Bar, the lower mouth. Each required, in the words of Admiral Lee, as many blockaders as Charleston.[6] He maintained that Wilmington and its adjacent inlets, with the intermediary points of Bermuda and Nassau, required more attention than all the rest of the coast.[7]

At New Inlet, the favorite of these entrances, the runners frequently could get in by hugging the shore. Even on a clear night, most of them were invisible against the land, and the

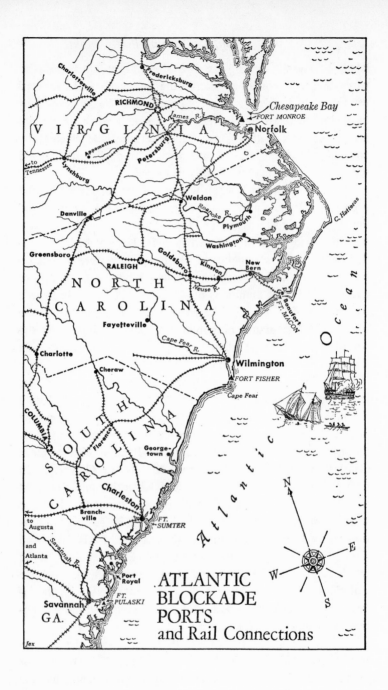

ATLANTIC
BLOCKADE
PORTS
and Rail Connections

roar of the surf drowned the noise of their screws and paddles. Because of their light draft, they could usually run well
inside of the blockaders. After getting past, they flashed a light
on their inshore side and then waited for a dim light to answer
from the beach, followed by another above and beyond the
first. These were the range lights for the channel. By getting
them in line, the incoming vessels could run straight in with
no further danger.

It was mainly for the purpose of signaling the runners that
the Southerners built, on Federal Point a mile or so from Fort
Fisher, an elevation that came to be known as The Mound. At
first it was reported to be a tower, for the blockaders could
see with their glasses a framework they judged to be sixty feet
high, diagonally braced and supported in the rear.[8] Then they
noticed a steam engine busily engaged in hauling sand along an
inclined railway to the top, where it was dumped, gradually
forming a huge mound. This was covered with brush and sod to
keep the wind from blowing it away. When finished, guns were
put in position there to throw plunging shot onto the decks of
any of the blockade vessels which got within range.

Sometimes, as runners tried to slip out in the dead of night,
an alert blockader would sense what was happening and flash
the signal to others. This usually was done with a rocket, which
was supposed to point out the direction the runner was taking.
But it was not a very satisfactory practice, for it was difficult
to tell which way the rocket was pointing, and often the runners
themselves would send up rockets, further baffling the blockaders.

Once a signal was given, several blockade vessels would go in
pursuit, each taking a different course and hoping to sight one
or more of the runners at daylight. This happened to the *Merrimac* the night she tried to get out of Wilmington, along with the
more fortunate *Eugenie* and *Emily,* both of which escaped.

The U.S.S. *Perry* was the blockader that discovered them,
and she and the U.S.S. *Mount Vernon* gave chase. From 2:00
A.M. until dawn, they ran up the coast along the land. At day-

light the *Perry* saw the *Merrimac* in the distance and, with the aid of an unidentified steamer, managed to run her down in four hours. The runner was loaded with six hundred forty-two bales of cotton, nine barrels of turpentine, seventy-seven kegs and thirty-four tierces of tobacco.

A day or two later, more complete information regarding the *Merrimac* was supplied to Admiral Lee. Originally built for opium smuggling on the China coast, she was fast—faster than the blockaders—and her capture had come about through too free use of rosin, which had filled her flues and caused the foaming of her boilers. But the big news concerning her came from the senior officer present, Captain Case: "I have the honor to inform you that the *Merrimac* was owned by the Rebel government and sold with the cotton by its agents to the late owners for $2,200,000 Confederate money." [9]

From the *Merrimac* thus came new evidence that the Confederate Government had gone into the blockade-running business.[10] As records would show, it had been forced in by the avarice of the private runners, who had found it much more profitable to bring in luxury items like corsets, toothbrushes, perfumes, and liquors than the war materials needed for government contracts—steel, iron, copper, zinc, ordnance, munitions, chemicals, and engines. Salt and coffee were other popular cargoes. Salt was worth $7.50 per ton in Nassau and $1,700 per ton at Richmond; coffee, $240 per ton in Nassau and $5,500 at Richmond.

The capitalists engaged in the blockade-running trade found themselves engulfed in a race to amass wealth rather than to aid a new government. Most of them were Englishmen, and quite a few were Northerners.[11] The odds were in their favor. In '61, it was estimated one runner out of every nine was lost. By '62, the average had dropped to one in seven, and by '63, one in four. But profits were so high that one successful run paid for the investment, leading to the statement that after two runs the investor could stand to lose his ship.

Efforts were constantly made by the Union to tighten the

blockade. Admiral Lee, who amassed a fortune in prize money, was most energetic in this respect, but even he could not offset the great odds on the side of the runners.[12] They still got through. In ten months, ninety vessels ran into Wilmington. One month, runners got in on an average of one every other day. One night, four appeared; another night, five. An officer under Lee wrote the Boston *Traveller:* "There ought to be ten blockade-runners caught where we now get one. We have fifteen miles to guard, and to do it we have sometimes four and sometimes only two vessels. Ten vessels is the least number we ought to have. The blockade seems to be a farce, and I am ashamed and disgusted with the whole thing." [13]

For days at a stretch, the blockaders met only with frustration, a great drain on their morale and patience. At nine o'clock one night, the U.S.S. *Victoria* made signals that a runner was coming out of Wilmington. She got within four hundred yards of her, so close she could make out a double-piped, long, low, side-wheel steamer. She slipped her chains and gave chase. Soon she was joined by the U.S.S. *Florida* and the U.S.S. *Montgomery*. Several times they thought they saw a light from the smokestack of the runner, but at dawn nothing but uncommunicative waves could be seen.

Later, in full daylight, the U.S.S. *Iroquois* spied a steamer steering to the northeast. Then at sunrise she saw the smoke of another to the southeast. The first vessel seemed to be a transport, so the *Iroquois,* having trouble with leaky boilers and coal mixed with slate, steered for the other. "We gained upon it steadily," reported her captain, Ludlow Case, "and at 8:00 A.M. could see she was a paddle-wheel steamer. At 10:00 A.M. we began to pass through bales of cotton which she was throwing overboard. We counted one hundred and fourteen bales and five bags. At sunset she was about six or eight miles distant from us, and we were fast coming up with her. The night was quite dark, there being no moon, and the only thing to guide us was the smoke, which was very uncertain. Before daylight, as I feared, we lost sight of her . . . she having in all probability stopped feeding her fires until we passed, and then steered another course." [14] The chase had continued for two hundred seventy miles.

While the *Iroquois* was meeting with failure, the *Florida, Montgomery,* and *Victoria* were having a similar experience. At seven o'clock that night, they spied a strange sail which they made out to be a small side-wheel, beam-engine steamer painted white. They gave chase. The stranger hoisted a dim light and stood to the westward. Suddenly the *Florida* saw another vessel bearing east, apparently with a light illuminating her bow. But as soon as the *Florida* started after her, the light was extinguished, and nothing more was seen of her. The *Victoria* had kept on the trail of the first runner until baffled. Whenever the blockader slowed down, so did the runner, showing a light each time and gradually working away to the westward out of sight.

The next day, things were a bit different in the way of luck for the blockaders. The *Hebe* attempted to run into Wilmington and was chased ashore on Federal Point, where her crew escaped in boats. A gale was blowing from the northeast, with a heavy sea, and the Federals saw no chance of getting her off, so they set her on fire. The boarding party sent to start the blaze was captured by Southerners, who opened an exchange from the nearby sand hills with rifles and two pieces of artillery, doing considerable damage. Three boats from the U.S.S. *Niphon* were sent to the rescue. They, too, were captured, after which the Confederates began hauling off a cargo of coffee, drugs, medicines, clothing, and silks.

One night off Wilmington, the *Niphon* discovered a runner passing inward along the beach, gave chase, and opened fire on her. The U.S.S. *Howquah* joined in, and between them they forced the runner to turn back to sea. Throughout the night the chase continued, and the next morning three other ships, the *Keystone State, Nansemond,* and the Army transport *Fulton,* were added to the pursuit. It was like two packs of hounds chasing the same fox. In the late afternoon they brought the fleeing vessel to, and found her to be the *Margaret and Jessie,* one of the most successful runners in the business. Eighteen times she had made runs between Nassau and Wilmington, amply repaying her owners and bringing fame to her commander, R. W. Lockwood, recognized as one of the best pilots on the coast. She was carrying a mixed cargo, most of which had been tossed overboard during the chase.

A boarding party left a picture of the way a champion runner usually accepted defeat, telling what happened to a once neat and trim iron steamer that had been drawn into the mad rush to make millions from the blockade-running business. Her deck was littered with cords of pine wood. Barrels of oranges were sitting around the sides of the bulwarks, some of them open and half empty. Her large saloon cabin, once fitted up with green plush settees, was now scarred and dirty, used as a cargo room. "A scene was unfolded which beggars description," wrote one member of the party. "Silks, gunpowder, hoop skirts, prints, hats, quinine, butter, brandies, cigars, clothing, toys, cases of gin, thread, needles, and in fact everything you can imagine, from a needle to an anchor, are heaped together in one disordered mass; trunks broken open and rifled, liquids spilled, and thousands of dollars worth of valuable goods destroyed." Crew members and passengers said Captain Lockwood had given them "unbounded liberty" in lightening the ship, encouraging them to throw overboard $70,000 worth of a cargo that had cost $300,000 in Nassau. In the ladies' cabin, once beautifully fitted, was found a dirty table on which were the remains of a half-finished meal, bits of bread, ham, plates of butter, empty brandy and gin bottles, all of which gave "ample testimony that drinking as well as eating furnished a portion of their pastime." [15]

The *Margaret and Jessie* was a marked exception. S. C. Hawley, U.S. consul at Nassau, wrote in alarm a few weeks after reaching his post: "Since I have been here there have been as many as one hundred and twelve voyages to Charleston and Wilmington and back, equal to two hundred and twenty-

four trips; but twelve steamers have been lost or captured.
. . . Under such circumstances England can set up a plausible
claim that the blockade is not such as to meet the demands of
public law, and make a good case to the foreign powers. The
fact is, success of the runners is the rule and capture the exception." [16]

Hawley at the start of his service got the idea that blockade-
running was an unprofitable business, an impression he soon
corrected. He cited that thirteen of a certain twenty-eight runners had been captured, a proportion that would seem too large
to allow a profit. But on investigation he found that the voyages
would average two to a steamer, a total of fifty-six, or one capture to every four and a third voyages. He cited a particular
vessel that had expenses of $115,000 on her outward journey.
On the return, she brought in cotton valued at $234,000, giving
her a profit of $119,000.[17]

Freight rates were enormous, ranging from $300 to $1,000 a
ton. But they had to be high in order to meet expenses. Wages
were also high, varying according to the reputation of the ship
captain. The more successful might receive $5,000 for a run,
half of it paid in advance. His chief officer would get $1,250;
the second and third officers, $750 each; the chief engineer,
$2,500; the crew and firemen, $250 each; and the pilot,
$3,500.[18] The pay scale developed as the business of blockade-
running became a science of much precision, and one that was
highly dangerous. An observer saw the runners in this light:
"The men who ran the blockade had to be men who would
stand fire without returning it. It was a business in which every
man took his life in his hands, and so he understood it. An ordinarily brave man had no business on a blockade-runner. He
who made a success of it was obliged to have the cunning of a
fox, the patience of a Job, and the bravery of a Spartan warrior. . . . The runners must not be armed and must not resist;
they must simply be cool and quick and watchful, and, for the
rest, trust to God and their good ship to deliver them safely to
their friends." [19]

Reports of the immense profits made from the business were highly tempting. This was confirmed in an intercepted letter that Alfred Judah wrote from Nassau to "My dear Papa." In it he stated: "There are men here who are making immense fortunes by shipping goods to Dixie, and on an average four out of every six vessels that start to run the blockade succeed, and goods of all kinds are worth ridiculous prices there. . . . There is one man here who commenced in this line of business as soon as the war broke out and he has made over $2,000,000. Six steamers left this port last week to run the blockade, and we have heard of the safe arrival in Dixie of five of them. . . . It is a speculation by which one makes either six hundred or eight hundred per cent or loses all." [20]

So the Confederacy, for self-protection, went in for blockade-running in serious fashion.[21] The chief intermediary point for shipping was Nassau in the New Providence Islands. Before the war, this British colony's business had been confined largely to fishing and wrecking. One observer who knew it well at that period recorded: "Nassau was scarcely worth a place on our maps. It was a small, dilapidated village inhabited principally by Negroes, who lived by wrecking, fishing and the spontaneous productions of the island." [22] But its harbor was shallow, of advantage to the runners, and war soon brought to its shores shipping, trade, merchandise, munitions, cotton, banks, brokers, government agents, gamblers, prostitutes, and lots of money. It was only one hundred and eighty miles from the Florida coast, five hundred and forty miles from Charleston, six hundred miles, or a three-day run, from Wilmington.

Judge J. S. Bosworth, Chief Justice of the New York Superior Court, visited Nassau during '63, and soon he wrote back: "There are over twenty swift, light-draft steamers running regularly between this and Charleston and Wilmington, mostly to and from Charleston. From nine to eleven days is the passage to and from. Over one million rifles and any quantity of cannon and ammunition have gone from this port, the steamers bringing back cotton and other cargo. Three steamers left here Saturday and two arrived Saturday night and Monday morning. It is known when they are to leave and when they are expected back." [23]

The New York *Herald* correspondent, with some violations of grammar, reported: "Charleston or Savannah, in their palmiest days, were never so overrun with cotton as is the city of Nassau at the present time. Every available place large enough to hold half a dozen bales is crammed full and running over. It is piled up six and eight bales deep on all the wharves, vacant lots and even on some of the lawns. It is literally laying around loose." [24]

This reporter was amazed at what he saw. "The blockade, reported to be so effective two weeks ago that it was impossible for a vessel to leave Charleston," he wrote, "would seem to be relaxed, judging by the arrivals here during the last ten days. The steamers *Charleston, Lizzie, Fanny, Alice, Raccoon, Ella and Annie, Banshee, Antonica, Beauregard* and one or two others, have all arrived here during that time from Wilmington and Charleston, with full cargoes of cotton, and some have left again for Dixie."

Fleet, rakish vessels shuttled back and forth, hauling cotton from Southern ports to the intermediary points, where it was loaded on heavy freighters for the trip to England. A reporter for the Buffalo *Commercial Advertiser* relayed word of what was happening: "Storekeepers put their stocks on shipboard and take their pay in cotton, on the return trip. Cotton sells for sixty cents per pound, specie, and Mr. Storekeeper gets rich." [25] His observations were cynical. "Every cargo of cotton," he added, "is worth from a quarter to a million of dollars, and as the *Antonica* has made six round trips and the *Leopard* the same, they may well put their fingers to their noses, and laugh about their packet and their ferry to Charleston. . . . The authorities here are of course not ignorant of all this. The clearances are taken to Halifax or St. John, but they know perfectly well the real destination."

At one period of '63 it was noted that the Confederacy's runners had made more than fifty trips out and back without a single loss. And then the luck changed, and for a time it looked as though private interests, angered at such strong competition, were tipping off the blockaders as to when the Government's vessels were scheduled to enter or depart.

The snooping may have had its start at Bermuda, where several Confederate runners were taking on cargoes. This was a slow process. There were only four public warehouses—Penno's, Munson's, Doctor Hunter's, and Mrs. Todd's. Attached to each was a wharf, capable of accommodating only one vessel at a time. Ships that drew ten or twelve feet of water could get no closer than thirty or forty feet of a wharf, which meant rigging and unrigging gangways. Cargoes could be loaded or unloaded only when customhouse officers were present, and there were only four of these. No carts or drays were available to move goods from one storehouse to another. Major Smith Stansburg, the Confederate agent at Bermuda, reported: "We cannot open boxes of arms, and clean and oil them, etc., or do any work of the kind—no room—no workmen—no tools—no conveniences—this is not a city nor a town, but a village." 26

One after another, and sometimes in groups, the Confederate runners came in to the wharves to load. The *Ella and Annie* stopped at Mrs. Todd's wharf and took on rifles, pork, bacon, lead, saltpeter, merchandise, wire rope, brandy, and rum. The *Robert E. Lee,* at another wharf, was stowed with Austrian rifles, brandy, gunpowder, cartridges, lead, army clothing, medical stores, sugar, tin, shoe thread, paper, hardware, and drugs. The *Cornubia,* the *Phantom,* and others came in and took their turns at loading.

The *Cornubia* made a run from Wilmington to Bermuda in September. She did it again in October, this time carrying as passengers the wife and two children of former President John Tyler. At Bermuda she found the *Alice,* the *Ella and Annie,* and the *Ella* in the harbor. The return was delayed by heavy rains. She left port on the night of November 4, trailed by the

steamers *A. D. Vance* and *Ella.* A private notebook kept by
J. T. Gordon, one of the passengers, had a rather routine entry
for the 7th: "Pleasant weather, number of sails in sight."

At midnight on the 7th, while lying in three and a half fathoms of water off Wilmington, about three miles south of Masonboro Inlet, the *James Adger* saw a vessel on her port bow heading east, and started in chase, but in half an hour lost sight of
the runner. The *Adger*'s captain, Commander T. H. Patterson,
concluded that if the ship he was pursuing was trying to run
the blockade it would steer in for the land, hug it close, and
make a dash for New Inlet, so he stood inshore himself, and
about 2:00 A.M. came up with a strange steamer that had run
ashore about eleven miles north of New Inlet. There she had
been chased by the *Niphon* and was blowing off steam.

Patterson recognized her as the *Cornubia,* an iron side-wheel
steamer he knew to be very fast. When he boarded her, her captain remarked to his executive officer that "though the *Cornubia* is a small vessel the Confederate Government could
better have afforded to lose almost any other vessel." [27] He
learned that her cargo was comprised generally of ammunition,
arms, saltpeter, and lead. A package of papers thrown over
her side was recovered by the Federals. They appeared to
have been in the care of C. E. Thorburn, a lieutenant colonel
in the Confederate Army who had been on leave of absence to
Europe, and they revealed that the Southerners had lost all confidence in intervention by England or France.[28] They also listed
the *Robert E. Lee, Ella and Annie,* and other vessels operated
by the Confederacy.

The next morning at early daylight, the *James Adger* discovered a steamer to the southeast. At about seven-thirty that
evening, she was overhauled and was found to be the *Robert E.
Lee,* which had left Bermuda five hours after the *Cornubia.* Her
capture implied a tribute to John Wilkinson, recognized as one
of the best blockade-runners in the business, for she had made
twenty-one successful runs under his direction, carrying out
from six to seven thousand bales of cotton valued at $2,000,000

in gold, and now she was on her first trip without him at her helm.[29] He was away on a secret venture that would go down in history as the Johnson's Island Expedition.

The *Robert E. Lee,* a Clyde-built steamer, had once been known as the *Giraffe,* and under that name she had plied as a packet between Glasgow and Belfast.[30] It was John Wilkinson who brought her from England. The Federals who captured her were not quite sure what to do with her. Someone on board told them she undoubtedly had treasure hidden on her somewhere and that it was understood that if she was captured, a Confederate agent in the North had instructions to purchase her and send her to Nova Scotia, where the treasure could be recovered.

Naval critics have blamed the loss of the *Robert E. Lee* on the timidity of Wilkinson's successor, R. H. Gayle, an officer from the Merchant Marine. After he had got past the inner cordon of blockaders, he attempted to turn the vessel over to the pilot, who refused to take the responsibility, as customary, until they had crossed the bar.[31] This indecision of command was of aid to the chasing gunboats.[32]

At 5:30 A.M. on the 9th, the *Niphon,* returning from an unsuccessful chase and steaming along the beach north of New Inlet, saw another vessel coming down along the shore. When the stranger saw it was intercepted, it headed directly for the *Niphon,* striking her about the forerigging and carrying away her bowsprit, stem, and starboard boats. At the moment of impact, a Federal boarding party went into action, and soon another prize was added to the Union list at the expense of the Confederate Government. It was the *Ella and Annie,* bringing another valuable cargo.[33]

Into the blockade bag the following night came the *Ella,* a small, fast steamer sent over from England in early '62. A shot across her gallows frame from the U.S.S. *Howquah* brought her to a stop. Her cargo was made up largely of canvas.

These captures in quick succession constituted a severe blow to the already dwindling fortunes of the Confederacy. They were evidence either of trickery or of greater efficiency on the part of the blockade, and they set the Government back in its efforts to monopolize a business that people came to look upon as fast degenerating into an illicit and unpatriotic practice. Within a matter of weeks the Confederate Congress passed an act prohibiting the importation of luxuries, and another stopping the exportation of cotton, tobacco, naval stores, sugar, molasses, and rice, "except under such uniform regulations as shall be made by the President of the Confederate States." [34]

Guerrillas on water

NOVEMBER-DECEMBER 1863

If fate ever deserted an individual's cause, it was that of John Yates Beall, gentleman farmer of Charles Town, West Virginia. He was able to say at the time of his death by hanging that he had given his life in the service and defense of his country. No follower ever worked more faithfully for the Confederacy, and no Southerner perhaps ever made more sacrifice in its behalf and got less in return.

The North first heard of Beall when word reached Norfolk in the fall of '63 that a band of guerrillas was alternating in their activities between Mathews County, Virginia, on the mainland, and Accomac and Northampton Counties, over on the Eastern Shore. Similar bands were operating west of Washington under the leadership of John Singleton Mosby, the "Gray Ghost," and others. But they were different, as the Union saw it: the guerrillas in Northern Virginia were partisan guerrillas, or Rangers, whereas guerrillas by sea were, in effect, following the practice of pirates.

This trouble on the Eastern Shore was guided by the fertile

brain of the twenty-eight-year-old Beall, graduate in law from the University of Virginia. In the spring of '61, he left the easy life of a gentleman farmer to serve in the ranks of Stonewall Jackson. During the fighting in the Shenandoah Valley the following October, a bullet tore into his chest, causing consumptive tendencies which ended his career as a soldier. While recuperating, he left the war area, and under the name of John Yates, entered the milling business at Cascade, Iowa, also serving there as a Confederate agent. Fearing disclosure, he fled to Canada, but he was a dedicated man, and his head was too full of ideas to remain long out of the country.

Early in '63 Beall was seen walking down the streets of Richmond.[1] He was there, it developed, to discuss with the Confederate Government a plan he believed held great promise. He suggested a secret expedition to the Great Lakes to capture a Union gunboat stationed at Johnson's Island, site of one of the main prisons to which Confederate captives were sent. But there was fear at that stage of the war that such an undertaking would endanger relations with England. Navy Secretary Mallory, one of those who heard him out, proposed, instead, guerrilla activities in the Chesapeake Bay area. This appealed to the enterprising Beall, and he accepted appointment as an acting master in the Confederate Navy.

His papers were issued in March. By April he had enlisted ten followers, most of them escaped prisoners. Two of them were Scotch, Bennett G. Burley and John Maxwell. Throughout the summer, Beall gradually added to his force, calling it the Confederate Volunteer Coast Guard and basing it in Mathews County. By September it had been increased to eighteen. Two boats were acquired, the *Raven,* painted black, and the *Swan,* white, the latter a mail boat captured from the Federals.

He led his band on its first attack in August. The lighthouse keeper at Eastville, Virginia, sent a telegram to Washington announcing that a small party of armed men was wrecking the lighthouse facilities along the coast. On the 3rd, they completely gutted the lighthouse on Smith's Island, carrying away the lamps, reflectors, and everything else removable. At that time a bystander overheard their plans to destroy the Hog Island and Cherrystone lights, and promptly relayed the information to Secretary Welles. Captain Guert Gansevoort, senior officer on duty in the area in which these lights were situated, was warned, but failed to take heed.

On the night of September 17, the *Raven* and the *Swan* sailed out of Horn Harbor in Mathews County and headed across the bay toward the Eastern Shore, Beall in command of one, Edward McGuire, the other.[2] They swung around Cape Charles and headed north for depredations along the Atlantic side. The following night they captured the schooner *Alliance,* its hold filled with supplies bound for Port Royal, South Carolina.

Hours passed while they lay out of sight in a cove. The night of the 20th, armed with revolvers, they climbed on board the *J. J. Houseman,* another schooner. Two others, the *Samuel Pearsall* and the *Alexandria,* also were captured. The sails were set on all three, their helms were lashed, and they were headed out over the bar at Wachapreague Inlet. Then the party set out around Cape Charles in the *Alliance,* their destination Milford Haven. But misfortune lay ahead of them. Before they could get clear, a blockader spied them and began firing. Before they went ashore, Beall directed his men to quickly unload a part of the cargo and set fire to the vessel.[3]

Telegrams flashed back and forth between Welles and Gansevoort. The latter gave warning to Lieutenant Commander James H. Gillis, senior naval officer at Yorktown, who immediately set out across the bay to learn what was happening.

Enough people had seen the raiders to be able to give specific information. Among these were Captain J. Bush and a man named Campbell, steward of the *Alliance*. Both said they had been captured and released, and both said they could identify all who took part in the raid. They reported that the Southerners appeared to have no organization and were not dressed in uniforms.

When Gillis prepared his report to Gansevoort, he was a disgusted man. "I tried to have an expedition sent out immediately after the Smith's Island lighthouse was burned," he wrote, "but could not succeed in prevailing on the military to send one. On my return today I immediately went to the headquarters of General Wistar[4] for the purpose of communicating with him, but found him too ill to attend to duty and was referred to his assistant adjutant general, who seemed to think that his acquainting himself with the contents of the last number of *Harper's Magazine* was of more importance than his public duties." [5]

Gansevoort relayed this report to Major General John G. Foster, commanding at Fort Monroe, and added: "Lieutenant Commander Gillis expresses the belief that this party will be on their way toward Richmond within the next three days, and that with a proper co-operating military force it can be broken up." [6]

Federal vessels spied the schooner *Samuel Pearsall* as it sailed eastward, its helm lashed in a stationary position. It was brought into Hampton Roads and placed in charge of the U.S.S. *Mystic*.

Admiral Lee, squadron chief, sent out instructions for the blockade vessels in Chesapeake Bay to be more vigilant, and then notified Secretary Welles that General Wistar at Yorktown had been ordered to confer with the senior naval officer at that point "as to the best means to take to break up this party of guerrillas." He also reported: "The Richmond *Whig* of yesterday's date has a report regarding this naval expedition, stating that it was under command of Acting Master J. Y. Beall, C. S. Navy, and captured on the Atlantic side of the Eastern Shore of Virginia three sloops and four schooners, one of the latter being the *Alliance,* whose cargo it is stated would alone have brought $200,000 in Richmond, about $10,000 worth being saved and the vessel burned." [7]

On the morning of October 5, two weeks after the Confederate Volunteer Coast Guard had made its raid on the Eastern Shore,

General Wistar left Yorktown with the Fourth U.S. Colored Infantry, detachments of Pennsylvania and New York cavalry, and two sections of artillery, marching them into Mathews County. The gunboats *Commodore Jones, Putnam,* and *Stepping Stones,* from the Navy, and four Army gunboats co-operated, covering avenues of escape by water from the peninsula between Mobjack Bay and the Piankatank. Gillis soon was reporting results to Admiral Lee: "It has been found to be a very difficult matter to break up the organization, for the reason that, as soon as our cavalry is seen approaching, they, the Rebels, take to the woods, and knowing every path, find no difficulty in eluding pursuit in almost every instance." [8]

The Federals stopped at the Tabb home, where it was reported Beall had his headquarters. There they found three compasses, assumed to have been taken from the vessels captured in Wachapreague Inlet.

After they left the Tabb home, gunfire sounded from the side of the road, and a Union soldier fell dead from his saddle. The man who had bushwhacked him was captured and questioned. The most that could be learned about him was that his name was Smith, that his house had been a rendezvous for the Coast Guard, and that he had been engaged in blockade-running. A drumhead court-martial was held, and he was hanged immediately. That night his brother was captured while riding along the road with a pair of pistols in his pockets. When questioned as to his business so armed, he replied that he had been out shooting crows. "His answer not being satisfactory," reported Gillis, "he was brought in, and his fate will probably be the same as that of his brother." [9]

For a month, nothing was heard from the sea partisans. Then, in the middle of November, they appeared in Tangier Inlet on the Eastern Shore. A schooner was captured, and Beall divided his party, sending some of the men away in the prize vessel. Through carelessness, the schooner fell into the hands of the Federals, and one crew member was frightened into talking. The details he related enabled Union soldiers to surprise

Beall and the Coast Guarders who had remained with him.

These developments were reported by Brigadier General Henry H. Lockwood, commanding at Drummondtown, to Major General Robert C. Schenck, commanding at Baltimore. "This is a highly important capture. . . . I would further call the attention of the major general commanding to the status of these prisoners. They are unable to show anything which, in my judgment, would entitle them to be considered or treated as prisoners of war. They are without orders and many of them without uniform. It appears by the shipping articles . . . that they are but partisans, receiving no pay from the so-called Confederate States, and trusting entirely for remuneration for their services to the possession of such property, public or private, as they may chance to capture. . . .

"I would respectfully suggest that they be tried either by military commission or that they be sent back here for trial by the civil authorities of Accomac and Northampton Counties, where the depredations have been committed, as is provided for in the Virginia Code, 1860. I am rather inclined to think the latter course would be the preferable one, inasmuch as some of the citizens seem to be considerably incensed against these raiders, and I think twelve men at least in the county of Accomac can be procured who will be disposed to deal with these fellows as their outrages deserve. . . ." [10]

The reply Lockwood received to these suggestions was satisfactory. "As to the prisoners themselves," it read, "they will be held for the present, not as prisoners of war, but as pirates or marauding robbers, until the further pleasure of the Secretary of War, to whom the matter will be submitted, shall be known. Not being protected by commissioners or any orders produced from the pretended Rebel government, they will probably be tried as pirates or as robbers, either in the United States court or the local court, unless ordered to trial by military commission." [11]

But the Confederate Government, hearing that Beall and his comrades were closely confined in irons at Fort McHenry at

Baltimore, intervened before trial could be held. Robert Ould, Confederate Agent of Exchange, wrote under date of December 15: "With whatever regret retaliatory measures can be adopted, the course of your authorities leaves no other alternative. In the hope, therefore, of inducing your Government to accord to these parties the treatment due to prisoners of war, I inform you that Lieutenant Commander Edward P. Williams and Ensign Benjamin H. Porter and fifteen seamen, all of the U.S. Navy and prisoners in our hands, have been placed in close confinement in irons and held as hostages for their proper treatment." [12]

Before many days passed, Beall and the captured members of his Coast Guard were on their way to Fort Monroe for investigation of their cases. Orders called for their irons to be removed and notice of the action to be sent to Exchange Agent Ould. This was the first step toward their ultimate release and toward a new career for Beall.

One man can spoil an expedition

JANUARY 1864

First official word that one of the South's brightest schemes had
failed was brought into Wilmington in the dead of night, January 7, by the little steamer *Presto*. The news was of a nature
not usually associated with the efforts of her captain, Virginia-
born John Wilkinson, looked upon as the king of blockade-
runners. No man had been more successful at eluding the Union
ships girding the Southern coast, a fact accepted as clear evidence that he was an unusual person and that he had certain
traits that set him apart from all other masters in this field of
enterprise.

Wilkinson believed his good fortune could be attributed to an
inviolate habit of doing things himself. Never at night did he
take off his clothes and go to bed. Chronometer readings he
made himself. Throughout the dark hours on a run into port,
he stood at his post and studied the stars and the coastal mark-
ings, both uncommonly familiar to him. He had done a coast
survey before the war, and the charts he studied were marked
with his own corrections. Slippers muted his footsteps as he

moved about deck. He spoke in whispers. Every light, even to that flickering over the compass, was shrouded in canvas.

But the care and perfection which brought him success as a runner could not be applied with the same completeness to his activities as the head of a secret expedition. Staring helplessly from their cell windows up in the Johnson's Island prison in Lake Erie near Sandusky, Ohio, were about two thousand Confederates, principally officers, who could attest to this. They had received a tip that Wilkinson was directing a plot to free them. And then they eventually heard of the human frailties that had caused it to fail.

Wilkinson was no haphazard choice to lead the expedition to Johnson's Island. Before calling him to Richmond for a conference, Secretary Mallory studied the Confederate naval rosters carefully. His ultimate selection was wise, for Wilkinson conducted the enterprise to the very brink of success. Blame for failure could not fairly be placed on his shoulders. A leader can be picked on a basis of past performance, but not so cautiously can be screened the men who are to follow him.

Originally, the expedition that Wilkinson led was not designed to free prisoners. Its purpose was to wreck the abundant Union commercial traffic shuttling back and forth across Lake Erie. The Southerners knew that only one gunboat, the almost twenty-year-old side-wheel steamer *Michigan,* by agreement with Canada, was being operated for the protection of traffic on the lake, and this vessel they hoped to capture. With it, they estimated they could do irreparable damage before they could be driven out of those waters.

Credit for origin of the scheme belonged to one of the nation's most energetic naval officers, Lieutenant William H. (Buck) Murdaugh. Stationed in Florida with the United States Navy at the start of the war, he had quickly resigned his commission and returned to his home in Virginia. On joining the side of the South, he was added to the staff of officers in whom the Confederate Navy Department placed its greatest dependence. There beside him were such stalwarts as Matthew Fontaine Maury, Hunter Davidson, Robert Carter, A. B. Fairfax, John Taylor Wood, Robert D. Minor, Catesby ap R. Jones, and Walter Butt, most of whom in another year would go down in history as members of the crew of the C.S.S. *Merrimack*.

While commanding a gun crew at Hatteras in August, '61, Murdaugh was badly wounded in his left arm by a shell fragment. But he was back on duty in a matter of months, and was soon headed for the coal and iron region of Alabama to establish a naval foundry.[1] By December, '62, he was in command of the gunboat C.S.S. *Beaufort,* and recommended for higher rank.[2]

Murdaugh first mentioned his plan for a raid on Lake Erie to two of his fellow officers, Lieutenants Carter and Minor, in February, '62. Both thought well of the idea and urged that it be brought to the attention of the Navy Department. The proposal was presented to Secretary Mallory and outlined carefully in a letter signed by Murdaugh.[3] Mallory, too, approved, but lack of funds caused it to be shelved. Finally, $25,000 was provided, and Murdaugh, Carter, Minor, and Lieutenant Butt were ordered to hold themselves in readiness to proceed on the duty. Then came an order to desist. The Confederate Cabinet had decided that operations in the Northern lakes might upset relations with England and prevent completion of war vessels building for the Confederacy in that nation's private shipyards.

The expedition thus appeared to be abandoned. Murdaugh was disheartened and sought other duty. Soon he, Carter, and Butt were ordered abroad, leaving Minor, assigned to the Naval Ordnance Works at Richmond, "as the only representative of a scheme whose prospects were so inviting and so brilliant." [4]

But by summer, reports began to come into Richmond that stirred new interest in the plan. In these it was revealed that Confederate officers, following the South's defeat at Arkansas Post, Vicksburg, and Port Hudson, were being crowded into the Johnson's Island prison, and this could mean only their demoralization and ultimate death. Numbers of others arrived after the battle of Gettysburg, further straining the facilities. Their life was said to be horrible, that they were forced to drink water from Lake Erie, the same body of water in which their latrines emptied. In August, Minor received a summons to a conference with Mallory and War Secretary James A. Seddon. He was asked for his views on the contents of a letter, part of which Seddon read to him. It proposed an expeditiion for the release of the prisoners.[5]

Minor quickly gave his answer, approving the plan. "I need not inform you, gentlemen," he added, "how much pleasure it would give me to be engaged upon such duty." [6]

A month passed before Minor heard again about the matter. Mallory sent for him and told him to organize the expedition, select the officers, and make all the necessary preparations. The Secretary suggested that Minor himself lead the party, but the young lieutenant refused. He suggested, instead, that the responsibility of leading the undertaking be placed upon his friend, John Wilkinson, with the proviso that if two lines of operations should be adopted, he himself should command one of them.[7]

By this time, President Davis was in thorough accord with the plan. Apparently there had been some talk of it in Montreal, and the President's opinion was that it would be better to fail than not make the attempt.[8]

Preparations were started immediately. A sum of $111,000 was set aside for the purpose. This was to be made up of $35,000 in gold and a cargo of cotton which could be sold at Halifax, Nova Scotia, for $76,000.

So John Wilkinson gave up his captaincy of the runner *Robert E. Lee* and came to Richmond to command the expedition. Officers selected to take part were some of the best in the Confederate Navy. Minor was second in command. Other participants included Lieutenants B. P. Loyall, A. G. Hudgins, J. M. Gardner, F. M. Roby, M. P. Goodwin, Patrick McCarrick, Otey Bradford, and George W. Gift;[9] Acting Masters William Finney, Henry Wilkinson, H. W. Perrin, and W. B. Ball, the last of whom had taken leave from his duties as colonel of the Fifteenth Virginia Cavalry; Chief Engineer J. Charles Schroeder; First Assistant Engineer H. X. Wright; Second Assistant Engineer John T. Tucker; Assistant Paymaster P. M. DeLeon; Assistant Surgeon William Sheppardson; Gunners Crawford H. Gormley and John Waters; John B. Tabb; and a man named Leggett, who afterward left the expedition at Halifax.[10]

As preparations proceeded, strict secrecy as to their purpose was maintained. Only Wilkinson, Minor, and Loyall knew the objective.[11] It was reported that the party was headed for England.

The participants gathered early in October at Smithville, North Carolina. On the 7th, twenty men walked quietly on board the *Robert E. Lee,* already heavily laden with cotton.[12] They slowly got the vessel under way and dropped down the river, trying to attract no attention; and on the 10th, Wilkinson took her out of port, but not without some misfortune. Before he could get clear, some of the blockaders got on his trail and fired at him. One shell struck the starboard bulwarks of the *Lee* and exploded, setting some of the cotton afire, wounding three men, and breaking a small hoisting engine into smithereens. But the runner got away and headed for Nova Scotia.

They reached Halifax on October 16, and the cotton was immediately sold. While it was being unloaded, word was spread that the vessel was on its way to England. Wilkinson in the meantime divided his party into two groups and directed them to proceed to Canada by different routes. They were to meet in Montreal on October 21.

Matters worked out as planned. Members of the groups came together under assumed names and went to scattered lodgings. Officers were directed to stay in quiet private boardinghouses, to avoid the hotels, not to be away from their rooms for more than half an hour at a time, and not to recognize one another if they met on the street.

Friends in Montreal, among them a man named Kane, a Johnson's Island escapee and former marshal at Baltimore, Maryland,[13] were contacted and their help solicited. Communication had to be established with the prisoners on the island, to let them know that an attempt was to be made to release them. This was easily accomplished through a plan devised by one of the captives, General J. J. Archer, who had written a friend in Baltimore to communicate with him through the personal columns of the New York *Herald*. This letter was delivered to Wilkinson by Mrs. P. C. Martin, a Baltimorean then living in Montreal, whose husband was active in sheltering escapees from the prison. A few days later, a "personal" in the newspaper informed "A. J. L. W." that his solicitude was fully appreciated, that a few nights after November 4, a carriage would be at the door, and to be ready, that all seeming obstacles were removed. The "obstacles" were the U.S.S. *Michigan* and the prison guard.

Wilkinson originally planned to lead his men on board one of the lake steamers at Windsor, opposite Detroit, and, when fairly out on the lake, to rise up against the crew, as the Confederates had done in capturing the *St. Nicholas* on the Potomac River in June, '61. But a Canadian named McCuaig advised against it, explaining that steamers seldom stopped at ports on that side of the lake, and then only at irregular intervals. This fellow had been introduced to ex-Marshal Kane by an acquaintance from Tennessee, a Mr. Hale, who identified him as "a good and reliable Southern sympathizer engaged in running the blockade and occupying a high commercial position in Canada." [14] So his advice was taken, and plans were made to embark from the American side.

One member of the party, familiar with the area, was sent to Sandusky to learn the strength of the garrison and to gather other information they would need to plan the attack. He returned with the news that there were four hundred troops on Johnson's Island, with no artillery except two small howitzers, one of which was on a ferryboat plying between the island and the city. The U.S.S. *Michigan* he found lying at anchor about two hundred yards offshore with her guns—six, it was reported —bearing upon the prison. Her captain, he was told, was Commander John C. Carter, a friend in the old navy days of Minor and others.

Preparations proceeded carefully. Wilkinson was informed that there were one hundred eighty escaped Confederate officers and soldiers hiding in the neighborhood, who would assist him, and he made plans to supply them with arms. Two small nine-pounder guns were purchased. The Colt Firearms Manufacturing Company at Hartford, Connecticut, through indirect channels, furnished the party with one hundred navy revolvers, as well as ample pistol ammunition. Dumbbells were substituted for cannon balls to avert suspicion. Powder, bullets, slugs, grapnels, and butcher knives were obtained in lieu of cutlasses.

Following McCuaig's advice, the party planned to take deck passage on a line of screw steamers running between Chicago and Ogdensburg, New York. Members would go in the disguise of mechanics and laborers bound for Chicago to work on the city waterworks.

A man was sent to Ogdensburg to buy tickets for twenty-five men and to make a blanket arrangement for passage for any other laborers who might be added to the group, this to be taken care of merely by presenting a ticket to the ship's captain. With this arranged, instructions were then given for all members of the party to assemble at St. Catharine's, a little port on the Welland Canal, and to go on board the same steamer. One member, who would appear to have no connection with the others, would take charge of the guns and ammunition, to be concealed in casks and boxes marked "Machinery, Chicago." When the vessel got out into Lake Erie well clear of British jurisdiction, they were to rise up and overpower the crew, mount their two nine-pounders, and push on to Sandusky, timing their arrival so as to reach the U.S.S. *Michigan* about daylight. As they approached, they would collide with this vessel as if by accident, board and carry her, train her guns on the prison headquarters, and send a boat on shore to demand an unconditional surrender of the island.

When they met at St. Catharine's, only thirty-two of the one hundred eighty escaped Confederates reputed to be in the area appeared. But this failed to upset the enterprise. With a total force of fifty-four, the opportunity appeared to be golden. Lieutenant Minor later described the situation as they saw it: "Major W. S. Pierson, the commanding officer, is said to be a humane man, and seeing the disadvantage at which we would have him, with the prisoners by this time clamorous for their release, he would have been compelled to surrender, and with the half dozen steamers at the wharf in Sandusky we could have speedily landed the whole two thousand prisoners on the Canada shore, distant only some forty miles; and then with the *Michigan* under our command, and she the only man-of-war on the lakes, with a crew composed of our fifty-four and some fifty others of such men as the Berkleys, Randolphs, Paynes, and others among the prisoners, we would have had the lake shore from Sandusky to Buffalo at our mercy, with all the vast commerce of Lake Erie as our just and lawful prey." [15]

The party of fifty-four assembled at St. Catharine's, confident of success. Hour after hour they waited. And then suddenly their bubble burst. Mayors of lake cities were notified by telegram from Secretary Stanton in Washington to be on their guard against a Confederate raid, which he had been informed by the Governor General of Canada was in progress. Troops stationed at Port Colborne, the Lake Erie terminus of the Welland Canal, were ordered to arrest any vessel passing through the canal with a suspicious number of passengers on board.

Fear of trouble at Johnson's Island had stirred precautionary action in October, and it now appeared to be justified. It was on the 22nd of that month that Welles ordered the *Michigan* to proceed to Johnson's Island. Commander Carter moved there immediately, and soon he was wiring back that "the necessity of the ship's stay here seems already to have ceased." [16] But he was told to stay, and a little later he was instructed: "Move the *Michigan* to a position near Johnson's Island, so as to be able to give immediate assistance in case of outbreak or trouble with the Rebel prisoners." And then on November 12 came the message that dispelled all doubt of the need for the presence of the gunboat: "Reliable information is furnished this Department that a project is on foot in Canada to fit out steamers and attempt a rescue of the prisoners confined on Johnson's Island. Use the utmost vigilance on board your vessel, and take every precaution against a surprise to yourself, as well as the garrison." [17]

Blame for the collapse of the Confederates' plan apparently lay with one man. Lieutenant Minor later wrote of it in a letter to Admiral Franklin Buchanan: "It appears that McCuaig, whom I believed to have been earnestly with us, became alarmed at the last moment, when our success seemed so certain, and fearing the ultimate bearing of it upon his own individual fortunes, involving perhaps failure, exile, loss of position, and imprisonment, betrayed us to Mr. Holden, a member of the Provincial Cabinet, who at once communicated it to the Governor General, and hence the discovery." [18]

And so the secret expeditioners turned back, sick at heart, and went about leaving Canada as soon as possible, but in "a dignified and proper manner." Wilkinson, Loyall, and Minor, under the respective names of Coleman, Kelly, and Brest, remained together in Montreal for several days, and then they came away, "leaving our poor fellows to bear the increased hardships of their dreary prison life for months to come." [19] They traveled in open wagons and buggies through the wilds of lower Canada and New Brunswick, "often looking into the houses on the Maine side of the river, with a desire to do to them as their people do to ours; but as our policy is different, and as we carry on the war more on principles of civilization, the feeling was a childish one, though the contempt one felt for the cowardly dogs who crossed the line to avoid the dreaded draft was only natural, and still more so when their daily papers poured such venom on our cause and all connected with it." [20]

Lieutenant Minor wrote a benediction to the Johnson's Island expedition in his letter to Buchanan: "So, but for treachery, which no one can guard against, our enterprise would have been the feature of the war, and our little Navy another laurel wreath of glorious renown."

★ 8

Opened with a prayer

What drew attention to Joseph Leuty was his account of the Confederates' activity in their capital. Leuty was one of six refugees from Richmond put on board the U.S.S. *Jacob Bell* on a wintry day, for delivery at Point Lookout, Maryland. But long before he got there he was talking so much that Acting Master G. C. Schulze, commanding the *Bell,* persuaded him to put his observations in writing.

"I am an Englishman by birth, a molder by trade," he wrote. "Have lived in the South for the last four years; for the last eight months I have been working in the artillery shop on Seventh Street, Richmond, where they are now making a shell which looks exactly like a piece of coal, pieces of which were taken from a coal pile as patterns to imitate. I have made these shells myself. I believe these shells have power enough to burst any boiler. After they were thrown on a coal pile I could not tell the difference between them and coal myself." [1]

In talking with the refugee, Schulze obtained other information which he passed on for what it was worth. The explosives were to be thrown among the coal in Northern depots by bogus refugees and spies. In addition, every blockade-runner would carry a supply, and if in imminent danger of capture, would throw the shells in with the coal in their own bins, in the hope of keeping the Union from using the ship.

All of this, as the war advanced into 1864, was recorded as additional evidence of the desperate fight the Southerners were waging. It showed they were cunning and ingenious, and that they were using every method they could think of to offset the North's superior strength in manpower and materials. It was not long before further Confederate initiative was reported, again from Richmond. George Gift was there, newly assigned to duty after his return from the Johnson's Island expedition, and he wrote his fiancée, Ellen Shackelford, a letter in which he showed no thought of censorship:

"Here I have been for a week now endeavoring to perform impossibilities in the way of procuring materials, etc., for the outfitting of the expedition. Today orders came for me to move to Goldsboro and I have not a car upon which to transport the boats; the Army people monopolize everything and yield up nothing. I have been from office to office looking up stores, munitions, etc., and with such poor success that I am not only tired bodily but mentally disgusted. . . .

"Of the coming expedition I know nothing save that I am very tired, and that we are to go to Goldsboro, which leads to the belief that we are going down the Neuse River to pounce on some Yankees. We will have between two hundred and three hundred men and twenty officers." [2]

George Gift's deductions were correct. The Confederates were planning a joint operation along the Neuse, and at the head of the naval contingent was to be John Taylor Wood, the former Naval Academy instructor and grandson of President Zachary Taylor.[3] It would be another effort to take New Bern, North Carolina, something already attempted with gloomy result in March, '63. Army forces under General George E. Pickett were to approach in three columns and take the works in New

Bern from the rear, while the Navy was to capture Federal gunboats in the Neuse and prevent reinforcements by water.[4]

On the next-to-the-last day of January, '64, Gift received
orders from Wood to move to Goldsboro without delay. Each
man with him was to be well clad and shod, to have a pea
jacket and blanket, three days' cooked rations, cooking utensils,
axes, a rifle, cutlass, and possibly revolvers.[5] At eight o'clock
that night, he started by rail, carrying two heavy launches—
each armed with a twelve-pounder howitzer—and two large
rowboats. His party consisted of one hundred twenty-five men,
led by ten or twelve officers. At eleven the following morning,
he was at Kinston. He found Wood, anxiously awaiting him.

Wood said he already had ten boats in the water. All in all,
they would have fourteen boats and about two hundred fifty
seamen, twenty-five Marines, and thirty-five officers. The attack
was to be made that night, and in the meantime they would
have to row sixty miles.

The launches Gift had brought were so heavy that Wood
left him and eighty-two men behind, with orders to get them
down as fast as possible. "I got them off the cars and hauled
them to the water with twenty mules," he wrote Ellen, "and a
right hard time I had of it. At three I was all ready, guns
mounted, arms loaded and men stationed. We left the landing
cheered by a great many pretty ladies. At five o'clock I was ten
miles down the river and there encamped to get my supper and
refresh before the long night's work. At sundown we were again
afloat and pulling away quite cheerfully, the eighty rowers
bending to their oars and sending the huge boats forward at
the rate of six or seven miles an hour. We had no pilot and not
a soul in the party had ever been down the narrow, lonesome
river before.

"With the night came clouds and mists and we could scarcely
see the banks, although the river was only about fifty or sixty
yards in width. Down and down we went, occasionally striking
upon sand bars and logs which caused much delay in getting off.
At three o'clock in the morning I concluded to stop as the men

were chilled, hungry and sleepy, and I was in doubt as to how far I was from the enemy at New Bern, and so far had not heard anything from the boats ahead." [6]

The plan of joint operation called for the Navy to board and carry the Union gunboats at New Bern, while the Army captured the works defending the town.

"Thus," wrote Gift, "we would make a joined victory, and beat the reprobates by land and sea."

At daylight Gift's party was aroused by heavy, sharp cannonading which he estimated to be about five miles distant. Soon the long, heavy roll of musketry began to mingle with the boom of the heavy guns, which led him to believe that the battle in front of New Bern had begun in earnest.

Gift feared that Wood would go into action before he arrived, so he immediately shoved off to continue to the point of rendezvous, a stream called Swift Creek. On arrival, he went into camp, finding no one else there and no signs of blood. A little later some Army officers arrived and informed him that Wood had not made the attack.

The day wore along without further news of the fleet. Gift was worried. Was Wood above or below? At night he stationed a picket on the bank of the river to watch for the boats, and an hour or so later this guard brought in a communication that had been relayed by the Army forces besieging New Bern. It revealed that Wood had searched the harbor from one end to the other the night before, but had found no enemy. Disappointed, he had returned up the river shortly before daylight and quietly hidden his party in a creek a few miles below the spot where Gift waited.

At eleven that night, the two parties met. By that time a single Federal gunboat had put in an appearance in front of New Bern. It anchored about one hundred yards from a land battery in the town and about five to six hundred yards from Fort Stevens, a formidable work mounting a number of heavy guns, and directly opposite Fort Anderson. In planning their attack, the Confederates realized that their advance and return would have to be between these fortifications.

"At half-past two A.M. of the 2nd instant," Gift wrote his fiancée, "we were near Fort Anderson peering into the darkness when we were fully enlightened by the striking of his bell. A faint light on his decks further informed us of his whereabouts. So the long column (formed two boats abreast, the launches bringing up the rear) turned its head and struck out steadily and noiselessly for our victim. As I stood up and watched the line it looked like a naval funeral procession. Not a sound could be heard save the dipping of the oars. Every ear was wide open for the first sound of alarm.

"At length a hurried voice came when the advance was about two hundred and fifty yards off—'boat ahoy'—thrice repeated quickly, and then the rattle sounded the alarm and call to quarters. As soon as we were hailed, Wood stood up in his boat and ordered his men to 'give way' and lay him aboard. The men sprang to their oars and we shot forward to the attack. Soon the enemy saw us and opened with musketry and pistols. I was about seventy-five or one hundred yards behind and I assure you that I feared for those in advance. The fire was quick and the distance close, still we bent forward, returning their fire with interest. At length we were alongside and the enemy was driven back on deck, the sharp, quick reports of pistols and the clash of cutlasses could be heard in all directions, accompanied with 'take that, you Yankee scoundrels,' etc."

Gift had orders not to board, but to hold himself in readiness for an emergency. It was all over before he got there.

"As soon as the enemy had surrendered," he related, "our crew commenced plundering and much confusion ensued. As soon as firing ceased, the forts became aware that the vessel had fallen into our hands and opened on her. The first shell passed through her upper works, and we soon found that it would be necessary to destroy the prize which we forthwith proceeded to do by setting her on fire and pulling away. The enemy shelling us and firing musketry as we fell back, we brought off our prisoners and wounded."

Much planning under Wood's direction had gone into the attack. Men had been gathered quietly at Kinston, and there they had waited, not knowing their assignment, but suspecting, from the small boats put in the Neuse, that it would be hand-to-hand fighting.[7]

Leaving Gift and the eighty-two men, Wood took his party down the Neuse the afternoon of January 31, landing on a small island at sunset. After they had eaten, all hands were assembled to receive instructions. Wood gave specific orders to each boat's crew. Then he announced solemnly: "We must now all pray." He himself gave the prayer. "I can remember it now, after the long interval that has elapsed since then," Dr. D. B. Conrad, fleet surgeon, recalled in later years.[8]

The party then re-embarked and continued downstream in one long line. At 4:00 A.M. they were in the estuary at New Bern, looking for enemy gunboats, but could find none. Fog partially obscured their view. As they moved back and forth, firing sounded from the land side of New Bern, and they knew that Pickett's forces were attacking. The near approach of daylight caused Wood to direct his men back upstream three miles to the shelter of a small island where they rested and slept all day.

About sundown they made out an enemy gunboat coming up the river. She approached steadily, and before dark they saw her anchor off the city at Foster's Wharf. She was low in the water, her guards scarcely clearing it, a factor that promised easier capture.

When Gift's party and the two launches arrived a little later, Wood resumed his plans to attack. Again the men were called together for prayer. A few minutes later, as they stepped into the boats, they kept their eyes on the lights of the gunboat in the distance and in youthlike gaiety, talked of the thrills ahead and chose mates for shoulder-to-shoulder fighting. But not all of them were gay. One of them stood erect and voiced a thought that sobered some of those within hearing: "I wonder how many of us will be up in those stars by tomorrow morning." He was Palmer Saunders, passed midshipman from Norfolk.[9]

They rowed off into the night, the lights on the masthead of the Union vessel their guide. Several factors were working in their behalf. The gunboat, later discovered to be the U.S.S. *Underwriter,* a side-wheel steamer of nearly three hundred fifty tons, had anchored and trained her guns on a bridge over the river. At full strength she had a crew of seventy-two men and thirteen officers. Nine of the crew were taken to the hospital at New Bern the hour she arrived, and others were sent off by boat for various duties and were expected back at varying periods. So it was only a routine hail that greeted Wood's party as it approached.

"This was a trying moment," related Surgeon Conrad with freedom of fantasy years later, "but Commander Wood was equal to the emergency. Jumping up, he shouted, 'Give way hard! Board at once!' The men's backs bent and straightened at the oars, and the Federal bluejackets at the same moment opened up on us with small arms. The long, black sides of the gunboat, with men's heads and shoulders above them, could be distinctly seen by the line of red fire, and we realized immediately that the only place of safety for us was on board of the gunboat, for the fire was very destructive. . . .

"The boat commanded by Lieutenant Loyall[10] had the deadly honor of being first on board. Leading his crew as became his rank, duty and desire, Loyall jumped into the gangway, now a blazing sheet of flame, and, being nearsighted (having lost his glasses), stumbled and fell upon the deck of the gunboat, the four men who were following close upon his heels falling on top of him stone dead, killed by the enemy's bullets, each one of the unfortunate fellows having from four to six of them in his body. Rising, Lieutenant Loyall shook off his load of dead men, and by this time our crew had climbed up on the wheelhouse, Commander Wood's long legs giving him an advantage over the rest of us. . . .

"I could hear Wood's stentorian voice giving orders and encouraging the men, and then, in less than five minutes, could distinguish a strange synchronous roar, the meaning of which I did not understand at first; but it soon became plain. 'She's ours! She's ours!' Everybody was crying at the top of their voices, in order to stop the shooting, as only our men were on their feet."

Wood hoped to take the *Underwriter* away with him, but engineers sent below soon returned with a report that her fires were so low she could not be moved within an hour. By that time, Forts Stevens and Anderson were firing at the vessel, so he gave orders for her to be set afire and abandoned.

Prisoners were hastily loaded into the boats. G. Edgar Allen, acting third assistant engineer on the *Underwriter*, was ordered into her whaleboat. As it pulled away upstream, he noticed that in the Southerners' hurry to get off, they had placed only two men over him as a guard. This he discovered as the steersman sitting next to him, alarmed over the number of captives on board, called to another boat to take some of them off. Allen snatched a cutlass from the fellow and told the other prisoners to pull for their lives. They landed at the foot of the breastworks on shore and soon were among friends.

At 5:00 A.M. the magazine of the *Underwriter* exploded.[11]

Gift was soon writing a letter to his friend Catesby Jones: "I am all admiration for Wood. He is modesty personified, conceives boldly and executes with skill and courage. The original design was to attack and cut out some four or five vessels that were accustomed to lay in the river, but unfortunately this one was all that could be found." [12]

The attacking party had consisted of thirty-three officers and two hundred and twenty men, not all of whom got into action. Six lay dead on the decks of the *Underwriter*, one of them Passed Midshipman Palmer Saunders—no longer wondering how many would be up in the stars, for his head had been "cleft in two by a boarding sword in the hands of some giant of the forecastle." [13]

When the attack was over and the *Underwriter* was in flames, John Taylor Wood took his dozen or so little boats back up the river. The Federals then realized the possibility of a new danger. "I think it quite probable," Commander H. K. Davenport, who had arrived off New Bern in the U.S.S. *Hetzel,* wrote Admiral Lee, "that the signal book of the *Underwriter* has fallen into the hands of the enemy. She had not the general, only the boat signal code. It would be well to change their numbers or their values." [14]

The peripatetic coffin

FEBRUARY 1864

Something low in the water off Charleston, coming from the sea toward the U.S.S. *Catskill* on her starboard quarter at twenty minutes to ten at night, was all Lieutenant Commander Greenleaf Cilley needed to press him into action. He hailed, and when his hail went unanswered, he waited no longer. He gave the signal to fire and then he leaned over the rail and stared into the semidarkness to observe the effect. He could see bullets from the guns kicking up splashes of silver in the reflection from the calcium lights burning over toward Morris Island. They struck dangerously close to the mysterious object, and it sheered off.

Shortly afterward, the object was seen approaching on the port quarter. Cilley repeated the hail. When silence again greeted his shouts, he once more gave the order to fire, this time directing the guns of the turret to be turned toward the cause of the disturbance.

"It kept off," Cilley said in his official account, "and I sent the picket boat to watch its movements. The boat returned shortly and the officer reported it a torpedo steamer. I immediately made signal and dispatched the picket boat to notify the ironclads. About half an hour afterwards observed firing of musketry in the direction of the ironclads." [1]

Cilley remained alert. At a quarter past eleven he saw what seemed to be the same low object moving close to the shore from Moultrie House toward Fort Moultrie. He followed it with his eyes until it disappeared in the darkness beyond the reflection of the calcium lights.

The lieutenant commander's experience on this particular evening was becoming more and more routine. Since the *New Ironsides* had received her blast from the torpedo boat and the Federals had learned beyond question that the Confederates were looking for ways to blow up the fleet blockading Charleston, pickets worked feverishly to maintain a constant guard against attack. Any object that came along, a rippling wave or a bit of flotsam in the form of a stick or plank, they watched to make sure it did not develop into a death-dealing device launched by the ingenious Rebels.

One evening, Acting Master Alvin Phinney of the mortar schooner *Racer* sent out a picket boat in charge of Acting Master's Mate D. B. Corey. Corey came back with a breathless report. All had been quiet until about 11:00 P.M., and then he had seen "something which appeared to be about ten feet long above the water, going very fast." From the ripple it made ahead and astern, he judged that it extended some distance under water. But it soon passed out of sight, and he saw nothing more of it. [2]

That same evening, at ten-fifteen, the sentry on board the schooner *Dan Smith* saw what he took to be a torpedo boat. He hailed and received no reply. When it was eighty yards off, he ordered the guns fired and called all hands to quarters. Whatever he was looking at had appeared to be trying to cross his vessel's bow, but it backed off when fired on and headed southward.

No matter how close a guard they maintained, the besiegers

of Charleston never could be exactly sure what was disturbing them at night. Deserters gave varied accounts of the new inventions the Confederates were adopting in an effort to offset the superior naval strength of the Union in that area. It was evident that more torpedo boats were under construction, and two deserters, in January, 1864, told of a device they called *Diver,* or *American Diver,* that was something to tax the imagination. She could dive beneath a ship and surface at will, and she could go for long distances under water. Because of her peculiar shape and sharp nose, she was sometimes referred to as *Fish Boat.*

A mechanic from Michigan named Belton, a settler in Alabama before the war, supplied details concerning the *Diver.* He had worked at Mobile until forced to take up arms, and then had joined the Navy at Charleston. Before leaving Mobile, he had seen the submarine in all stages of construction. Sometimes he had been engaged near her in the same shop. He described her as thirty-five feet long, five and a half feet high, with a propeller at the rear end, turned by hand from inside. Entrance was through two manholes at the top, about twelve to fourteen feet apart. He estimated she could be driven at a speed of five knots without exertion of the men propelling her.

This deserter also had been on hand when the submarine was dismounted for shipment from Mobile to Charleston on two railroad flat cars. At the time he was questioned by the Federals in January, 1864, he said she had drowned three crews, one at Mobile and two at Charleston, a total of seventeen men. But he attributed her failures to lack of understanding on the part of those handling her. He believed she could be operated successfully. He had seen her raised after the last sinking, had seen her refitted, and had watched her submerge again. While he looked on, she dived beneath the C.S.S. *Indian Chief* twice, making about a half mile with each dive. And then he saw her go under the C.S.S. *Charleston.* Each time, she remained below about twenty minutes.[3]

Another deserter, George L. Shipp, also had been a close

observer at Charleston of what the submarine could do. He stood by while she submerged and stayed under water long periods at a time, and he was looking at her the day she went under and failed to come up again. Nine days later she was brought to the surface, and just thirty yards separated him from her when seven bodies were taken from her hold. In a week, she once more was moving about the harbor, but with a promise to the crew that she would not submerge.[4]

The story of the submarine went back to the siege of New Orleans, at a time when the Confederates, to keep such a device they had built from falling into Federal hands, were forced to scuttle her. The men who may have been pioneers in the project were James McClintock and Baxter Watson, munitions and steam-gauge makers,[5] who were associated in the undertaking with Horace L. Hunley, a thirty-seven-year-old Sumner County, Tennessee, native, brought to New Orleans while he was still a child. Backed by private funds, they had started building an undersea craft sometime in 1861, in the hope of operating against two Union steamers on Lake Pontchartrain.

These men labored heatedly in the months when the war clouds were darkening.[6] By early February, '62, their submarine was ready to take to the water. She was named *Pioneer,* and they took her out in Lake Pontchartrain for trial. Twenty feet long, four feet in diameter, and six feet deep, she was made of quarter-inch iron sheets fastened with rivets. Her propeller was turned by cranks, operated by two or more men facing one another. Rudders were at both ends, worked by a single shaft.

In her trials, the *Pioneer* destroyed a barge used as a target, and she immediately was looked upon as a success. Her principal investors were Hunley; his brother-in-law, Robert Ruffin Barrow, a wealthy sugar-cane planter; John K. Scott; and Henry J. Leovy. They obtained a letter of marque in March and were prepared for business. But Farragut, pushing up the Mississippi with his huge fleet of Federal ships, soon brought an end to the career of the *Pioneer*.[7]

The submariners fled from New Orleans, going to Mobile,

where they received a friendly reception. Major General Dabney H. Maury, commanding the Department of the Gulf, gave them full co-operation. So convinced was he of the value of the undersea craft that he assigned to them, as helpers, two young engineers from the Twenty-first Alabama Infantry—Lieutenants George E. Dixon and William A. Alexander, the latter born of Scotch parentage in London in 1837 and an emigrant to America in 1859. They began building another *Pioneer,* again on private capital, this one a longer and more tapering vessel, designed from plans furnished by Hunley, McClintock, and Watson. It was completed in the machine shops of Park & Lyons in early '63.

A major contributor was Horace Hunley. Graduated from Tulane University in 1849, his business career was divided between sugar-cane planting, in association with his brother-in-law, Robert Barrow; law practice at New Orleans; and the duties of a special deputy collector of customs for the port and city of New Orleans.

When finished, the second submarine, possibly never named, had a short career. While being towed off Fort Morgan where she was to be manned for an attack, she foundered and sank. No lives were lost.

Undaunted, the *Pioneer*'s designers promptly started work on still another undersea craft, this the one the deserters referred to as the *American Diver.* They began with an old iron boiler about twenty-five feet long and four feet wide. This they cut in two, lengthwise, inserted twelve-inch iron strips in the sides to provide height, and added wedge-shaped end sections fore and aft to give her an over-all length of thirty-five feet. Bulkheads were riveted across the bow and stern to form water-ballast tanks equipped with sea cocks and force pumps for raising and lowering the craft. For ballast, flat castings were fastened to the bottom on the outside. These were attached by means of bolts that passed through stuffing boxes to the inside, so they could be loosened and dropped when necessary.

Lateral fins were controlled by means of a lever on the inside.

A wheel, attached to rods that ran the length of the boat, operated the rudder. Depth of the boat when submerged was indicated by a mercury gauge. A compass, installed near the wheel, provided direction.

The crew entered through hatchways at each end, fitted with coamings eight inches high. Glass panes in the coamings permitted a view of the outside. An air box and pipe between the hatchways made it possible to let in air while on the surface without opening the hatches.

Nine men comprised a full crew. As they prepared to enter, they divided into two groups, one passing in through the forward hatch, with the skipper entering last. Seven members took their seats at the propeller shaft. When all was in readiness, the skipper lit a candle, both for purposes of illumination and as a device to warn them when the oxygen supply was running low. Then the officers fastened down the hatch covers, let water into the ballast tanks, and closed the sea cocks. With this routine completed, the second officer took a seat with the crew at the shaft and gave a hand at turning the propeller.

When completed, the third submarine was taken for trial to Mobile River, rather than to Mobile Bay. There she gave promise of success. Towing a floating torpedo, a ninety-pound copper cylinder, she dived under an old flatboat and blew it to pieces. But subsequent trials in the bay indicated a dubious future in choppy waters, so plans were made to move her to Charleston where the bay was calmer.[8]

The submarine arrived at Charleston about August 15, 1863, weeks before the torpedo boat made its attack on the *New Ironsides*. She was under the management of B. A. Whitney, Baxter Watson, and James McClintock. Soon McClintock received a letter of advice and encouragement from Horace Hunley:

"I have been extremely anxious about your experiment at Charleston. It is not at all on the question whether you will succeed in blowing up a vessel of the enemy, for I think that more than probable and of itself only a small matter. It is whether your success will be made available in effecting a real solid benefit to the Confederacy and conferring glory on its originators. I am anxious first and above all for a dead silence on our part that the enemy may be lost in uncertainty and misery which is more dreadful than any understood evil of even the greatest magnitude. Secondly, while in a panic if you succeed, the enemy, if properly pressed before he can make preparations to resist the consequences of your success, might be possibly driven entirely from Morris Island, his works destroyed and guns spiked even if it be not possible to take and permanently hold the island and prevent it from being retaken. . . . Remind your crew of Manassas and Shiloh and the consequence of faltering in the hour of success, and make one grand effort and you may have cause to rejoice as long as you live over the fruits of your labor. . . ." [9]

At Charleston, the submarine, now called the *H. L. Hunley,* became an immediate curiosity. But she still had accomplished nothing by August 23. That evening at sunset she started out, but returned shortly afterward because of an "accident." Three days later, Chief of Staff Thomas Jordan assigned C. L. Sprague to the *Hunley* as a torpedo expert; and in another day or two, Lieutenant John A. Payne of the C.S.S. *Chicora,* an Alabamian who already had distinguished himself for valor, was detached to take command of the undersea vessel.

Payne got together a crew from his shipmates on the *Chicora,* and on the evening of August 29, he prepared to go out for a dive. The men he had enlisted climbed slowly down into the hold. When all had gotten in except Payne, the submarine became entangled in some way with ropes of the U.S.S. *Etiwan* near by, was drawn on her side, filled, and went down. Five seamen were drowned, and from then on she was given the nickname of "Peripatetic Coffin."

This sinking at Charleston gave the impression the *Hunley* was having trouble solely because her crew did not know how to operate her. So logical did this seem that her chief benefactor, Horace Hunley, came up from Mobile, bringing a crew that had

had experience with her there.[10] On September 19, he applied to General Beauregard, commanding in the area, for permission to refit and manage the submarine. Three days later, Chief of Staff Jordan directed that the "boat be cleaned and turned over to Hunley for refitting, the repairs to be made at the expense of the Confederate States."

Hunley soon had the submarine in operation again. She moved about, demonstrating that she was slow in turning, but that she could dive at a moment's notice—and sometimes without it.[11] Then, on the morning of October 15, after making several successful dives under the receiving ship *Indian Chief,* she failed to surface. On board, in addition to Hunley, were Robert Brookbank, Joseph Patterson, Thomas W. Park, Charles McHugh, Henry Beard, John Marshall, and Charles L. Sprague.[12]

Weeks passed. While the *Hunley* lay at the bottom, the Federals renewed their bombardment at Charleston, continuing it without break day or night for forty-one days. This was in lieu of an attack, which a majority of the commanding officers opposed in a council of war called by Admiral Dahlgren after receiving an inquiry from Secretary Welles.[13] Most of the fire was concentrated on Fort Sumter. Of four hundred thirty-five shells fired during a seven-day period, three hundred fifteen took effect in or on the fort, already so battered that Dahlgren himself wrote: "Of itself Sumter is nothing; its cannon, if any are mounted, as rumor has it, would make but a poor show against the ironclads, but it stands at the very entrance to the harbor; is at such a convenient distance from Moultrie and Johnson that their fire sustains and protects it, while its own fire of musketry and artillery (if it has any) is sufficient to keep the crews of the monitors under cover and prevent them, and of course boats, when we enter, from promptly removing the rope obstructions that extend across the entrance from Moultrie to Sumter." [14] The only original feature left was the northeast face; the rest appeared to be a pile of rubbish.

But Beauregard wrote on November 10: "Total number of

shots since 26th ultimo, when attack recommenced, is nine thousand, three hundred and six. Fort is still in a defensible condition." [15]

Inside the city, numerous dwellings, stores, and public buildings were damaged, and several were burned. Three women, including a Negro slave, and two men were killed by shells.

Before the bombardment stopped on December 6, the *Hunley* had been brought to the surface again and once more was being refitted, this time under the direction of Lieutenants Dixon and Alexander, the two Alabama Infantry engineers assigned to help the submariners after their flight to Mobile from New Orleans. Beauregard himself had been an eyewitness when the submarine was dragged from the bottom. The scene he pictured as "indescribably ghastly." Members of the crew were contorted into horrible attitudes, some clutching candles as though they had been trying to force open the manholes, others lying grappled tightly together, and all with expressions of despair and agony on their blackened faces.[16]

After such an experience, Beauregard was at first deaf to argument, maintaining that the submarine was not worth the toll it was taking in human lives. But Dixon and Alexander made an impassioned plea, citing that their efforts would be in the nature of a memorial to the men who had died in the *Hunley,* bringing good out of tragedy and supplying aid to the desperate Confederacy. Finally, mainly upon the suggestion of General Jordan, Beauregard consented, but only on the condition that the *Hunley* operate on the surface as a David.

The two engineers studied the *Hunley* closely when she was brought to the surface. She had been found with her nose in the mud at the bottom of the river, her stern pointing upward at an angle of about thirty-five degrees. Considerable air and gas escaped when the hatches were raised. Bolts holding them had been loosened. Hunley's body lay forward, his head in the hatchway and his right hand extended, in evidence that he had been trying to lift the cover when he died of suffocation. A candle was in his left hand. The sea cock on the forward ballast tank was open. In the after hatchway was found the body of Thomas Park, second in command and a member of the firm at whose shop the submarine had been built. It was in much the same position as that of Hunley. The bolts fastening the iron keel ballast on the bottom had been loosened, but not enough to release it.

Dixon and Alexander were able to surmise what had happened. When Hunley set the fins to go down, he determined he needed more ballast for the dive, and without stopping to light the candle, opened the sea cock on the forward tank. This caused the boat to sink below the glass panes in the coamings, plunging the interior in darkness. The boat sank before Hunley could light the candle.

With this grim story as a background, Dixon and Alexander refitted the submarine. Then they sought a crew. Jordan referred their request to Beauregard, who consented for them to seek volunteers from the *Indian Chief,* provided they gave each man enlisted a full account of the drownings that already had occurred on the *Hunley*.

The engineers did as instructed, but stressed that misuse of the submarine's simple machinery was to blame. They got a crew and, by December 14, were ready to attack. On that date, Beauregard issued Special Orders No. 271, Section 7 of which stated:

"First Lieutenant George E. Dixon, Twenty-first Regiment Alabama Volunteers, will take command and direction of the submarine torpedo-boat *H. L. Hunley,* and proceed tonight to the mouth of the harbor, or as far as capacity of the vessel will allow, and will sink and destroy any vessel of the enemy with which he can come in conflict. All officers of the Confederate Army in this department are commanded, and all naval officers are requested, to give such assistance to Lieutenant Dixon in the discharge of his duties as may be practicable, should he apply therefor." [17]

Dixon's first request was for a vessel to tow the submarine down the harbor, and Flag Officer Tucker assigned the task to the David, captained by Chief Engineer Tomb, one of the four heroes of the *New Ironsides* incident. But there is no record that the *Hunley* succeeded in making an attack on the night of December 14. Two or three times more, Tomb towed the submarine, and after the last trip he came back and prepared a report criticizing her method of dragging torpedoes. He was stirred by the fact that the torpedo used on the last venture had got foul of the David and almost blown it up. A safer way to do it, he advised, would be on the same plan as that employed by the David—on a spar, with the boat on the surface, the torpedo lowered to eight feet. "Should she attempt to use a torpedo as Lieutenant Dixon intended, by submerging the boat and striking from below," he added, "the level of the torpedo would be above his own boat, and as she has little buoyancy and no power, the chances are the suction caused by the water passing into the sinking ship will prevent her rising to the surface, besides the possibility of his own boat being disabled." [18]

Dixon took the crew out on an average of four nights a week, the frequency depending largely on the weather. Alexander made a record of their routine on these ventures:

"We would leave Mount Pleasant about 1:00 o'clock P.M., walk seven miles to Battery Marshall [19] along the beach—this exposed us to the enemy's fire, but it was the best walking—take the boat out, and practice the crew for two hours in the Back Bay. Dixon and myself would then lie down on the beach with the compass between us, and get the bearings of the nearest Federal vessel as she took her position for the night. We would ship up the torpedo on the boom, and, when dark, go out, steering for the ship we had marked. We would proceed until the condition of the men, the sea, the tide, the moon, the wind, or the approach of daylight compelled our return to the dock. Then we would unship the torpedo, put it under guard at Battery Marshall, walk back to quarters at Mount Pleasant, and cook breakfast." [20]

Week after week they went on in this manner. And then

someone raised the question of how long they could stay under water. They decided to find out in Back Bay off Sullivan's Island. It was agreed that they would sink the boat and let her remain on the bottom until someone cried "up," at which time they would rise to the surface.

"We noted the time and sank for the test," Alexander related. "Twenty-five minutes after I had closed the after manhead and excluded the outer air, the candle would not burn. In comparing our individual experience afterwards, we found that each man had determined that he would not be the first to say 'up.' Not a word was uttered except the occasional 'How is it?' between Dixon and myself, until at last, as the voice of one man, 'up' came from all nine.

"We started the pumps. Dixon's worked all right, but I soon realized that mine was not throwing. From experience I guessed the cause of the failure, took off the cap of the pump, lifted the valve, and drew out some seaweed that had choked it. While I was doing this, the boat was considerably by the stern. Thick darkness prevailed and all hands had already reached what they thought was the utmost limit of their endurance. Some of the crew almost lost control of themselves. But a moment later we had the boat to the surface and the manhead opened.

"We had been on the bottom two hours and thirty-five minutes—more than two hours after the candle went out for lack of oxygen. The sun had been shining when we went down, and the beach lined with soldiers, as it usually was when we were practicing in the bay. It was now quite dark, with one solitary Confederate gazing at the spot where he had seen the boat go down. When I called to him, he told us that we had been given up for lost, and that a messenger had been sent to General Beauregard to inform him that the torpedo boat had gone to the bottom again." [21]

Week after week, through November, December, January, and early February, they went on in this manner. In their tests it was determined that the *Hunley* could cover more than twelve miles on a night when the sea was comparatively quiet, a distance that would take them out to the Union ships beyond the bar.

The weeks of January passed without unusual development for the submarine.[22] In the meantime, rumors, plus information received from the deserters Belton and Shipp, were keeping the Federals constantly alert. Ever dutiful, Dahlgren passed on to Welles the intelligence he had obtained from Belton describing in some detail the types of torpedo vessels the Confederates were planning to use. "There being every reason to expect a visit from some or all of these torpedoes," he concluded, "the greatest vigilance will be needed to guard against them." [23]

A week later, Dahlgren wrote Welles a longer letter about the torpedo vessels. He said there were ten building in Charleston, and that one was ready. With this, plus the original David that had damaged the *New Ironsides,* and the *H. L. Hunley,* which he referred to as the *Diver,* there were three machines they would have to fear.

And fear them they did. Dahlgren reported that additional precautions had been put into effect. Outriggers and submerged nettings protected each monitor, and at night the water around them was patrolled by steam tugs and cutters inside a ring of scout boats.

"If those who so ignorantly or basely endeavor to persuade the public that the monitors here are idle could witness one night of such vigils," he assured Welles, "they would feel disgraced at having so wantonly traduced the officers and men who give themselves to such incessant and hard service; a battle would be far preferable." [24]

Dahlgren frankly looked upon the Confederate devices with sincere appreciation. "There is, no doubt, much to be apprehended from these torpedoes," he wrote, "and I have already suggested to the Department an extensive use of similar means. I again respectfully urge on your consideration the most prompt resort thereto; nothing better could be devised for the security of our own vessels or for an examination of the enemy's position. . . . With the ample mechanical means of the North it seems that in one month five or six could be gotten into service." [25]

More than two weeks of February passed, during which Dixon waited for a dark night and smooth water suitable for him to attack some of the blockading vessels outside the Charleston bar that were unprotected by outriggers and submerged nettings. Around him were gathered a crew of six—Arnold Becker, C. Simpkins, James A. Wicks, F. Collins, and a man named Ridgeway, all of the Confederate Navy, as well as Corporal J. F. Carlsen of Captain F. W. Wagener's artillery. In the meantime, Alexander had left him, called back to Mobile on February 5 to help in developing a special gun.

On the night of February 17, Dixon decided to wait no longer. The weather was clear, the sea smooth, and the tide at half ebb. Only one factor was against him, and that he ignored: the moon cast a brightness that reduced the chances of concealing any craft approaching a victim on the surface of the water. Beauregard agreed with Dixon that an attack should be made.

Out in the North Channel opposite Breach Inlet, where the submarine was stationed, lay the U.S.S. *Housatonic,* two and a half miles from the nearest land. At 8:45 P.M. Acting Master J. K. Crosby, on duty as the ship's officer of the deck, paced back and forth, remaining constantly alert. Officers of the fleet felt more or less on their own, for everyone knew that the Admiral had gone off to Port Royal. Six lookouts were on duty around the ship. [26]

Only a little more than two years had passed since this vessel on which Crosby was stationed, a sloop of war, first had slid down into the waters at the Boston Navy Yard. [27] She lay at anchor in twenty-eight feet of water, with Fort Sumter bearing W.N.W. six miles away. Her head pointed toward the fort. In all directions, the waves rippled in a silvery peace, perhaps deceiving, that extended to the murky curtain of darkness in the distance.

But suddenly an object caught Crosby's attention. The lookout stationed at the starboard cathead, on the starboard bow of the ship, saw it at the same time. It was about one hundred yards away, had the appearance of a plank with two protuberances, and it moved directly toward the ship, in the direction of the starboard quarter, at a speed of three or four knots. Only a slight ripple trailed it.[28]

During the next two or three minutes, the alarm was given on board the *Housatonic,* the chain was slipped, engines backed, and all hands called to quarters. Several shots were fired from small arms in the direction of the mysterious object.[29] Then there was a terrific explosion forward of the mizzenmast, on the starboard side, in line with the magazine. The crew had been helpless to fend off the object, for the after pivot gun was pivoted to port and could not be brought to bear upon it. The vessel sank stern first and heeled to port as she went down, the sailors on her deck struggling frantically up the rigging to save themselves.[30]

At 9:20 P.M. a boat from the *Housatonic* reached the side of the *Canandaigua* and reported what had happened. The latter vessel hurried to the scene and found the stricken ship with her hammock nettings under water. Twenty-one officers and one hundred twenty-nine men were rescued from the rigging. Missing were Ensign Edward C. Heseltine, Captain's Clerk Charles O. Muzzey, Quartermaster John Williams, Second Class Fireman John Walsh, and Landsman Theodore Parker.[31]

The news spread slowly, for the explosion under water had made little noise. On the 19th, a Confederate picket boat captured a boat from the U.S.S. *Nipsic* off Fort Sumter and learned from the six men in it of the *Housatonic's* fate, but it was hours later before definite announcement was made in Charleston. In the meantime, Lieutenant Colonel O. M. Dantzler, commanding the Confederacy's Battery Marshall, sent off a message with implications: "I have the honor to report that the torpedo boat stationed at this post went out on the night of the 17th instant and has not yet returned. The signals agreed upon to be given in case the boat wished a light to be exposed at this post as a guide for its return were observed and answered." [32]

The Charleston *Daily Courier* on the 20th had little to tell, and most of what it was able to publish had come from the crew of the picket boat captured off Fort Sumter. It reported that the loss of the *Housatonic* had caused great consternation in the Union fleet, that all wooden vessels were ordered to keep up steam and go out to sea at night, and that picket boats had been doubled and the force in each boat increased. "This glorious success of our little torpedo boat, under the command of Lieutenant Dixon of Mobile," it added, "has raised the hopes of our people, and the most sanguine expectations are now entertained of our being able to raise the siege in a way little dreamed of by the enemy." [33]

As the hours passed and the *Hunley* failed to return, the mystery concerning her grew. Those familiar with her tried to estimate what had happened. "I am of the opinion," wrote one officer, "that, the torpedoes being placed at the bow of the boat, she went into the hole made in the *Housatonic* by explosion of torpedoes and did not have sufficient power to back out, consequently sunk with her." [34] John Payne, who had had a narrow escape in the submarine, shared this conviction. Time and again, he had said, the boat would go into the hole she created in the side of an enemy ship; and he had urged that the torpedo staff be lowered to a level below the *Hunley* so she would strike above the damaged area. [35] At Mobile, Alexander, realizing his transfer had saved him from a watery death, reasoned that the movement of the *Housatonic* as soon as the alarm was given had caught Dixon by surprise, that she had backed down on the submarine, and that the combined momentum of the two vessels had brought them together sooner and with greater impact than Dixon had anticipated.

Captain J. F. Green of the *Canandaigua* was ordered out on the 20th to examine the wreck of the *Housatonic*. He reported that her spar deck was about fifteen feet under water and that the afterpart appeared to have been entirely blown off.

Dahlgren, returning from Port Royal, was highly alarmed over what had happened. He ordered outriggers and nettings for all vessels in the fleet and then wrote Welles: "I desire to suggest to the Department the policy of offering a large reward of prize money for the capture or destruction of a David. I should say not less than $20,000 or $30,000 for each. They are worth more than that to us." [36] Cruisers outside the harbor were instructed to keep constantly under way. "With an increased number of steam tugs and some torpedo boats like those of the Rebels added to the measures already taken," he advised, "I should feel no apprehension whatever from this style of Rebel warfare." [37]

As the Southerners waited for definite news concerning the *Hunley,* Beauregard issued an order: "As soon as its fate shall have been ascertained, pay a proper tribute to the gallantry and patriotism of its crew and officers." [38]

But the fate of the *Hunley* would have to be assumed. Divers sent down to look for her in November, 1864, dragged the area for five hundred yards around the wreck of the *Housatonic* without finding the submarine.[39] And yet traditional reports say she was discovered years later, pointing to the spot a hundred yards away where the *Housatonic* had gone down.

★ *10*

Feeble efforts

The crew of the U.S.S. *Memphis,* a screw steamer captured
by the Union while trying to get out of port with a cargo of
cotton, stared in alarm at what they could see coming through
the water toward them at one in the morning. It looked like
"a ship's boat in the water bottom up." [1] When first seen, it was
about fifty yards distant, approaching rapidly on the port quarter
from upriver.

Recognizing the sort of emergency they watched for every
night, the alarmed sailors beat to quarters and slipped the
chain. There was not much else they could do, for the object
was so close they could not bring a heavy gun to bear upon it,
but the watch was armed and did let loose a rapid fire from
muskets, revolvers, and pistols, aiming at what looked like a
hatchway in its center.

The fire seemed to check for a moment the progress of whatever was out there in the water. It went a few feet astern of the
vessel, and then darted forward again, its ripples an ominous
sight on the silvery surface of the murky river.

"At the same time," reported Acting Master R. O. Patterson of the *Memphis,* who assumed "the object" to be a torpedo boat, "we rang to go ahead, and our propeller, I think, must have caught and broken some of her gear, as she appeared to be disabled and drifted up river. In a few moments they showed a light, at which we fired a twelve-pounder shot; she then disappeared and an armed boat was immediately dispatched to search for and capture her if possible, but returned without success." [2]

Unaware of it at the time, the vessel Patterson commanded had just escaped a fate that might have been worse than that of the *New Ironsides.* The "object" was the same David that had made the earlier attack, and her commander was James H. Tomb, one of the four men who had taken her out at that time. Since then, she had been fitted with an attachment to permit the torpedo she was carrying to be lowered to any depth just before striking. She also had been covered above the water line with a coating of quarter-inch iron, and an adjustable cap had been placed over her stack to prevent water from drowning out her fire. These were all measures taken at Tomb's direction, to eliminate faults found in her as a result of her first trial. [3]

When the torpedo boat once more was ready for duty, Tomb had been ordered to take her to the North Edisto to attack the *Memphis,* the sight of which anchored out in the river rankled the Southerners. They could see with their glasses that she was well armed,

A few days before receiving his orders, Tomb met Captain Theodore Stoney, one of the fathers of the David, and Francis D. Lee, captain of engineers and the man in charge of torpedo production at Charleston. In discussing the plans for the David, Lee suggested that the torpedo the boat then was carrying might not be reliable, having been exposed for six months to every vicissitude of weather and climate, and he offered to furnish a new one that he considered far more perfect. [4]

But Tomb couldn't wait. He left Charleston on March 3 and

headed toward the North Edisto. With him were Pilots A. Coste and Walker Cannon, the latter of whom had taken part in the *New Ironsides* attack, and Fireman James Lawless. Captain Stoney, it was agreed, was to have a section of artillery sent down the river to draw attention away from the torpedo boat after she had struck.

Next day the David was at Church Flats, and from there it proceeded toward the *Memphis*. Just as it came in sight of the vessel, about midnight, the pump on the torpedo boat broke down, and the tiny craft had to be taken back up the river for repairs.

The following night, at about the same place and about the same hour, the pump again failed. This time, Tomb decided to anchor in the marshes, let the steam go down, and make repairs. At an hour after midnight, the David started out into the river again.

"We proceeded in the direction of the *Memphis,* whose lights were plainly in sight from our position up the river," Tomb recorded. "When close aboard they hailed us, and since we paid no attention to their hail, they began a rapid fire with their small arms. As we were so near, they could not make use of their big guns or howitzer. The hail of shot struck the steel covering of the David and did us no harm. The next moment the David struck the *Memphis* under the port counter some eight feet below the surface, and it was a splendid blow but did not explode the torpedo. We then turned to port and came at her on the starboard quarter, but as the *Memphis* was working her engine and going ahead pretty fast our blow was but a glancing one. We passed under the counter and carried away a portion of our stack, but did not explode the torpedo. Realizing that we could do nothing more under the circumstances, as the *Memphis* was well on her way, we turned upstream. The *Memphis* then opened fire with her heavy guns, but all her shells passed well beyond us." [5]

After the David was tied up, an inspection revealed that Captain Lee's advice was sound. The first blow had been an especially good one, smashing the tube containing the acid and flattening the torpedo, but it was too weatherworn to explode.

Fitted with a new torpedo, the David ran out of Charleston one night in April. Captain John De Camp, commanding the U.S.S. *Wabash,* picked up her trail:

"I have to report that last night, at about 9:45, an object was discovered by Ensign Charles H. Craven, the officer of the deck, on the starboard quarter, distant about one hundred and fifty yards, which corresponded in shape and movements to the torpedo boat which sank the *Housatonic.* It moved rapidly up against the tide, till about the mainmast, then, turning, stood directly for the ship.

"Ensign Craven opened fire with musketry, beat the gong for the crew to assemble at quarters, rang four bells for the engine to go ahead, opened fire with the watch, with the starboard battery, and gave orders for slipping the chain.

"The men rushed quickly to their quarters, the ship moved ahead, the chain was slipped, and when the object was being left in the quarter, distant at the time about forty yards, a round shot is supposed to have struck it; at all events the second shot struck in its immediate vicinity, and it was seen no more." [6]

Confederate officer Tomb gave a different explanation as to why the David failed to damage the *Wabash* on this occasion: "We headed for her three times, but the heavy swell rolling over and into the David compelled us to return to the harbor." [7]

These occasional appearances of the torpedo boat spread alarm through the Union fleet surrounding Charleston Harbor. Ship captains were instructed to surround their vessels with nets that hung down at least eight feet below the surface of the water, to "use great vigilance, row guard, and keep your people at or near their guns" at night, giving them rest during the day.[8]

More torpedo boats in the region of South Carolina were on their way to harass the Federals. They would be under command of Captain Stoney, and notice for their protection went out to all Confederate officers, Army and Navy, in the vicinity: "Their signal at night will be two flashes of a white light." [9]

Confederate torpedoes and torpedo boats were heard from at a succession of points. The wharf boat at Mound City, Illinois, filled with reserve supplies of ammunition and stores for Union vessels, was blown up by an explosive equipped with a timing device to fire its detonating cap. Similarly, the U.S. Army transport *Maple Leaf* was destroyed in St. John's River in Florida. Five days later the transport steamer *General Hunter* met the same fate on almost the same spot. A floating torpedo put an end to the Federal ironclad *Eastport* in the Red River shortly afterward.[10]

Precautions against torpedo boats in Charleston Harbor were not applied with the same diligence in all areas. The U.S.S. *Minnesota,* Admiral Lee's flagship at the time, lay off the mouth of the James River. A young surgeon, Dr. John M. Batten, went on board her for an overnight stay. He was extremely tired and sought his bed early. Around two in the morning he was aroused by a noise and the trembling of the vessel. He dressed quickly and went to the gun deck.

"I soon learned what was the cause of the excitement," he wrote. "It was the explosion of a one-hundred-pound torpedo under the bottom of the *Minnesota,* which had been borne thither by a torpedo boat manned by Confederates from somewhere up the James River. . . . The damage to the *Minnesota* was considerable. Her guns were dismounted, her partitions were broken down, her doors jammed, her chairs and tables upset, and her crockeryware broken." [11]

Though unknown by them at the time, the Federals on board the *Minnesota* felt that night another blow at the hands of an old foe of the James River sector, Hunter Davidson. It would bring him a citation from Secretary Mallory and the Confederate Senate "for gallant and meritorious conduct as the engineer officer of the torpedo boat *Squib,*" and along with it, promotion to commander in the C. S. Navy.[12]

Davidson had caught the *Minnesota* riding to the ebb tide. The attention of Acting Ensign James Birtwistle, officer of the watch on the Federal vessel, was attracted to a dark object slowly passing about one hundred fifty yards away. The sentry at the gangway hailed. The answer came back "Roanoke!" Birtwistle stared more intently. The object was directly abeam, seemingly without power of locomotion. Then he hailed, and the reply that was returned was indistinct. He went down off the bridge and hailed from the quarter. Again the answer was "Roanoke!"

"Don't come alongside!" shouted Birtwhistle.

"Aye! Aye!" came out of the darkness.

The union tug *Poppy* lay astern, supposedly keeping guard. Birtwistle yelled at her three times, ordering her captain to see what the object was.

The *Poppy*'s commander shouted "Aye! Aye!"

Birtwistle looked again. He was puzzled, because he could see no oars. He sent a messenger to call the *Minnesota*'s captain, Lieutenant Commander J. H. Upshur, and then shouted at the object: "Keep off or I will fire into you!"

He repeated the order, only to notice that the object was approaching rapidly. He yelled at the *Poppy:* "Run that boat down!"

"I then saw the glimmer of a light," Birtwistle reported. "The quartermaster said he could hear her puff. I jumped to a convenient gun, called for help to train it; the sentries on the gangways and forward fired three shots at her; but before I could fire the gun, she was inside of range. I jumped back from the gun and the explosion followed." [13]

On board the *Poppy,* her captain, Acting Ensign Isaac Miller, found himself in a helpless situation. By his routine, he remained on deck daily from 4:00 A.M. to 8:00 P.M. At eight the night before, he had gone to the engine room and instructed the engineer to have things ready to start at a moment's notice. The officer of the deck was cautioned to keep a good lookout.

Then he lay down on the settee in the cabin without undressing and soon fell asleep.

But the captain apparently was the only one on board who was particularly concerned about the danger of an attack. The *Poppy* had been assigned to guard the ironclad *Roanoke,* anchored near by, a duty that required it to circle the larger vessel occasionally, just to make sure no enemy was stealing up on it. When orders came for the tug to tie up near the flagship, in the center of the fleet, her crew got the idea they no longer had to maintain a rigid guard.[14]

When Miller was awakened by shouting during the night, he rushed on deck and heard the order from Birtwistle: "Run that boat down!" He jumped into the pilothouse and rang the bell to go ahead. But there was no motion. Down in the engine room the engineer was caught in a jam. But, anyway, his fires were banked to keep the steam at a level of twenty pounds, which would not have been enough to help in this emergency. Everyone on board knew the *Poppy* had orders to be careful about disturbing Admiral Lee's sleep. There was to be no blowing off steam at night.[15] The *Poppy*'s exhaust made so much noise the officers on the *Minnesota* complained that their orders could not be heard. Fleet Engineer Benjamin F. Garvin reported that he frequently had protested against the ban on the blowing off of steam, warning that the *Poppy* would not be ready to move at a moment's notice unless her pressure was maintained at a higher level.[16]

The Federals watched as the object disappeared in the darkness after the explosion. Some of them had thought it the picket boat from Norfolk, for it resembled her very much. As it went away, they could hear its exhaust and see the sparks from its smokestack.

Hunter Davidson's report of what he had done that night was brief: "Passed through the Federal fleet off Newport News and exploded fifty-three pounds of powder against the side of the flagship *Minnesota* at 2:00 A.M. She has not sunk, and I have no means yet of telling the injury done. My boat and party escaped without loss under the fire of her heavy guns and musketry and those of a gunboat lying to her stern." [17] With him on board the *Squib* were six men who would talk about the experience long afterward: J. A. Curtis, acting master; G. W. Smith, acting master; Thomas Gauley, acting boatswain; H. X. Wright, first assistant engineer; Charles Blanchard, first fireman; and William A. Hines, pilot.

A much longer report of the affair was prepared by John W. Grattan, crewman on board the *Minnesota,* and mailed next day to his parents.

"I suppose you have heard of the attempt by the enemy to blow up this frigate," he began. "I can feel very thankful that I am alive to relate the narrow escape we have had from destruction."

About 2:15 A.M. this morning, I was thrown out of my bunk by the concussion of an immense torpedo. I heard the sound and in a second afterwards the hatch gratings and gangway ladders came tumbling down the cockpit. I immediately guessed what was the matter, as I could hear the ring of the torpedo striking the side of the ship below the water line. The ship tottered and rolled like a small boat in the sea. The whole ship was lifted completely out of the water and came down with a tremendous jerk. As soon as the gratings and heavy hatch braces had stopped tumbling down the hatch, I picked myself up, being pretty severely bruised, and arranged to hobble to within a few feet of the cockpit ladder, when I struck my shin and had just got from under the hatch when a heavy iron bar from the spar deck came rattling down, just grazing my head. There was no light, everything dark as midnight, and I could hear the rush and heavy tread of five hundred men on the decks above.

Everyone thought the ship was sinking. In about five or ten seconds after the explosion, I was on deck with all the officers and men, not one in fifty being dressed. The night being very raw and cold, I rushed below as quick as possible (all the ladders being down and some of them broken) and managed to get my pants and boots on when I heard another explosion that shook the vessel. I rushed on deck with my coat and cap, and found out that it was one of our guns. I looked over towards the port quarter and could see a small segar-shaped steamer, about the size of the captain's gig, moving very rapidly towards the Rebel shore. Several shots were fired at it, but it was soon out of sight. It was some five or ten minutes before we could get up steam, and as soon as the engines were ready the cable was slipped and we were under way. It was soon ascertained that the ship was not sinking, only leaking about an inch per hour, and we anchored again and all hands ordered to man the pumps.[18]

The situation at Cherrystone on the Eastern Shore of Virginia seemed to have been made for guerrilla warfare. There a Union telegraph operator, William H. Dunn, had his instruments in operation day and night; and off two miles or so, busily laying a telegraph cable across Chesapeake Bay, were the *Titan* and the *Aeolus,* Army tugs otherwise of no particular fame.

There was mention of this operation in the newspapers. No special attention was paid to this notice until afterward, and then it was credited with the responsibility of causing a party of Confederate guerrillas to steal across the Piankatank River in open boats, conceal themselves for two days, and launch forth on a campaign of mischief that would go in the records as new evidence of Rebel defiance.

The *Aeolus* was the first to feel the effects of their plan. It came unsuspectingly in to the wharf at Cherrystone, and there was boarded and captured without a shot. Hastily the guerrillas donned the clothing of their prisoners, and thus were ideally disguised for the capture of the *Titan* when it arrived a short while later.

Dunn, the telegrapher, had only time enough to throw his instruments in the bay. Later he managed to conceal himself on the *Aeolus,* but was discovered and paroled. Before they departed, the guerrillas cut the telegraph wires, killed all the horses they could find, and burned the guardhouse and a lot of commissary stores. Then they took three thousand dollars from the captain of the *Aeolus,* bonded and disabled the vessel, and sailed away in the *Titan.*

Despite the hazy weather, the *Titan* was seen at the mouth

of the Piankatank. The telegraph on the mainland broadcast that she was "a lead-colored tugboat, without a flag, and steaming up the river fast." A chase was organized, but failed for lack of competent pilots. Others were brought in from St. George's Island, arriving at two-thirty in the morning, two days after the guerrillas had left Cherrystone. They went on board the *Commodore Read, Jacob Bell, Fuchsia, Freeborn,* and *Currituck,* and the little fleet hurried up the Piankatank, shelling the woods along the way for a stretch of twenty-two miles. At Freeport, a tiny village at the head of navigation, they found the *Titan* burned to the water line.

Back came the fleet, still shelling the woods. Further pursuit and investigation failed to reveal the identification of the guerrillas. The Federals were forced to record the incident as a total defeat, but official reports mentioned that it was probably the work of the nemesis, John Taylor Wood.[19]

Yazoo City, in Mississippi, where the dreaded Confederate ironclad *Arkansas* once lay at anchor, festered with trouble for the Federals. The Southerners there refused to remain quiet. At 9:30 A.M. one March day, they came charging into the city, catching part of the Eleventh Illinois Volunteers gathered around a twelve-pounder rifled howitzer in a redoubt and the remainder stationed with a Negro regiment around the outskirts. There was hot firing for a time, until a shell became jammed in the gun and could not be removed. The U.S.S. *Marmora,* standing by in the Yazoo, sent one of her rifled howitzers to replace it. Mounted on a field carriage, it was hauled to where there was hand-to-hand fighting. Officers hoped the gun could be placed in the redoubt, but the Confederates were there in force, so the piece was placed in position in the street, behind a barricade of cotton bales, and there it did much toward saving the day for the Union.

At one time the crew was driven from the gun, but the Federals rallied and retook the howitzer, losing three men in the charge. The fight went on until four in the afternoon, with the

Marmora, Petrel, and *Exchange* shelling the city in support of the Union regiments until the Confederates withdrew.

During the day, there had been many instances of individual bravery, both on the part of the Army and the Navy. But there also had been some examples of cowardice. One of these had been set by Ensign Shepley R. Holmes of the *Petrel,* placed in charge of the howitzer when it was sent ashore. At the first fire he deserted his post and ran back to his ship, causing her commander, Acting Master Thomas McElroy, to write: "He has sent in his resignation. I hope it may be accepted." [20]

But Ensign Holmes was to see more action and to show more cowardice before he departed from the Navy. The post at Yazoo City, intended only as a support to Sherman's winter drive in the neighborhood of Meridian, was abandoned after the attack. A few weeks later, someone got the idea that the Southerners were storing cotton in the area, and a new expedition was organized to confiscate it. An Army force under Colonel Hiram Scofield was to march overland from Haynes' Bluff, while the Navy would co-operate by sending the gunboats *Petrel* and *Prairie Bird* and the Army transport *Freestone* up the Yazoo.

The vessels moved up to Yazoo City in the afternoon, cautiously inquiring at plantations along the way as to the numbers of the enemy. A crowd of women and children could be seen on the levee, but no soldiers were in sight, so Acting Master Thomas McElroy in the *Petrel* ran up to the city, and there guns opened on him from the bluffs. Realizing he could not turn around, he ran on past, to a point where he could reverse his course. There, finding that the other gunboat had not followed him, he decided to wait until he could investigate.

Next day, Colonel Scofield's forces still had not appeared, and the *Prairie Bird* still lay below the city. McElroy called his officers into conference and kept moving his vessel back and forth to deceive the Confederates. At one that afternoon, he ran up the river two and a half miles and sent a detail on shore to gather fence rails, some for the protection of his boilers, others to be used in the furnaces in order to do away with the coal smoke that was so revealing to the enemy. At 2:20 P.M., McElroy sat down to eat. He had just gotten up from the table and gone on deck when two twelve-pounder Parrotts opened on his vessel at four hundred yards from a point astern concealed by undergrowth. Hastily he gave orders to turn around, but before this could be done, a shot passed through the stern, cutting off the steampipe and disabling the engine. Another shot cut off the legs of a gunner's mate.

The fire from the *Petrel's* gunners at this time was slow because the Rebel sharpshooters were pestering the loaders. McElroy noticed that Ensign Holmes was not encouraging his men and was behaving very badly. Another shot came through the stern, this one raking the gun deck and exploding the boilers. Officers and men jumped for the bank.

McElroy found that only Pilot Kimble Ware and Quartermaster J. H. Nibbs had remained behind with him. As soon as the escaping steam died down, they got the wounded ashore and then prepared to set fire to the *Petrel,* with the dead still on board, but the Southerners were upon them before they could succeed. McElroy and his companions were captured, never receiving a message from Scofield to the effect that "it was not deemed prudent to move the land forces to Yazoo City." [21]

Among those who fled across the fields was Ensign Holmes. A dishonorable discharge from the Navy was in store for him.

These episodes were examples of the desperation with which the South was fighting as the war moved into its fourth year. No bright hope for the Confederacy's future could be cited. In Virginia a new Union Commander, Ulysses S. Grant, had taken charge of the army facing Robert E. Lee's starving Confederates and was preparing to push them back against Richmond. The Confederacy was cut in two. Along its coastline stretched a tightening blockade. And overseas, all hope for relief from foreign powers appeared to have vanished. It was now well known that England would supply nothing that could not be paid for in cash or in cotton—cotton that the invading Northern troops were tying up tighter than the bales themselves. And the faithful Confederate agent abroad, James Bulloch, ordered to have two fast paddle steamers built, sent word: "It is with much regret that I am forced to postpone the construction of these vessels for the present, in consequence of the large excess of the outstanding liabilities of the Navy Department over the amount thus far realized from the sale of cotton, which now constitutes the only source from which I can obtain money." [22]

The ram born in a cornfield

APRIL-MAY 1864

Nothing in the experience of Gideon Welles and the Union Navy remained a mystery as long as did the *Albemarle,* the ironclad the Confederates were said to be building in a cornfield somewhere up the Roanoke River in North Carolina. Reports so conflicted they were useless. Just how strong the vessel would be, how unusual its dimensions, or even what it would look like could not be determined. But there was one rumor that persisted. This formidable craft was to spearhead a drive by the Southerners to break the blockade along the Carolina coast.

For months the Federals had been toying with an idea that they could keep the *Albemarle* from coming down the Roanoke by blocking the stream with old hulks. As early as the fall of '63, Commander H. K. Davenport, senior Union officer in the sounds of North Carolina, began sending derelict ships to be scuttled where they could obstruct the channel. No matter how powerful the ironclad, it would be of little threat locked up in an inland waterway.

Despite rumors, there seemed to be little need for any particular hurry about efforts to stop the *Albemarle*. Lieutenant Commander Charles Flusser, officer in charge at Plymouth, nearest town to the point at which the river would be blocked, was one who saw no cause for haste. When reporting that some of the vessels sent to be scuttled were so shallow they would serve no purpose, he added: "I think we will have time to put things in good order before our friend from above ventures down." [1] And besides, he relayed, Admiral Lee, the squadron chief, thought it scarcely worth while to block up the river.[2]

That was back in November. December arrived and passed with the Union as badly off as ever for information about the *Albemarle*. Brigadier General Henry W. Wessels, the military commander at Plymouth, sent word he could learn nothing about the ram and could do nothing to clear up the contradictory rumors. "My own impression is that the ram has no engine, is not plated yet, and will not be ready for some months," he wrote. It was his information that the ironclad was supposed to be near Halifax, North Carolina.[3]

Meanwhile, Confederate plans in the North Carolina area did indeed center around the *Albemarle*. The ram was like a time clock that would set off an explosion. All activities were controlled by it, and the scheduled offensive awaited its completion. For that reason, the Navy Department at Richmond was concerned over the fact that the contractors to build it were hired by the day, a circumstance that might cause the project to be unduly protracted. To offset this, it was decided to do the same thing that was done in the case of the *Arkansas:* send an officer to superintend and to assume all responsibility for its construction.

On January 15, an order went out from Secretary Mallory's office to Commander James W. Cooke, instructing him to go to North Carolina where the cornfield was located and to take charge of the completion of the ram. He was to leave nothing undone to effect this objective.

Cooke was a man in the class of Isaac Newton Brown, the

officer who had pushed the *Arkansas* to completion. Born at Beaufort, North Carolina, he lived before the war at Portsmouth, Virginia, joined the U.S. Navy in 1828, and resigned as lieutenant May 1, 1861. After a month in Virginia's naval forces, he was transferred to the service of the Confederate Navy and assigned to blockade duty on the Potomac at Aquia Creek. Next he was shifted to command of the small steam tug *Ellis,* formerly a canalboat, and ordered to the North Carolina coast. There, in the fighting around Roanoke Island in '62, he fought so desperately that it was said of him he would "fight a powder magazine with a coal of fire." Wounded in the arm by a musket ball and in the leg by a bayonet, he refused to surrender and finally was overpowered by main force. He seemed the ideal commander for such a fighting ship as the *Albemarle.*

In February, after Cooke had taken over his new duties, Union Commander Flusser gave a report on his progress in blocking the Roanoke River. "There seems to be no need for great haste in the matter," he repeated, adding that he did not think the *Albemarle* would be finished for some months.[4]

But Admiral Lee, while reporting no concern about blocking the river, was bothered by lack of information. He wrote Gideon Welles, reviewing the latest reports on the ram and revealing that he had asked General Butler, in over-all command of the troops in North Carolina, to obtain exact intelligence about the *Albemarle,* as well as about an ironclad said to be building on the Neuse River farther downstate.[5]

A few days later, Flusser struck at the food supply of the Confederates on duty along the Roanoke above Plymouth. The men working on the *Albemarle* were existing mainly on a diet of coarse meal and bacon. Flusser determined to take away from them their corn meal, and he sent a party to burn the mill where it was ground. After accomplishing their mission, the raiders came back with an assortment of reports. They said, among other things, that the ram would never venture down without the support of a land force.[6] Added to this was a bit of news passed on by a man who came into the Federal

lines from Raleigh. He reported that the Southerners thought
the Union troops at Plymouth had mounted several three-
hundred-pounder Parrotts, guns whose fire the *Albemarle*
could not endure, and for that reason she would be assigned
to auxiliary defense at Rainbow Bluff higher up the Roanoke.

Mixed reports concerning the ram continued during March.
Davenport talked with a Confederate deserter, a cavalry ser-
geant, and was informed by him that the vessel was about
ready and that there was a plan to attack Plymouth, Parrotts
or no Parrotts.

Shortly afterward, Flusser got word from a man just down
from Hamilton that the *Albemarle* had arrived there and that
a large force of soldiers was near by. "Further," the lieutenant
commander reported to Lee, "the floating battery, about which
I had heard nothing for a long time and hoped had died a
natural death, is said to be very near completion. The present
report makes her octagonal, with seven inches of iron, lined
with two tiers of cotton bales. The ram, or whatever it may be
called, is also said to have seven inches of plating. I think the
reporters are putting on the iron rather heavy. I am inclined
to believe her armor is not more than stated in one of my
former letters—three inches. The people in the country above
and below us, who have better means than we possess of gain-
ing information, anticipate an early and severe attack by land
and water here." [7]

In answer to Admiral Lee's request for "exact intelligence,"
General Butler sent a scout to Hamilton. This spy remained in
the town only half an hour, during which time he was informed
that the *Albemarle* was aground ten miles down the river and
twenty-five miles from Plymouth, and that she was so stuck in
the mud the Rebels had removed her guns in an effort to
lighten her. With this information, Butler suggested that an
expedition be sent to burn her. Lee at first concurred, but
later, on advice from Flusser, decided that the plan was inad-
visable. [8]

Flusser now became alarmed, and his messages began to take

on a note of urgency. He had indications that an attack was imminent. For example, he was informed that the Rebels had removed the torpedoes they had placed in the Roanoke below Williamston, that their land force in the vicinity recently had been increased, and that they were closing their lines to prevent information reaching the Federals. "It is also stated," he reported to Davenport, "that their boat is eighty feet long and, something more serious, that her armor is four and a half inches instead of three, as formerly represented." [9]

Flusser had at his command four vessels. The most powerful was his flagship, the *Miami,* the double-ender side-wheeler jokingly referred to as the "Miasma." Next in power was the *Southfield,* a ship of the same class. The other two, the *Ceres* and *Whitehead,* were much smaller craft and suitable mostly for picket duty. None of them was protected by iron.

But a day or two later, Flusser's alarm was calmed by a man just in from Kinston who recently had quit as a cavalry lieutenant in the Confederate service. The deserter—"his statement is clear and full, and I am disposed to give it great weight"—said no attack would be made within five or six weeks and possibly two months. The information was relayed through General Wessels, who concluded: "This man's statement is so open and unreserved that I believe it, particularly as I am informed as to his antecedents." [10]

More intelligence of this sort was brought toward the end of March by two Union cavalrymen who had escaped from the Rebels. In their travels, they had encountered a Negro who had worked in the navy yard at Halifax and who said the ship would not be finished before July. He also reported that iron was being placed on her, but that not so many men were at work on her as in the past. Flusser was present when the cavalrymen were interviewed, and he immediately wrote Lee: "I think there is no immediate prospect of the ram's appearance."

April brought an odd twist to reports. Flusser learned that

the ram, after receiving her plating, did not draw enough water to submerge her armor to a safe extent and so had to be careened and sheathed lower down. "This information is correct," he informed Lee. "It makes her of such light draft that she may pass over our obstructions in the river without touching them." [11]

On April 10, General Wessels was informed that the *Albemarle,* although not entirely covered with plating, had been floated down as far as Rainbow Bluff. This news he passed on to other commanders, even though he admitted the ram was "too well watched for me to obtain positive and reliable information." [12]

Flusser began to anticipate approaching trouble. Two days later he notified Lee: "From three distinct sources we have reports today that the Rebel ram is several miles below Rainbow Bluff; that she is accompanied by a land force of eleven thousand men, and that an attack will be made during this week on Plymouth." He said he thought the report false, but would act as though he considered it true.[13] That same day he wrote his young sister: "I shall have a formidable antagonist, Little One, but I shall not fail to ask God's aid." [14] Earlier he had written her: "As for me, you may expect me to do my duty. All that I am I owe to my country." [15]

On this day the Confederacy officially put in channels the final order for the projected offensive. Brigadier General Robert F. Hoke, commanding troops at Kinston, North Carolina, was notified that he was to direct land forces in an attack against Plymouth, the strong point along the Roanoke, and that he was to send notice to the commander of the *Albemarle* so he could co-operate. With Plymouth captured, the next objective would be Washington and New Bern.[16]

General Wessels, on the 13th, revealed he was so disturbed over the reports of an impending attack that he considered it wise for him to be reinforced with five thousand men and the gunboat *Commodore Perry,* then on duty in the James River. He pointed out that the water in the Roanoke was unusually high and thus favorable to naval operations, while the condition of the creeks and swamps was not favorable to movement of troops.[17]

But as late as the 14th, Admiral Lee was toying with the idea that the Confederate operations in Virginia, as Grant launched his drive against Richmond, would force every man available to be sent from North Carolina. The following day he added: "We have no certain information of any sort respecting the Rebel ram reported to be on the Roanoke. The reports about her have been conflicting, especially as to the thickness of her iron plating. Should this ram attack Plymouth, no doubt it will be vigorously fought by the *Miami* and *Southfield,* with which success will, in the absence of any ironclad or torpedo boats, depend on its speed and plating." [18] He also announced that he had found there were two other routes the *Albemarle* might follow in approaching Plymouth, either of which would enable her to avoid the obstructions in the Roanoke.

About 2:00 P.M. on the 17th, Acting Ensign G. W. Barrett, commanding the U.S.S. *Whitehead,* was ordered to take his vessel up to the blockade near Hyman's Ferry, nearly three miles above Plymouth, beyond Fort Gray on the left bank of the river, and to relieve the *Ceres* on picket duty there. All afternoon he and his crew stood at their posts, watching the obstructions to see that they were not tampered with, and looking upstream for signs that the ram was coming. At 5:30 P.M., they heard firing behind them, in the direction of town, and forty minutes later the *Ceres,* noted for bad luck, arrived with a report of what had happened. A Confederate battery of field-pieces had suddenly opened on her while she was on her way back with a dispatch from Flusser announcing that the Rebels were approaching along the Jamesville road. Two dead and seven wounded lay on her decks.[19]

Upstream at Hamilton, the dreaded *Albemarle* was at last on her way to battle. Commander Cooke had been asked by General Hoke to co-operate in the attack on Plymouth. Mechanics still worked at various points about her, some fastening on additional armor, some adjusting her machinery. Anticipating a breakdown, portable forges were brought along for use in such an emergency.

At ten o'clock that night, the bolts fastening the main coupling of the ram's center shaft were wrenched loose. Six hours later she was able to get under way again. Next the rudderhead broke off, causing a delay of four hours. The river was at a level which residents said was the highest in their recollection. Because of the numerous bends and difficult navigation, the ironclad was forced to move stern foremost, a huge chain dragging from her bow for steering purposes.[20] It was slow progress, but the *Albemarle* was definitely on her way.

Back at Plymouth, Flusser was preparing for an attack at dawn. He brought the *Miami* and *Southfield* side to side and lashed them together to make them more formidable against the ram.

The night passed quietly. At dawn the desultory fire of a skirmish line began to develop on the outskirts of town. But there was no over-all attack, and up at the obstructions, the *Whitehead*'s crew was still watching for the approach of enemy vessels.

Throughout most of the 18th, the picket fire continued. Realizing the Confederates were in force, the Federals in the town evacuated women and children, contrabands, and other noncombatants. Twice during the day, the Army transport *Massasoit* made trips to Roanoke Island, her decks crowded with refugees. In the late afternoon, the attack on land grew hotter, and continued until the Southerners withdrew about nine that night. In order to co-operate, the *Miami* and *Southfield* were separated and taken to points where they could shell the enemy, the former ship below town and the latter above. One naval casualty in the meantime lay in twenty feet of water at the Plymouth wharf. She was the Army transport *Bombshell,* struck in several vulnerable places during the day by the Confederate fieldpieces.

A few minutes after 8:00 P.M., the *Whitehead,* patrolling

the river above the blockade, saw the lights of two steamers coming around a bend. Acting Ensign Barrett, by instruction, sent up a rocket to warn the Federals at Plymouth of the enemy's approach by water. A moment later, a rocket arose from one of the Rebel vessels, and Barrett assumed the Confederates had taken the first signal to be from their own forces near town. At any rate, the *Albemarle* and the merchant ship *Cotton Planter,* carrying sharpshooters, came to a halt and lay perfectly still in the beauty of an April night that seemed a much more fitting occasion for a moonlight cruise than a battle between two forces of a divided nation.

At nine-thirty that night, Flusser sat down and wrote Admiral Lee the last letter he would ever write. He told about the fighting that had continued off and on during the day, and of the Federals' final success in beating back the Confederates. If he knew about the rockets that had risen into the dark skies up the river earlier in the evening, he made no mention of it. He did say he was fearful for Fort Gray and the protection of the town.[21]

Flusser had six hours to live. Before preparing his final message to Lee, he wrote a note to Davenport in which he said: "The ram will be down tonight or tomorrow. She was just after daylight this morning foul of a tree six miles above Williamston. I think, if she doesn't stay under cover of their battery established above Fort Gray, that we shall whip her." [22]

At the moment Flusser was writing Admiral Lee, the *Albemarle* was approaching the obstructions. She had turned around and now was moving bow first.

This movement by the ironclad threw some degree of panic into Acting Ensign Barrett. He tried to flee by way of Upper Thoroughfare. The current threw his vessel against the bank, and there his stern remained immovable. In this emergency, the ensign ordered the engines stopped, cautioned his men to keep perfect silence on board, and stood waiting in high tension until the ironclad, in full view, went on past and came to anchor, still above the blockade. It was ten o'clock.

Commander Cooke hoped to hear from General Hoke specific instructions as to the best manner in which to co-operate with the land forces. When no signal or contact was made after a wait of more than an hour, he took matters into his own hands. With him on the *Albemarle,* as volunteer aide, was Gilbert Elliott, the young North Carolinian who had been given the original contract to build the ironclad. At his own suggestion, this aspiring individual was sent in a small boat with a pilot and two men on a reconnaissance. He was to go down as far as Plymouth, sounding the river as he went, especially at the point where the hulks had been sunk.

Barrett in the meantime succeeded in getting the *Whitehead* free again. She passed Plymouth by twelve-thirty in the morning, went on below a half mile or so to where Flusser was waiting on the *Miami,* and reported to him that the ram was coming.

Flusser repeated the preparations for battle he had made on the 17th. The *Southfield* was brought alongside the *Miami,* and the crews of both vessels were set to work lashing them together with chains.

At 1:00 A.M. Gilbert Elliott returned to report to Commander Cooke. This was his account:

"We set forth in a small lifeboat, taking with us a long pole, and arriving at the obstructions proceeded to take soundings. To our great joy it was ascertained that there was ten feet of water over and above the obstructions. This was due to the remarkable freshet then prevailing. . . . Pushing on down the stream to Plymouth, and taking advantage of the shadow of the trees on the north side of the river, opposite the town, we watched the Federal transports taking on board the women and children who were being sent away for safety, on account of the approaching bombardment. With muffled oars, and almost afraid to breathe, we made our way back up . . . reporting to Captain Cooke that it was practicable to pass the obstructions provided the boat was kept in the middle of the stream." [23]

Cooke waited an hour and a half longer and then weighed

anchor. The ironclad moved downriver, floating over the old hulks without so much as a scrape of the keel. A short distance later, Fort Gray opened on her, firing several shots, but none of them damaged her. The *Cotton Planter* remained above the fort.

It was 3:45 A.M., according to Acting Master W. N. Welles of the *Miami,* when the *Ceres,* which had been coaling at the wharf at Plymouth, ran down and gave the alarm that the *Albemarle* was coming.[24] In a few minutes the ram could be seen steaming down along the far bank of the river, in the shadow of the trees. She continued to a point almost directly opposite the two vessels on which men were still working in a frantic effort to get them securely fastened together, and then she swung out obliquely and headed across the stream.

Flusser gave orders for the *Miami* and *Southfield* to attack her. Starboard chains were slipped and bells rung to go ahead fast.

The waters churned as the chained vessels swung into action. Flusser ran forward to a nine-inch Dahlgren in the bow of the *Miami.* The *Albemarle* was only yards away.

In a matter of minutes after she was first seen, the ram plowed into the Union vessels. She hit the *Miami* on the port bow near the water line, gouging through two planks for almost ten feet, and bounced off, striking the *Southfield* slantwise, her sharp prow ramming her victim's side clear through to her forward storeroom and into her fireroom.

Almost at the moment of contact, the two Federal vessels opened with their guns. Solid shot fired at close range bounced harmlessly off her sides, making indentations of no more than soupspoon depth. From the nine-inch Dahlgren, Flusser sent a shell. Then another. The third had a short fuse. It struck the ram's heavy armor and shattered, and pieces of it flew back into the crew around the gun from which it had come. Flusser fell dead, fragments piercing his chest, face, and skull—"one piece cutting his heart out," General Butler reported.[25] Men around him dropped, some of them badly wounded. Musket fire was mixed with that of the great guns in an angry outburst from the *Albemarle,* for Cooke had ordered all his crew not otherwise engaged to open with muskets from the top deck.

The *Southfield* began to sink rapidly. The one hundred seventeen men on her decks made a mad rush to get into small boats or to leap across to the *Miami.* The forward lashings were parted by the force of the collision; those aft were quickly cut.

When freed, the *Miami* swung around to starboard. Her engine was reversed to straighten the vessel in the river and prevent her going into the bank.

On board the doomed *Southfield,* men who had not managed to leap to the *Miami* were fighting over her small boats. Some, at the last moment, dived into the water and started swimming for shore or for the chains hanging from the *Miami.*

Cooke was having serious trouble. He had begun backing the engines of the *Albemarle* in an attempt to extricate her prow from the sinking vessel. Before he succeeded, the weight of the *Southfield* depressed the forward deck of the ram to such a degree that water ran into the forward port. With the ram in this condition, Cooke realized he was unable to work his great guns and he sent his men to the top deck with muskets. One of them, named Harris, was killed with a pistol shot, becoming the ironclad's only casualty.

In a few minutes—some sailors said three, others fifteen—the *Southfield* went down, taking her six guns with her. Her crew had fled from her decks with only the clothes they wore. Among those who leaped across to the *Miami* was her commander, Acting Volunteer Lieutenant Charles A. French. Finding Flusser dead, he took over in his place and headed downriver. The *Albemarle* fired two shells after the *Miami* as she fled.

"Had I not been confident that this boat would have met the fate of the *Southfield,* had I come in contact the second time," he later reported, "I should never have left her, but after having had so severe a test, I became satisfied that our shot had no effect, and it was worse then useless, in my opinion, to attempt to run on her prow. She has two propellers and can be managed very expertly, and has a great advantage over a vessel of this kind." [26]

On the morning of the 20th, the *Albemarle,* virtually undamaged, steamed up and down the Roanoke in the Plymouth area, shelling the shore batteries and works wherever she could find them. If by this time Cooke had heard of the death of Flusser, it must have been with some regret. Just two years back, when Cooke had refused to leave his vessel in the fighting around Elizabeth City, it was his old shipmate Flusser, storming aboard with a party from the *Commodore Perry,* who insisted on capturing the resisting Confederate instead of shooting him.[27]

The fighting around Plymouth went on in a joint operation. During the night, Gilbert Elliott had stolen along a path through swampy country around Plymouth to notify Hoke that he should attack from the land side. Throughout the 20th, the fourth day, the battle raged, and at 10:00 A.M. on the 21st, General Wessels surrendered the town unconditionally. "Heaven has crowned our efforts with success," Jefferson Davis' aide-de-camp, John Taylor Wood, wired his chief.[28]

The *Miami* and other vessels were down at the mouth of the Roanoke in Albemarle Sound waiting for the ram to come down, assuming that in waters where there was more room in which to maneuver, they would be able to avoid her prow. The Federals feared the Confederate attack would now be pushed toward Roanoke Island and New Bern, with the ultimate loss of all of eastern North Carolina.

Dispatches flew back and forth. General Butler reported "great consternation" at Beaumont, with Wilmington a principal blockade point.[29] The aim was to keep the *Albemarle* in the Roanoke, but, assuming that she might get down to the sounds, Lee offered this advice:

"The great point is to get and hold position on each side of the ram. Have stout lines with small heaving lines thereto to throw across the end of the ram, and so secure her between two of our vessels. She will then have no use of her ram, and must

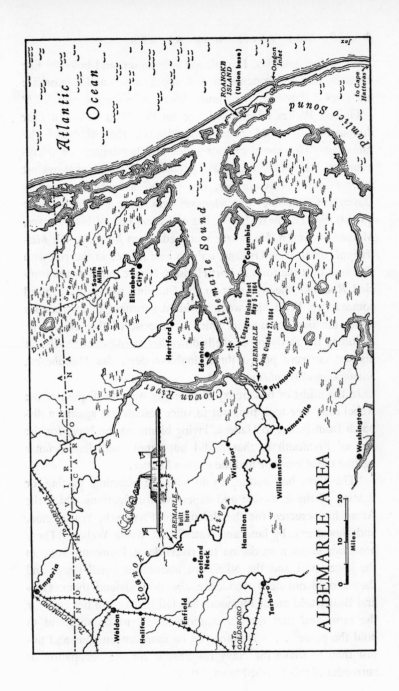

ALBEMARLE AREA

yield to our batteries. Her plating will loosen and bolts fly like canister, and the concussion will knock down and demoralize her crew if they keep their ports down, as in the late attack." [30]

Gideon Welles telegraphed Lee on the 22nd to ask if four double-enders would be able to destroy the *Albemarle* by ramming. "Her speed of four miles and her battery of thirty-pounders," he observed, "make her not very formidable against several rams." [31] In answer, Lee got off a fretful message to Davenport, advising that whatever was done should be done quickly.[32] The next day Welles called on one of his veterans, Melancton Smith. He it was who had taken his ship, the *Mississippi,* up to New Orleans, only to lose it later in the run with Farragut past the forts at Port Hudson. Now captain of the iron-clad *Roanoke,* he was sent to the Carolina sounds as over-all commander. With him went a wide assortment of instructions about the best manner in which to dispose of the *Albemarle,* including the throwing of shells down her smokestack.[33] Also at his service were placed three double-enders, the *Mattabesett, Sassacus,* and *Wyalusing.*

In the midst of this frenzy of planning ways to dispose of the Rebel ram, Lee took time out to voice resentment against a dispatch from Butler to Halleck, laying blame on the Navy for the loss of Plymouth in that it did not supply sufficient defense against the *Albemarle* and the *Cotton Planter.*

"The Navy had nothing to do with the planning, placing, or fighting of the extensive and expensive fortifications which the Army had erected for the defense of Plymouth, Washington, and New Bern, by land and water," Lee wrote Welles. "There are three earthen works on the riverside at Plymouth—one in the lower part and the other two above this small town, and they should not need wooden gunboats to defend them. General Butler told me at Plymouth last fall that he did not care for the ram, and that the fortifications ought to be sufficient to hold the place. . . . Nothing can be more ungenerous and unjust than to make the Navy responsible for the occupation or surrender of this fortified town." [34]

By the 25th, the Federal vessels watching at the mouth of the Roanoke were kept under way constantly at night. This was because of information that the Confederates were sending down launches, manned by about three hundred men and each armed with a howitzer, to co-operate with the ram. Another change of command followed, and another veteran of the Mississippi campaign, Lieutenant Commander Francis A. Roe, was sent to take charge in Albemarle Sound, with specific orders to keep the ram from coming out of Roanoke River.

Toward the end of April, Captain Smith arrived on the Carolina coast with the *Mattabesett* and *Wyalusing*. At the same time, Lee got information from Butler that the Rebels had evacuated Plymouth and were leaving the state, and the House of Representatives at the Union capital passed a resolution calling for an investigation of the successes of the *Albemarle*.[35]

Three days of May went by with no particular excitement, and then Butler upset the quietude by notifying Lee that the Confederate ram had come out of the Roanoke River into Albemarle Sound. But at ten-thirty in the morning two days later, Melancton Smith sent word that the vessel was still in the Roanoke and that he was making every arrangement to capture it.[36] He was well aware of her position because the *Ceres* had even been chased by her a few days earlier.[37]

The U.S.S. *Commodore Hull* was the first to spy the *Albemarle*. In the early afternoon, the Union vessel had gone up to the Roanoke, in company with the *Miami, Ceres,* and Army transport *Trumpeter,* to put down torpedoes. Just as they neared the buoy at the mouth of the river, the *Hull,* in advance, saw the ram coming down, followed by two steamers, the *Cotton Planter* and the raised *Bombshell,* each laden with troops. It developed later that they were on their way to attack New Bern, but what happened within the next few hours put an end to these plans.

The *Trumpeter* was immediately sent back to notify Captain Smith that the Confederates were coming. Then the *Miami, Ceres,* and *Commodore Hull* slowly fell back, timing their movements so they could keep constant watch on the movements of the enemy vessels.

When notified a few miles down Albemarle Sound of the approach of the ram, Smith immediately steamed in that direction in the *Mattabesett,* followed in order by the *Sassacus, Wyalusing,* and *Whitehead.* This was in accordance with a plan of action he had passed out to the officers of his fleet on May 2. The larger vessels were to pass as close as possible to the ironclad without endangering the huge revolving wheels at their sides, were to center their attack on the enemy's stern, and to foul up her propellers with a fish net. The *Miami,* fitted with a torpedo on the end of a spar, was to try to get close enough to explode it against the side of the ram. And if the ironclad managed to sink her prow into any of the Federals, that would be the signal for the others to gang up on her.

It was four-forty in the afternoon when Smith came within range of the Confederates. The ironclad fired the first gun, sending a shell that destroyed the *Mattabesett*'s launch and wounded several men around the forward rifle. A second shot cut away some of the rigging.

Before the action started, Commander Cooke ordered the *Cotton Planter* and the *Bombshell* to retreat. The former read the signal correctly and turned back, but the latter missed it and followed the *Albemarle.* Five minutes after the first shot was fired, the *Mattabesett, Wyalusing,* and *Sassacus* turned their guns on the small steamer and forced her to surrender.

At 4:50 P.M. the *Mattabesett* fired a broadside at the ram from a distance of one hundred fifty yards. Its chief damage was to the aftergun on the Confederate ship, one of two Brooke one-hundred-pounder rifles, each on a pivot so it could be fired out of three different ports. A shell fractured the muzzle of this gun, taking off twenty-three inches of the barrel on the bottom side, but its crew continued to fire it. The Federal vessel passed around the stern of the ironclad and swung wide down the sound.

Fifteen minutes later, the *Sassacus* spearheaded the attack.

She had been drawn off some little distance in her operations against the *Bombshell*—three hundred to four hundred yards —and this gave her opportunity to build up a good headway.

"Seeing the favorable moment before me," reported her commander, Francis Roe, "I ordered full steam and open throttle and laid the ship fair for the broadside of the ram to run her down."

He estimated his vessel was making a speed of nine to ten knots—his executive officer said eleven—for her wheels were turning at the rate of twenty-two revolutions a minute on thirty pounds of steam, but he later admitted that it might have been only five knots.[38] As she struck, the *Albemarle* sent a shot through her from starboard bow to portside on the berth deck. It was fired from the after gun, so near as to cover the bow of the *Sassacus* with smoke and burned powder.

One of the seamen on board the *Albemarle,* John B. Patrick, captured the following month, told the Federals about the collision of the two vessels as the Confederates viewed it. "We saw her coming and thought she carried a torpedo," he related, "and made preparations to get overboard by getting near her ports and hatches. The order was given to stand by small arms and repel boarders. The shock was not great; at the after gun we felt it, but not much. It heeled her over some; the water came over her shield. There was a good deal of confusion. About eight men ran the gun out and fired into her. Most of the men left their station and ran around. Captain Cooke was standing in the hatch and was knocked down. He looked kinder scared like." [39]

Roe considered that the effect of the impact upon the *Albemarle* was more serious. "The collision was pretty heavy and the ram careened a good deal, so much so that the water washed over her deck forward and aft the casemate," he reported. "At one time I thought she was going down. I kept the engine going, pushing, as I hoped, deeper and deeper into her, and also hoping it might be possible for some one of the boats to get up on the opposite side of me and perhaps enable us to sink her, or at least to get well on to her on all sides. I retained this position a full ten minutes, throwing grenades down her deck hatch and trying in vain to get powder into her smokestack, and receiving volleys of musketry, when the stern of the ram began to go around, and her broadside port bearing on our starboard bow, when the ram fired and sent a one-hundred-pounder Brooke rifle shot through the starboard side on the berth deck, passing through the empty bunkers into the starboard boiler, clear through it fore and aft, and finally lodging in the wardroom." [40]

Steam blinded sailors on the *Sassacus* from the hurricane deck down to the fireroom. A coal heaver, Thomas Johnson, died instantly. Several men were seriously scalded and would die later. The first assistant engineer, James M. Hobby, was standing at the starting bar in the path of the steam and received bad scalds, but remained at his post. Roe ordered the signal books thrown overboard.

The engine of the *Sassacus* continued to run, with no one below to control it. Roe threw the helm hard aport. As the vessel came around, her starboard wheel passed over the *Albemarle*'s stern, crushing a launch she had been towing and damaging the buckets and braces on her hull. Before she got too far away, the wheel badly damaged, men manned her guns despite the stifling vapor. One shot they fired struck the *Albemarle*'s port sill and broke into fragments, some of the pieces falling back on the deck of the Federal ship. Another hit the flagstaff and dropped the Confederate colors.

The battle, for the last two hours a general engagement, continued for three hours and fifty minutes. On board the *Albemarle,* the men were suffering from heat. Ventilation was to be gained through a four-foot-square trap door on her house on top, but Cooke was afraid it would be seen and fired into if opened. When it was closed, the guns could not be fired too rapidly because the smoke would suffocate the crew. The trap door remained shut, and the sailors inside sweated and choked, while the temperature outside was a pleasant sixty-three degrees.

At times the Federal vessels found themselves in the line of fire from one another's guns and were forced to change direction. The *Wyalusing* was struck by shells several times and was damaged so seriously she falsely signaled she was sinking, but it was found finally that she was leaking no worse than usual. The *Miami* never had succeeded in exploding the torpedo she was carrying.

"I saw the *Sassacus* running into the ram," explained her captain, Acting Volunteer Lieutenant Charles A. French, "and immediately headed for them both, with the intention of exploding under the ram the torpedo rigged on my bow. Before I could get to her, however, the *Sassacus* became disabled and dropped down from her; the ram had changed her course and I could not work to advantage on account of the fire of our own vessels." [41]

After the firing had been going on for about an hour, French made a new attempt to use the torpedo. He steamed ahead, keeping up a rapid fire, until he got within a ship's length of the *Albemarle*. There he tried to get to her, bow on, but the *Miami* was so unwieldy and hard to steer that the ram succeeded in keeping clear by going ahead and backing and turning.

Toward the last, the *Mattabesett* rounded to port, working her port battery. When nearly abeam of the *Albemarle,* she received from the ram a six-inch shell that entered on the portside below the wheelhouse guards and abaft the wheel, and wound up in the small-arms locker, so severely wounding two men, en route, that they died soon afterward. This shot was preserved on board, marked with the name of John M. Brooke, inventor of the rifle from which it was fired.[42]

By 7:30 P.M. darkness had settled so deeply that firing was useless. In the gloom, the *Albemarle* steamed away and headed for the mouth of the Roanoke. Each of the seven vessels that had engaged her bore evidence of her might. All of them were damaged, the *Sassacus* worst of all, but the *Miami* had so many holes in her sides that she was taking on five inches of water per hour. Some of her injury had been inflicted by her own shells ricocheting back from the ram.

The *Albemarle* went out of action with comparatively little damage except to her smokestack. That had been riddled and shot away, making it so difficult to keep up steam that she was able to leave the scene only by burning nearly all the bacon, lard, and butter she had on board.[43] She had been struck on the casemates by forty-four solid shot, but they had left no more than glancing scars.[44] Two timbers had been broken, the port shutters carried away, one gun disabled, some plating knocked off, and the stack riddled.

She would be talked about frequently in the months ahead while undergoing repairs and alterations—talked about and argued over and feared. On one thing could all of those who had fought against her agree: she was formidable, perhaps more so than the *Merrimack* had been. They had clear recollections of the manner in which solid shot had been fractured against her sides. Melancton Smith sent Admiral Lee a fragment of a one-hundred-pounder rifle ball fired from the *Sassacus* at close range and with it the observation that "the various reports heretofore made of the invulnerability of the ram have not been exaggerated." [45]

★ *12*

That tricky Red River

MARCH-MAY 1864

It was a sure thing, in talk along the Red River, that the water level of the stream would rise in springtime. Only once in the memory of the older folks had this failed to occur, and that was back in 1846, in itself quite a year, for it marked the beginning of the War with Mexico and the period in which the Mormons, refusing to give up their idea that a man should have more than one wife, pushed toward the West under the leadership of Brigham Young. Union strategists took stock of all this as they went about plans for a new assault in the Louisiana-Texas area.

The rich farm lands along the Red had beckoned for a long time. Even during '62, when the drive against Vicksburg was in its earlier stages, Admiral David Porter had written his military friend, General William Tecumseh Sherman, that by the time that stronghold was taken he hoped to have his light-draft boats ready to push up the river, "where the Rebels have all their supplies." [1]

But things hadn't worked out that way. There had been some offensives up the Red, one leading to the fall of Fort De Russy,

165

main stronghold along the river. Yet nothing was of a permanent nature. An expedition during September of '63, under General William B. Franklin, failed completely; and two months later, an army led by General Nathaniel P. Banks began pecking away along the Rio Grande River. It had moderate success. The Stars and Stripes were raised at Brownsville, Texas, opposite the Mexican city of Matamoras, and later at the entrance to Matagorda Bay. But lack of sufficient troops to hold these points caused a withdrawal.[2]

Suddenly it became urgent that the United States flag be restored over the state of Texas. In Mexico the French, under Archduke Ferdinand Maximilian, began threatening the border, and the Union realized it would be unwise to leave an area so near in Confederate hands. Abraham Lincoln saw the need for action. The French might support the independence of the Lone Star State or demand its return.

Banks had scarcely hung up his sword at New Orleans, after the Brownsville-Matagorda campaign, when he had orders to lead another thrust up the Red River, this time a combined naval and military operation. It would be aimed at Shreveport, at the head of navigation, three hundred fifty miles away.[3] The usual time of highest water fixed the date for the offensive at around the middle of March.

Banks had an army of ten thousand. On March 1, General Sherman, over-all commander in the West, visiting New Orleans, agreed to lend a force of similar numbers and to assign as its leader the veteran A. J. (Whiskey) Smith. But there were conditions: These men must be returned in time to take part in the concerted drive against the South planned by the new Union commander in chief, General U. S. Grant.

As projected, Banks's plan of campaign seemed simple. Toward Shreveport would move two armies, that of Banks and another under General Frederick Steele, this latter to come in from the direction of Arkansas. Banks would advance by way of the Red, in a step-by-step development. The fleet under Porter would convoy the troops sent by Sherman, landing them at

Simsport on the Atchafalaya, for an assault on Fort De Russy from the rear, while other vessels went up the Red to remove obstructions and advance on the fort from the front. With that stronghold out of the way, the ships would proceed to Alexandria, where Banks would meet them on March 17 for the joint movement by land and by water to join Steele for the grand offensive at Shreveport.

By March 7 Porter had a fleet of fifteen ironclads waiting at the mouth of Red River. Included were such battle-scarred veterans as the *Essex, Benton, Louisville, Carondelet, Pittsburg,* and *Mound City.* Lighter boats on hand were the *Lexington, Gazelle, Cricket,* and *Black Hawk.*[4]

Before things could get under way there was a mishap, and involved in it, of all people, was that slave to misfortune, Lieutenant Commander Thomas O. Selfridge. He had been sent with the *Conestoga* to Vicksburg for ammunition. On the way back, on March 8, his ship, having the right of way, was struck by the steamer *General Price.* Down the *Conestoga* went, in four minutes. It was a shocking development. Her captain had gone to bed several hours before the collision, leaving a pilot in charge, but, luckily, everybody was overboard before the ship sank.

Thus for the third time during the war, Selfridge was on a doomed ship. His last experience had been with the *Cairo,* sunk by torpedo in the Yazoo in the fall of '62. Before then, he was on the ill-fated *Cumberland,* victim of the *Merrimack* in Hampton Roads.[5]

On the 11th, A. J. Smith's troops—two divisions of the Sixteenth Corps and one of the Seventeenth—began to appear in transports at the mouth of the Red. Early next morning, in darkness, the fleet started up the river, the vessels showing no lights, beating no drums, striking no bells, and moving single file at a distance apart of not less than three hundred yards. But when daylight came, they abandoned their caution. A sailor recorded: "The water is quite a muddy red and looks anything but inviting. The ships move majestically—slow—

but onward. The transports from the head belch out three bellowing whistles which is caught up by the next, and sometimes two or three vie in an euphonious concert much resembling the bellowing of cattle at the smell of blood." [6]

There was just sufficient water to allow the larger boats to pass. Lieutenant Commander S. Ledyard Phelps had been sent ahead in the *Eastport,* with seven other vessels, to remove obstructions and to keep Fort De Russy busy until the Army could be landed at Simsport and marched thirty miles to attack the rear of the works.

Following this plan, the *Benton, Pittsburg, Chillicothe, Louisville, Mound City, Carondelet, Ouachita, Lexington,* and *Gazelle* turned off to the left up the Atchafalaya to land the troops. Simsport was reached about noon of the 13th. Next morning the Army was ashore and drove the Confederates back toward the fort. There was little excitement. Some of the transports were tied up at the banks and stood by while the soldiers went through battalion drill, marching over plowed ground.[7]

As soon as he learned the Federals had debarked at Simsport, the Confederate department commander, General Kirby Smith, sent out a call for all available troops in Arkansas, Texas, and Louisiana to hurry toward Shreveport and the Red River. Even Indian forces in the general area were included. He could see from the character of the country that Banks and Steele would not be able to form a junction, and as they advanced, he hoped to refuse one and fight the other with his entire force.[8]

Off in another direction, the *Eastport* and other vessels were busy removing obstructions up the Red. These consisted of heavy piles driven into the mud, clamped together with heavy iron plates and chains, and carefully braced. They were supposed to be impassable, but demolition crews removed them in a matter of hours.

At four on the afternoon of the 14th, the *Eastport, Osage, Fort Hindman,* and *Cricket* managed to get through the barricade and move up to Fort De Russy. General Smith's troops were already there, and a brisk musketry and artillery fire was in progress.[9] Only three hundred Confederates had been left to defend the fort. Attacked from the rear, it fell within a short time, yielding eight heavy guns and two fieldpieces. The Confederates had hoped it would stop an advance by water and had assigned some of their best engineers to fortify it, but the Union offensive came before their plans could be completed.[10] The Southerners managed to escape, marching seventy miles through country thick with pine trees.

Porter reached Alexandria on the afternoon of the 16th, ahead of schedule, and there found time to write Gideon Welles a report in which he made fun of the Confederates:

"The efforts of these people to keep up this war remind one very much of the antics of Chinamen, who build canvas forts, paint hideous dragons on their shields, turn somersets, and yell in the faces of their enemies to frighten them, and then away at the first sign of an engagement." [11]

The Confederates' "antics" had been forced by the difficulties under which they operated. They had made their way above the falls at Alexandria, losing one vessel, the steamer *Countess,* set afire after it grounded. With them they took all their transports, as well as all pilots able to steer boats over the falls. This left Porter with the problem of feeling his way up as best he could.

"It is not the intention of these Rebels to fight," Porter wrote Welles. "The men are tired of the war, and many of their officers are anxious to go into cotton speculations. A large trade has been carried on between this and New Orleans, the Rebels receiving supplies for their cotton. There is a surprising abundance of every kind of food in this country, and no suffering among the people except for luxuries; it would be folly to suppose they could all be starved out. The only way is to take possession of this rich region, hold it with a strong military and naval force, and enforce the laws." [12]

While the Navy pushed along rapidly, the Army was having

trouble. Rain poured for days, making the roads impassable. Smith was a day late reaching Alexandria, and Banks's army, under General Franklin, was still arriving on the 26th.

While they waited at Alexandria for the Army to come up, the sailors had a chance to go ashore. William R. Stewart, of the steamer *John Rains,* was one of them, and he wrote of the experience in a diary: "Saw quite a number of the ladies from Pine Village opposite Alexandria. Two in particular were out on a display promenade, one of which had a beautiful black squirrel which ran all over her, up her dress sleeves and under her lace cape into her bosom with a familiarity that made me envy the little favorite and sent a thrill that did not feel very bad through all the little veins in my body, exciting desires not over complimentary to the fair exhibitor." [13]

Miles up the river, the Confederates were taking desperate steps to block the Federal advance. Kirby Smith realized that the Red River Valley was the only practicable line of operations by which the Union could penetrate the country under his command.[14] With this in mind, the steamer *New Falls City* was taken to the foot of Scopern's Cutoff and there held in readiness to be scuttled. Another steamer, with a special crew, moved down near the falls below Grand Ecore, to place thirty torpedoes in the path of the oncoming vessels.[15] These steps were taken at a time when the Union was issuing orders to shoot on the spot anyone seen attempting to use torpedoes defensively.[16]

On the 23rd, Banks reached the mouth of Red River in the transport *Black Hawk.* With him were a number of cotton speculators licensed at Washington, among them agents from the concern of Butler & Casey, the name Butler standing for none other than General Ben Butler of the Union Army.[17]

Before continuing up the river, Banks asked for a convoy. None was available, so he had to be satisfied with borrowing a twelve-pound howitzer. The following day he set up headquarters at Alexandria. Already, boats were bringing in supplies they were capturing from the countryside—cotton worth $400 a bale on the New Orleans market, barrels of molasses, and bales of wool.

Soon, more specific instructions from General Grant arrived. His all-out offensive was to be undertaken by eight Union armies, including those under Banks and Sherman. The Red River invasion could be pursued, provided it did not interfere with the more extensive campaign. Smith's forces must be returned to Vicksburg by April 10 to aid Sherman in a march on Atlanta, while Banks, his Red River drive either accomplished or abandoned, should be ready by that time to move toward Mobile. Banks decided to gamble on his progress up the Red.

The immediate problem was that of getting the gunboats past the falls at Alexandria. For nearly three days the *Eastport* hung on the rocks before she finally got over. The hospital steamer *Woodford,* following her, was wrecked.[18] It was April 3 before the last of thirteen gunboats and thirty transports were finally taken above the rapids. The water was rising, but slowly.

After the falls were traversed, a supply depot was set up at Alexandria, and a fleet of wagons was provided to haul the supplies around the falls for reshipment to points higher up. Now assured of food, the Federals pushed on, some by land, some by water, with Confederates under General Richard Taylor falling back before them to Bayou Boeuf, covering Alexandria.

"The Rebels are retreating before the Army," Porter notified Welles, "and, as usual, are destroying everything that can fall into our hands, treating public and private property alike. This is the last hold they will have in this country, and they seem determined to wreak their vengeance on the unoffending inhabitants who have some little cotton to dispose of. Their destructiveness has been a death blow to the rebellion in this state, and General Dick Taylor has left a name behind him to be execrated when the rebellion is long past." [19]

At 6:40 P.M. of the day they got above the falls, men on board the U.S.S. *Chillicothe* and the U.S.S. *Lexington* saw a quantity of cotton aflame on the left bank of the river beyond Grand Ecore. Two shots were fired by the *Lexington* to drive the burners away. The *Chillicothe* neared the spot twenty minutes later, and as it passed, a guerrilla hiding behind the bank shot an officer as he stepped from the ladder to the turret. He was the ship's commander, Acting Volunteer Lieutenant Joseph P. Couthouy. The ball passed through the starboard chimney before it hit him. At eight-ten the next morning he died, after expressing the hope that he would not be accused of reckless exposure.

Couthouy's death was an indication of the desperate resistance made by the people in the land he was invading. They fought as men fight with their backs to the wall. Some had never seen a gunboat, nor did they know of the power possessed by the guns strapped to the decks of these chugging vessels that nosed up along the log-infested rivers skirting their pioneer homes. Yet they showed their defiance, running to the water's edge to fire pop-gun volleys from their ancient weapons and then falling back to the undergrowth while mighty weapons on shipboard roared at their backs.

Except for occasional bull's-eyes from the banks and occasional grounding of boats, things for Porter were going fine. But all were keeping their eyes on the water. It would surely rise.

By April 3, Banks's army had gathered at Natchitoches. The fleet, with the stores and A. J. Smith's corps, arrived at Grand Ecore, four miles away, the same day. It was there that General John M. Corse overtook the expedition, with special orders emphasizing that Sherman's troops should be returned by April 10.[20] The decision was to proceed: Shreveport was only four marches away.

The division, under Union General Kilby Smith, was left with the transports, to go as far as Loggy Bayou, near Springfield Landing, one hundred ten miles above Grand Ecore. The remainder of the army was to move by land. It was expected to reach Springfield by April 10.

The troops started marching on the 6th. Their route led through pine country, miles of it, traversed by a narrow road. The congestion along this line was terrible. It became worse the next day when A. J. Smith's ten thousand followed.

At the head of the column moved six thousand infantry, organized as mounted cavalry under General Albert L. Lee. Behind it came a train of wagons, two hundred fifty in all. Still farther back were the Nineteenth Corps under General Franklin, some Negro regiments, and the Thirteenth Corps, under General Thomas E. G. Ransom.

The advance of the cavalry had a skirmish with the Confederates the night of the 7th, and drove them back. Next morning, Lee sent Franklin a message asking for two thousand five hundred men to annihilate the enemy. Franklin, in answer, reminded Lee that he was not sent out to bring on a battle, that there was danger of getting his army into a fight when it was not prepared for one.

Then General Banks rode to the front, and what happened next was an incident David Porter said "the management of which would be discreditable to a boy nine years of age." He wrote this to General Sherman, adding: "You need not blush, however, for anything that was done by your troops." [21] He was referring to the battle of Mansfield, or Sabine Cross Roads.

If Porter had had respect for Banks in the past, he lost it on this occasion.

"Lee's messages reached Banks," Porter reported to Sherman, "and he ordered Ransom with two thousand, five hundred men to reinforce Lee. Ransom protested against this disposition of his men, stating that they would be sacrificed, but General Banks ordered the movement. Franklin then prepared for the consequences which he knew were to follow. In a short time the cavalry, emboldened by the small support, brought on a fight. The part of the Thirteenth Corps did its best to support them, but, opposed to about fifteen thousand infantry, were swept away almost to a man. The cavalry broke and fled back on the wagons, the wagons stampeded and blocked up the road, when such a scene ensued as was never seen before except at Bull Run.

"Franklin opened his ranks and let the flying mass through, and received the Rebels with such a murderous fire that they were soon dispersed, leaving many killed and wounded on the field. The Rebels fought well that day, indeed desperately, coming up to the charge in a compact body and filling up their ranks as their men fell like veterans. It was just such a time as our men would have desired in the open field, but the panic created by the disorder at first was too great to get the men to do their work thoroughly. There was enough done, however, to allow us to hold our position and recover our lost trains. To expect to recover again the eighteen guns we lost was out of the question. They were mixed up with the trains, and the Rebels had secured them with one hundred rounds of ammunition each. Three of the best batteries in the army were lost and most of the men killed or wounded." [22]

The Army retreated during the night to Pleasant Hill, fifteen miles away. Porter heard that when Banks arrived there, he lost all command of himself.

"I do not wonder at that," he wrote Sherman. "An uneducated soldier may be cool and pleasant enough in the hour of victory, but the true general is best known in the hour of defeat. General Banks lost all his prestige, and the men talked so openly of him that our officers had to check them and threaten to have them punished." [23]

Next morning the Confederates continued their pursuit until General Smith's men appeared on the scene. Then the tide turned, and the Confederates fell back. But so did the Federals, leaving the field to the dead and wounded. Smith protested the retreat in vain.[24]

"The general will never get over it as long as he lives," wrote Porter. "He cried like a child at having to leave his poor fellows on the field." [25]

While this fighting on land was going on, the fleet was making its way slowly up the river, around snaggy bends, through loggy bayous, over shifting rapids, and down rapid chutes. Porter had his flag on board the *Cricket.* Five other gunboats, the *Osage, Neosho, Fort Hindman, Lexington,* and *Chillicothe,* also were along. And there were twenty transports, carrying stores and the Sixteenth Army Corps under General Kilby Smith, a part of A. J. Smith's forces. Another part of the fleet was made up of six vessels that Porter charged were sent by Banks "for the purpose of taking on board cotton." [26]

The Confederates moved ahead of them, destroying cotton. Millions of dollars worth of property went up in smoke so dense it covered the land and obscured the sun, almost turning day into night. But corn and cattle were left, enabling the Federals to live off the country and save their rations.

At one point, some of the fleet's officers stopped at a little wharf in front of a handsome plantation house to talk with a man they had seen waving a white handkerchief. Tearfully he identified himself as the brother of Captain Edward R. Colhoun of the United States Navy. He said he was too old to fight, but not too old to lose a fortune overnight. The destructive Southerners had set fire to five thousand bales of his cotton and a cotton gin valued at thirty thousand dollars.[27]

Frequently the vessels drew up to the bank to refuel. Their coal supply was exhausted, and they now had to depend upon the rail fences of the Southern plantations. Soldiers and sailors ranged over the fields, each returning with two rails. So often was this done that the Confederates were wondering whether it would not be more advantageous to destroy fences instead of cotton.

Porter reached Springfield Landing on schedule. There he found something that made him laugh. It was the *New Falls City,* scuttled and lying across the river, her bow resting on one shore, her stern on the other. The ship had broken in two, and a sand bar was making below her. A sign on her side invited the Federals to attend a ball in Shreveport.

He brought his gunboats to anchor. While discussing ways to get the *New Falls City* out of the channel, a courier arrived from General Banks with orders for him "to return without delay."

It was a thing easier said than done. "We had disembarked the troops," Porter reported, "none dreaming of anything but victory to one of the best appointed armies I ever saw in the field, and after getting in our pickets and getting the troops on board, I reversed the order of steaming and with a heavy heart started downward, anticipating that the Rebels, flushed with victory, with our army in full retreat before them, would come in on our flank and cut us to pieces." [28]

They did. At Coushatta the banks were high above the pilothouses, and sharpshooters had a field day. In front, slowing the fleet's progress, were ten large steamers Porter had expressly stipulated were not to come up the river. The Confederates continued to attack in small bands, peppering the transports with heavy fire whenever they grounded. It was their practice to attack at one point, and then hurry across the numerous necks of land in the bends of the winding river to intercept the invaders at another point.

At three in the afternoon, Porter drew up with two of his gunboats at Graff's Bluff. He had been told that a battery was waiting there, and he shelled the woods in all directions. There was no response.

Suddenly a tremendous fire of musketry and heavy cannon broke out two or three miles behind him. It had all the sounds of a heavy battle, and it lasted so long that Porter turned back to investigate. Soon he was met by a gunboat that informed him the Confederates under command of General Thomas Green, Indian fighter, Mexican War hero, and one of the South's best and most respected soldiers, had attacked at Blair's Landing. They had come charging to the very edge of the river, shouting and yelling like madmen.

The attack, it developed, was brought on by the grounding of the *Osage,* captained by T. O. Selfridge. As the transport *Black Hawk* came alongside to tow her off, two thousand muskets opened from along the banks, driving the Federals to the safety of the monitor's casemates. The gunboat *Lexington* doubled back to help, and her guns and those of the *Osage* opened a murderous fire on the charging Rebels.

"I am told that their hootings and actions baffled description," Porter reported. "Force after force seemed to be brought up to the edge of the bank, where they confronted the guns of the iron vessel, only to be cut down by grapeshot and canister."

The Federals knew there must be a reason for this foolhardy fighting—muskets against the heavy guns of the vessels—and when the firing stopped at sunset, they thought they had the answer. Canteens scattered along the bank were filled with Louisiana rum, and some of the bodies of the Confederates actually smelled of the intoxicating liquor.

For a mile back from the river, the ground was covered with dead and wounded, and with muskets, canteens, and knapsacks. General Green lay among the dead, his head severed by a cannon ball.[29]

Night came on, with a bright moon shining, and Porter hurried the transports along, following them up with the gunboats. The water seemed to be falling instead of rising.

They got back to Grand Ecore on the 13th. Scenes there were not pleasant. "Wounded men were all the time being brought in, some on stretchers and some on foot," one man recorded. "General Ransom went past on a stretcher, with one knee bandaged and bloody. Right behind him walked a man with one arm gone, and who was joking with another who was carrying his cut off arm in his hand. I got out among them to try and hear what had happened and what I heard was not altogether complimentary to General Banks." [30]

Porter wrote Welles on the 14th, outlining for him a picture that was already dark and might get darker:

"I found the fleet at Grand Ecore somewhat in an unpleasant situation, two of them above the bar, and not likely to get away again this season unless there is a rise of a foot. I could not provide against this when over one hundred miles up the river. If nature does not change her laws, there will no doubt be a rise of water, but there was one year—1846—when there was no rise in the Red River, and it may happen again. The Rebels are cutting off the supply by diverting different sources of water into other channels, all of which would have been stopped had our Army arrived as far as Shreveport." [31]

The next day he poured out his wrath against Banks in a letter to Sherman: "I cannot express to you my entire disappointment with this department. You know my opinion of political generals. It is a crying sin to put the lives of thousands in the hands of such men, and the time has come when there should be a stop put to it. This army is almost in a mutiny and not fit to go into a fight." [32]

A few hours later, Porter waxed even more caustic in a three-thousand-five-hundred-word report to Sherman in which he praised A. J. Smith and denounced Banks:

"Had Banks been victorious, as any ordinary general would have been, we would have had no trouble at all, but he has led all hands into an ugly scrape. I did all I could to avoid going up this river with him, but he would have thrown all the blame of failure on me had I failed to go. I have risked a great deal and only hope for a rise of water to get over the falls." [33]

The deadline for A. J. Smith to report to Sherman at Vicksburg had passed. There was no repercussion about it.[34] The Union was faced with too great an emergency to wrangle over miscues. One of its most important fleets was bottled up in a river that for the first time in eighteen years—and no one could remember how long before then—refused to produce enough water to float vessels over the falls at Alexandria. Usually, at this time of the year, the river was high from melting snows and rains. Now it was falling at a rate of three inches per day.[35]

The ironclad steam gunboat *Eastport,* once the property of the Southerners, left Grand Ecore on April 14, her captain hoping he could get her to Alexandria. A mile downstream she grounded on a bar and did not get off until the 15th. Eight miles farther along, with the ship drifting in water only a foot deeper than her draft, she received a severe shock forward.

Her captain, Ledyard Phelps, ordered her run into shoal water, and there set all hands to pumping and bailing water. The *Lexington* and towboat *B* came alongside and aided with siphon and other pumps. But six days passed before they could make enough headway on the leakage to float her again, for she had struck one of the Confederate torpedoes. Porter hurried to Alexandria in the hope of providing more pumps for her, sending a dispatch vessel for two pump boats, the *Champion No. 3* and *Champion No. 5*.

The drive to save her went on night and day, while the river around her continued to fall. Finally she started downstream again, with carpenters from different ships working around the clock to confine and stop the leak. The effort was wasted. It took her two days to move three miles, owing to the frequent groundings on logs and sand bars. Phelps's crew was worn out, and many of them were sick. Porter, after two visits to her decks, finally ordered Phelps to transfer his men to the *Fort Hindman* and destroy the *Eastport*.

Phelps placed eight barrels of powder under the foot of her forward casemate, and an operator from the Army went on board to set off the charges with a galvanized battery. He failed in two attempts. More powder was placed about her machinery and in her stern, and trains of it were laid fore and aft—in all, three thousand fifty-five pounds—in such a manner that a match could ignite the different mines—eight of them—in quick succession, utterly destroying her.

Phelps was heartbroken. "The act has been the most painful one experienced by me in my official career. She was the finest vessel of your squadron and one of the best possessed by the government." [36] He was the last to leave her deck, after applying the match himself, and fragments of wood fell in the boat in which he fled from the explosion.

"As perfect a wreck as ever was made by powder," concluded Porter. "She remains a troublesome obstruction to block up the channel for some time to come." [37]

Just before she blew up, the Confederates made an attack

from the right bank. Twelve hundred muskets, Porter estimated, blazed from the hands of men who rose suddenly from
cover and then made a rush to board the *Cricket*. But in five
minutes they were beaten back, riddled by a cross fire of grape
and canister.

Porter continued on his way, determined to get his ships to
Alexandria where Banks was waiting with the Army. Upstream,
the Confederates, virtually in the driver's seat, were doing what
they could to stop him. "When the Rebels heard we had arrived
at Grand Ecore," he informed Welles, "they commenced turning
the source of water supply off into the lakes, which would have
been remedied had the army succeeded in getting to Shreveport.
I cannot blame myself for coming up at the only season when
the water rises. All the rivers are full and rising, but the Red
River is falling at the rate of two inches a day, a most unusual
occurrence, this river always being full until the middle of June.
Whether we will yet have a rise it would be impossible for anyone to foresee. It seems like an impossibility that we could be
caught in such a predicament in the time of rising water, but
such may be the case." [38]

Twenty miles farther down the Red, at a point above Cane
River, Confederate cannon—eighteen in all—opened as the
vessels in close order rounded a bend. Porter, on board the
Cricket, found her guns firing rapidly and stepped on the gun
deck to see what was the matter. "As I stepped down," he reported, "the after gun was struck with a shell and disabled, and
every man at the gun killed or wounded. At the same moment
the crew from the forward gun was swept away by a shell exploding, and the men were wounded in the fireroom, leaving
only one man to fire up. I made up a gun's crew from the
contrabands, who fought the gun to the last moment." [39]

Porter next noticed that the engine was not running. He went
into the engine room. There lay the chief engineer dead. He
went to the pilothouse and found that a shot had gone through
it and wounded the pilot. He himself took hold of the wheel
and ran the vessel past the Confederate battery. In five minutes

she was struck thirty-eight times, and half her crew of fifty were killed or wounded.

Both the light-draft *Juliet* and her tow, the pump boat *Champion No. 5,* whose pilot had abandoned the wheelhouse, lay close in to the bank where they had drifted, the *Juliet* with her steampipe cut. The *Fort Hindman* was firing from above. Suddenly the boiler of the pump boat *Champion No. 3* exploded, killing all but fifteen of her crew of four engineers and two hundred Negroes.[40] Sight of the escaping steam spurred Porter to further action. He headed downstream, for a point where he had ordered the *Osage* and *Lexington* to stand by for an emergency. The emergency was at hand.

But before going far, the *Cricket* grounded and remained so for three hours, taking fire when a cartridge box struck by a Confederate bullet exploded. It was after dark before the fire was extinguished and she was able to proceed. Porter found the *Osage* and *Lexington* shelling a Rebel battery, the *Lexington* already hulled fifteen times, and he gave up any hope of getting back upstream that night.

Next day the *Fort Hindman* drifted into view, turning around and around, her wheel ropes cut away and her decks littered with debris. Behind her came the *Juliet,* cut to pieces in hull and machinery, with fifteen dead and wounded on board. The *Champion No. 5* had been disabled, set afire, and destroyed.

By the 27th the fleet was back at Alexandria, and there Porter wrote Welles in stunned reaction, again looking to the Almighty to do something about the river:

"The difficulty about water is a most unusual one, and we must certainly have a rise of the few feet we want before the end of the season; all the rivers are booming at this time, and it should be so here. I am no more responsible for the failure of water here than I would be if the Mississippi went dry at this season, a thing that never happened yet. I came up here with the river on the rise, and water enough for our largest vessels, and even on my way up to Shreveport from Grand Ecore the water rose, while it commenced falling where I left the largest gunboats. Falling or not, I could not go back while in charge of the transports and the material on which an army of thirty thousand men depended; nothing would justify me in doing so. I have still confidence in a good Providence, which I am sure will not desert us, and confidence that the nation will not permit this fleet to be sacrificed, when it has so well performed its part in what should have been a complete success." [41]

As he wrote, the water on the falls at Alexandria stood at three feet four inches. Seven feet would be needed to get his ships over. He knew that no amount of lightening the vessels would accomplish the object. Ten of them lay helpless above the falls. They were the *Mound City, Louisville, Pittsburg, Carondelet, Chillicothe, Osage, Neosho, Ozark, Lexington,* and *Fort Hindman.* Kirby Smith in the meantime had intercepted a message from Sherman to A. J. Smith, telling him to return to Vicksburg. The Southern leader, correctly fathoming that Banks would fall back on Alexandria, promptly turned his attention toward Arkansas in the hope of destroying Steele and taking Arkansas Valley and the powerful fortifications of Little Rock. [42]

Porter was bitter about the situation. "This fatal campaign has upset everything," he wrote Welles. "It has delayed ten thousand troops of General Sherman, on which he depended to open the state of Mississippi; it has drawn General Steele from Arkansas and already given the Rebels a foothold in that country; it has forced me to withdraw many light-clad vessels from points on the Mississippi to protect this army that would desert me without notice, when a man of ordinary abilities would have marched triumphant to Shreveport." [43]

Porter could get apoplectic, looking back over the campaign. He and A. J. Smith were to meet Banks at Alexandria on March 17. They were there on the 16th. Banks did not leave New Orleans until the 22nd, never left Alexandria for Natchitoches until April 2, and never left Natchitoches until the 6th, four days before Sherman expected his troops back in Vicksburg. He wrote bitterly:

"There is no foreseeing what other calamities may arise from the errors of one man, who, absorbed in his own interests, and diseased with political aspirations, cares little or nothing for the lives of those he has sacrificed, or thinks of anything but the effect this may have upon his future career." [44]

Soldiers and sailors by the thousands now jammed into Alexandria, which one of them described as ". . . a pretty place. . . . The streets are wide, and the houses are not crowded up against each other. Nearly every house has a yard and one or more shade trees in it." [45] But confusion took over. Soon, Porter was writing: "A ring of fire surrounds Alexandria tonight. It is said our forces are working in and burning everything as they come." [46]

This diarist made notes as battle-scarred veterans, accustomed to action, were forced into a period of idleness while they waited for the water in the Red to rise. Alexandria, already an Army base, became now a huge center of soldiers and sailors, with din and noises and sins strange to this bucolic Louisiana countryside. "A man fishing from the boat this afternoon," it was recorded in the diary, "hooked onto something which when pulled up proved to be a dead soldier with his skull smashed in. The boatmen remembered him as one who had a quarrel with a deck hand last night, and as he, too, is missing, it is thought he killed this soldier and after throwing him in the river cleared out. I could not get his name or regiment, but am sure he did not belong to the 128th. It is easy to die here, and there are many ways of doing it. A dead man was found on the upper deck of the *Mattie Stevens* yesterday. He was thought to be asleep until a comrade went to wake him up and found he was sleeping his last sleep. He was shot through the heart, but as no shot had been fired on the boat it is supposed it came from some distance away, missing the thousands that are here and finding only this sleeper. He was of the Thirty-third Massachusetts." [47]

One day soon after Banks returned to Alexandria, a flag of truce came in from the Confederates. The bearer delivered a note addressed to Union Colonel James Grant Wilson and signed by General John A. Wharton, commanding the South's Army of Western Louisiana that had taken part in the fighting at Sabine Cross Roads. It read: "After the damned good licking we gave you Yanks the other day, I discovered some baskets and boxes bearing your familiar name. As no one in this army appeared to have as good a claim to the grog as your old College Hill classmate 'Texas Jack,' otherwise 'Red-headed Jack,' I levied upon the same and sent it to my quarters, where the wine was drunk with great gusto by Dick Taylor and our other generals. Nothing so good has gone down our gullets for a long time; and if you will come to Galveston after 'de wa' is ober,' you will be paid back with compound interest." [48]

On April 29, Acting Ensign T. A. Quin of the *Carondelet,* for fourteen years a civil engineer, came forward with a plan to relieve the fleet: By building a cofferdam to shut off the water over one part of the falls, he would blast out the rock and cut a channel deep enough for all of the vessels shut up above to pass. Two hundred fifty men would be needed for the work. He estimated it would take thirty days to cut the channel after the dam was completed.[49]

But Quin's plan never had a chance. Before it could be put into effect, a better one was offered by Lieutenant Colonel Joseph Bailey of the Fourth Wisconsin, chief engineer on the staff of General Franklin. A thirty-seven-year-old logger from the Northwest, he knew what they did back home when the water got so low logs wouldn't float downstream. He said that with the manpower available he could throw up a set of dams that would float the vessels over the rapids in less than half the time it would take Quin to build a cofferdam. "I wish I was as sure of heaven as I am that I can save the fleet," he said.[50]

On April 30, Bailey was ordered to proceed.[51] "There seems to have been an especial Providence looking out for us, in providing a man equal to the emergency," Porter wrote.[52]

Time was the factor influencing decisions. Food was short, and forage was almost exhausted. On the face of things, the supply situation would force the Army to start marching in ten days, leaving the Navy to rescue or destroy what amounted to the best part of the Mississippi Squadron. Bailey said he would have the water at a satisfactory level within that period.

The logger already had shown some ability at marine salvage. After the capture of Port Hudson, he saved two transports by use of wing dams and a central boom. Now he looked out on a stretch of river that was mostly rocks. The current ran through a channel barely twenty feet wide, at a speed of nine miles an hour, over two sets of falls, these about a mile apart, with a drop of thirteen feet between them. Where he proposed to build the dams, the stream was seven hundred fifty-eight feet wide.[53] His minimum goal was to raise the water to a depth of at least seven feet, nearly four feet higher than it was at the moment.

The dams Bailey proposed were of three classes. From the north bank he would build tree dams, some of them three hundred or more feet long, formed by tying together the butts of large trees, raised by cross logs, their tops toward the current and kept in place by weighting with stone and brick. From the opposite bank, where large trees were rare, he would construct cribs of logs and timber and fill them with stone, bricks, and pieces of machinery taken from neighboring sugar houses and cotton gins. The third type would be made of logs raised at the lower end on trestles and sheathed over with plank. Four large coal barges would be filled with stones and scuttled to fill in a part of the gap in the center.

Banks placed at Bailey's disposal all the men he requested —three thousand from Maine and New York—as well as between two and three hundred wagons.[54] Crews spread out over the countryside, tearing down neighboring steam mills and other buildings for materials. Soldiers from Maine, accustomed to the woods, were put to work felling timber. Everything became a beehive of activity. Teams snaked in the large trees as they were dropped and trimmed to specifications, and wagons rolled back and forth in all directions, hauling stone and brick. Stone from quarries opened above Alexandria was brought down on flatboats especially built for the purpose. Forges of the fleet were kept busy making bolts with which to fasten the cribs. Night and day men worked in water, sometimes up to their necks.

"Every man seemed to be working with a vigor I have seldom seen equaled, while, perhaps, not one in fifty believed in the success of the undertaking," Porter wrote. "These falls are about a mile in length, filled with rugged rocks, over which at the present stage of water it seemed to be impossible to make a channel." [55]

While crews worked on the dams, others were engaged in lightening the vessels. Armor was stripped from the larger ironclads and, to keep it from falling into the hands of the Confederates, was taken up the river after nightfall and dropped in a deep hole. Guns were moved ashore.

Almost constantly during the daylight hours there was skirmishing in the outskirts of the community. Kirby Smith, confident that the advance on Shreveport from along the Red had been stopped, sent off a major portion of his troops after Steele, but there was still a strong force around Alexandria, and the Southerners were convinced Porter's fleet was bottled up for months to come. The dam they looked upon as a joke, and so did all but a small percentage of the Federals who stood on the riverbank and watched its construction.

Night scenes were especially memorable. One officer recalled: "The fires burning on both banks of the river and at different points on the dam; the thousand swarthy figures at work on land and water, passing to and fro; the campfires of the Army which surrounded us on every side; the loud commands of the officers superintending the work; the noisy shouts of the teamsters; the sound of the falling trees, and the roaring of the rushing waters. . . . Mingled with these sounds we often heard, as we passed on our rounds among the men, the sweet strains of 'Annie Laurie,' or the martial notes of the 'Battle Cry of Freedom,' while at the other end of the dam, among the dusky members of the Corps d'Afrique, the popular refrains of 'John Brown's body lies a-mouldering in the ground,' and some of those peculiar and plaintive plantation melodies of the South." [56]

One night an aged contraband, silver-haired and wrinkled, came upon the scene. He had just been brought into the lines, and he looked down upon the bedlam in wonder before throwing up his hands and crying, " 'Fo Gawd, whut won't de Yankees do next!" [57]

On the morning of May 4, three vessels that had remained below the falls—the transport *John Warner,* loaded with cotton and troops, and the gunboats *Covington* and *Signal*—were sent toward the mouth of the Red. They never got there. Along the way, the Confederates attacked them with artillery and infantry, sinking the trio and killing many of the men on board before they had gone more than twenty miles.

By the 8th, the dams were far enough along to cause the water to begin rising. The level rose to a depth of five feet, four and a half inches that day, and three of the light-draft vessels—the *Fort Hindman, Neosho,* and *Osage*—passed the upper falls.[58] It was anticipated that the others would be able to get through the following day.

General Banks was among those who stayed up late that night to watch. Between sundown of the 8th and one A.M. of the 9th, the water had risen two feet, and was still rising. But Banks, visiting the upper fleet after midnight, noticed that the pressure of the current was terrific. He also observed that the ships appeared to be idle, all of them anchored with scarcely a light showing or a man stirring. He returned to his headquarters and sent Porter a telegram telling him about the situation. He also warned that the vessels should be ready to take advantage of the high water, advising that things above the falls were so quiet that there might be unnecessary delay in getting started.

Banks's advice was in order. At five the next morning the pressure of the current became so great that it swept away two of the coal barges sunk in connection with the lower dams. Porter was watching and immediately leaped astride a horse and rode above the falls to order the *Lexington*—the only vessel ready to move —to attempt to pass before the water got too low.[59]

"The *Lexington* succeeded in getting over the upper falls just in time," Porter wrote Welles, "the water rapidly falling as she was passing over. She then steered directly for the opening in the dam, through which the water was rushing so furiously that it seemed as if nothing but destruction awaited her. Thousands of beating hearts looked on anxious for the result; the silence was so great as the *Lexington* approached the dam that a pin might almost be heard to fall. She entered the gap with a full head of steam on, pitched down the roaring current, made two or three spasmodic rolls, hung for a moment on the rocks below, was then swept into deep water by the current and rounded to, safely into the bank. Thirty thousand voices rose in one deafening cheer, and universal joy seemed to pervade the face of every man present." [60]

The *Neosho* tried it next, but failed to fare as well. Her pilot became frightened as he approached the gushing torrent, and stopped her engine. For a moment her hull disappeared below water, but she rose, was swept along over the rocks, and escaped with a hole in her bottom so insignificant that it was repaired within an hour. The *Fort Hindman* and *Osage* came through without scraping.

Bailey returned to work, and this time the crews under his direction had more faith in what they were doing. They had seen that his plan would work. To offset the tremendous pressure, he decided to leave the gap in the dam at the lower falls and to raise the river by directing all of the water into a narrow channel through wing dams at the upper falls.

Early on the morning of the 10th, the side-wheel steamer *Chillicothe,* her armor removed, made it over the upper falls, stern first. At one point she went aground on the rocks, but she was pulled free and came to anchor above the lower dam.

By the 11th, eight to twelve inches of water were still needed to get all the vessels over, Porter estimated. He was laid up with rheumatism, an attack so bad it was only with pain that he could ride a horse. A part of the day was spent in writing Banks a letter in which he tried to stem his impatience over the forage and food supply. "I hope, sir," he wrote, "you will not let anything divert you from the attempt to get these vessels all through safely, even if we have to stay here and eat mule meat." [61]

The water was rising at the rate of two inches every six hours. At a few minutes before 7:00 P.M. on the 12th, the *Ozark* managed to get through the rapids. Behind her, the *Mound City* built up steam, battened ports and hatches, and stood for the falls. She went through with some damage to her starboard rudder, causing her to ground across the channel below. The night was spent in freeing her.

On the 13th, the remaining vessels were able to get through, and the ammunition taken from them to lighten their draft was moved back on board. That afternoon they headed downstream, while behind them the town of Alexandria was swept by flames of undetermined origin. The Federals were departing at a fortunate time. In another week the Confederate forces that had driven Steele back to Little Rock were once more on duty along the Red.[62]

As the vessels moved away, one soldier watched them go with light heart. He had saved a fleet valued at nearly two million dollars. Navy Secretary Welles soon was suggesting to War Secretary Stanton that he recommend to Congress that it give a vote of thanks to Joseph Bailey, which was done.[63] His fellow servicemen in the meanwhile began raising a fund to testify to the Mississippi Squadron's high appreciation. The fleet presented him with a silver vase valued at sixteen hundred dollars, and Porter gave him a seven-hundred-dollar sword and recommended that he be promoted to brigadier general.[64]

No one would sing the logger's praise more loudly than Porter. "Words are inadequate to express the admiration I feel for the abilities of Lieutenant Colonel Bailey," he said in his report. "This is without doubt the best engineering feat ever performed. Under the best circumstances a private company would not have completed this work under one year, and to an ordinary mind the whole thing would have appeared an utter impossibility." [65]

Porter was so relieved at saving his fleet that he almost forgave Banks for his part in the failure of the Red River campaign. Only once during the expedition did he have anything nice to say about the military leader, and that was after the ships had managed to get past the falls: "To General Banks personally I am much indebted for the happy manner in which he has forwarded this enterprise, giving it his whole attention night and day, scarcely sleeping while the work was going on, tending personally to see that all the requirements of Colonel Bailey were complied with on the instant." [66]

The Army had repaid the Navy for at least one of the times the Navy had saved soldiers from defeat.

★ *13*

The eruption at Deep Bottom

MAY 1864

Deep Bottom was just another section of the James River below Richmond. Where it got its name, no one had recorded. Its main distinction was the straightness of the channel at that point, for this stream, after it passed the falls at Virginia's capital, wound about in a serpentine manner. In places it almost met itself, and thus it was slow running, murky, and amply bordered with mud flats. But this was not true at Deep Bottom, for there it seemed to take on some degree of respectability.

The Confederates attached particular importance to Deep Bottom. There, in a sheltered pit near the southern bank, were stationed three men who for months had done little but wait. Occasionally they might be seen moving about among the bushes, whiling away the time, but mostly they remained out of sight, watching for the approach of Union vessels from downriver toward the east, toward Newport News and Norfolk and the coastal region whence had come the armada that had worn itself out against Drewry's Bluff in '62.

One of the three men always remained on duty in the pit, a

four-foot-square box containing the points of connection that could touch off a dreadful explosion out in the middle of the river. It was arranged snugly out of sight, its exterior peaceful, but its interior characterized as sinister by several wires that twisted in various directions and ran out through auger holes to disappear beneath the surface of the earth.

In the box were two large wooden plugs, a half-inch hole bored in each and filled with mercury. Buried wires extended from the plugs to the river's edge and from there were suspended below the surface of the water by a rope weighted down with sections of chain. This rope ran in two directions, a part of it toward the channel directly opposite the pit, the other to a point farther upstream.

To the left rear of the box, along a footpath leading higher up the bank, other wires were buried. These connected with two sets of batteries, a crude assemblage of zinc cups containing sulphuric acid and water, surrounding porous clay cups filled with nitric acid, all attached by clamps and thumbscrews. One touch of the wires from the batteries to the mercury in the wooden plugs down in the pit, and the surface of the James would erupt in a sudden, violent turmoil as thousands of pounds of powder were ignited.

The month of May was not far advanced when rumors came that the Union's new commander in chief, Ulysses S. Grant, was planning a grand offensive, one part of which would call for a fleet to move up the James. The Confederates had been preparing to meet such a maneuver for a long time.

This military and naval evolution, as planned at Washington, would resemble in some respects the '62 advance when the Southerners drove back the *Monitor, Galena,* and other Union vessels. But this time the accent would be on the Army, with the Navy participating at least a part of the way. Troops would be convoyed to Bermuda Hundred and there debarked to take up a land offensive against the Confederate capital.

Hunter Davidson, of the Confederacy's Torpedo Service, had

worked steadily during the intervening months to make sure the Federals would find that two years had made a difference. In '62 the Union ships had reached Drewry's Bluff with interference only from riflemen along the banks; now they would find that the Southerners were relying heavily on water mines to impede an invasion.

The Confederate Navy Department gave the first warning that the enemy fleet was on its way. On May 5, it wired Davidson that monitors, gunboats, ironclads, and transports were coming up the river.

At Newport News, at an early hour that morning, the advance started. Ben Butler's army was loaded on transports. Never again would the James present such a scene: forty thousand soldiers moving by water in almost every type of craft. First came seven gunboats, then the vessels with the Army units —coastal and river steamers, ferryboats, tugs, sloops, schooners, barges, and canalboats—and finally the ironclads, the monitors *Tecumseh, Canonicus, Saugus,* and *Onondaga,* and the casemated ram *Atlanta,* a captured Confederate ship.[1] On board the warships were one hundred seven guns.[2]

The Confederates created no trouble along the way. The log of the Federal gunboat *Aroostook* recorded in almost routine fashion: "At three-twenty weighed anchor and proceeded up James River, with U.S. ironclad *Canonicus* in tow. All the fleet under way, steering up James River, in company with army transports. Passed many transports, all steering up river. Grapnels over the stern, dragging for torpedoes."[3] By sunset the first brigade had been landed at Bermuda Hundred, and others were on their way. Not a water mine had been sighted.

But on the morning of the 6th, the picture changed. A runaway slave came on board one of the gunboats and reported that numerous mines were up ahead, especially in the vicinity of Deep Bottom. He had seen the Confederates working at them, and he knew they were there.

The gunboats moved slowly forward, crews in open boats

rowing in advance and dragging for mines. Their rate of advance after leaving Bermuda Hundred was half a mile every twenty-four hours.[4]

Noon arrived, and the day moved toward 2:00 P.M. The *Commodore Jones, Commodore Morris,* and *Mackinaw* were in the lead. Commander J. C. Beaumont of the *Mackinaw* was the senior officer. On board his vessel was the runaway slave, eagerly pointing out the exact spot where he knew mines were located. When within five hundred yards of the position, Beaumont anchored and signaled to the other gunboats to approach no closer.[5]

An armed boat's crew, under Acting Master's Mate J. F. Blanchard, landed on the right bank of the river and began to search for wires and galvanic batteries. Beaumont in the meantime maneuvered for a better position farther down the river. Suddenly a terrific explosion rent the air. It shook the area in a manner remindful of an earthquake and sent water and bits of the *Commodore Jones* flying hundreds of feet into the air.

"It seemed as if the bottom of the river was torn up and blown through the vessel itself," wrote one eyewitness. "The *Jones* was lifted almost entirely clear of the water, and she burst in the air like an exploding firecracker. She was in small pieces when she struck the water again." [6]

While debris was still settling down on the ruffled surface of the water, three men were seen to run out of the bushes along the bank of the river. A coxswain in a cutter, dragging for mines, shot one of them dead.

Blanchard headed his boat toward the spot where the men had been seen. He found the batteries, fully charged and arranged on shelves. Back to Beaumont he went to report, and was ordered to return and trace the wires.

On shore again, Blanchard went to the batteries and disconnected them. Then he began to trace the wires, following them for about seventy-five yards, when they turned directly to the river. They led to the little square box, and in it he found the two surviving Confederates, concealed and waiting for an opportunity to explode another mine.

Taken on board the *Mackinaw,* the prisoners identified themselves as P. W. Smith and Jarvis Johnson. Smith admitted there were other mines in the river, but refused to tell where they were. Johnson, who claimed he was forced into the Confederate Army and had chosen the torpedo service so he could be near his home at Deep Bottom, also refused to talk at first, but changed his mind when placed in the bow of a gunboat searching for the mines. He said that the *Commodore Jones* had been destroyed by two thousand pounds of powder placed out in the river the preceding fall, and that there were other charges like it, naming the points at which they were to be found. He also revealed that Hunter Davidson himself, with twelve men, was on the opposite shore when the explosion occurred.[7]

It would be days before an exact count could be made of the casualties caused by the mine. On May 12, there was a light breeze from the northeast, and then thunder, lightning, and rain. During the late afternoon, a body was seen floating down with the tide. It was towed ashore and there recognized as that of Thomas King, ordinary seaman on the *Commodore Jones.* The next day a body was found on the bank, but identification was not possible. It was much bruised about the head and shoulders, the right arm and left leg were broken, there was a wound on top of the head, and it was scalded from head to foot.[8] It was originally given out officially that the total dead from the explosion was sixty-nine.[9]

The Confederates were relentless. Only hours after the *Commodore Jones* was destroyed, the Union gunboat *Shawsheen* steamed toward Turkey Bend to look for mines along the shore. At eleven-twenty, anchor was dropped in six feet of water, and the crew was allowed to eat before landing. Twenty minutes later, a battery of Napoleons and howitzers and four companies of infantry opened on the vessel from woods along the bank. The fire riddled her and finally struck her steam drum.

Men poured over her sides, among them her captain, Acting Ensign Charles Ringot. As he swam toward shore, a rifle ball struck him in the right eye. He turned back toward the tug, shouted for a white flag to be hoisted, and then went out of sight. His body was found four days later.[10]

By the 13th, residents of Richmond were listening to another bombardment from the direction of Drewry's Bluff. But this time the fighting was on land. Beauregard, who had just taken over command of the Department of North Carolina and Southern Virginia on April 23, was himself on hand. For four days there was battle, and then Butler's troops began the march back to Bermuda Hundred. Richmond was still safe from attack from the direction of the James.

★ 14

Cushing demands attention

MAY 1864

At dusk one May evening, blockaders off Wilmington Bar watched four Confederate steamers moving along the North Carolina waters of New Inlet behind Fort Fisher. They were about three miles distant, one of them an ironclad ram, and the others, seagoing vessels. They created more than ordinary interest, for it was generally known that the Rebels in that area had been working for months to bring out two mailed ships, one to be known as the *North Carolina,* the other as the *Raleigh.* Could the ironclad be one of these?

Acting Volunteer Lieutenant Samuel Huse, commanding the U.S.S. *Britannia,* decided to find out. He ran in closer than usual to Fort Fisher, and the fact that he was not fired on confirmed his suspicions that the Confederates were up to something that was not routine. In the growing darkness he could see red, green, and white lanterns blinking as they led the ironclad cautiously toward the fort in a manner quite different from anything he had seen before.

As suspicions increased, the U.S.S. *Mount Vernon* steamed

down to her night station off the end of some woods on Bald Head. Other blockaders sought their posts, alert and ready to flash signals to one another at the first alarm.

At 8:00 P.M., with water high and darkness deepening, a vessel the Federals took to be the ram came out over the bar and began firing at the *Nansemond* and *Britannia,* doing neither any damage. Against the skyline behind her, the ghostly form of one of the other vessels they had watched at dusk could be seen running off to the northeast. The Federals took particular notice. Heretofore this second craft had been identified as a gunboat, but now it was realized she was a blockade-runner. The U.S.S. *Nereus,* stationed just outside a buoy off the bar, and the U.S.S. *Howquah* gave chase.

New Inlet rapidly became a scene of confusion. Rockets and gunfire broke the darkness. Signals flashed in all directions.

At eight-thirty, two rockets soared into the air in the vicinity of Fort Fisher, followed by the flashes of five guns. The *Mount Vernon* steamed ahead under full speed, steering to the southward and eastward in the hope of intercepting any runner that might be trying to escape. But her crew could make out nothing, and she soon was turned inshore again.

Ten minutes later, Lieutenant Commander Pendleton G. Watmough, commanding the U.S.S. *Kansas,* saw a blue light and heard the report of two guns. They were bearing S.W. by S. He held to his station.

In another half hour the U.S.S. *Howquah,* Acting Master J. W. Balch, returning from the chase after the runner, neared a steamer running N.E. by E. Balch stood for her and challenged her with night signals. When there was no answer, he fired a thirty-pounder rifle, and this time he got a reply. She was the *Nansemond.*

Midnight neared. White and blue lights flashed. More rockets zoomed into the blackened skies. Across the water, guns roared in full echo. Acting Ensign J. H. Porter of the *Nansemond* saw a vessel bearing E. by S. He steamed up toward her and gave the challenge light. In answer, a white flash cut the darkness, and the sail started ahead, steering northeast and crossing the *Nansemond*'s bow. Porter put his helm hard astarboard to prevent a collision, and challenged again. The answering flash was in red, and he could see the other vessel was coming directly toward him. He made a third challenge, using a Coston signal. This time there was no reply. He fired a twenty-four-pounder howitzer aft. Back from the sail came a shot that passed over and near the Federal's walking beam. The two vessels were not over five hundred yards apart, and Porter could see the outline of the stranger's hull and the white water from her propeller. He fired another shot and received one in return.

Porter now put on more steam to get out of range. As he moved away, he ordered aloft a blue light, which the other vessel fired at as long as it was burning. When the light went out, the sail disappeared in the darkness.

Other vessels circling in the area, the *Tuscarora, Howquah,* and *Britannia,* saw the flashes in the dark between the *Nansemond* and the stranger and heard the reports of guns. This caused them to run about in general confusion, challenging at random. The ram had not been heard from since her initial outburst.

As day began to break at 4:00 A.M., Acting Volunteer Lieutenant James Trathen of the *Mount Vernon* steamed cautiously toward Fort Fisher.[1] He could see nothing. But twenty-five minutes later, the *Howquah* made out the *Nansemond* bearing east by north, a mile and a half distant, and saw a steamer following a course in line with the fort. She was burning soft coal. Commander Balch saw she was a ram and thought her the *North Carolina.* The Confederate ensign was flying above her, and back of her lay one armed steamer and two tugboats.

Balch of the *Howquah* called all hands to quarters. He could see the ram making toward him at a speed he estimated at six knots. She seemed to be a large vessel cut down to the water line and refitted with a plated house having three ports on each side and one at each end. She had one smokestack and a small flag post aft. He and others remarked at her resemblance to the *Atlanta,* the ironclad screw steamer captured from the Confederates in the Savannah area during the summer of '63. She was formidable and dangerous looking.

Toward the *Howquah* the ram continued to come. Balch headed offshore and commenced firing. The shot struck near the ironclad. She answered with a blast from her bow gun, the shell exploding close to the Union ship's starboard quarter.

The fight went on, out toward the buoy, the vessels still exchanging shots. Balch gave a signal. The *Mount Vernon* saw it, hoisted her colors, and started toward the two vessels, clearing for action as she came. Soon the *Kansas* arrived on the scene and opened up with one-hundred-pounder rifles and nine-inch guns.

It was approaching 5:00 A.M. As daylight grew fuller, the other vessels could be seen closing in from various directions —the *Tuscarora, Britannia, Niphon, Fahkee,* some of them remaining out of fighting distance and merely reconnoitering.

The ironclad steamed about, advancing and retiring, firing first at one vessel and then another. A shell tore through the smokestack of the *Howquah* about two-thirds of the way up. Sailors stared at the hole it left—twenty-three inches by sixteen inches—and estimated it to have been caused by an eight-incher. This was the ram's last shot, a fitting finale, for it had created a triumphant image for the Confederates to be remembered by. The sailors on the *Howquah* were furious. They fired fourteen thirty-two-pounder solid shot, two thirty-two-pounder percussion shells, and three shells from a twelve-pounder howitzer. Two of them found their marks, but did no damage.

Nearly an hour had passed since the ironclad's first appearance in the early dawn. She now seemed to be fed up with the fight. She veered her course and steamed back toward Fort Fisher. At 7:00 A.M. she was across the bar. The atmosphere was so hazy that the Federals were unable to determine whether the red flag she hoisted was an English ensign or a common battle flag. As she passed the fort, nine guns were fired as a salute.

But the day for her was not one of glory. Had the Federals been able to follow the ram as she steamed up New Inlet, they would have seen her ground at a point known as "The Rip." There she stayed, just as the Confederates had feared she might, for her draft seemed considerable for the Carolina sounds. Soon they were taking off her equipment and her four guns, and removing her iron, resigned to the loss of a vessel on which they had worked for nearly two years. None was sadder than her commander, Pembroke Jones, or Flag Officer Lynch. A court of inquiry would find them not guilty of negligence or inattention, and their conduct proper.[2] But in the meantime, the *Raleigh* was on the bottom of the river.

The Federals still thought the ironclad that had given them such a lively time during the early-morning hours of a May day was the *North Carolina*. So sure of it were they that a plan for the destruction of the *Raleigh,* assumed to be still at Wilmington, soon was forthcoming. It was the brain child of the zealot, William B. Cushing, who had come out of Philadelphia in '61 in the U.S.S. *Minnesota* and much of the time since then had been stationed off the North Carolina coast. Young, ambitious, member of a fighting family, he was constantly on the lookout for some way to distinguish himself. In February he had made a daring raid on Smithville, North Carolina, and returned in triumph without losing a man. Now, he said, he would be willing to steal up toward Wilmington and knock out the *Raleigh*.

"I write unofficially to you to say that, having just learned the particulars of the mortifying affair off Wilmington," he wrote Admiral Lee from Beaufort, "I deem it my duty to leave for the point of danger at once. I feel very badly over the affair, sir, and would have given my life freely to have had the power of showing my high regard for you and the honor of the service by engaging the enemy's vessels." [3]

He outlined his plan to Secretary Welles:

"Selecting a time when the ram is anchored at Smithville, I can, as I have often done, take boats by the forts and up to the anchorage, and, covered by the darkness, approach to within a short distance of the enemy. The *Raleigh's* low, flat decks are very favorable to boarders, while there are but two small hatches communicating with officers' quarters and berth deck. The lookouts can easily be swept away and these hatches guarded, while the main force, rushing through ports and hatch, will secure the unprotected gun deck, which will give us the engine room and magazine hatch." [4]

He admitted it had been pointed out to him that, once on deck, he would be unable to reach the lower part of the vessel and the crew. To take care of this, he would equip himself with long-fused shells and a slow match. One shell down each hatch would be likely to bring all hands to terms.

Cushing's plan was approved within a week. "I applaud the spirit manifested by you," wrote Lee.[5] Gideon Welles was equally as enthusiastic: "Risks to accomplish an important object ought to be undertaken without hesitation, and will never be disapproved by the Department if well arranged and intrusted to good officers." [6]

Cushing pushed off on reconnaissance one night in a cutter from the U.S.S. *Monticello,* the ship he commanded. His every move was mysterious. A slender six-footer, with smooth face and with hair falling to his shoulders, he sat in the bow of the boat, gazing upstream. With him, besides fifteen crewmen, were two officers, Ensign J. E. Jones and Acting Master's Mate William L. Howorth. Both had been his companions on other daring enterprises.

Soon he unknowingly passed in the darkness the sunken hulk of the very vessel he was on his way to sink. At one point, a blockade-runner stealing through the darkness almost ran him down. And later, when the moon came out brightly, sentinels hailed from the bank and fired muskets, causing him to take a hand in rowing madly toward the safety of the shadows on the opposite side. Shortly before dawn he hauled his boat into the marshes seven miles below Wilmington.

Lying there in the reeds, Cushing watched Confederate

Unaware for six months that the war had ended, the C.S.S. *Shenandoah* fought on alone. Here she is pictured in the Arctic Ocean before her captain relinquished his command in Liverpool, England.

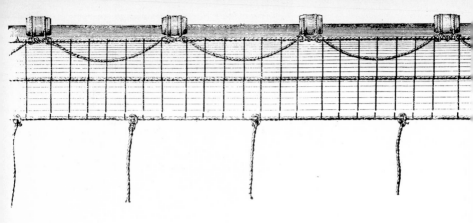

The Southerners put great faith in the rope and chain obstructions placed across river channels to stop the invading Union gunboats. Some of the most intricate found between Fort Sumter and Sullivan's Island are shown in these drawings.

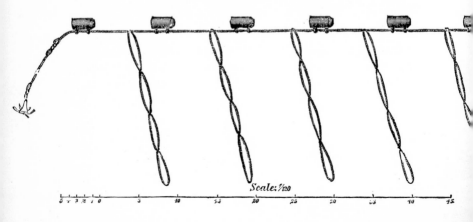

Scale: 1/120

This early submarine, now on display in New Orleans, is generally thought to be the *Pioneer,* which was scuttled in Lake Pontchartrain on April 27, 1862, to keep her out of Federal hands. Some say, however, that this is not the *Pioneer* but an earlier craft of Confederate design.

This painting of the *H.L. Hunley,* first submarine to sink a ship, gives the best indication of what the undersea craft actually looked like.

A pen-and-ink artist made this sketch of the C.S.S. *Albemarle,* the formidable ironclad the Southerners built in a cornfield and then launched against the Union blockading fleet.

In her first appearance, the Confederate ironclad ram *Albemarle* attacked a Union fleet at Plymouth, North Carolina, on the Roanoke River, sank the U.S.S. *Southfield,* pictured here as she went down, and helped in recapturing the strategic military point.

An artist's conception of the ramming of the Confederate *Albemarle* by the U.S.S. *Sassacus* during the fierce battle fought in Albemarle Sound in the Spring of 1864.

The U.S.S. *Cricket,* a tinclad, saw much action in the Red River campaign of 1864. Admiral Porter used her at times as his flagship.

An artist traveling with Admiral Porter's Union fleet down the Red River made this sketch as the *Lexington* passed over the falls created by the dams thrown up under the direction of Lieutenant Colonel Joseph Bailey.

Lieutenant William **B.** Cushing, the zealous young Union officer whose greatest feat perhaps was the sinking of the C.S.S. *Albemarle*.

Bearded Admiral John J. Winslow led the U.S.S. *Kearsarge* into battle against his friend, Admiral Raphael Semmes of the Confederate Navy, and sank the latter's vessel, the C.S.S. *Alabama*.

Credit for firing the shot that disabled the C.S.S. *Alabama* and sent her to the bottom is given this well-polished gun, shown on board the U.S.S. *Kearsarge* in front of some of the ship's officers.

Under Farragut's direction, Union sailors worked carefully at night to remove Confederate water mines and open a way for the Union fleet. Here an engraving shows a crew at work hauling the explosives on board a raft.

An entire fleet surrounded the C.S.S. *Tennessee* in the Battle of Mobile Bay and forced her to surrender. Here the U.S.S. *Lackawanna* is shown ramming the *Tennessee*.

The double-turreted monitor *Onondaga* was one of a class of vessels constructed by the Federals to aid them in their advance up Southern rivers.

This vessel, the U.S. *Black Hawk*, flagship of the Mississippi Squadron, caught fire from coal oil the morning of April 22, 1865, and burned rapidly.

The fleet standing off Fort Fisher in the attack of January 15, 1865, part of which is shown here, was the greatest ever assembled on the American coast up to that time.

The Mound at Fort Fisher, a man-made elevation from which the Southerners could fire plunging shot at passing vessels, was a key point of action in both battles.

The C.S.S. *Tallahassee* was a cause of much alarm during the latter months of the war when she took to the high seas after Union commerce.

The Confederates scored a major triumph in their mine warfare during the closing months by sinking this vessel, the U.S.S. *Harvest Moon*. She was Admiral Dahlgren's flagship.

steamers plying up and down the river. Commodore Lynch's flagship, the *Yadkin,* passed within two hundred yards. Boats continued to go by throughout the day. He studied them all and was impressed by the fact that they did not seem to have many men on board.

Just after dark, as he prepared to move out, two boats rounded the bend from below. They were captured and found to be conveying a party of fishermen back to Wilmington. Cushing took all of them along with him as guides.

Near Wilmington he came upon three rows of obstructions in the channel and turned off into a creek until he reached a road he was told connected with the main routes from Fort Fisher. Leaving half his party at that point, he went with the remainder two miles farther and at dawn went into hiding.

Toward noon a courier came along on horseback with a mail-bag, and was captured. Soon another appeared from the opposite direction, but managed to spy one of the Federals before he reached them and immediately turned in flight. Cushing rode after him on the captured courier's horse, but abandoned the chase after a ride of two miles.

As the day wore along, more prisoners were captured. One of them reported that a store was located only two miles down the road. Howorth was chosen to go there for food, and off he went, dressed in the courier's coat and hat. When he returned, he brought a supply of milk, chickens, and eggs.

That night Cushing rejoined the other members of his party, and they made their way back to the river. While he was trying to land his prisoners on an island, a steamer passed so close that he and his crewmen had to jump overboard to keep from being seen. Later, miles downstream, the fishermen he was using as pilots pointed out where the *Raleigh* had been wrecked.

"She is, indeed, destroyed," Cushing reported to Lee, "and nothing now remains of her above water." [7]

So William B. Cushing's ambitions were for the moment frustrated, mainly because he had mistaken his ships. The

North Carolina, he learned, was at anchor off Wilmington and was not worth bothering about. "She is but little relied upon, and would not stand long against a monitor," he reported.[8]

Blockade-runners stealing past the *Raleigh* on their way out to sea invariably ran wide of the spot where she had gone down. One that did this was spied by the U.S.S. *Niphon* at four-thirty in the morning. The runner was heading southwest, going fast. Day was just breaking, and the two vessels were only two and a half miles apart. The *Niphon* threw up rockets and opened with all her guns, forcing the runner to change her course to northeast by east and to commence throwing cargo overboard. For two hours the air was calm and there was no difference in speed, and then a breeze sprang up from the south. The ship in front began to gain. By noon she was six or seven miles ahead, and at 1:30 P.M., in hazy weather, she dropped out of view. The Federals had noted that she was a large, long, side-wheel steamer, painted a greenish white, and that she looked much like the *Robert E. Lee.*

The *Minnie,* bound for Bermuda with a cargo of cotton, tobacco, and turpentine, came along next. She was seen and chased by the U.S.S. *Connecticut.* After a run of more than four hours, with shells falling near her, the *Minnie* hoisted English colors and stopped her engine. Federals swarmed over her decks. In addition to her mixed cargo, they found on board a quantity of gold.

Next day the *Connecticut* saw another suspicious-looking steamer following the course toward Bermuda. Two hours later the Union vessel was within gunshot range, and after a couple of shells had been fired, the stranger surrendered. She proved to be the *Greyhound,* built at Liverpool in 1863. On board were eight hundred bales of cotton, thirty-five tons of tobacco, and twenty-five casks of turpentine. Twenty bales of cotton had been thrown overboard.

When the chase came to an end, a woman passenger on board the *Greyhound* went below to destroy, in the ship's fires, official dispatches she was taking to England from the Confederate

Government. The *Connecticut*'s log identified her as "the famous Rebel lady, Miss Belle Boyd, and her servant." [9]

There was other intrigue on board. The *Connecticut*'s master, Commander John J. Almy, reported: "The captain represents himself as George Henry, but his real name is George H. Bier, whom I formerly knew as a lieutenant in the U.S. Navy." [10]

A prize crew was sent on board the *Greyhound*. It was in charge of Acting Ensign Samuel Hardinge, Jr., a young man whom fate was to give a sharp turn. In the days ahead, he would fall in love with Belle, even though he knew her reputation as a Confederate spy. He listened to her entreaties, made it possible for "George Henry" to escape and, for it, was dismissed from the Navy. She in the meantime had been banished from the United States, and her choice of destinations was England, to be reached by way of Canada. Hardinge followed as soon as he could. He found her in London and there, on August 25, three months and two weeks after he first had met her, they were married.

It was to be a marriage of short duration. When Hardinge returned to the United States the following month, he was imprisoned. Behind bars he received treatment that broke his health, and he died a few months after his release.

★ 15

The bewitched witch

JUNE 1864

The U.S.S. *Water Witch* could not be described as a large ship. She was a wooden side-wheel steamer, three hundred and seventy-eight tons burden, a fourth-class vessel with four guns—two howitzers and two rifles—and a crew of seventy-seven officers and men. Where she was anchored in Ossabaw Sound on the coast of Georgia, half a mile north of the mouth of Bradley's River, there seemed nothing to worry about. For months the area had been peaceful, and a long period had passed since anyone had been seen who looked as though he might be an enemy—or, for that matter, it had been a long time since anyone had been seen. This was low country, thinly populated, an area so deserted it gave the *Witch*'s captain, Lieutenant Commander Austin Pendergrast, a false sense of security. It was his frequent boast that neither he nor his ship would ever be taken.

So much the worse for Pendergrast's feelings the morning his watch hailed in the dark and heard, first, "Who the hell are you hailing?" and then, "Go to hell, you sons of bitches."

Just the night before, the U.S.S. *Massachusetts* had steamed up and transferred to the *Water Witch*'s deck a new store of supplies, enough to last her for weeks.

Pendergrast was a careful man. A Kentuckian trained at the Naval Academy, his first baptism of fire had come in Hampton Roads on board the old frigate *Congress* when she was attacked by the *Merrimack* in '62; and since then he had been assigned to the *Water Witch*. For twelve months she had been on blockade duty in Ossabaw Sound, watching the mouth of the Great Ogeechee River leading up into the heart of cotton-rich Georgia. The waters about him were so quiet and so devoid of suspicious incidents or appearances that he had trouble remembering there was a war. But he never dropped his guard. One watch was always on deck, fully armed; and the guns were kept loaded. Each evening at quarters, four rounds of ammunition for each gun were brought up. Fires were heavily banked. Every half hour the engines were turned over to make sure they were in order. Chains were constantly prepared for slipping. Discipline was excellent, even though most of the men were being detained past their terms of enlistment. They liked their skipper.

The night of June 2 was a damp, squally evening, set off by occasional flashes of lightning and peals of thunder, a spell of weather not given to blockade purposes. It was so dark that Pendergrast and his men could scarcely see the length of the one-hundred-and-fifty-foot *Water Witch,* except when lightning flashed.

At the usual hour, Pendergrast went to his berth. Before doing so, he checked the ship personally to make sure everything was in order—just a quick walk around like a mother tending her children. This was habit. It had been ages since anything had happened to cause him alarm.

Equally as conscientious was the executive officer, Acting Master Charles W. Buck. At 8:00 P.M. he began his routine. He examined the buoy rope on the ship's cable, looked at the shackle and pin, saw that the hammer and chain punch were convenient, and that everything was ready and easy to slip at a moment's notice. He gave the customary night orders to the officer of the deck, and before signing off, made the evening report to the commander.[1]

The officer of the deck, as the hours moved into the early morning, was Acting Master's Mate E. D. W. Parsons, a man considered trustworthy enough, although it was realized he was rather short on naval experience. He was standing watch alone, a circumstance that had been brought about by the recent departure of a part of the crew, sent home for discharge. Pendergrast was reluctant to make acting master's mates stand watch by themselves, but there was nothing else he could do.[2]

So Parsons was on duty, and he was making his rounds and staring off frequently into the murky darkness. Men could charge, but no one ever was able to prove, that Parsons was not dutifully alert this particular night. It was the weather, some of them admitted, that was against him, for who could see through such darkness? He was to be commended, they conceded, for seeing a boat as far away as thirty yards, even if it were illumined by a flash of lightning.

And then came that abusive language, threatening and violent and angry: "Go to hell, you sons of bitches."

Parsons sprang the rattle for quarters, and the pilot in the pilothouse rang the bell to go ahead. Some of Parsons' fellow officers later would say he gave the alarm in such a manner as to have little effect in assembling the men. Parsons said he gave it and then advanced, firing his pistol at the approaching foe.

At any rate, Pendergrast heard the firing. Like an automaton, he slipped on his trousers and shoes, and sprang up the companionway.

"What's the matter?" he shouted to Parsons.

The answer came from a disorderly group of men who were storming over the ship's sides and shouting, "Rebels! Rebels!"

Pendergrast yelled: "Call all hands to repel boarders, slip the chain, and start the engine!"

Then he fled back to his stateroom for more clothing and his arms. As he rushed again on deck moments later, someone

struck him over the head with a cutlass and knocked him senseless.

For the next twenty minutes there was a melee of cursing
and confusion from stem to stern. Men, armed with cutlasses
and pistols, hacked and fought and died in the darkness. During
this period, Pendergrast partially regained consciousness, stumbled to the hurricane deck, rang the bell to go ahead, heard the
engines make half a revolution, and then fell to the deck,
weakened by loss of blood.

Executive Officer Buck had gone to bed with his air port
open, and he plainly heard the yelling outside before he heard
the rattle. He sprang out of his berth, jerked on trousers and
slippers, snatched up side arms, and rushed on deck. It was so
dark he could not distinguish one person from another, but a
flash of lightning suddenly revealed men crawling over the rails
and boarding nettings, and he could tell by the discharge of
small arms, the yelling, and the cries of surrender that the enemy was on board.

He heard Pendergrast's cry for the chain to be slipped and
the engine started.

Before Buck could move ten feet, he was blocked by the
hand-to-hand fighting. Somewhere in the darkness he heard the
voices of Paymaster Luther Billings and Ensign Abner Stover.
He fired all six charges from his revolver at men climbing over
the rails; he believed every one took deadly effect. He tried to
get past the wardroom skylight, and failing to do this, attempted
to swing the howitzer into action. He thought the paymaster
tried to assist him, but at that moment someone pushed him
down, breaking his grip on his cutlass and pistol. He fought to
get to his feet, and this time he was knocked senseless by a
blow on the forehead. When he came to, he was lying on the
poop deck aft, his hands fastened behind him and a sentry
standing over him. This was not a great day for Executive Officer Buck.

Acting Third Assistant Engineer Isaac A. Conover later told
with sincere innocence of the role he had played: "I went up

to the hurricane deck and to the bell, which was my station at quarters. I stayed there a minute or two, then I found there was no one there to give me any orders, and they was a-firing at me, for the balls was a-coming all around me. I then looked which way I should go down again. I went through the hurricane deck skylight to the engine room, then down the back stairs to the fire room." [3]

Henry Hill, the quartermaster, overpowered a Confederate and locked him in the pilothouse. Soon he, too, was a captive and had to stand by helplessly and watch his prisoner released.

Officer of the deck Parsons may have been somewhere in the crowd fighting, but fellow officers later could not recall having seen him.[4] Also missing were the men down below, Pendergrast reporting that they "evinced no desire to come on deck and defend the ship." [5]

Acting Assistant Surgeon W. H. Pierson was asleep in the wardroom. When awakened by the firing, he slipped on trousers and boots and was about to make his way to the sick quarters between decks forward when Acting Ensign Chase Hill came limping in with a dangerous-looking wound. Behind him appeared John Parker, gunner's mate, also wounded. The doctor had pocket case, lint, and bandages at hand, and he attended them on the spot. Before he could finish, other disabled men began to appear in rapid succession. Pierson applied bandages with the speed of experience, assisted by a Confederate surgeon, Dr. C. Wesley Thomas, who had joined him.[6]

A Confederate officer, gun in hand, leaped into the wardroom, his eyes flashing, and stood motionless as he watched the surgeon at work. A moment later the *Water Witch*'s chief engineer, Samuel Genther, appeared, without arms.

The Confederate directed his gun at Genther.

"I surrender! We surrender! The ship surrenders!" Genther cried.

Pierson turned in surprise. "What, Genther, is the ship surrendered?"

"Yes," said Genther.[7]

Down in the engine room the engineers and firemen and a Negro contraband named Peter McIntosh hovered miserably. A Confederate suddenly burst in upon them and ordered them on deck. They went willingly, the Negro moving with set purpose, for he had scarcely gotten above before he rushed forward and dived into the water.[8] As he did so, he heard a member of the *Water Witch*'s crew say, "My God, I am shot!" [9]

When he came to the surface, McIntosh saw four boats that looked like cotton barges around him. He kept low in the water and headed toward Ossabaw Island. For a mile and a half he swam before emerging on a beach, there to lie in sight of the ship until daylight.

When dawn arrived, the *Water Witch* was still at her same anchor. The contraband studied her. Whoever the men were who had stormed up on her during the night, they seemed to him at the moment to be having a "grand jubilee" on board.

Later that morning the U.S. bark *Fernandina,* steaming up the sound, saw a man making signals from the south end of Ossabaw Island. A boat was sent to pick him up, and on board he identified himself as Peter McIntosh and told with wide-eyed excitement what had happened during the night.

Thus came the news to the Federals, brought by the only member of the seventy-seven-man crew to escape. The *Fernandina*'s skipper, Acting Master Lewis West, made up his mind that his vessel should remain off the bar in order to keep it out of the grasp of the Southerners. But, on reflection, it occurred to him that it was highly important the other blockaders in the sound should know what had happened and that a report should be made to Rear Admiral Dahlgren, commanding the squadron. So, after waiting for hours, he bore up and ran for Wassaw in the dead of night. At daylight he found he was to leeward of it, and finally gave up his plan and sent an acting master's mate in a boat to Tybee Island with a verbal communication.

When he received word, Dahlgren reacted by sending four gunboats to Ossabaw Sound. They had orders to retake or destroy the *Water Witch*.

The Southerners, in the meantime, were rejoicing. What had looked at one time to be a failure had turned out to be a glorious success—with exceptions. The exceptions were the six dead, among them First Lieutenant Thomas P. Pelot, commanding the expedition, and seventeen wounded. The Federal losses were two dead, fourteen wounded, and sixty-one captured.[10]

Pelot, who had organized the party, received his orders on May 31. The *Water Witch* then lay at the mouth of the Little Ogeechee River. He was directed to surprise and capture her with seven boats carrying fifteen officers and one hundred seventeen men.[11]

That afternoon the *Water Witch* shifted to St. Catherine's Sound. Pelot trailed her. He was at Beaulieu Battery on June 1, and from there sent out scouts to watch for the enemy vessel. When last seen she was to the southward of St. Catherine's. Pelot was out all night searching for her.

At nine on the evening of the 2nd, the expedition got under way and proceeded to Raccoon Key, there picking up scouts who reported that their prey lay on the other side of Ossabaw Sound, about three miles away. Men at the oars pulled into the dark, shuddering inwardly every time lightning lit up the rolling surface of the sound.

The advance on the *Water Witch* was in two columns, one on the port side and one on the starboard. As the boats came alongside, the fire of small arms from the ship was severe, and it was then, while the boarding netting was being cut, that most of the casualties occurred. Pelot was the first to gain the deck, and there he fell, shot through the heart.

Also found among the dead when the fighting ended was Moses Dallas, the Negro pilot who had directed the expedition from the forward boat, and this caused a problem. He alone among the Southerners knew the tricky channels of Ossabaw Sound. Who now was to steer? In desperation, someone brought the Southern-born pilot of the *Water Witch,* Rufus B. K. Murphy, a badly wounded man, and forced him to direct the vessel up toward Beaulieu Battery. But for his wound, he might have been shot for treachery when the ship grounded in Green Island Sound.[12] She would be lightened sufficiently to enable her to run up to Savannah, and at all times in her hold would be kept at least one hundred pounds of powder—enough to blow her up and prevent her recapture.[13]

Dahlgren tried to defend the crew of the *Water Witch:* "It is to be apprehended that long and undisturbed possession has relaxed the vigilance of our blockaders, and that, in some instances, precautions have been omitted because they seemed needless in places where, as far as the eye can reach, not a living soul is to be seen for months that looks like an enemy." [14]

But Gideon Welles could not be tolerant over such news. "No number of vessels will make good the want of vigilance," he wrote back sarcastically. "The *Water Witch* was a steamer, and it cannot be claimed, as in many instances, that her capture was owing to her being a sailing vessel without steam power. It was not a deficiency of men nor of coal, but from what at present appears as carelessness and neglect, that occasioned her capture." [15]

The prisoners captured by the Confederates were taken to the naval hospital at Savannah and to hospitals at Macon and Andersonville. From Savannah, Pendergrast wrote: "The wounded are well cared for in this hospital, the surgeons manifesting much kindness toward us." [16] Surgeon Pierson added: "I know that while at Savannah I tabled with the Rebel surgeons in the hospital, and thus, during all my stay there, nearly six weeks, we had coffee never, tea only five or six times, butter about as often, and to the credit of the surgeons, be it said, that while they denied themselves the luxury of tea at $30 or $40 per pound, they had it furnished to our wounded, and generally fed them better than they fed themselves." [17]

In time, most of the *Water Witch*'s officers were exchanged, Pendergrast returning to stand trial at a general naval court-martial. He was found guilty of a charge of "culpable inefficiency in the discharge of duty," and sentenced to suspension from duty, with loss of rank, for two years. This, despite the care with which he maintained guard on board his ship and his oft-repeated declaration that he would never be captured. The court thought he should have stationed picket boats to guard his vessel at night, or that he should have kept her under way.

The end of the Alabama

JUNE 1864

No duel at dawn ever was conducted with more formality than
the one between the C.S.S. *Alabama* and the U.S.S. *Kearsarge*. It was avoidable, and yet brought on with premeditation,
the site and the time settled on in advance.

Raphael Semmes of the Confederate ship, the challenger, a
slightly built man whose waxed, pointed mustaches caused
him sometimes to be mistaken for a Frenchman, acted with
the inordinate and relentless desire for revenge of a man whose
feelings have been hurt beyond repair. And in answer, North-
Carolina-born John Ancrum Winslow of the Union vessel, na-
ture-lover blinded in his right eye by disease, steamed out for
the contest, going far enough to sea to keep the shells from falling on shore. Then he went quickly about the task of sinking
his old friend, now his enemy. In the Mexican War they had
been shipmates, messmates, and roommates.[1]

After she received her death blow, it took the *Alabama* only
minutes to sink. A part of the crew went down with her. On the
Kearsarge, only a few were wounded, one fatally. And when

Confederate prisoners came on board the Union vessel, they were surprised to find they had been fighting a virtual ironclad, for chains, forming a coat of mail, hung along the side of the ship to keep shells from tearing into her vital parts, a defense measure Farragut first had employed in his passage of the forts below New Orleans in '62.

A phenomenal person, this man Semmes. He was a hated man in the North, and in turn he gave back a bitterness of feeling with venom that poured from his facile pen. "Future generations will be astonished at the folly and fanaticism, want of principle and wickedness, developed by this war among the Puritan population of the North," he wrote in his journal. "A people so devoid of Christian charity, and wanting in so many of the essentials of honesty, cannot be abandoned to their own folly by a just and benevolent God." [2] And again: "The hyenas of the North will receive their reward under the inevitable and rigorous laws of a just government of the world." [3]

In a three-month period, Semmes captured twenty-six Union ships, and twenty-one of them he burned. The North wanted him so badly it detached some of its strongest vessels from important stations and sent them around the world on his trail.

These ships, sent afar, were searching for a deeply religious man. Semmes's faith and motivating principles were revealed in his diary: "The Almighty, for a wise purpose, hides future events from the eyes of mortals, and all we can do is to perform well our parts and trust the rest to His guidance. Success, as a general rule, attends him who is vigilant and active, and who is careful to obey all the laws of nature." [4] On the wheel of his ship was inscribed in Latin: "God helps those who help themselves."

As Semmes marked off his birthdays, he realized gradually that he was "supremely disgusted with the sea and all its belongings." [5] At fifty-five he was past the age when men ought to be subjected to the hardships and discomforts of naval life. "The very roar of the wind through the rigging, with its accompaniments of rolling and tumbling, hard, overcast skies, etc., gives

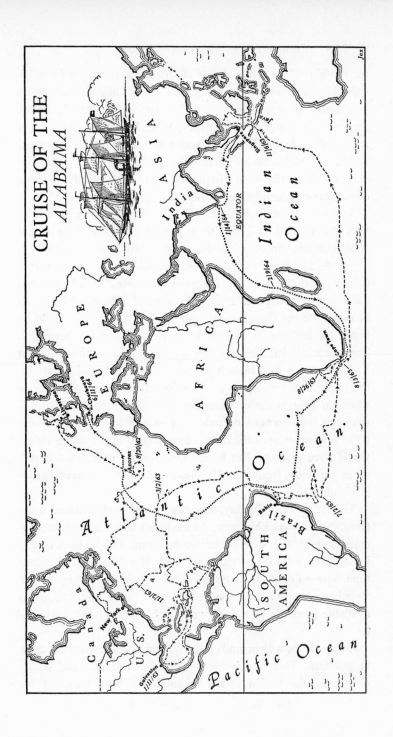

CRUISE OF THE *ALABAMA*

me the blues," he wrote. Some of this obvious fatigue from his unbroken war service may have influenced him as he steered his *Alabama* into Cherbourg, France, on June 11, 1864, and asked permission to refit her. What his vessel needed was recoppering, refastening, and boiler repairs. This he estimated would take two months.[6] Weeks earlier he had written that the ship was like "the weary foxhound, limping back after a long chase, footsore, and longing for quiet and repose."

Semmes entered port shortly after noon. His first step was to visit the vice-admiral maritime prefect, an official he found courteous but unreceptive. In response to Semmes's request, the prefect commented that Confederate vessels were showing a "marked preference" for the ports of France. Then he pointed out that Cherbourg was exclusively a naval station, all its docks belonging to the Government, and he suggested that it would be better for the cruiser captain to go to Le Havre or Bordeaux. Semmes reminded him that this was the first time the *Alabama* had been taken to a French port for repairs and, besides, it was the practice of nations to admit ships of war into public docks when no private docks were available. The prefect's final answer was that the matter would have to be referred to the minister of marine, who at the moment was not in Paris, so the visitor would have to wait.[7] But he did give permission to land thirty-seven prisoners from the *Alabama,* and these were sent ashore at nightfall.

The next day, a Sunday, was cloudy and cool. Semmes mustered and inspected his crew. As the hours advanced, matters remained quiet. A few visitors came on board, but Semmes stayed in his cabin, affected by cold and fever. His sailors in the meantime were enjoying their hours in port. They were there in the strawberry season, and the berries were large and fine. Also available in ample quantities were beef, mutton, milk, and butter.

On the 13th, a clear and cool day, Semmes exercised his crew at quarters. This was because he had heard that the U.S.S. *Kearsarge,* the Union vessel he knew had been watching for him for months, was on her way and would arrive in a matter of hours.

The information was correct. On the 14th, the *Kearsarge* arrived off the Cherbourg breakwater. Winslow, a balding man two years Semmes's junior, stopped her engines at the entrance to the harbor and sent a boat to communicate with the American consul. It came back with a report that led to the terse entry in the ship's log: "Found the Rebel privateer *Alabama* lying at anchor in the roads." [8]

The weather was cool, with an occasional spitting of rain. Sight of the *Kearsarge* caused great excitement on board the *Alabama*. The Union vessel first was seen off the entrance of the breakwater at about eleven in the morning, and Semmes immediately sent an order on shore for one hundred tons of coal. Then, as he recorded in his journal, he "sent down the yards on the mizzenmast and the topgallant yards, and otherwise prepared for action." [9] During the day he also directed to Paris this message to Flag Officer Samuel Barron, senior Confederate officer in the area:

"The *Kearsarge* is off the port, which I understand, of course, as a challenge. As we are about equally matched, I shall go out to engage her as soon as I can make the necessary preparations, which will probably be tomorrow. As the issue of combat is always uncertain, I have deposited four and a half sacks of sovereigns, containing about 4,700, and the paymaster's last payroll with Mr. Ad. Bonfils, of Cherbourg, a gentleman known to Mr. Slidell." [10]

Later that day he sent a message to his old friend, Winslow: "I hear that you were informed by the United States consul that the *Kearsarge* was to come to this port solely for the prisoners landed by me, and that she was to depart in twenty-four hours. I desire you to say to the United States consul that my intention is to fight the *Kearsarge* as soon as I can make the necessary arrangements. I hope these will not detain me more than till tomorrow evening, or next morning, at the farthest. I beg she will not depart before I am ready to go out." [11]

An aide-de-camp from the admiral prefect arrived on the 15th to say that the request for coal must imply a withdrawal of the application for repairs. Semmes agreed that it did, and that afternoon he commenced coaling. While the music of scraping shovels permeated the ship, he wrote in his journal: "My crew seem to be in the right spirit, a quiet spirit of determination pervading both officers and men. The combat will no doubt be contested and obstinate, but the two ships are so equally matched that I do not feel at liberty to decline it. God defend the right, and have mercy upon the souls of those who fall, as many of us must. Barometer low, and weather unusually cold and blustering for the middle of June." [12]

The coaling continued during Thursday, the 16th, a cool and cloudy day with occasional rain. It also went on during the 17th. By the 18th, Semmes had his coal on board and was ready to leave. He set his departure for the morning of the 19th, a Sunday, in the meantime sending his valuables and the collection of chronometers from prize ships on shore for safe-keeping.[13]

The *Alabama* left Cherbourg at 9:30 A.M. A moderate breeze was blowing from the west. The sky was blue, with a few scattered clouds. Nearly an hour later the *Kearsarge* saw her coming, and fearing the question of jurisdiction might arise, steamed to sea for a distance of six or seven miles. There she rounded to and headed directly toward the Confederate ship.

Here were two vessels ostensibly equal in power. Both were third-class screw steamers of about the same tonnage and length, and both were powered by two engines. The *Alabama*, with a crew of one hundred forty-nine, had eight guns, among them "the only successful rifled one-hundred-pounder yet produced in England." [14] The *Kearsarge*, manned by one hundred sixty-three men, carried seven guns. But there were differences. Most important of these were the chains draped along the sides of the Union ship.[15] And on board the *Alabama*, the magazine was so near the condensing apparatus used to distill water for the crew that her powder frequently became moist from steam.

It was partly that way at the moment, although the powder was stowed in copper tanks.[16]

At 10:57 A.M. the *Alabama* began the action with her starboard broadside at a distance of about a mile. The shot cut some of the *Kearsarge*'s rigging. Winslow ordered more speed. Two minutes later, Semmes sent another broadside, and followed it with a third, damage still occurring only to the rigging. At that point the Union vessel sheered and opened with her guns.

"The position of the vessels was now broadside and broadside," Winslow related, "but it was soon apparent that Captain Semmes did not seek close action. I became then fearful lest after some fighting he would again make for the shore. To defeat this I determined to keep full speed on, and with a port helm to run under the stern of the *Alabama* and rake, if he did not prevent it by sheering and keeping his broadside to us. He adopted this mode as a preventive, and as a consequence the *Alabama* was forced with a full head of steam into a circular track during the engagement." [17]

Semmes had a different explanation for the circles: "To prevent our passing each other too speedily, and to keep our respective broadsides bearing, it became necessary to fight in a circle, the two ships steaming around a common center and preserving a distance from each other of from a quarter to half a mile." [18]

The two ships became enveloped in smoke, and vessels from afar began steaming in that direction to watch the fight. Thousands of spectators looked on from the French shore. A war that for years had been going on across the Atlantic suddenly was brought to their door. Some of them had come in that morning from Paris by excursion train, for Semmes had made no secret of the fact that he meant to fight.[19]

For eighteen minutes the action continued without casualties. Then a shell passed through the starboard bulwarks of the Union ship, below the main rigging, and exploded on the quarter-deck, wounding three members of a gun crew. The worst hurt was William Gowin, ordinary seaman, injured in the leg. Next was John W. Dempsey, quarter gunner, who was quickly anesthetized with chloroform, and had his right arm amputated.

When Semmes got within good shell range, he changed from solid shot to shell. At one point in the action, the *Alabama*'s spanker gaff was shot away and her ensign came down by the run. Another soon was placed at the mizzenmast head.

"The firing now became very hot," Semmes related, "and the enemy's shot soon began to tell upon our hull, knocking down, killing and disabling a number of men in different parts of the ship. Perceiving that our shell, though apparently exploding against the enemy's sides, were doing but little damage, I returned to solid shot firing, and from this time onward alternated with shot and shell." [20]

Noon passed, with the fight still raging. The ships made seven giant circles as they pursued the battle. On the last, the *Alabama*'s speed was lessened. She winded, setting fore-trysail and two jibs, with head inshore, and presented her port broadside. The guns of the *Kearsarge* roared, sending fatal shots. At 12:10 P.M. Winslow thought he saw the *Alabama*'s flag come down, but he was unable to tell whether it had been hauled down or shot down. Then he noticed a white flag displayed over her stern, and ordered the fire reserved. But two minutes later, according to his version, the Confederate opened again with two guns on her portside. Seeing that Semmes was making all available sail, apparently with the intention of running back to Cherbourg, Winslow ordered the fire resumed, steamed ahead, and steered across the bow of the *Alabama* for raking. Soon he saw that the white flag was still flying, and once more he halted the shooting.

This last outburst of fire brought a serious charge from Semmes: "Although we were now only four hundred yards from each other, the enemy fired upon me five times after my colors had been struck, dangerously wounding several of my men." [21] In his formal report he added: "It is charitable to suppose that a ship of war of a Christian nation could not have done this intentionally."

But, flag lowered or not, the *Alabama* had received her death blow. Water was coming in through holes in her sides at such a rate that the fires in her furnaces were extinguished. There was no longer any doubt that she would have to be abandoned.

Semmes had a vision of his crew then that he never forgot. "A remarkable spectacle presented itself on the deck of the sinking ship," he later wrote. "There was no panic, no confusion among the men. Each stood, waiting his doom, with the most perfect calmness. The respect and affection manifested for their officers was touching in the extreme. Several gathered around me, and seemed anxious for my safety. One tendered me this little office of kindness, and another that." [22]

Arthur Sinclair, master of the *Alabama,* went below to get a bottle of brandy for a wounded man. There he came upon the acting surgeon, David Herbert Llewellyn, working over the wounded, in water up to his waist.

"Pills," cried Sinclair, "you better get yourself and the wounded out of this, or you'll all be drowned!"

"I must wait for orders, you know," calmly replied Llewellyn.

Other men came below, and the doctor and his patients were moved to the deck, where the wounded were placed in a boat to be rowed to the *Kearsarge.*

When Winslow saw Semmes lowering his boats, he feared a ruse, but it was now too late for such a thing. Soon the wounded were brought alongside, and among them stood a master's mate who announced that the *Alabama* had surrendered and was rapidly sinking. He asked that boats be sent immediately to rescue the crew.[23]

The *Kearsarge* had only two boats that were not disabled, the sailing launch and the second cutter. These were lowered, and the officer who had come to announce the surrender was permitted to return to aid with the rescue.[24] Standing by within hailing distance was an English yacht, the *Deerhound,* owned by John Lancaster, a wealthy gentleman of Lancashire, England, who had brought his family out from Cherbourg to watch the fight. Winslow yelled to him: "For God's sake do what you can to save them!" The yacht immediately steamed toward the stricken vessel. Two French pilot boats also hurried to the scene.

Even before her boats were lowered, the *Alabama*'s crew began jumping overboard, obeying an order for each man to save himself. There they threshed about, some swimming, some drowning, and all trying to get away from her side. Someone happened to remember that Dr. Llewellyn, now on deck, was unable to swim. Two empty shell cases were strapped beneath his arms, and he took to the water, there to die when one of the improvised life preservers came loose from its fastenings. A boat from the *Deerhound* was pulling toward him at the time and was only a few yards away.

At 12:24 the *Alabama* went down, in forty fathoms of water. Her mainmast, shattered by shot, broke as she sank, and her bow rose high out of the water as her stern began to settle. With her went a keg of wine from the Cape of Good Hope that Semmes planned to send Mrs. Slidell as soon as he went into dock.

Semmes was threshing about in the water near his first officer, John McIntosh Kell. He turned to get a last look at the *Alabama*. "A noble Roman once stabbed his daughter rather than she should be polluted by the foul embrace of a tyrant," he wrote afterward. "It was with a similar feeling that Kell and I saw the *Alabama* go down. We had buried her as we had christened her, and she was safe from the polluting touch of the hated Yankee!" [25]

Suddenly, Winslow noticed that the *Deerhound*, which had been busy picking up men from the water, was edging to leeward and moving away. "I could not believe that the commander of that vessel could be guilty of so disgraceful an act as taking our prisoners off," he reported, "and therefore took no means to prevent it, but continued to keep our boats at work rescuing the men in the water. I am sorry to say that I was mistaken; the *Deerhound* made off with Captain Semmes and others, and also the very officer who had come on board to surrender." [26]

Semmes could credit his rescue to two men. First was William Roberts, chief steward on the *Deerhound.* He had recognized Semmes in the water, having seen him once on board the *Sumter* at Gibraltar, and had dragged him on board. There Semmes came under the wing of his first officer, Kell, who had been rescued a moment before and who directed him to lie flat on the bottom of the boat to prevent recognition. When a boat from the *Kearsarge* approached and someone called, "Where is Semmes?," Kell, wearing a *Deerhound* crewman's hat, replied, "He is drowned."

Serious charges later would be made against the *Deerhound.* It was reported that she was a consort of the *Alabama,* that the night before, she had received on board all the personal effects of Semmes, that boats were seen going to and fro between her and the Confederate ship, and that the following morning she had brought to Semmes several men, supposed to be from the naval reserve, who were made captains of guns. This complicity Lancaster denied in a letter to the London *Daily News.* In his defense, he stated that Winslow had asked him to aid in saving the *Alabama*'s crew, but had made no mention of turning those rescued over to him. He added: "My own opinion is that a man drowning in the open sea cannot be regarded as an enemy at the time to anybody, and is therefore entitled to the assistance of any passerby." [27]

Seventy men were taken to the *Kearsarge,* and when they reached her they stared in astonishment. Semmes told about it in a report: "Her midship section on both sides was thoroughly iron-coated, this having been done with chains constructed for the purpose, placed perpendicularly from the rail to the water's edge, the whole over by a thin outer planking, which gave no indication of the armor beneath. This planking had been ripped off in every direction by our shot and shell, the chain broken and indented in many places, and forced partly into the ship's side. She was most effectually guarded, however, in this section from penetration." [28]

In his official report, Winslow had an explanation for the chains. He said the *Alabama* was so heavily laden with coal—three hundred fifty tons, including one hundred and fifty taken on at Cherbourg—as to be brought down in the water. The *Kearsarge*, on the other hand, had only one hundred twenty tons, "but as an offset to this her sheet chains were stowed outside—stopped up and down as an additional preventive and protection to her more empty bunkers." [29]

The one man fatally wounded on the *Kearsarge* was William Gowin. He had dragged himself to the forward hatch, refusing to allow the men to leave his gun to assist him. He lay dying when the *Alabama* surrendered. When he heard the cheers from his shipmates, he insisted that the doctor working over him should go up on deck and join them, saying he would be willing to bear a dozen such wounds to hear that sound. Gowin would not be forgotten. A monument in his memory was planned at Cherbourg, and resident Americans in Paris got together a sum of money to pay for a similar memorial in his native town in Michigan. [30]

As the *Kearsarge* came out of action, an unexploded one-hundred-pound rifle shell in her sternpost gave Winslow concern. Had it exploded when it struck, the vessel would have foundered fifteen minutes after the fight started. [31] But there it stayed, until the post was sawed off at the Boston Navy Yard the following January and the part containing the shell boxed and sent to Gideon Welles for presentation to President Lincoln, who had expressed a desire for it. [32]

One hundred seventy-three shots had been fired by the *Kearsarge;* the *Alabama,* it was estimated, used twice that many. [33] On board the latter, the carnage was terrible. Some of her crew were literally torn to pieces by an eleven-inch shell, and others were mutilated by splinters. The final official count was thirteen dead and seventeen wounded, but men on both sides estimated the total was nearer forty.

In July, Winslow received notice from Gideon Welles that he was to be advanced to the grade of commodore and to receive a vote of thanks from Congress. "I congratulate you on your good fortune in meeting the *Alabama,* which had so long avoided the fastest ships and some of the most vigilant and intelligent officers of the service," the Secretary wrote, "and for the ability displayed in the contest you have the thanks of the Department." [34]

In later communications, Welles advised Winslow against paroling prisoners, reminding him that they were generally recruited in Great Britain and had received superior training on board her Majesty's gunnery ship, the *Excellent.* He also scored Semmes, whom he described as "their ignoble leader" and "a deserter from our service and a traitor to our flag," who for nearly two years had been making piratical war on unarmed merchantmen. "That the wretched commander of the sunken corsair should have resorted to any dishonorable means to escape after his surrender," the Secretary observed, "that he should have thrown overboard the sword that was no longer his; that before encountering an armed antagonist the mercenary rover should have removed the chronometers and other plunder stolen from peaceful commerce, are not matters of surprise, for each act is characteristic of one who has been false to his country and flag." [35]

Semmes in the meantime was enjoying himself at Southampton, England. The *Deerhound* had brought him and thirty-nine others to the shelter of a neutral flag. As they steamed toward shore, some of the officers began to express their appreciation to Lancaster. The wealthy man replied: "Gentlemen, you have no need to give me any special thanks; I should have done exactly the same for the other people if they had needed it." [36]

The doughty Semmes was nursing a slight wound in the hand. His defeat he blamed on the *Kearsarge*'s chain armor and the deterioration of his powder and fuses.[37] The weeks ahead would be weeks of leisure, while he enjoyed the social life of England

and prepared to return to the war in which he had played such a prominent role. But his career on the high seas was ended; henceforth the Confederacy would keep him closer to shore. This was no discredit, and it would not affect his reputation. The record he had set during his years abroad in the *Sumter* and *Alabama* would stand for future generations to study: three hundred five ships overhauled; ten bonded for $562,250; and fifty-five, valued at $4,613,914, burned—a contribution to the war effort in money and destruction of better than five million dollars.

Damn the torpedoes!

AUGUST 1864

Northerners and Southerners were alike in their thinking by the summer of 1864 that action was long overdue around Mobile Bay, one of the major channels through which the Confederacy was getting its support from abroad. If David Glasgow Farragut had had his way, it would have been closed off from the sea in '62, immediately after the fall of New Orleans. But his efforts to bring this about failed.

Even while his ships, a few days after the New Orleans episode, moved up the Mississippi to pound Vicksburg, he argued with Navy officials at Washington that he should be going in the opposite direction, toward the Gulf of Mexico, to capture the harbor of Mobile before the Confederates could make it a stronghold. The goal he had in mind at the time was control of the bay rather than capture of the city, for he suspected that his heavy vessels might have trouble getting up to the wharf.

But more than two years passed before Farragut had his way.[1] In the meantime, Admiral Franklin Buchanan, recovered from his wound received while commanding the C.S.S. *Merri-*

mack, had been sent to organize the naval defenses of this important Southern port.

Mobile was thirty miles from the Gulf of Mexico, at the northern end of a bay that widened from six miles at the upper end to fifteen at the lower. Separating this body of water from the Gulf were narrow arms of sand—Mobile Point, extending out from the mainland, on the east, and Dauphin Island, three miles farther west. The main channel, the route Farragut would have to follow, ran between them, curving in close to Mobile Point. Off to the northwest about six miles was another entrance, through Grant's Pass, but this was navigable only by light-draft boats.

Three forts protected the lower bay. The major work was Fort Morgan on Mobile Point, on the site of old Fort Bowyer that had repelled the British in 1814. It was a pentagonal bastioned fortification of brick, intended to be armed with guns both in casemates and *en barbette,* but the Confederates had made changes, one of which provided an exterior water battery. Next in importance was Fort Gaines, on the eastern tip of Dauphin Island, too far away from the main channel to provide much of a threat. The third was Fort Powell in Grant's Pass, still only partially completed, although it had several guns in position and ready for action. Farragut knew he would have to worry only about Fort Morgan. He was also aware that the Southerners had been busy sinking piles and laying water mines from Fort Gaines eastward, leaving open only a part of the main channel nearest Fort Morgan, this chiefly for the benefit of blockade-runners. Three lines of mines had been floated, the eastern extremity marked by a red buoy one hundred and sixty yards west of Fort Morgan.

Reports brought in by refugees toward the end of '63 indicated to the Federals that the Confederates were placing much of their faith for a successful defense of Mobile in ironclads. One, the C.S.S. *Tennessee,* was said to be building at Selma, Alabama.[2] She was reported to be about two hundred feet long, covered with four inches of iron, fortified with compressed cot-

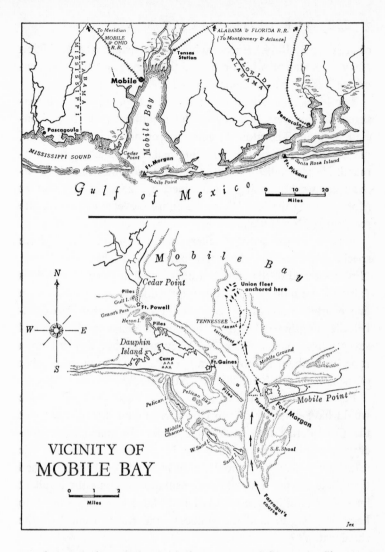

VICINITY OF
MOBILE BAY

ton between her timbers, and to carry eight guns. She was
thought to be more dangerous than the *Merrimack*.[3]

At this time, Farragut, sojourning in New York, was preparing to return to active duty. When news of the Rebel strength
amassed at Mobile reached him at the Astor House, where he
was stopping, he went over to the Navy Yard and stepped up
plans to sail. He expected to be ready for sea by the evening

of January 3, 1864.[4] Encouraging his departure was the Union Navy Department, which repeated the intelligence that the *Tennessee* was more formidable than the *Merrimack*.[5]

The blockading squadron at Mobile at the start of '64 consisted of nine vessels, some of them gunboats, but none ironclad. Captain Thornton A. Jenkins, senior officer in the area, made strong note of the "present weakened state" of his command. He also called special attention to a rumor that the Confederates were planning a combined operation by the fleet at Mobile and in the Red River, the entire movement aimed at the recapture of New Orleans.[6]

Jenkins passed along further information that would have special significance when the battle of Mobile developed: "From the end of the piles that cross the flats from Fort Gaines (about three months ago), thirty torpedoes were laid down on a line bearing southeast by compass across the main ship channel; they are shaped like a can buoy, with a chamber in each and seventy-five pounds of powder. They are anchored with manila rope, with about the third of a bar of railroad iron. A number of them broke adrift and floated up the bay." [7]

Farragut arrived at Pensacola Navy Yard January 17. He would have gone directly to New Orleans but for a report that the Confederate fleet at Mobile, under Buchanan's great energy, was planning to attack the blockade at that point.[8] He asked emphatically for monitors, at least two of them. "If I had them," he wrote, "I should not hesitate to become the assailant instead of awaiting the attack. I must have ironclads enough to lie in the bay to hold the gunboats and rams in check in the shoal water." [9]

On the 18th, Farragut reached Mobile, there to be met with a report that the dreaded *Tennessee* was on the bar off the mouth of Dog River,[10] where she was prevented from entering the lower bay by a draft that was two feet greater than the depth on the bar. The Confederates, it was said, were trying to float her with camels.[11]

Two days later, he made a reconnaissance, going in over the

outer bar in the gunboat *Octorara,* with the *Itasca* accompanying. The day was fine and the air clear, and he managed to get within three to three and a half miles of Forts Morgan and Gaines, so close that with his glasses he could count the Rebel guns and the men who stood by them. He also could see a line of piles extending out from a point near Fort Gaines, forcing ships to keep close to Fort Morgan. No enemy vessels other than a transport were visible.

Back at his flagship, he wrote Welles: "It is depressing to see how easily false reports circulate out here, and in what a state of alarm the community is kept by the most absurd rumors. If the Department could get one or two of the ironclads down here it would put an end to this state of things and restore confidence to the people of the ports now in our possession. I feel no apprehension of Buchanan's raising the blockade of Mobile; but with such a force as he has in the bay it would be unwise to take in our wooden vessels without the means of fighting the enemy on an equal footing." [12]

By the end of January the guns were all in the *Tennessee,* and Buchanan had ordered a few officers and men on board. She was even stronger than the reports leaking to the enemy had said, for six inches of iron instead of four covered the most vulnerable part of her. But she had several defects that could have been avoided. One of these concerned her port shutters, which opened and shut on a pivot and were apt to be jammed in battle. A more serious fault was in her rudder chains, which were exposed on the afterdeck. Still another was her lack of speed. Her engines had been taken from the old river steamboat *Alonzo Child* and were too weak for their task when she was weighted down with battery, ammunition, and fuel. But the big worry at the moment was getting her over the Dog River Bar. She seemed to draw about fourteen feet, while ten feet of water on the bar was considered a very good tide.[13] Meanwhile, there was no evidence that the Federals were pressing for an attack.[14] Despite this, the Confederates were not to be caught napping. They were looking for Farragut from the waterside and an army, perhaps under General McPherson, then in Mississippi, from the landside. For these developments they could wait. At hand were enough breadstuffs to take care of twenty thousand men, and sufficient grain to afford rations for four thousand horses for six months. Ammunition was not so plentiful, but blockade-runners were slipping in with new supplies at every opportunity.

For a time, during February, the Federals were without information on the *Tennessee,* although they were positive she was not yet over Dog River Bar.[15] But work on her was progressing. By the 16th she was ready to be commissioned, and her colors were hoisted at nine that morning. Most of her officers and a sixty-three-man crew were on board. Four days later, Admiral Buchanan visited the ship and remained three hours. In a little run up the river, it was evident that a lot of lifting would have to be done to get her over the bar, for she grounded twice. Her personnel problems would soon be relieved by the War Department, which had agreed to transfer men from the Army.[16]

Farragut passed these days impatiently. He was asking for the *Brooklyn* and the *Galena,* for two thousand men to attack Fort Gaines in the rear, and especially for an ironclad: "If I had one ironclad I would go up and destroy the *Tennessee* where she lies." [17] On clear days he could see a considerable distance up the bay, but no Rebel vessels were in sight. Yet he knew they were busy. Captain J. B. Marchand of the *Lackawanna,* on the basis of information gained from six deserters, wrote him that the enemy was employing an assortment of water mines, generally made of sheet iron. Some of these, from being long in the bay, had rusted and sunk, or been washed away. "I learned that they have twenty torpedoes on the wharf, made of copper," he added, "but they do not intend to plant them until they see our vessels collected to make an attack; then it is thought they will be closely placed in the Main Ship Channel near the fort." [18]

Preliminary action occurred at Grant's Pass on February 23. Some mortars and light-draft vessels, brought over from the

Mississippi River, opened on Fort Powell and for three days continued the bombardment. It was a waste of ammunition.[19]

On March 1, the ironclad appeared. Farragut wrote Welles about it: "In my last dispatch I informed you that the ram *Tennessee* in Mobile Bay had not yet crossed Dog River Bar; but today to our great surprise she appeared in full view in the bay opposite Grant's Pass, where I was at the time, having been at work all day yesterday shelling Fort Powell. This morning at 7:00 A.M. we perceived three gunboats and two ironclads lying near the fort; about one hour afterwards the *Tennessee* made her appearance, coming down the bay. The wind freshened and she came to an anchor." [20]

Farragut was becoming increasingly impatient. In a message to the Army he warned of a night attack by the *Tennessee,* and in another he said: "You will readily understand that she can be in shoal water alongside of the beach inside of the peninsula and prevent the approach of your troops toward Fort Morgan, and that our ships, even after passing the forts, will not be able to get at her, at least none but the small vessels, who would not be able to make any impression upon her, so that now Mobile will have to be left until the arrival of the ironclads. When that will be, God only knows." [21]

But a day or two later, Farragut was reversing his information about the *Tennessee.* A spell of bad weather set in. At first he wrote: "We are in the dark as to the fate of the ram *Tennessee;* some say she had not yet crossed Dog River Bar; some that she has come down, I among the latter; those who were looking at her when the norther struck her say (some of them) that she went down, others that she went up the bay in tow of the other steamers. The deserters I will send you will say that she never came over the bar, but I saw a vessel that I do not believe could be anything but the *Tennessee.*" A little later he announced that he had been mistaken. He had authentic news that the ram was alongside the wharf at Mobile, with camels attached, and that the Confederates had little hope of raising her sufficiently to get her over the bar.[22] He described her as three hundred feet long, protruding three feet above water.

The Confederates were indeed having trouble. The camels they constructed lifted the vessel only twenty-two inches, whereas the lowest calculation indicated she would have to be lightened at least four feet.[23] Engineers now were building sectional docks, hoping they would give the added lift.

The work went on around the clock. Then at midnight one night, a mechanic dropped a lighted candle into a parcel of cotton used for calking and started a fire that destroyed three of the docks.[24] The building of new docks was started immediately.

On April 4, Farragut wrote a letter home:

"I suppose you saw the notice of me as 'Jack the Giant Killer,' declaring that, when I had taken Mobile, they would give me a suitable force to take Charleston, and then run me for President of the United States! As if a man who had toiled up the ladder of life for fifty-two years and reached the top round in his profession did not need a little rest. My own opinion is that, if I survived these two engagements, there is little doubt that a Presidential campaign would finish me. No, after I have finished my work, I hope to be allowed to spend the remainder of my days in peace and quiet with my family on the banks of the Hudson.

"This is a day to try men's hearts. It is blowing a perfect gale. The wind is howling, the rain is pouring down in torrents, and the quick flashes of lightning and heavy peals of thunder all combine to create melancholia. . . . My cabin is all afloat with rain running down from the heretofore undiscovered leaks." [25]

Soon he was temporarily disabled: "I write flat on my back. I am just getting over a boil that would humble the greatest hero that ever fought a ram." [26]

May arrived, and with it, heat that Confederate and Federal alike long remembered. "Whew! How hot it is!" an officer on board the C.S.S. *Gaines* wrote his sweetheart. "Not a breath of air does the wind-sail send down. It is much cooler below than on deck." [27]

While waiting for action everyone knew someday would come, this fellow spent his time at song:

> "You had better stay at home with the girl you love so dear
> "Than venture your sweet life in the bold privateer."

Sometimes he wrote glowingly: "Five of our guns can whip a fleet of Yankees." Food now and then was good: "I had such a breakfast this morning! Hot coffee and nice rolls, stewed oysters, fried croakers, and tomatoes." And so was the fishing: "I have four splended sheepheads and a pair of red fish in our bathtub." But eventually his tastes changed: "It is really quite a relief to get rid of the interminable fishing and oystering (we have got tired of them) and the nightly beating to quarters and making extensive preparations for an enemy that never comes, and we will never go to him." At night he lay with others on deck and watched the blackened runners slip through the darkness out toward the sea, and his eyes invariably turned toward the great U.S.S. *Colorado* whose lights loomed above those of the smaller blockaders five miles away. Occasionally across the water wafted the notes of a calliope on board a steamer at the wharf, with "Dixie" the tune most often played. One day he went ashore and found Mobile swarming with strangers from New Orleans, Memphis, and other points, and with two companions, paid thirty-two dollars and fifty cents for a dinner that was plain, except for a dish of scalloped oysters and a stale, sour pineapple. Daily his admiration centered on Buchanan, and he eventually forwarded this description of the Admiral to his sweetheart: "He is probably sixty-five years old, though his form, appearance and remarkable energy would not induce you to take him to be over forty-five. He is bald on top of his head, has blue eyes, a large roman nose, which is rather a 'hawk-bill,' and a clear, fine, youthful complexion. In his manner he is quick and positive, and I take him to be very impulsive. He is by no means an old man. So far I am very much pleased with him."

Out among the blockaders, Farragut was not so resigned to his fate as this animated young Southern sailor. The veteran Admiral wrote Welles in disgust: "It appears that it takes us twice as long to build an ironclad as anyone else. . . . While the Rebels are bending their whole energies to the war, our people appear to be expecting the war to close by default, and if they do not awake to a sense of their danger soon it will be so." [28] In a letter home, he revealed that he was depressed by the bad news from every direction. "The enemy seem to be bending their whole soul and body to the war, and whipping us in every direction," he wrote. "What a disgrace that, with their slender means, they should, after three years, contend with us from one end of the country to the other, after we had taken nearly half of their land!" And a few days later he said in a note to his son: "One thing appears to be certain, that I can get none of the ironclads. They want them all for Washington. We will trust in God, as we have always done before." [29] He had information that Buchanan would be out in a week. [30]

On May 18, the *Tennessee* got over Dog River Bar. That night, a night so full of moonlight that sailors could sit on deck and write in their diaries, [31] Buchanan wanted to give her a run against the enemy, but his plan was upset when he found her hard aground. [32] Two days later she appeared in the lower bay. To a point near Fort Morgan she steamed, and there dropped anchor, surrounded by several smaller vessels.

At ten o'clock on the morning of May 22, Admiral Buchanan hoisted his flag on the ram, inspected the crew aft, and addressed to the members a few remarks aimed to curb their impatience. [33]

The tenseness around Mobile Bay tightened. Confederates placed more torpedoes at various points, and Buchanan notified the Army: "It is likely that torpedoes will soon be placed at Fort Morgan also, extending from the west bank easterly toward the fort, so as to occupy three-fourths of the channel's width." [34]

The Federals were watching with concern. Farragut ran in-shore on May 24 and took a good look at the *Tennessee.* He saw the blue flag of Admiral Buchanan, stared at the ominous ports of the ironclad, having information that seven-inch Brooke rifles and ten-inch columbiads were to be fired through the openings, and he examined with much concern a torpedo fix-ture on her bow. News of the formidable Confederate water mines had been of growing concern to him, and at this stage he wrote Welles: "Torpedoes are not so agreeable when used on both sides; therefore I have reluctantly brought myself to it. I have always deemed it unworthy of a chivalrous nation, but it does not do to give your enemy such a decided superiority over you." [35]

The next day he got off a letter on the subject to Acting Rear Admiral Theodorus Bailey, commanding the East Gulf Squad-ron: "I am watching Buchanan in the ram *Tennessee;* she is a formidable-looking thing. . . . I can see his boats very indus-triously laying down torpedoes, so I judge that he is quite as much afraid of our going in as we are of his coming out, but I have come to the conclusion to fight the devil with fire, and therefore shall attach a torpedo to the bow of each ship and see how it will work on the Rebels—if they can stand blow-ing up any better than we can." [36]

By the first of June the weather was so hot that Confederate officers were accorded a bit of humane consideration: they could wear their gray flannel frock or sack coats with navy buttons, gray pantaloons, and vests—a bit of respite, but not much.

As June advanced, the Federals expected Buchanan to run out any dark night. In turn, Buchanan was looking for Farragut to run in, and he was aware that his forces had never been able to obstruct the channel effectually against such a thing. Farragut was becoming more impatient than ever, declaring in a letter home: "I am tired of watching Buchanan . . . and wish from the bottom of my heart that Buck would come out and try his hand upon us. This question has to be settled, iron versus wood; and there never was a better chance to settle the question as to the sea-going qualities of ironclad ships. We are today ready to try anything that comes along, be it wood or iron, in reasonable quantities. . . ." [37]

The Confederates looked out toward the sea on July 5 and counted seventeen ships in Farragut's fleet. There were rumors from Charleston that monitors were on their way to join him. For several days there had been an exchange of fire at long range between the fleet and Fort Morgan, and some of the Federal shells had been aimed at the runner *Ivanhoe,* which had run ashore near the fort. It was reported in Mobile that Union General Edward Canby, who had succeeded Banks after the unsuccessful Red River campaign, had been to see Farragut, preparatory to attacking the city by land with an army of twenty thousand to thirty thousand men. The effective Southern force to combat an offensive at the moment was four thousand three hundred thirty-seven. [38]

In the face of this diversity of strength, the Confederates put down more water mines. Farragut again was watching. In a supplementary general order he warned the fleet: "There are certain black buoys placed by the enemy from the piles on the west side of the channel across it towards Fort Morgan. It being understood that there are torpedoes and other obstructions between the buoys, the vessels will take care to pass eastward of the easternmost buoy, which is clear of all obstructions." This "easternmost" buoy was the red buoy one hundred and sixty yards west of Fort Morgan, and from that day on, Federal eyes watched it intently. [39] They knew there were three lines of torpedoes, none east of this buoy. But the channel left open to the attackers would bring their fleet too near the guns of Fort Morgan. Farragut knew he would have to open a way farther west.

Two Army officers arrived on board the *Hartford* on the 8th. They were Generals Canby and Granger, and they had come to discuss plans for a joint operation against Forts Morgan and Gaines. It was agreed that all the troops that could be spared would be sent to co-operate with the fleet.

So impatient was Farragut for action that as early as July 12 he prepared orders outlining preliminary battle plans: "Strip your vessels and prepare for the conflict. Send down all your superfluous spars and rigging. Trice up or remove the whiskers. Put up the splinter nets on the starboard side, and barricade the wheel and steersman with sails and hammocks. Lay chains or sand bags on the deck over the machinery, to resist a plunging fire. Hang the sheet chains over the side, or make any other arrangement for security that your ingenuity may suggest. Land your starboard boats or lower and tow them on the port side, and lower the port boats down to the water's edge. Place a leadsman and the pilot in the port quarter boat, or the one most convenient to the commander." [40]

The flagship was to lead, steering from Sand Island north by east until abreast of Fort Morgan. There it would turn northwest half north until past the Middle Ground, then north by west into the bay. The ships were to open fire the moment the Confederates did and, when within three hundred or four hundred yards of the fort, were to use grape.

By the middle of July, Farragut was like a lion in a cage. He wrote Admiral Bailey about his concern over Buchanan's inactivity: "Now is the time; the sea is as calm as possible and everything propitious for his ironclads to attack us; still he remains behind the fort, and I suppose it will be the old story over again. If he won't visit me, I will have to visit him. I am all ready as soon as soldiers arrive to stop up the back door of each fort. I can form no idea when we will make the attack. . . ." [41]

For some time, Farragut had been working out his battle plans. This he did with little wooden blocks shaped like boats that he had had a carpenter make for him. These were experimented with on a table on which the points of the compass had been traced, the objective being to find the best position of the vessels with reference to each other in entering the bay. [42] As finally worked out, he would go in with fourteen vessels, lashed together two and two as at Port Hudson. As they advanced, the ships would be under low steam, on the flood tide of the morning, with a light southwest wind, the ironclads on the eastern side next to Fort Morgan to attack the *Tennessee,* and the gunboats toward the west, ready to go after the Rebel fleet as soon as they were past the forts. Other vessels would be left outside to assist the Army in landing on the beach and flanking the enemy.

Farragut at this period also began to give some attention to the water mines. He believed that many of them were leaky and would not explode, and also that a good many probably had drifted from their moorings.[43] With this in mind, he began sending out boat crews at night under command of his young flag lieutenant, John Crittenden Watson, grandson of John Crittenden, the eminent statesman and anti-secessionist from Kentucky. This officer was the Admiral's favorite. Often he sat patiently reading to the fleet commander from the Bible. When someone had to be sent out on an important mission or to carry a message, Watson got the nod.

The boat crews, working after dark, would row until they found the line of buoys, then fumble around until they located the torpedoes anchored a few feet under water. The next problem was that of sinking them, lifting them from the water, or cutting adrift the buoys to which they were anchored. Ropes were freely used, and efforts were greatly aided by the fact that many of the explosives were duds. On the night of July 25, boats from the *Hartford, Monongahela,* and *Sebago* went out into the channel to work at this risky business, and the last of the three did not return until 4:00 A.M.[44]

Meanwhile, Farragut tried to goad Canby into action: "As the winds give some evidence in the last three days of an early fall, time is very precious with us, and I can not urge too strongly upon you the necessity of bringing all your forces up into Mississippi Sound and landing a force first in the rear of Fort Gaines. The menace is good, for they are now transporting everything over to Morgan from Gaines and doing everything they can to increase the strength of Morgan. But my reason is stronger than that. Gaines must fall to make my communication good. When I once get inside I can approach within three-fourths of a mile, with the vessels, of Gaines, and as close as I please with the New Orleans monitors." [45]

The Confederates, on July 27, watched Union boats sounding near the channel abreast of Fort Morgan. It was noticed that they kept constantly clear of the line of torpedoes, which would indicate their knowledge of the location. Directing them was Watson, aided by Martin Freeman, the flagship's pilot. They went up toward Little Pelican Pass and placed buoys, and later in the day they buoyed out an anchorage for the monitors over near Sand Island. Towing them was the little steam tug *Cowslip*. [46]

A few hours later, a Federal monitor and two small gunboats steamed inside of Sand Island and anchored, and then a double-turreted monitor came from the westward and stopped close in to the north of the island. [47]

Farragut was almost wild with anticipation. Captain Percival Drayton, in command of the flagship, wrote a fellow officer: "The admiral talks as usual as if he were going in in the morning, but he can't go against fate, which is here represented by the Army and the ironclads. I think myself it would not be a bad thing to get also an idea of the obstructions, which, so far, on account of the weather, it has been impossible to manage, for it is evidently on them, not on the guns, the enemy depends for safety." [48]

Again, on the 28th, the *Cowslip* towed Watson and his crew into position, and they remained out all day, busily sounding and marking with buoys. It was 7:30 P.M. when they returned. [49]

They were back on the job on the 29th. That day the *Hartford*'s crew was engaged in getting up starboard sheet chains and hanging them over the starboard side to protect the ship from the fire of Fort Morgan. Once more, on the 30th, they were out in daylight, marking locations. [50]

On the 31st, the three Confederate ships could be seen moving in behind Fort Morgan. That night, Watson led an expedition out into the channel to feel for torpedoes. He was in a large cutter, armed and equipped for action, moving with muffled oars.[51] They labored so diligently that it was five-thirty in the morning when they returned to their ships.[52]

The first day of August the Confederates noticed a decided increase in the number of vessels waiting outside the bay. They had been stripped of the nonessentials. One eyewitness observed: "They appeared like prize fighters ready for the ring." [53]

The following night, Watson continued his dangerous task. He repeated it on the 2nd, going out so far this time that he was able to return with five deserters from Fort Gaines.[54]

August 2 was a day of strain for the Federals. Frequently they cast their eyes in the direction from which the *Tecumseh* would come. Drayton hurried off a message to Captain Jenkins, who had gone to Pensacola to escort the monitor: "We are anxiously looking for you all. . . . I don't believe the admiral will wait much longer, but go in with the force he has, which will get in if any can. . . . The Army lands tomorrow, and today was an excellent one for our going in." [55] The day before, General Granger, a partly bald officer with a face full of whiskers, had had dinner with Farragut.

Drayton repeated, on the 3rd, his efforts to stir Jenkins: "If you can get the *Tecumseh* out tomorrow, do so; otherwise I am pretty certain that the admiral won't wait for her. Indeed I think a very little persuasion would have taken him in today, and less tomorrow. The Army are to land at once, and the admiral does not want to be thought remiss."

As predicted, a division of Federal troops under Granger landed on August 3 on the west end of Dauphin Island and began preparations for a siege of Fort Gaines. Watching them, Farragut wrote: "I can lose no more days. I must go in day after tomorrow morning at daylight or a little later. It is a bad time, but when you do not take fortune at her offer you must take her as you can find her." At nine o'clock that night, a severe squall set in, and for a time the sailors enjoyed the beauty of a sea of white caps illuminated by flashes of lightning.[56]

As darkness settled that evening, Watson led another crew out to remove the mines. With him this time went Alexander McKinley, Farragut's secretary, as well as Pilot Freeman.[57] It was 8:15 P.M. when they shoved off in two boats from the *Hartford* and the second cutter from the U.S.S. *Manhattan,* the latter under command of Acting Ensign C. W. Snow. At 9:10, signal lights began flashing from the forts, and the men in the open boats began to wonder if they had been discovered. But no gunfire followed, and they worked on through the hours of darkness, boring holes to deactivate some of the explosives, sinking others. They started on the return at daylight and were all back on board their ships at 7:05 A.M.[58]

Entrenchments were thrown up on Dauphin Island on the 4th, and that afternoon Farragut made a reconnaissance in the steam tender *Cowslip,* running inside of Sand Island where the monitors were anchored and within easy range of both forts. With him were the commanding officers of the various ships, outstanding among them Captain Drayton, the South Carolinian who had opposed his brother, Thomas, in the battle of Port Royal.[59] A fellow officer described him as "the man of all men to be Farragut's chief of staff, gentlemanly and courteous to all, a man of marked intellect and power." [60]

What Farragut saw on this final trip to look around made no change in his determination to force his way into Mobile Bay. Just around Mobile Point, behind Fort Morgan, he could see three gunboats and the *Tennessee.* "She looks like a great turtle," wrote Lieutenant John C. Kinney, signal officer on the *Hartford.*[61]

On the return, Farragut called a council of war. He already had consented to let the *Brooklyn* lead the line of advance because it was equipped with a cowcatcher, or torpedo-removing device.[62] His officers had argued, too, that the flagship should not be too much exposed. He was reluctant to give in at first, and later said in a report: "This I believe to be an error, for apart from the fact that exposure is one of the penalties of rank in the Navy, it will always be the aim of the enemy to destroy the flagship." [63]

As he planned it, the ships would be lashed together in pairs, one floating the other in case it became disabled. They were to proceed in this order, with the first-named vessel on the right, next to Fort Morgan: *Brooklyn* and *Octorara, Hartford* and *Metacomet, Richmond* and *Port Royal, Lackawanna* and *Seminole, Monongahela* and *Kennebec, Ossipee* and *Itasca, Oneida* and *Galena*. Farther to the right and a little in advance would move the monitors: the *Tecumseh, Manhattan, Winnebago,* and *Chickasaw*. Twelve wooden ships would be left outside for purposes of blockade and external co-operation.

At some time during the day, Farragut worked carefully over a personal message. "My dearest Wife," it read, "I write and leave this letter for you. I am going into Mobile Bay in the morning, if God is my leader, as I hope He is, and in Him I place my trust. If He thinks it is the proper place for me to die, I am ready to submit to His will, in that as all other things. My great mortification is that my vessels, the ironclads, were not ready to have gone in yesterday. The Army landed last night, and are in full view of us this morning, and the *Tecumseh* has not yet arrived from Pensacola. . . ." [64]

It was now obvious to the Confederates that the enemy was ready to attempt the passage of the forts.[65] Before sunset the *Tecumseh* appeared. She was a single-turreted monitor, a formidable vessel not quite a year old. Sight of her boosted the morale of the fleet. She worked her way up to the other monitors, and there dropped anchor. Southern eyes four miles away stared at her and at the other monitors. Thick, black smoke rose above their lengthy, dark lines, appearing at times, as swells blocked the view, to rise out of the sea itself.

The day closed at 10:45 P.M. with two loud reports of heavy guns from Fort Gaines. Off and on throughout the morning and afternoon, the fort had had brief exchanges with the monitor

Winnebago, action brought on by the Federals when they saw infantry being unloaded on the beach.

Farragut hoped to get under way by daylight, but sometime after midnight a dense fog developed, delaying the movement of vessels in forming line. Despite this setback to plans, all hands were called at 3:00 A.M., hammocks were stowed, and breakfast served. A Coston light burning in the center of the fleet was signal for activity, and so were red and green lights on the flagship. Sailors on board some of the vessels saw a comet flare up and bear northeast, in the direction they soon would follow to get into Mobile Bay, and they wondered if it were a celestial omen from the Almighty.[66]

At dawn a light breeze came on, scattering the fog and leaving a clear, sunny August day. At fifteen minutes before six o'clock, the *Brooklyn,* in the lead, started moving out of Pelican Bay toward the channel leading into Mobile Bay. Near Sand Island, she and the *Octorara* lashed to her stopped, and her crew was mustered on the quarter-deck. When the men had all assembled, Captain Alden directed the executive officer to read a prayer. At its end, the captain addressed them briefly, speaking against a background of noise from the gulls and the pelicans and other aquatic fowl resentful of this interference in their normally peaceful lives. He said the fleet was about to go into battle, that the sailors knew him better than he knew them, but that he was sure they were going to hand the Rebels what they called "Jessie," and that before going further they would give three cheers. Voices rang loudly across the misty waters on a day that would make history, and the cheers were picked up by sailors on board the other vessels following at intervals of two hundred to three hundred yards.[67] Off to the right a golden summer sun was climbing above the horizon, promising heat, and at the moment the wind had stiffened and was blowing from the west, so that it would take smoke from the fleet's guns directly into the eyes of the men in the fort.[68]

Perhaps never had there been such a disparity of strength

between two hostile fleets about to engage in battle. Union vessels, including those left on the outside, numbered thirty, four protected by iron, with a total of two hundred fifty-two guns, including howitzers, and crews totaling three thousand men. The Confederates had a lone ironclad and three gunboats, with twenty-two guns and four hundred seventy men, exclusive of the guns and the garrisons in the forts. Their gunboats had been hastily constructed: all were unarmored except for light iron plating around their boilers and machinery, their frames were of unseasoned wood, and their engines were much too small.[69]

At 6:22 A.M. the *Tecumseh,* leading the monitors by several yards, fired the first shot.[70] It was a fifteen-inch shell filled with sixty pounds of powder and cylindrical flathead bolts. It exploded over Fort Morgan. The fort replied at 7:06. A surgeon on board the U.S.S. *Lackawanna* had a lasting impression from the view of this first shell from Mobile Point. "It is a curious sight to catch a single shot from so heavy a piece of ordnance," he recalled. "First you see the puff of white smoke upon the distant ramparts, and then you see the shot coming, looking exactly as if some gigantic hand had thrown in play a ball toward you. By the time it is half way, you get the boom of the report, and then the howl of the missile, which apparently grows so rapidly in size that every green hand on board who can see it is certain that it will hit him between the eyes. Then, as it goes past with a shriek like a thousand devils, the inclination to do reverence is so strong that it is almost impossible to resist it." [71]

A few minutes later the entire fleet came within range and began firing. They were answered by the fort and by the Confederate ships around the point behind the fort.[72]

At sight of the approaching fleet, Buchanan assembled the officers and crew of the *Tennessee* on her gun deck and made a little speech. It was broken and rambling, but effective because of its sincerity:

"Now, men, the enemy is coming, and I want you to do your duty; and you shall not have it to say when you leave this vessel that you were not near enough to the enemy, for I shall meet them, and then you can fight them alongside of their own ships; and if I fall, lay me on the side and go on with the fight, and never mind me—but whip and sink the Yankees or fight until you sink yourselves, but do not surrender." [73]

The wooden vessels in Farragut's line moved more rapidly than the heavier monitors. As they arrived opposite the fort, the *Brooklyn* came abreast the rear monitor, the *Chickasaw,* and, to keep from taking the lead, stopped and began making signals. Signal Officer Kinney on the *Hartford* read them: "The monitors are right ahead. We cannot go on without passing them. What shall we do?" [74]

Farragut told his signal officer to reply: "Go ahead." [75]

Still the *Brooklyn* did not advance, but began backing. The eyes of the Federals were turned suddenly in another direction. Drayton of the *Hartford* recorded: "About 7:35 I heard the cry that a monitor was sinking, and looking on the starboard bow saw the turret of the *Tecumseh* just disappearing under the water, where an instant before I had seen this noble vessel pushing on gallantly in a straight line to attack the enemy's ram *Tennessee,* which had apparently moved out to give her an opportunity." [76]

"Sunk by a torpedo!" reported Captain James Alden of the *Brooklyn.* "Assassination in its worst form! A glorious though terrible end for our noble friends, the intrepid pioneers of that death-strewed path. Immortal fame is theirs; peace to their names." [77]

Down with the *Tecumseh* went all but a score or so of her crew, as well as her captain, Tunis Augustus M. Craven.[78] In the last few seconds that the vessel was afloat, he met his pilot, John Collins, at the foot of the ladder leading to the top. The vessel was careening so that water was pouring in the turret.[79]

Collins drew back. "Go ahead, Captain!"

"No, sir," said the captain. "After you, Pilot. I leave my ship last."

Collins hurried up the ladder. As he reached the top rung, the *Tecumseh* sank beneath the surface.[80]

Onlookers noted the position where she went down and re-marked that Craven in the excitement of battle had allowed his ship to veer from the designated course.[81]

On Farragut's orders, a boat put out from the *Metacomet* to rescue survivors, some of whom could be seen floundering in the water. The roar of battle went on, but no shells from Fort Morgan were aimed at the rescuers. This was the work of the fort's commander, General Richard L. Page, a Virginian brought up in the U. S. Navy, serving a part of the time with Farragut.

But Page, transferred from the Confederacy's Navy to its Army, made sure that the fire from Fort Morgan aimed at the ships was murderous. On the *Hartford* the men were falling one after another. Bodies of the dead were placed in a row on the portside, while so many wounded were sent below that the surgeons' quarters overflowed. A solid shot from the fort struck a gunner in the neck, beheading him. Another took off the legs of a man, and as he fell forward, still another shot carried away both arms.

Finding his view blocked by the low-hanging smoke from the guns, Farragut climbed the rigging of the mainmast as far as the futtock shrouds immediately below the maintop. From the deck below, Captain Drayton saw him and ordered Signal Quartermaster Knowles to tie a rope around him to prevent his falling. Farragut at first protested against this precaution, but finally consented, himself passing two or three turns of the rope around his body and fastening the end.

The Admiral now turned his attention to the *Brooklyn,* still backing and starting. Alden, her commander, later explained this action: "We were now somewhat inside of the fort, where shoal water was reported, and at the same time, as the smoke cleared up a little, a row of suspicious-looking buoys was discovered directly under our bows." [82]

Informed by the pilot, Martin Freeman,[83] directly above him in the maintop, that there was enough water for the *Hartford* to pass to the left of the *Brooklyn,* Farragut shouted, "I will take the lead!" [84]

Someone reminded him of the torpedoes.

"Damn the torpedoes!" he shouted. "Full speed ahead!" [85]

And ahead he went, to the left of the *Brooklyn,* to the west of the red buoy, over the ground where boat crews at night had worked so diligently. The other ships of the fleet followed him.

As the *Hartford* ran up into the bay, the *Tennessee* swung out into the main channel and followed her. Already the Confederate ship's pilot was out of action, injured by the fall of the trap door to the pilothouse when it was struck by a shell; and his place was taken by Commander Johnston.[86]

Off on the starboard bow, the *Selma, Gaines,* and *Morgan* were inflicting galling punishment, demonstrating with the rapidity of their fire, from a distance of seven hundred to a thousand yards, that their gunnery crews were well practiced. In the log of Farragut's flagship were written in ink these terse lines: "Very sharp engagement of the *Hartford* with the *Morgan, Gaines* and *Selma.* Our men falling rapidly."

Cheer after cheer, some Northern, some Southern, were flung out on the air as the battle raged. Now in the broader waters of the bay, some of the smaller vessels in the Union line were cast loose from their larger mates, and, although hampered by scarcity of competent pilots, they concentrated their attack on the three Confederate gunboats. It was a sideline action that went on for nearly an hour, interrupted at one point by a sudden squall that came up out of the Gulf, but it eventually ended in dismay for the Southerners. After a lively chase, the *Selma* was overtaken and forced to surrender by the *Metacomet.*[87] The *Gaines* was disabled and run ashore, and soon was enveloped in flames. More fortunate, the *Morgan* was in position to run back under the protection of the fort, and from there, after dark, she ran toward Mobile, keeping close inshore.

The chase between the *Tennessee* and the *Hartford* continued only a short distance. Easily outrun, the ironclad turned back toward the *Brooklyn* and the *Richmond,* both close together. The other ships in the line waited expectantly; if she struck either of the vessels, the concussion would throw her portside to their advantage, so that they could sink her. But they were disappointed. When a hundred yards or so away from the Union ships, the ram sheered off and sent two shots through the *Brooklyn*'s sides, doing considerable damage. Quickly the *Richmond* fired at her three broadsides, but there was no apparent effect.

The *Tennessee* now headed toward the *Lackawanna,* next vessel astern. The *Monongahela* had anticipated the move and was waiting, ready to charge. The blow, by quick maneuvering on the part of the Rebel vessel, was glancing and ineffective. Grazing the bow of the *Kennebec,* damaging her planking and dropping a boat on her deck, the *Tennessee* continued toward the end of the line. There she fired two broadsides into the *Oneida.* One of the shells struck the starboard boiler and, exploding, caused death by scalding of nearly the entire watch below of firemen and coal heavers. Another shell entered at the water line, exploded in the cabin, and cut both wheel ropes. The *Tennessee* ran past, only two hundred yards away, and, astern, delivered a raking fire that severely wounded J. R. Madison Mullany, the *Oneida*'s commander. She then steamed toward Fort Morgan and rounded the point.

Four miles into the bay the *Hartford* ran before dropping anchor, shortly after nine o'clock. There she soon was joined by the other vessels of the fleet, with the exception of the *Port Royal, Kennebec,* and *Itasca,* which remained behind to watch the *Morgan* and *Tennessee.*

Farragut again had run past some of the most formidable forts in the Confederacy, and there was much elation. For the fourth time, as at New Orleans, Vicksburg, and Port Hudson, he had demonstrated that fortifications on shore could not block hostile steam vessels handled in concert and determined to pass. The one dark cloud in this new day of success for the veteran sea dog was the *Tecumseh.*

The fleet's cooks began preparing a second breakfast for crews made hungry by battle action. Down below, surgeons were busy attending the wounded, while matters on deck were approaching some degree of normality. Debris was cleared away, and the tension of the last two or three hours seemed a thing of the past—when suddenly, like a discordant note at high pitch, the cry rose above the noise of the decks: "The ram is coming!"

For half an hour the *Tennessee* had remained out of sight while Franklin Buchanan and his crew got a breather from the terrible conditions in the ironclad. The men around him watched his face closely, especially his mouth. They knew his peculiarities, and they had seen before that when he was full of fight, the corners of his mouth drooped until the thin line of his lips formed a perfect arch around his chin. They stared at him as the minutes ticked by—fifteen, twenty, thirty. Suddenly he straightened and called to the ship's captain: "Follow them up, Johnston! We can't let them off that way!" He spoke through arched lips.[88]

Around the point in the distance the Confederates could see the Union ships resting on the water like a flock of ducks. They seemed numerous, rocking gently with the waves, smoke pouring lazily from their funnels, activity on board turned from the horrors of making war to the more domestic routine of feeding hungry men.

Captain Drayton found Farragut on the poop and reported that the ironclad was headed outside to destroy the little nest of ships left as a diversion south of Fort Morgan. "Then we must follow him out," the Admiral immediately replied. But a moment later, taking up his glasses, he said: "No! Buck's coming here. Get under way at once. We must be ready for him." [89]

Preparations were made by the Union fleet for a general attack. The monitors were too slow, so wooden ships were designated to begin the battle. The *Monongahela* and the *Lackawanna,* with false iron prows, were given specific orders to run down the ram.

A young soldier, Lieutenant John L. Rapier, who had fought with Stonewall Jackson in Virginia and was now with a Confederate battalion on Dauphin Island, was looking on and described the scene shortly afterward in a letter to a friend:

"Here comes the *Tennessee!* Yes, here she comes—right for

the enemy's fleet—they scatter before her—yes, three ironclads and fourteen wooden vessels mounting two hundred guns would run from one—with six guns—did not shame and the scarcity of water prevent them. . . . Now comes a fight that throws all others in the shade. I have gazed, as upon a picture, upon the greatest fight that ever took place. . . . Well, they scatter before her. She makes for the flagship. She nearly reaches her, but Farragut glides from in front of her prow. . . . The whole fleet gathers around her—starboard, port, beam, bow, quarter —on every point. What a noise! The *Tennessee* fires with great rapidity—chiefly the broadside guns. . . . The bay for a mile around is boiling with the ricochet of the shot and shell. The *Brooklyn* moves past, delivers her broadside, then the *Hartford,* followed by the *Richmond,* but that is nothing. They make no impression. That brave old Admiral Buchanan, in contempt of danger, stands on the shield, when the *Brooklyn* at thirty yards delivers her broadside. The concussion knocks him over, but he is not hurt, and some fellow from the tops of the *B.* in his rage dashes his opera glasses at him." [90]

When the *Tennessee* approached, moving as awkwardly as a raft of logs, she headed for the *Hartford,* while still using her guns on the other vessels. Before she could strike, the *Mononga-hela,* going at full speed, struck her amidships, doing no damage to the ironclad, but tearing off her own prow and cutwater. The *Lackawanna,* close behind, delivered a similar blow, only causing the ram to lurch to one side.[91]

The two flagships approached each other, bow to bow. "The port bow of the *Hartford* met the port bow of the ram," an eyewitness related, "and the ships grated against each other as they passed. The *Hartford* poured her whole port broadside against the ram, but the solid shot merely dented the side and bounded into the air. The ram tried to return the salute, but owing to defective primers only one gun was discharged. This sent a shell through the berth deck, killing five men and wounding eight. The muzzle of the gun was so close to the *Hartford* that the powder blackened her side." [92]

Farragut stood on the quarter-deck when the vessels came together. After they parted, he jumped to the port quarter rail, holding to the mizzen rigging, a position from which he might have jumped to the deck of the ram as she passed. Seeing him in this position and fearing for his safety, Flag Lieutenant Watson slipped a rope around his waist and secured him to the rigging, the second time during the day that this had been done.

The *Tennessee* was fighting the entire fleet. The torrid heat of August was developing as the sun climbed, and the men inside the ironclad were breathing powder smoke in an atmosphere superheated to one hundred and twenty degrees. Shot was pounding her sides, and the enemy vessels were trying repeatedly to run her down.

In the *Tennessee,* the wounded were brought below in increasing numbers to Fleet Surgeon Daniel B. Conrad. Some of them, when stripped to their waists, presented a sight that at first puzzled the doctor. Beneath their skin he could see dark blue elevations which he found hard to the touch. He cut into them and found unburnt cubes of cannon powder. "Their sufferings were very severe, for it was as if they had been shot with red-hot bullets," he reported.[93]

The *Hartford* had been a primary target all morning. As fast as men fell, others stepped into the gaps; almost two entire gun crews had been swept away.[94] She turned to make for the ram again and was struck on the starboard side, amidships, by the *Lackawanna,* a collision that crushed her planking and caused general confusion. The cry rang out over the deck of the Union flagship: "Save the admiral! Save the admiral!" It was thought the ship was sinking. The port boats were ordered lowered. In their frenzy of excitement, some of the sailors cut the falls, dropping two of the cutters into the water wrong side up. Farragut loosened the ropes around his waist and sprang into the starboard mizzen rigging, and from there stared over the side at the damage. He saw the planking had been broken to within two feet of the water. Again he ordered the ship full speed ahead.

Over on the *Tennessee,* a shell struck the cover of a stern port, jamming it against the shield. Buchanan, assisting with the gun at that port, sent to the engine room for a machinist. While this fellow worked in an effort to remove the bolt of the cover, another shot struck directly above him. Sailors gathered up his remains in buckets and dumped them overboard.

This same shell that killed the mechanic sent a shower of iron splinters flying inside the shield. One struck Buchanan below the knee and broke his leg.

The water churned as the vessels swung about in a mad turmoil. The *Lackawanna* straightened out and struck the *Tennessee* again, and then came once more into the path of the *Hartford.* Farragut yelled to his signal officer: "Say to the *Lackawanna* for God's sake to get out of our way and anchor!" [95]

The flagstaff of the *Tennessee* was shot away. Most of her smokestack was missing, having been knocked down close to the top of the shield by the concussion of collision with other ships, and her steam was rapidly going down. The monitors were pounding her with eleven- and fifteen-inch solid shot. A fifteen-inch gun on the *Manhattan* made a conspicuous dent in her side. The two quarter ports, from which were fired the aftergun, were jammed. The bow port cover and the cover of the forward port on the portside were damaged, and two of the broadside port covers were entirely unshipped. Her gun primers repeatedly failed. And then a shot from the *Chickasaw* cut the ram's rudder chain, and she would no longer mind her helm. Several days before the battle, this exposed part of her steering gear had been noticed by her captain, Commander James D. Johnston, and he had reported it to Buchanan, but there had not been time enough to make alterations. [96] The chain ran along the upper side of the afterdeck, or fantail, and it should have passed under the deck, where it would have been protected.

"She was at this time sore beset," Farragut wrote in his report of the *Tennessee* at this point. "The *Chickasaw* was pounding away at her stern, the *Ossipee* was approaching her at full speed, and the *Monongahela, Lackawanna,* and this ship were bearing down upon her, determined upon her destruction." [97]

On board the *Tennessee,* Johnston went below and reported conditions to Buchanan. The Admiral, gritting his teeth with pain, listened and then instructed: "Do the best you can, sir, and when all is done, surrender." [98]

Johnston went to the top of the shield and took down the ensign, which had been fastened to the handle of a gun scraper and stuck up through the grating. Several shots passed close to him. He went below to order the engines stopped, his footsteps hurried by the noise of the battle still raging on the outside. "I then decided, although with an almost bursting heart," he later reported to Buchanan, "to hoist the white flag, and, returning again onto the shield, placed it in the same spot where but a few minutes before had floated the proud flag for whose honor I would so cheerfully have sacrificed my own life if I could possibly have become the only victim." [99]

On seeing the white flag, the *Ossipee* reversed her engine, but a harmless collision could not be avoided. As though at a general signal, the terrific cannonading now ceased, and over the waters from the victorious Federal fleet rang cheer after cheer. "Such cheers as rent the air then I never heard before," a sailor on the *Brooklyn* wrote.[100] The first shot that morning had been fired at 6:47 A.M.; it was now ten o'clock.

A voice hailed the *Tennessee:* "This is the United States steamer *Ossipee.* Hello, Johnston, how are you? Le Roy—don't you know me? I'll send a boat alongside for you."

A boat soon came across and conveyed the commander of the ironclad to the *Ossipee.* At the gangway, he was met by his life-long friend, Commander William E. Le Roy.

"I'm glad to see you, Johnston," Le Roy said. "Here's some ice water for you—I know you're dry. But I've something better for you down below."

In his cabin he placed a bottle of sherry and a pitcher of ice water before Johnston.

Soon the Confederate was on his way to the Union flagship.

"I'm sorry to meet you under such circumstances," Farragut said when they met.

"You're not half as sorry as I am," Johnston replied.

Percival Drayton spoke up: "You have one consolation, Johnston. No one can say that you have not nobly defended the honor of the Confederate flag today." [101]

One of Farragut's first acts after the cessation of battle was to send his fleet surgeon, Dr. D. B. Conrad, to attend Buchanan.[102] The medical officer was rowed to the *Tennessee,* climbed through an iron port, ascended a ladder, and found Buchanan lying "in a place like the top of a truncated pyramid." Someone announced the doctor.

"I know Dr. Conrad," Buchanan said gruffly but politely, extending a hand.

"I'm sorry to see you so badly hurt," greeted Conrad. "I'm here to learn your wishes."

"I only wish to be treated kindly as a prisoner of war."

"Admiral Buchanan," said Conrad, "you know perfectly well you will be treated kindly."

Buchanan was dejected. "I am a Southern man, an enemy and a Rebel," he said.

Conrad was for a moment offended at Buchanan's tone, but he ignored the feeling and proceeded professionally. "Admiral, you are wounded and disabled, and I shall try to have your wishes filled. Admiral Farragut will take you on board the *Hartford,* or send you to any other ship you prefer."

"I don't pretend to be Admiral Farragut's friend and have no right to ask favors of him," muttered Buchanan, "but I'll be satisfied with any decision you reach."

When Conrad returned to the *Hartford* and reported Buchanan's irritated feeling, Farragut seemed hurt, remarking that the Southerner had once professed friendship for him. Sensing an embarrassing situation, the surgeon suggested that the wounded be taken to Pensacola, and this was arranged.[103]

In his report, Mallory summed up the action in a single paragraph: "Naval history records few contests between forces so unequal in ships, guns and men, and but few in which the weaker party displayed equal heroism. Apart from graver considerations this contest possesses peculiar interest for all who are watchful of the progress of naval affairs, it being the first in which the modern and improved means of naval warfare, offensive and defensive, have been tested.[104]

Farragut's wooden fleet had plenty of evidence of the power of an ironclad. A sailor on the *Brooklyn,* on whose decks lay eleven dead and thirty wounded, walked through the ship and then wrote in his diary about the "terrible sight" that met his eyes. "The berth deck was completely riddled," he recorded. "Mess chests, bags of clothes, timbers and splinters, the greater part of the galley, shots and pieces of shells were mixed up in confusion, and these, covered with blood and mangled flesh, presented a sickening sight. All hands had worked with unprecedented bravery and so completely were we exhausted that little was done in putting things in order. We turned in as best we could, expecting on the morrow we would see the Stars and Stripes floating over some or all of these forts." [105]

The *Brooklyn* had been struck fifty-nine times in her hull, rigging, and spars. One of the shells exploded on the berth deck forward and killed or wounded every man at the two shell whips. Another whip was rigged, and men were stationed at it, only to be cleared away by a second shell that struck in almost the same place as the first.

Estimates of casualties would vary. Farragut said in his report that "this great victory cost the Union fleet three hundred and thirty-five men." A subsequent breakdown by Federal officers placed the total at one hundred seventy-two killed and one hundred seventy wounded.[106] Confederate Navy Secretary Mallory gave the South's losses as twelve killed, twenty wounded, and two hundred forty-three captured.[107]

Before going to bed that night, Farragut penned a letter to his wife: "The Almighty has smiled upon me once more. I am in Mobile Bay. . . . The *Tennessee* and Buchanan are my prisoners. . . . It was a hard fight, but Buck met his fate manfully. After we passed the forts, he came up in the ram to attack me. I made at him, and ran him down, making all the others do the same. We butted and shot at him until he surrendered. . . . They made a gallant fight, but it was all to no purpose. My ship is greatly cut up—twenty-five killed and twenty-eight wounded. I escaped, thank God! without a scratch." [108]

News of the battle was slow getting to Washington. At nine o'clock on the night of the 6th, Assistant Secretary Fox wired General Ben Butler, commanding along the Virginia coast: "Please try and get a Richmond paper to see how Farragut is getting on at Mobile. He went inside about the 1st and is attacking Fort Gaines." Butler replied next morning, relaying word of the landing of troops on Dauphin Island. It was the afternoon of the 8th before he was able to send a terse report on the outcome.

A contrast in the fighting spirit of individual officers developed in the Mobile Bay area after the battle on the 5th. That night Fort Powell was surrendered, after much of it had been blown up by the Confederates. Next morning the *Chickasaw* began shelling Fort Gaines, and the following day the fort's commander, Colonel C. D. Anderson, asked Farragut for terms. They were unconditional and were accepted without further struggle, eight hundred eighteen prisoners, including forty-six commissioned officers, twenty-six guns, a large amount of ordnance stores and ammunition, and subsistence stores for a garrison of eight hundred men for twelve months going into the hands of the Federals.

But over in Fort Morgan, fiery fifty-seven-year-old General Page was determined to defend his post to the last extremity. Farragut sent two men to talk about surrender, and was surprised at the answer he got: "I am prepared to sacrifice life and will only surrender when I have no means of defense." Page also complained that while he was being communicated with under flag of truce, the captured *Tennessee* was towed up within range of the fort.[109]

The Federals immediately began a siege, and under the worst conditions. Granger's troops found it a severe task to get guns in position along Mobile Point, owing to the great distance involved. Everything had to be packed in on men's backs. The wind and the surf and the shallow water were no help, and nearly the entire peninsula was a quagmire of deep sand, "hot enough during the day for roasting potatoes." [110]

Shelling began on the 9th. Ships took turns. The *Tennessee,* armed with guns that once had had Southern hands on their lanyards, fired from 2:00 to 4:00 P.M. one day. From 4:00 to 6:00, the *Winnebago* took over, and from 8:00 to midnight, the *Manhattan* threw occasional shots at the fort. Next morning the *Chickasaw* sent over a shell every thirty minutes, and later in the day, other vessels stepped up the pace to one every twenty minutes. Now and then the fort answered angrily, showing the determination of its commander.

At three in the morning of the 15th, while the moon was setting, a perfect rainbow was visible in the east against a heavy cloud bank. Union sailors fired their occasional shots with eyes upon it: the Bible told that there once had been a star in the east. . . . And inside the fort, young men thought of the old legend, so strong among superstitious Southerners, that a pot of gold lay at the end of the rainbow.

Fort Morgan kept up its resistance. At intervals during the 21st, a shell was fired from it every five minutes. Late in the afternoon, a bright light, low down, was seen on the east end of the fortification. Its outbuildings, to give better range for its guns, had been burned weeks earlier.

The firing from both sides kept up during the night of the 22nd, and at five o'clock next morning the bombardment became general from the Union fleet and shore batteries. Throughout the day it continued—three thousand shells in twelve hours —the *Brooklyn, Ossipee, Monongahela, Richmond, Galena, Seminole, Octorara,* and *Lackawanna* moving in close. That night a large fire broke out in the fort, followed by another shortly before midnight. At 5:00 A.M., the Confederates replied with a couple of shots, and then there was silence. Around 6:00 A.M., a heavy explosion occurred in the fort, and a few minutes later a white flag appeared.

Captain Drayton and Lieutenant Watson visited the fort at 7:00 A.M. Page handed them a note addressed to Farragut. "The further sacrifice of life being unnecessary, my sick and wounded suffering and exposed," it read, "humanity demands that I ask for terms of capitulation."

Page had reached his decision only after the situation in Fort Morgan became completely hopeless. The enemy parallels had reached the glacis of the fort, the walls were breached, and all but two of his guns were disabled. Fires started by shells so endangered the magazines that he had the powder—eighty thousand pounds of it—brought out and flooded.

That afternoon, at two o'clock, the surrender took place inside the fort. Farragut was furious over what he found. Every gun and carriage had been damaged, and everything of value in the fort, including arms, ammunition, and provisions, had been converted into a mass of debris. Moreover, Page and his officers —"with a childish spitefulness" in Farragut's opinion—had thrown away or broken their swords.

But six hundred Southerners became prisoners, adding the final touch to the closing of one of the Confederacy's remaining important ports. Only two—Charleston and Wilmington—still were open, and the offensive soon would be aimed against them. It was easier now for the Union to concentrate its forces, making the hope for the South a dying gasp. Still, the end was not at hand. There were other men like Richard Page to fight beneath the Stars and Bars, and somewhere in the North Carolina coastal waters, the dreaded *Albemarle,* most successful of the ironclads, was still at large.

Bottoms to the bottom

AUGUST 1864

C.S.S. *Tallahassee!* This name, in August, '64, flared on the horizon of war news in the manner of the *Merrimack* and the *Arkansas* and the *Albemarle.* Within a matter of hours after the Southern defeat in Mobile Bay, she began her remarkable career: thirty-three Union vessels of commerce burned, scuttled, bonded, or released in ten days, and more slated for similar treatment in the weeks ahead.

Official Washington was shocked. Welles stormed, and ships went running out from many ports to search for her. In the very beginning, it was known that she was commanded by President Zachary Taylor's grandson, John Taylor Wood, a "first family" scion already heard from many times since he gave up his teaching chores at the United States Naval Academy to join the South. The *Tallahassee* was a paragon of Confederate desperation.[1]

Sailors on blockade duty off Wilmington the night of August 6 stared until darkness at four vessels near Smithville. They were long and low, of light color, so designed as to be invisible at even short distances. Nothing about these vessels indicated any intention to escape. They lay in a group, still, close together.

At 9:10 that night, the U.S.S. *Montgomery,* patrolling off the Western Bar, with the Bald Head light east by north, saw a ship moving very slowly in a southeasterly direction three or four miles from the picket station on Oak Island beach. Suddenly, excitement erupted: a rocket toward the northeast rose in a southerly direction, and the flashes of several guns broke the darkness.

The *Montgomery* went to quarters and spread her fires. Five minutes later she was disturbed by the sight of a vessel on her port bow, moving rapidly southward. Her helm was put to port, and she steamed ahead at full speed. Soon the *Montgomery* challenged twice, but received no answer. "I think we challenged too soon," her commander, Acting Volunteer Lieutenant E. H. Faucon, reported. His opinion was based on the fact that the stranger disappeared almost immediately, and no further trace of her was seen. Another ship was sighted on the starboard bow, apparently standing to the southeast. A rocket soared in the darkened skies to the northwest, with nothing to identify it either as a signal from a blockader or a deceptive stroke by a runner. The *Montgomery* headed in that direction, her quartermaster imagining he saw vessels close inshore. But nothing developed.

The U.S.S. *Vicksburg* came even closer to one of the ships causing the disturbance. Challenges being unanswered, a rocket was fired, and a thirty-pounder percussion shell barely missed the fleeing vessel. She turned northward, then westward, then northward, standing inshore. Soon she was lost to view.

Another blockader that came close enough to send up rockets and fire guns was the U.S.S. *Emma.* But by ten o'clock she, too, had lost the trail and returned to her station.

Next morning they looked up the river toward Smithville, toward the spot where the four vessels had been seen at sunset the evening before. Only three were still there.

Off at sea, clear of the Wilmington blockaders, John Taylor

Wood was raising his admiration for the *Tallahassee,* formerly the *Atlanta,* a two-screw steam sloop cruiser his Government had entrusted to his care. British built, she was two hundred twenty feet long, with two smokestacks, three guns, and a crew of one hundred twenty men. But the most amazing thing about her was symbolized by the white foam that marked her trail. She could make seventeen knots, a factor that influenced her purchase by the Confederacy after she had made several blockade-running trips from Bermuda to Wilmington. Her one failing was her consumption of fuel—difficult to supply for a commerce-destroyer with two home ports blocked by hostile vessels. Sacrifice of some of the customary neatness about a ship was made in order to get on board all the coal possible. This caused one officer to write his sweetheart: "Most people have very romantic notions concerning the gallant *Tallahassee.* They think her perfection in everything. So she is as regards model and power, and consequently speed. But there the matter ends. We are overcrowded with men, and officers have very small quarters and plenty of dirt. It is impossible to keep clean. The coal dust on deck and from the firerooms fills the air with a fine powder which settles in and upon everything in a most pro-voking and disgusting manner." [2]

Thus laden with coal, the *Tallahassee* had to wait two days to get out of Wilmington. On her eventual run, she passed five blockaders, two of which sent shells in her direction.[3] And then next morning she was sighted by four of the offshore fleet. One ship fired at her, but she easily outdistanced them all.

For five days she ran northward, speaking and overhauling a number of vessels, all found to be European. On the 11th, eighty miles off Sandy Hook, she fell in with a Union ship, the schooner *Sarah A. Boyce.* She kept extremely busy. Before the day ended, another schooner, two brigs, two pilot boats, and a bark were added to the bag. Five of them were burned, one scut-tled, and a schooner, to which were transferred the prisoners, bonded for ten thousand dollars.

Next day the captures included three schooners, a brig, a bark, and the ship *Adriatic,* bringing immigrants to New York. Three were burned, two bonded, and one was scuttled.

And that day, messages of alarm began reaching Washington. One was from Admiral Hiram Paulding, commandant of the Brooklyn Navy Yard: "Pirate off Sandy Hook capturing and burning." Additional information followed: "They strip everybody of everything valuable. Crew badly dressed and of all nationalities." He had sent three ships in pursuit, and was readying two more.[4]

Another telegram spreading alarm bore the signature of B. S. Osbon, reporter for the New York *Herald.* "New pirate *Tallahassee,* painted white, two funnels, two screws, two hundred and thirty feet length, twenty beam, fore-and-aft schooner rig, three guns, crew one hundred and twenty all told, most soldiers," it read, "escaped from Wilmington six days ago. . . ."[5]

Admiral Lee, commanding the North Atlantic Blockading Squadron, informed the Navy Department that a two-smoke-stack steamer had escaped from Wilmington, and added: "It is quite probable, from comparison of dates, descriptions, and distances, that this was the *Tallahassee.*"[6] He was notified five days later by Secretary Welles that the *Tallahassee* had been spoken by a British brig off Cole Harbor, Nova Scotia, that she had "inflicted serious injury on our commerce," and that "increased vigilance should be exercised."[7]

Wood ran into Halifax, Novia Scotia, for coal, on August 18. He had only forty tons on board.

Within minutes after the *Tallahassee* put in her appearance, the U.S consul at Halifax, M. M. Jackson, wired Secretary Welles that she had just come into port and that he would protest her being coaled there.

The consul's protest was partially successful. Barely had Wood dropped anchor before he was given definite evidence of the change in Great Britain's attitude toward the Confederacy— a change that had been taking place for months. No one came to offer him the courtesies of the port. He found there the H.M.S.

Duncan, bearing the flag of Rear Admiral Sir James Hope, and promptly made a call. Neither on arriving or leaving was he extended the honors of the side. When he entered the ship's cabin, Hope did not rise, shake hands, or offer the visitor a seat. His manner and tone were offensive.

Wood went next to see the Lieutenant Governor, Sir Richard MacDonnell, and again the reception was "uncivil and cold." When the Confederate officer explained his need of fuel, the Lieutenant Governor replied that he might remain in port twenty-four hours, or such time as might enable him to obtain a reasonable quantity of coal, the tonnage to be estimated by Admiral Hope. He cited the proclamation of the Queen, orders in council, and other authority to sustain him, and no matter how much Wood protested, there was no relenting.

When Wood returned to the *Tallahassee,* he found, standing by to enforce the Governor's orders, eleven armed boats. Immediately he complained, knowing they had come from the frigate *Galatea,* a vessel in quarantine on account of smallpox on board. MacDonnell ordered them away.

Next day at the expiration of the twenty-four hours, the Governor saw that the *Tallahassee* was still taking on coal, and he was informed that one hundred eighty tons already had been shipped. He sent a note of protest, and Wood quickly replied that he had not yet taken on the prescribed one hundred tons and asked further time, some of it needed to ship a new mainmast. MacDonnell granted it.

That night, forty hours after she had come into port, the *Tallahassee* steamed out again, without the mainmast. But she had on board one hundred twenty tons of coal, including the amount in her bunkers when she arrived at Halifax. This was enough to get her back home, although not enough to enable her to strike along the Capes of Delaware, as Wood had planned.

Her departure was just in time. About noon the following day, the U.S. gunboat *Pontoosuc* entered the harbor at Halifax, while outside lay five other Federal cruisers, all part of a fleet of thirteen which had been started from U.S. ports as soon as the American consul in Nova Scotia telegraphed information about the arrival of the *Tallahassee.*

Wood headed straight for Wilmington, capturing and burning along the way the brig *Roan;* and on the night of the 26th, he ran in, engaging the blockading fleet as he passed. It was so dark the effect of his shot could not be seen.

Lee heard about the *Tallahassee*'s return, and immediately ordered Captain B. F. Sands, his divisional officer, to "use the utmost vigilance to prevent her escape." [8]

Confederate Navy Secretary Mallory also heard about the *Tallahassee.* In his next departmental report he devoted an important part of it to an account of her activities, and reasoned: "The immediate losses inflicted upon the enemy by these captures were greatly enhanced by the delay and detention of his commercial ships in port from a feeling of insecurity, and by the augmentation of the rates of marine insurance." [9]

In two months the North would hear more from the *Tallahassee.* She would make another run out of Wilmington, this time under the name *Olustee,* and once more she would strike heavily against Union commercial shipping. But that would be her last experience as a destroyer. In December, under command of John Wilkinson, the captain with the uncanny ability for avoiding the blockaders, she would go to sea again, this time as a runner laden with cotton. The career facing her would make her one of the last of the Confederate vessels to surrender.

Lake Erie again!

AUGUST 1864

As the summer of '64 faded, the South turned in desperation to a greater variety of stratagems. One of these pointed again to the U.S.S. *Michigan* on Lake Erie and to another attempt to release the prisoners on Johnson's Island. This effort would approach nearer its goal than did the first.

The desperation of the South spread further, even into the national election. Theorists believed the war could be brought to a quick close by a "bold, vigorous, and concerted movement" that would afford the Northwestern States, especially Illinois, Indiana, and Ohio, an opportunity "to throw off the galling dynasty of Washington and openly to take ground in favor of State rights and civil liberty." [1] Such a development would enable the border states of Kentucky and Missouri to be put on their feet, and in sixty days the hostilities would end.

Under this belief, based on the mighty power of politics, the Confederate Government at Richmond called into its confidence two ardent Southerners. One was Jacob Thompson, of Mississippi, Secretary of the Interior under President Buchanan, former schoolteacher, member of Congress, and at one time Inspector General of the Confederate Army. The other was Clement Claiborne Clay, of Alabama, a United States senator who surrendered his seat in Washington to join the Confederate Congress. Jefferson Davis gave these two agents verbal instructions in April, '64, and sent them off to Canada. For a time they operated together and then, because of Clay's poor health, they were forced to separate and to remain in touch with each other at a distance.[2]

Thompson, the more active of the two, soon got in touch with an organization known as the "Order of the Sons of Liberty in the Northern States." This brotherhood was ideal for the purpose at hand. Its organization was essentially military, and its objects were political. Members believed that the Government was based on the consent of the parties to it, that the states were the parties and were sovereign, that there was no authority in the "General Government" to coerce a seceding state. They also had a feeling that it was useless to hold a Presidential election, that Lincoln had the power and would certainly re-elect himself, and that, consequently, there was no hope but in force.

The Order received Thompson cordially. He obtained its support with little effort. Plans for a day of action were discussed. Before these could be developed, the national Democratic Convention was postponed from July 4 to August 29. As a result, July 20 was selected as the date, but later, a council was called and it was decided that August 16 would be a better time for a general uprising. Open meetings were scheduled, to prepare the public mind—one at Peoria, another at Springfield, and a third at Chicago, this last to come on the day of the uprising. The Peoria gathering was a decided success. One leading idea swayed the mind of the multitude attending—peace. Then the belief began to spread through the North that the South would agree to a reconciliation, and politicians conceived the idea that on such an issue, Lincoln could be beaten at the polls. This led to a feeling that the ballot box should be relied upon for a redress of grievances before a resort to force.

But the project began to collapse. The Springfield meeting, at which speakers endorsed the idea of voting before rising up, was a failure. Some of the leading lights of the Sons of Liberty began to relax and to lose the drive that had formerly sparked their efforts. A large lot of arms intended for Indianapolis was discovered, and some of the most influential members were charged with planning the arming of members for treasonable purposes. Treachery was apparent. J. E. McDonald, candidate for Governor of Indiana, learning of the date set for the movement and believing that it would affect his chances of election, threatened to expose the entire plan unless it was abandoned.

August 16 came. The crowd at the Chicago meeting was immense—peace a unanimous desire. General McClellan's nomination followed. And so did the arrest of prominent members of the Sons. The day of uprising was forgotten.

In the meantime, the Lake Erie plot proceeded, but with an unexpected development. Captain Charles H. Cole, of General Nathan Bedford Forrest's Confederate command, escaped from prison and sought out Jacob Thompson. He wanted to help, and Thompson accepted his offer. Soon Cole was sent around the Great Lakes with instructions to travel as a lower-deck passenger and to learn, among other things, the best way to capture or destroy the U.S.S. *Michigan*. After an absence of several days, he returned with a satisfactory report. He was sent back, this time with orders to put himself in communication with the officers of the vessel and to attempt its purchase. These efforts failed, mainly through insufficient guarantee of payment. Cole next asked permission to organize a band to capture her by force. It was granted, and to his assistance was sent Acting Master John Yates Beall, the University of Virginia graduate who had upset official Washington with his guerrilla activities on the Eastern Shore the latter part of '63.

Cole moved into Sandusky and put up at the West House, the most popular inn in town. He tossed money about at random, posing as a wealthy, retired oil operator from Pennsylvania. His guests for wining and dining were numerous, among them the officers of the U.S.S. *Michigan.* But his attention strayed, to his own undoing. He became interested in the niece of George Marsh, a leading merchant of the community. She was on a visit from Louisville, Kentucky, true to the Union, and she agreed to do what she could to confirm the suspicions of a United States Secret Service man, who had been sent into the area on the chance that Cole might be a Confederate agent.

The Southerners planned carefully. Escaped prisoners from Johnson's Island told that the men behind bars had formed an organization for the purpose of surprising the guard and capturing the island, but that the main obstacle was the presence of the *Michigan* with her fourteen guns. This obstacle, Cole and Beall were determined to eliminate. It would be done by seizure, in a beautiful example of teamwork. Cole would divert the attention of the ship's officers with another of his frequent champagne parties, while Beall would acquire a boat, load it with enough Confederate soldiers to board and take the *Michigan,* and would be ready to move in when Cole gave him the signal.

The night of September 19 was set for the attempt. That morning the *Philo Parsons,* a steamer plying between Detroit and Sandusky, left on a routine trip. Five or six passengers were on board, one of them John Yates Beall. At Malden, more passengers got on board, bringing with them a heavy box. Shortly after leaving Kelley's Island, Beall broke open the box and passed out revolvers and hatchets to his confederates. Without a single shot, the ship was captured, and toward the mouth of Sandusky Bay she was steered, there to wait after dark for a signal from Cole.

But no signal was flashed out of the night. Cole was in jail, locked up by the Secret Service agent, on information supplied by George Marsh's niece. In the early afternoon the agent had appeared at the West House. The desk clerk on duty was named Sullivan, an accommodating individual who, when asked, obligingly led the Secret Service representative down the street to a restaurant on the south side of Water Street, where sat Cole.[3]

When no signal was seen from Cole, Beall assumed something was wrong and he started back toward Canada. At Middle Bass Island he stopped for fuel. Residents who pushed on board were promptly confined, to keep them from spreading word of what had happened to the *Philo Parsons*. While there, another steamer, the *Island Queen,* on her way to Toledo with thirty-two vacationing soldiers from the One Hundred Thirtieth Regiment of Ohio Volunteer Infantry, drew alongside to take on wood. She was promptly captured and her passengers paroled, after which she was taken out into deeper water and scuttled.

Again Beall ran the *Philo Parsons* toward the mouth of Sandusky Bay and waited for a signal from Cole. After a long wait without results, he turned about and ran toward the Detroit River, beaching the vessel on Fighting Island. Then he and his men rowed to the Canadian shore and disappeared into the countryside.

Other segments of the master plan to upset the national political picture succeeded or failed in varying degree. On money advanced by Thompson, an agent was able to destroy several Federal steamboats at St. Louis. Efforts at incendiarism in New York City came to naught because of too much reliance on Greek fire, a chemical compound that failed to live up to expectations. A raid on St. Albans, Vermont, netted several horses and more than $100,000 from three bank robberies.

But a chance is a chance. Failure of the *Philo Parsons* did not discourage Thompson in his plans to upset the shipping on the Great Lakes. He backed Dr. James T. Bates, of Kentucky, an old Mississippi River steamboat captain, in the purchase of the steamer *Georgian,* hoping to fit her up as a ram, arm her, and send her out on the lakes. Before this could be accomplished, word of what was under way leaked out, and immediately the wildest consternation prevailed in the border cities. At Buffalo, two tugs were fitted out with cannon, and four regiments of soldiers were rushed there to stand by for action. Church bells were rung at Detroit. The whole lake shore was a scene of wild excitement.

"The bane and curse of carrying out anything in this country is the surveillance under which we act," Thompson reported. "Detectives, or those ready to give information, stand at every street corner. Two or three cannot interchange ideas without a reporter." [4]

The sea takes a rose

SEPTEMBER-OCTOBER 1864

"Confound an Englishman anyway."

Midshipman Clarence Cary of the C.S.S. *Chickamauga* wrote those words while waiting at Wilmington late in September. Near by was the C.S.S. *Tallahassee,* also, like his own ship, watching for an opportunity to run out of port. His tirade against the British was prompted by the uproar from captains of the runners at anchor, most of them of English connection, when it was announced that each should give a day's supply of coal toward the operation of the two cruisers.

"They hope we will be captured, I have no doubt," Cary added.

Never had Wilmington been so lively. The ordinarily sedate town had become greatly demoralized by the war. Speculators were there in hordes, waiting for the weekly auction of cargoes safely landed. Desperate characters were everywhere, and robbery and murder were common. Fights occurred in the streets in daytime, and at night, only the foolhardy went into the suburbs. Often, bodies were found floating on the surface of the

275

river near the town. People associated with the blockade-running business lived in the most magnificent style. Many of the residents went elsewhere, renting their houses at sky-high prices. Ladies were seldom seen in public. Some of those brave enough to venture out formed a society to care for the wounded and convalescent passing through. On a marshy flatland across the river from town were the cotton presses. There the runners loaded and unloaded while sentries paced the wharves day and night to keep stowaways from slipping on board.[1]

As the North closed its blockade on the South, more and more runners turned toward Wilmington. They knew the chances of getting in were best there because they could run up Cape Fear River and, if successful in passing the outer line of blockaders, could soon get under the protective gunfire of Fort Fisher. It was a center that at the moment was the mecca of some of the most experienced men in the business. John Maffitt was there, waiting on the moon and killing time by casually visiting from ship to ship. So was John Wilkinson, commanding the *Chickamauga.* In a few weeks he would run out in the *Tallahassee,* after her name had been changed to *Olustee.*

The men gathered at the port knew that the odds were against them. In the last fourteen months, fifty runners had been captured and nearly half of them destroyed along the Cape Fear.[2] In view from Fort Fisher were the wrecks of many —the *Stormy Petrel, Kate, Modern Greece, Hebe, Venus, Sophia, Arabian, Annie, Fanny Lewis, Ella,* and *Bendigo.* They were the unluckies. Some of the more fortunate were watching for a chance to run to sea again. In the meantime, there was a thrill in waiting throughout the daylight hours for the approach of night, to see what ships got out and which came in. It was like a game of skill, a sports contest, with cheers and celebration the reward of those successful in making port. "It looks pretty (when you are safe inside)," wrote Midshipman Cary, "to see the rockets, calcium lights and flashes of guns over the bar at night, whenever a vessel is discovered running out or in. The Yankees know perfectly well that we are waiting to go out, as we are in sight from their mastheads. . . ."

There was no despondency. The *Tallahassee,* as she stood by, was gaily dressed with flags, and while coal heavers threw precious fuel on board, a brass band on deck serenaded them with the liveliest tunes of the day.[3] Some of those who saw her, watched in disapproval. "There can be no question," wrote an Army man, "that in the past four weeks the loss of seven of the very finest and fastest of the trading fleet is due, directly or indirectly, to the expedition of the *Tallahassee.*" [4] Directly, he charged, because she had been the cause of their giving up anthracite and taking on soft coal from North Carolina that left behind a trail of black smoke; indirectly, because her recent successes had led the Union to strengthen the blockade fleet off Wilmington.

The weather cooled, the leaves fell, and the weather-wise watched the skies for evidence of impending autumnal storms. One night the crew of the U.S.S. *Howquah,* stationed a mile and a half from Fort Fisher, saw a rocket and heard the reports of three guns. Fires were spread, all hands called, and she headed eastward. Soon she made out a side-wheel steamer with two smokestacks standing to the northeast with two blockaders in chase. The *Howquah* tried to run her down, but the strange steamer was too fast.

An uproar of gunfire shook the silent night. The *Howquah*'s helm was put to starboard, bringing the two ships side by side about one hundred yards apart. Two thirty-pounder shells were fired from the Union vessel. Their explosions so illuminated the runner that parts of her could be seen flying in all directions after she was hit.

Suddenly, guns were turned on the *Howquah.* The fleeing vessel fired twice, and there was a constant blast from shore batteries. A shell struck the *Howquah*'s main rail on the starboard bow, cutting it through; tore into the forward end of a thirty-pounder pivot carriage, disabling it; glanced over, hit the main rail on the portside, and fell on the deck. It did not explode, but on its passage it killed one seaman and wounded four others. So hot was the fire on the Federal ship that it was almost impossible to keep her crew, most of them new to the service, at the guns.

Soon the *Howquah* was out of action, and so was the runner, which headed toward the beach, so badly damaged that she could not continue, and there, near Half Moon Battery, she burst into flame. At dawn the blockaders began fishing bales of cotton from the water. With their glasses they could make out her name—*Lynx*.[5]

Midshipman Cary of the *Chickamauga,* on September 30, wrote in his journal: "Last night was thought very probable for running the blockade and a steamer tried coming in, but was much cut up and had to be beached. I have not heard her name." The vessel in question was the *Night Hawk,* a thirty-thousand-pound investment fresh out of Liverpool. She was a long, low side-wheel, fitted with two smokestacks and two masts. She could make a speed of fourteen knots and carry eight hundred bales of cotton.

The U.S.S. *Niphon* saw the *Night Hawk* early in the evening. She was coming out of New Inlet, running hard. The *Niphon* gave chase, and seeing the stranger was getting ahead, brought her abeam and opened fire. She was only forty yards distant, and four shots took effect, causing her to display lights. At the same time, Fort Fisher threw up rockets, to confuse the fleet, and fired three guns.

Seeing the lights, Acting Master Edmund Kemble of the *Niphon* thought the runner had surrendered, and stood for her. But when he got near, she steamed full speed to the southeast and in a few moments disappeared.

Kemble went back to his station. At 11:15 P.M. he saw a steamer standing in toward New Inlet. This time he gave chase, went to quarters, opened fire on her, and in fifteen minutes caused her to run ashore on Federal Shoals. A crew sent to board found her to be the *Night Hawk,* bound for Wilmington with a general cargo from Bermuda; they set her on fire after pouring several cases of spirituous liquor about her cabin and hold.

Her destruction was not without repercussions. The British minister charged that members of the *Night Hawk*'s crew who had been unable to escape, some of them wounded, had been inhumanly treated by the boarding party. But the North was too sure of winning the war to be bothered. A court of inquiry was held, no misconduct was found, and the matter ended with a routine official report.

Hours after the *Night Hawk* met her fate, a vessel steered toward her in the dark. It was near daylight. The U.S.S. *Niphon* had sighted the approaching craft as she tried to get into New Inlet, given chase, fired at her five times, and struck her once. But she kept going, only to run suddenly upon the hulk of the *Night Hawk* and, mistaking it for a blockader, she swerved so suddenly that she went ashore on Swash Channel Bar.

Next morning, men staring from Fort Fisher and from the blockading fleet saw this victim of circumstances. The name was easily readable—*Condor*. She was of rakish build, very long, narrow in beam, equipped with three low funnels and two short masts, her hull painted a lead color. It was obvious that she was of light draft and great speed.

Since early September, blockaders along the Cape Fear had been watching for the *Condor*. A warning telegram had come from M. M. Jackson, the U.S. consul at Halifax, Nova Scotia: "British blockade runner, iron steamer *Condor,* three hundred tons, forty men, arrived here today from Ireland via Bermuda, with very large and valuable cargo. Will take on coal and doubtless proceed to Wilmington with steamer *Flamingo,* already reported." [6]

A few days later, he telegraphed that the *Condor* had left for Washington, a part of her cargo being clothing for the Confederate Army. He also revealed that she was commanded by Captain William N. W. Hewett, late commander of the British ship of war *Rinaldo* and still an officer in Her Majesty's service, even though he was sailing under the assumed name of Samuel S. Ridge. An honored man was he, the records would show. He had been awarded the Victoria Cross for his work in the Crimea and been knighted by Queen Victoria for his distinguished service as ambassador to King John of Abyssinia. But as for the vessel, she was designed expressly for running the blockade—registered at Glasgow and insured by David McGregor of London.[7]

Sometime after daylight, a soldier walking along the beach near Fort Fisher came upon the body of a woman washed up on the sand. He stared. Tragedy struck often in these precarious times and in this area of promise for blockade-runners. But what caught his eye was a leather reticule around her neck. In it he found two thousand dollars in gold. Later in the day, when her identity was known, he turned in his loot with embarrassed apologies. No Confederate could in good conscience steal from Rose O'Neal Greenhow, dead or alive.

Thus, on Cape Fear River, along the stretch where the hulks of wrecked runners spotted the sands, ended one of the most remarkable careers of the war. Newspapers had told in glaring headlines of the work of this woman who before the war had moved only among the socially elite of Washington, entertaining Presidents and congressmen on the friendliest of terms. A beautiful and charming widow, it was not difficult for her to learn the military plans of the Union as the nation went to war, and these she passed on to her beloved South. Allan Pinkerton, Abraham Lincoln's celebrated detective, got on her trail, sending her to Old Capitol Prison, a building familiar to her because it had been a boardinghouse operated by her aunt. Released during '62, she was sent to Richmond. There, for her services to the Confederacy, she was awarded a special appropriation of twenty-five hundred dollars by President Jefferson Davis.

Big things were in store for Mrs. Greenhow. The Confederacy sent her to England on a special mission, and she left by runner on August 5, '63, carrying with her the manuscript of a book she had written about her experiences. This was published in London under the title, *My Imprisonment, or the First Year of Abolition Rule at Washington.* It was a financial success, and it brought her international fame. She met Napoleon III in Paris.[8] Queen Victoria received her. Then, in August, '64, she decided to return to America. With her in the leather reticule she brought in gold the royalties from her book.

Captain Hewett was as much disturbed by her death as anyone. When the *Condor* ran aground, Mrs. Greenhow became frantic, crying that direst punishment awaited her if she were captured. Against his protests, she insisted that a boat be lowered to take her ashore. Hewett refused over and over, citing the raging surf beating against the ship. But she finally had her way. Several men stepped into the boat with her. It went only a short distance from the *Condor* before a breaker overturned it. The men managed to get ashore, but the woman, weighted down by her gold, was drowned.

Of much concern to the Confederacy were certain dispatches she had concealed in her clothing. Some were from Confederate Commissioner John Mason in London.[9]

Mrs. Greenhow was given the honors which were her due. Her body was taken to Wilmington on October 2 and buried with Catholic rites in a grave marked by a small cross that bore her name. A Confederate flag was her shroud.

Cushing apes the enemy

OCTOBER 1864

Acting Master's Mate John Woodman of the U.S.S. *Commodore Hull* parted the bushes at a point on the bank of the Roanoke River opposite Plymouth. The scene he saw caused him to stiffen, his eyes fixed on the dreaded ram *Albemarle*. It was ten in the morning, an hour for full light, but the day was hazy, and the grass and foliage were rank and thick. Since midnight he had been struggling upstream and over swampy countryside on a reconnaissance, his second in a matter of weeks. How well he knew the Union's great concern over the fierce ironclad. From the lowest serviceman in the North Carolina sounds to the highest Navy Department official in Washington, the question uppermost was: When will the ram appear again?

He could see her lying at a wharf, near a steam sawmill that occasionally let off a small tower of vapor. No one seemed to be at work on the vessel's deck. On the top of the casemate house stood a figure he took to be that of the quartermaster, idling in the sun. Even the town in the background seemed quiet. A few persons could be seen moving about, and from some low buildings near the river he could hear the familiar noises of blacksmiths and carpenters, hammering and clanking and puttering in an apathetic manner.

With the confidence of military routine, Woodman turned to take his field glasses from young Henry Hatch, the sailor delegated to follow him across the island from Middle River. Henry was not there.

For a moment, Woodman was stunned. He looked about before calling softly, "Henry." Then a shade louder, "Henry! Henry!"

Only silence came from the bushes. He was puzzled. He had told Hatch to follow closely. Odd he had not missed the sounds of the younger man as they fought their way through undergrowth and swamps, he realized, but this might be blamed on the pain of diarrhea gnawing at his vitals. His rundown condition, which he feared might cause him to require assistance, was the main reason for bringing the other fellow along.

Assuming Hatch was off somewhere, observing from a more advantageous point, Woodman turned back to look once more across the river. Downstream a mile or so he could see the U.S.S. *Southfield,* sunk in the attack by the *Albemarle* back in April. He found her in the same condition as when last seen, except that her hurricane deck appeared to be about three feet higher out of the water. Her smokestack, lookout ladder, and forward pilothouse were standing, and there was a barge on her starboard and a schooner on her portside. But he could see on them no purchase rigging that might be used in raising the sunken vessel, nor were there any persons at work on her.

Woodman waited for half an hour before again calling softly for Hatch. When there was no answer, he concluded that the sailor had returned to the cutter in which they had made their way up Middle River. Confident no mishap had occurred, he started back across the island himself. Eventually, after another torturous trek through the swamps, he came to the boat, concealed in bushes along the bank. He found seated in it the two sailors who had remained behind, but Henry was not there.

Four hours Woodman waited, until the pain in his stomach became almost unbearable. He then started downstream. Before leaving, he placed two days' rations in a prominent spot and protected it by rocks from wild animals. He also left a message telling the missing man where he should wait until they came for him.

Henry Hatch would go down in history as another missing warrior whose eventual fate would be left a mystery in official records. He was another victim in another desperate attempt by Union forces along the North Carolina sounds to prevent a surprise by the *Albemarle.* Since her last appearance in May, fear had been growing, and there was more and more determination to destroy her.

Captain Melancton Smith, who had commanded the fleet that battled the ironclad in Albemarle Sound in May, was of the opinion at that time that the *Southfield* would be raised by the Southerners and would accompany the ram if she came out on another expedition. To repel such an attack, he had the *Mattabesett, Wyalusing, Miami, Ceres, Whitehead,* and *Commodore Barney,* all wooden except for the *Whitehead,* which was lightly armored.

Captain Cooke, commanding the *Albemarle,* was in the meantime taking stock of her faults. She had been struck at musket range forty-four times without serious damage. But he was convinced she drew too much water to navigate the sounds well, that she had not sufficient buoyancy, that she was slow and not easily managed, that her decks were dangerously near the water, and that she needed two broadside guns.[1] None of these deficiencies were evident to Acting Ensign John R. Peacock, formerly of the U.S.S. *Southfield* and one of the first to follow the course taken by John Woodman. Peacock had gazed at the ram from the bushes and noticed that she was as formidable as ever, except that her smokestack, shot off in the battle, was still missing. She seemed to have been lightened, for she was much higher out of the water than when he last had seen her, but it was not noticeable to him that her plating had been damaged at all.

Smith hoped that the ram might be enticed into the broader waters of the sound, where his vessels would have more room to maneuver. He estimated that Cooke would make an effort to "outgeneral" him by slipping up on him at night through the Cashie River, and for that reason he gave instructions for the mouth of that stream to be guarded carefully.[2]

A reconnaissance, a few days after the battle at Plymouth, resulted in the information that the ram's smokestack had been repaired and replaced. Men could be heard at work on her. Members of the party who watched her from the bushes across the river could see only her starboard side, which appeared to be completely free of damage. The *Southfield* was still where she had sunk, her upper deck just awash.[3]

A week later, the *Albemarle* appeared at the mouth of the Roanoke. She came down within sight of the Union picket boats on duty there, turned her head upstream, and stood by while a rowboat pulled several times diagonally across the river, apparently dragging for torpedoes. The *Whitehead* fired one shot at her from a distance and withdrew. Smith relayed the news of this incident and, with it, reports about the ironclad he was getting from contrabands and refugees: her plating was much damaged, four Federal shells had penetrated her outer armor, the concussion at the time was so severe it was impossible to keep a light burning in her.[4]

The *Albemarle*'s end might have come on May 25. That night, five volunteers from the *Wyalusing*—Coxswain John W. Lloyd, Firemen Allen Crawford and John Laverty, and Coal Heavers Charles Baldwin and Benjamin Lloyd—followed the route taken by Peacock and Woodman. During the afternoon they had left their ship and gone up Middle River in a boat, taking with them two torpedoes, each filled with one hundred pounds of powder. These explosives they carried through the swamps on a stretcher, arriving on the bank of the Roanoke opposite

Plymouth at eleven at night. There John Lloyd and Baldwin stripped off their clothes and swam out into the river, drawing the torpedoes behind them. At a point above the town, they fastened the explosives together with a bridle, after which Baldwin began guiding them downstream. It was his intention to place them across the bow of the *Albemarle* and then signal to Crawford, who would explode them from the swamps on the opposite side. A few yards away from the ram, the line by which Baldwin was pulling them fouled a schooner. The scraping noise drew the attention of a sentry. He fired, setting off a volley of musketry.

Thirty-eight hours later, after a day and night of rain, the two Lloyds and Laverty returned to their ship. But Baldwin and Crawford were still missing, and for two days, parties searched unsuccessfully for them. On the 29th they appeared, tired, dirty, and hungry. Behind them, they said, they had destroyed all traces of their plot to blow up the *Albemarle*.

This failure did not put an end to the Federals' plans to destroy the ram. Early in June, Melancton Smith began experimenting with explosives. One day he blew two old boats to pieces with a single charge, and happily dreamed of doing the same to the ironclad. He even placed mines along the Roanoke and had selected men standing by during the day with trigger wires to explode them in case the *Albemarle* came down. He had an idea she would never appear at night, for fear of getting aground.

After the mines were placed—nine feet from the surface, twelve feet apart, straight across the river, a lock string extending from each to the swamp on the right-hand side going up—the U.S.S. *Commodore Barney* and the U.S.S. *Whitehead* were sent upstream to throw a few shells, in the hope that they might bring the ram down. But the Confederates refused to budge. They were having trouble with the command of the *Albemarle*. Cooke's health had failed under the strain, and orders had been issued for John Maffitt, then at Wilmington, to replace him.[5]

Another reconnoitering party watched the *Albemarle* from the bushes across the Roanoke from Plymouth on June 24. It returned with a report that the work on her appeared to be completed. Her guns were mounted, the smokestack she was using had come from the *Southfield,* and everything about her appeared to be in readiness for an attack. A refugee from Plymouth added the news that Maffitt had assumed command. This information was in no way encouraging, and it further dampened the spirits of Union ships' crews suffering from intense heat and dysentery and diarrhea.[6]

It was true that Maffitt had taken over. Aggressive by nature, he was making plans, in compliance with verbal instructions from Secretary Mallory, to stage another attack in Albemarle Sound.[7] But he soon ran into trouble. Confederate Army officials in the area protested in concert. If the ram ventured out into the sound, they argued, she would in all probability be captured or destroyed and, with her out of the way, Plymouth would be certain to fall. "It is risking much, with fearful odds against us, for the doubtful prospect of an inconsiderable advantage," wrote one officer.[8] The appeal went directly to Mallory, who disposed of the complaint with this endorsement:

"It is evident from these papers that the military authorities immediately in charge at Plymouth regard our tenure of 'Plymouth, Washington, and the rich valley of the Roanoke,' as dependent upon the ironclad *Albemarle;* and hence their 'protest' against the alleged verbal orders given her by the Navy Department to 'attack the enemy.' The importance of this vessel in holding the country she greatly aided to recover is apparent, even if the water fronts of Plymouth were strengthened; but she was not designed to act as a floating battery merely, and while her loss must not be lightly hazarded, the question of when to attack the enemy must be left to the judgment of the naval officer in command, deciding in view of the relations she bears to the defenses of North Carolina." [9]

A change in Federal command occurred the first week in July. Melancton Smith was ordered elsewhere, and into his place stepped W. H. Macomb of the U.S.S. *Shamrock,* next in seniority. Scarcely had he taken charge of the fleet before the Confederates quietly carried off a party of men dutifully standing by to explode the mines at the mouth of the Roanoke. Their boat was found in its usual place, but the occupants were gone and there was no trace to indicate what had become of them.[10] The new commander promptly ordered removed or exploded all the mines requiring attendants.

On July 5, the aspiring young lieutenant, William B. Cushing, arrived at Hampton Roads. He had come to present to Admiral Lee a report of his reconnaissance in the Wilmington area, to look for the C.S.S. *North Carolina* and the C.S.S. *Raleigh.* Lee listened, congratulated him on his efforts, and then asked him why he had not attempted to destroy the *Albemarle.*[11] Cushing exuded eagerness to undertake such a project.

"I submitted in writing two plans," he related. "The first was based upon the fact that through a thick swamp the ironclad might be approached to within a few hundred yards, whence India-rubber boats, to be inflated and carried upon men's backs, might transport a boarding party of a hundred men; in the second plan the offensive force was to be conveyed in two very small low-pressure steamers, each armed with a torpedo and a howitzer. In the latter (which had my preference), I intended that one boat should dash in, while the other stood by to throw canister and renew the attempt if the first should fail. It would also be useful to pick up our men if the attacking boat were disabled." [12]

The torpedo-boat plan was agreed upon, and Cushing was ordered to Washington for further conferences. Lee wrote Welles: "Lieutenant Cushing, who desires to superintend the fitting of the boats he may have, is instructed to report to the Department. . . . I have enjoined secrecy and discretion upon him. He is entirely willing to make an attempt to destroy the ram, and I have great confidence in his gallantry."

In this letter to the Navy Secretary, Lee enclosed a statement from Cushing that was marked "confidential." It read:

"Deeming the nature of destruction of the rebel ram *Albe-marle* feasible, I beg leave to state that I am acquainted with the waters held by her, and am willing to undertake the task.

"If furnished with three low-pressure tugs, one or more fitted with torpedoes, and all armed with light howitzers, it might be effected, or if rubber boats were on hand to transport across the swamp to a point immediately abreast of Plymouth. If detailed for this work, I would like to superintend the outfitting of the boats. . . ."

When Cushing presented his plan in person at the Navy Department in Washington, he failed to receive complete approval. Assistant Secretary Fox doubted the "merit" of the undertaking, but he at last consented to send the young officer to New York to purchase "suitable vessels." [13]

At New York, Cushing found some boats built for picket duty that he estimated would serve his purpose. They were approximately forty feet long, nine and a half feet in beam, with a draft of forty to forty-one inches. Their engines were small, and they were propelled by a screw. Two of these were selected. Each was fitted with a fourteen-foot boom for the torpedo that swung by a gooseneck hinge to the bluff of the bow, and was so arranged that it could be detached and placed out of view in the front of the boat.

Weeks passed, with Union fears over the *Albemarle* constantly mounting. Some of this was caused by her nightly appearances at the mouth of the Roanoke.[14] On August 6, she was first seen a few minutes before four in the morning. Commander A. D. Harrell, in the U.S.S. *Chicopee,* stood slowly out into the sound, expecting her to follow. At 5:00 A.M. he sent a telegram to Commander Macomb: "From the number of people in sight on the beach, no doubt it was expected that an engagement would ensue. . . . The ram is now lying in the river blowing off steam. I do not think she will advance. Should she do so, however, I will endeavor to draw her down toward the fleet. I shall now pay my respects to the gentlemen on the beach in the shape of a few shells." [15]

But the *Albemarle* could not be enticed into the sound. Next morning at 2:25, she was discovered again, this time outside the buoy at the mouth of the river. Lieutenant Commander W. T. Truxton, who was standing picket duty, reported to Macomb:

"It is my impression that these nightly expeditions on the part of the ram are made with the hope of picking up one of the small picket boats, or ramming one of the double-enders, and then returning. So far the ram has, in every case, turned back as soon as she was discovered, which looks as if she did not at present mean fight. . . ." [16]

Whether the *Albemarle* meant battle or not, three Union vessels, the *Ceres, Sassacus,* and *Valley City,* remained at the mouth of the Roanoke, constantly patrolling the waters at night. If the ram appeared, the ship first discovering her had instructions to fire one gun and then steam toward the fleet, anchored six miles out in the sound.[17]

Toward the end of August, John Woodman was sent back to peer at the *Albemarle* from the bushes opposite Plymouth. He left at eight at night, going by dinghy, accompanied by two sailors from the *Wyalusing* and two from the *Valley City.* At midnight they entered a creek flowing into Middle River and concealed their boat. There they waited for the hours to pass, and at daylight Woodman left his companions and started across the swamp toward Plymouth, arriving at his customary observation point at 10:00 A.M.

Across the water, Plymouth baked peacefully in the August sun. The *Albemarle* lay alongside the wharf where Woodman last had seen her, but now he noticed that she was protected by a shield of single cypress logs chained together. The Confederates, he realized, had either learned or suspected that the Federals were thinking about torpedoing the ironclad.

Before leaving, he dropped down the island to a point opposite the *Southfield.* He noticed the water was higher than on his last visit, for only about eighteen inches of her hurricane deck could be seen. A barge and two schooners stood by while a number of men worked with heavy tackle and four large pieces of timber. He was unable to determine what they were trying to do, but he assumed all of their efforts were aimed at raising her.

Woodman's report was to Macomb's satisfaction. The following night, Army gunboats took a body of armed men up the Chowan River, for the purpose of landing and slipping into Plymouth to destroy the ironclad. But lack of stealth upset their plans, and the project was a failure.[18]

At Richmond on September 9, an order was prepared by the Navy Department that would bring happiness to John Maffitt. It informed him that he had been detached from command of the *Albemarle* and was to report to Wilmington for duty on board a blockade-runner. To an officer whose reputation even among the Federals indicated he was "not the man to sit down at Plymouth," [19] this was a welcome transfer. Maffitt looked upon his duty on the ram as more that of a river guard.[20] He was replaced by Lieutenant Alexander F. Warley, whose naval career was highlighted by the months he had spent as commander of the ironclad C.S.S. *Manassas* in the Mississippi River earlier in the war.

Warley took the ram down to the mouth of the Roanoke in broad daylight on September 23. It was 12:30 P.M. when she first was sighted by the *Valley City,* which fired a signal gun and steamed back into the sound. But the *Albemarle* was not to be trapped that day. When the Union fleet steamed up to the mouth of the Roanoke in answer to the signal, she already had returned upstream. Behind her she left much excitement. The Federal ships steamed about until 6:00 P.M. before returning to their anchorage.[21]

By October, Cushing had matters connected with his plan to blow up the *Albemarle* pretty well in shape. Around the middle of the month, he started southward with his two torpedo boats. The plan worked smoothly until he reached Chesapeake Bay, but misfortune caught up with him there, and one of the craft was swamped and lost.

Cushing continued with the remaining boat, proceeding down the Chesapeake and the Albemarle Canal with a crew of seven, including himself. Halfway through, he reached a point where the canal had been filled up, but this failed to stop him. He managed to get around this section by working his way through a nearby creek. His next barrier was a milldam, and there he waited for high water and ran the boat over it. Still farther on, the craft grounded. Getting a flatboat, he removed the gun and coal and in two days got her through. Reaching Roanoke Island, he stopped for the night and was assigned a bed in a room with three officers who had come ashore from the *Valley City,* anchored a mile out in the sound, and had been unable to return to their ship because of hurricane winds. They were especially impressed with him, a twenty-two-year-old, modest, reserved, and showing himself to be an individualist by the long light hair falling to his shoulders. When these men awoke next morning, he was gone.[22]

Another reconnaissance was considered necessary at this time, and the call again went to John Woodman. He left one afternoon in a cutter with seven men, drew alongside the *Valley City* at the mouth of the Roanoke after dark, and waited there until 2:00 A.M. before heading up Middle River. At daylight, following his customary pattern, he started across the swamp toward Plymouth, and at 10:00 A.M. was looking at the ironclad from the bushes. She was still moored alongside the wharf, head downstream, apparently with her fires out. The logs placed around her to protect her from torpedoes were still there. Before leaving, he dropped down and took a look at the *Southfield.* The only change he could see in her appearance was that her smokestack had been removed. Four vessels were around her, still trying to raise her.

Several other reconnaissances were made as the date for Cushing's attempt neared. One of these was by a boat's crew under Acting Ensign Rudolph Sommers of the U.S.S. *Tacony,* like Woodman a frequent visitor to the neighborhood of Plymouth

since May. On the return, their boat was ambushed by Southerners, and they were driven into the swamps, with one killed
and one badly wounded.[23]

On October 22, Admiral David Porter, who on the 12th had
relieved Lee as commander of the North Atlantic Blockading
Squadron, sent Macomb a message that bespoke his usual dis-
trust of a project engineered by someone other than himself. In
it he revealed that he had instructed Cushing to go down in a
steam launch and destroy the *Albemarle* with torpedoes, adding:
"I have no great confidence in his success, but you will afford
him all the assistance in your power, and keep boats ready to
pick him up in case of failure." [24]

Cushing reached Macomb's flagship, the U.S.S. *Shamrock,*
in the late afternoon of October 24.[25] The next two days were
extremely busy for him. He conferred with Macomb about his
final plans, and then he began to make additions to his crew.
Knowing the Confederates at Plymouth kept a picket on
board one of the schooners anchored beside the *Southfield,* he
decided it would be best to take the cutter of the *Shamrock* in
tow with a crew of two officers and ten men, these to silence this
guard in case his plan of capturing the *Albemarle* failed.

On the night of the 26th, he drew up in his launch beside
the U.S.S. *Otsego,* doing picket duty near the mouth of the
Roanoke. This was his last stop before proceeding up toward
Plymouth, and members of the crew were warned against any
noisy outburst. One of these, Acting Ensign Thomas S. Gay,
approached Cushing and proffered his services. They were accepted. Others did the same thing, some of them offering as
much as a month's pay to change places with the men in the
launch and cutter, but there were no takers.[26]

Off into the night Cushing steamed, with luck against him.
In the darkness his craft grounded, and so much time was taken
to get her free that he realized it was too late to make the attempt. It was six-thirty in the morning when he returned to
the *Otsego.*

The daylight hours of the 27th were passed impatiently by Cushing and his crew. At 11:28 P.M. he started up the river again. In the launch with him were fourteen men. One of them, Acting Ensign William L. Howarth of Cushing's own U.S.S. *Monticello,* had been with him on other adventures and had earned his complete confidence. Gay was there, and so were Acting Assistant Third Engineer William Stotesbury, First Class Fireman Samuel Higgins, and Lorenzo Deming, Henry Wilkes, and Robert H. King, landsmen, who, with Cushing and Howarth, had composed the crew of the launch when it made its way through the canal. Others were Acting Assistant Paymaster Francis H. Swan and Acting Third Assistant Engineer Charles L. Steever, both of the *Otsego;* Acting Master's Mate John Woodman of the *Commodore Hull;* Richard Hamilton, coal heaver, of the *Shamrock;* and William Smith, Bernard Harley, and Edward J. Houghton, all ordinary seamen of the *Chicopee.* In the cutter behind were Acting Master's Mate Wilson D. Burlingame, Acting Gunner William Peterkin, and ten men.

Ahead of them lay eight miles of river they would have to travel before they would reach the ironclad. The night was dark and stormy, with occasional heavy downpours.

Up at Plymouth, Alexander Warley, recognizing the added danger to the *Albemarle* on such a night, had doubled the watch on board the ironclad. He also had strengthened the pickets along the shore. But he had little faith in what he was doing. He knew there was no reason why the town might not be captured by the Federals any day.[27] The guns commanding the river were in no condition for use, and a new detail of soldiers had just that day arrived to take charge of them. Warley had gone in person to see their commanding officer, bringing a message of alarm. People lower down the river reported they had seen and heard a steam launch the night before.

As Cushing and his men moved upstream at low speed, running cautiously under the trees on the right bank, little noise could be heard above that of the water swirling around them. A heavy tarpaulin covered the engine, shutting out the sound of its mechanism. Its exhaust was below surface, further deadening the sounds of their progress.

Most of the men stood or sat in the forward part of the launch. Cushing was on the right, Howarth next to him, and Woodman, who knew the river perhaps better than any of them, on the left by the wheel. Gay was on the deck by the twelve-pounder howitzer. Swan was directly behind Cushing. Squatting in the bottom of the boat was Acting Third Assistant Engineer Stotesbury, attending the engine. He had never been under fire.[28]

It was Cushing's intention to land below the ram, board her from the wharf, and, after overpowering her crew, bring her down the river. If they were discovered before this was accomplished, he then planned to use the torpedo.

After the first mile or two, complete silence was maintained. One o'clock passed. Two o'clock. Shortly before three, they rounded the bend below the point where the *Southfield* lay. Not a light was visible to mark the location of vessels or even the town.

Cushing checked details to make sure they were ready for action. In his hands he held five lines, one to adjust the spar, another to detach the torpedo, and still another to pull its trigger pin. The other two were for the control of the boat, one fastened to the wrist and the other to the ankle of the engineer. The management of all these lines, it was said, required as much exactness and delicacy of touch as a surgical operation. A single error in their employment, even a pull too much or too little, would spoil the entire expedition.[29]

The launch passed within yards of the *Southfield*. Men in the two small boats held their breath, but there was not a sound from either the steamer or the schooners.

Farther along they came in view of a small open fire burning a short distance back from the bank, its flames reflected faintly on the crest of the water. The launch steamed along, with a ghostly swish, almost silently. Woodman, at Cushing's direction, steered toward the landing below the wharf. They were counting the seconds until they reached land—and then would come the rush, the storming of the *Albemarle* a few yards above, a hurried assault, to be followed by up-anchors and away, in what would surely be recognized as one of the most amazing feats of the war.

The yards to the landing were decreasing steadily, and hopes were on edge. Suddenly the situation changed. A dog barked. A sentry, abruptly aroused, glanced out over the water, discovered the boat, and hailed. Receiving no answer, he hailed again.

Like a flash of gunpowder, Cushing changed his approach. His idea of capturing the *Albemarle* was abandoned, and efforts at stealth were dismissed. In a loud voice he called out, "Ahead fast!" He turned toward the stern and ordered the cutter cast loose, to go downriver and capture the pickets at the *Southfield.*

He directed the launch toward the dim outline of the *Albemarle,* approaching on the port bow. Suddenly a large bonfire flared up on shore, pointing out to him the boom of logs around the ironclad. He saw instantly that his boat was too near to rise over them at the sharp angle of his approach, and he directed that it be sheered off, to circle and come in head on.

The alarm along the bank and on the *Albemarle* now became general. Rattles were sprung, bells were rung, and bullets flew about, kicking up silvery splashes in the yellow reflection from the fire. Swan gasped as a bullet tore into his flesh. Three bullets ripped Cushing's clothing, but his skin was not touched.

Out into the river on a wide sweep ran the launch, its engine at full speed. As it came around, it straightened, and headed bows on for the *Albemarle.*

Cushing shouted at the top of his voice: "Leave the ram, or I'll blow you to pieces!" [30]

The air seemed full of flying lead. Warley on the *Albemarle* was having trouble. His officers and men—sixty in all—were at quarters, but the launch was so near the broadside guns of the ironclad they could not be brought to bear.[31]

Cushing gave the signal for the howitzer to be fired, and a charge of canister rattled against the side of the ram. Confederate riflemen up in her shield singled him out. A burst of buckshot tore off the tail of his coat, a bullet ripped into the sole of his shoe. Another struck him in the left hand just as he jerked on the control cords.

"In a moment," Cushing reported, "we had struck the logs, just abreast of the quarter port, breasting them in some feet, and our bows resting on them. The torpedo boom was then lowered, and by a vigorous pull I succeeded in diving the torpedo under the overhang and exploding it at the same time that the *Albemarle*'s gun was fired. A shot seemed to go crashing through my boat, and a dense mass of water rushed in from the torpedo, filling the launch and completely disabling her." [32]

Warley yelled from the deck of the *Albemarle*. There was no answer. He yelled again. Still no answer.

Then Cushing's voice sounded above the confusion. "Men, save yourselves!"

He threw off his side arms, coat, and shoes, and dived into the water. The chill of frost had settled on it, and it was cold, chilling his blood. He swam with others toward the middle of the stream. The fire from the ironclad and from the shore grew hotter, bullets splashing in the water around them.

Cushing headed for the opposite shore. As he swam, a man near him gave a gurgling yell and went down. It was Samuel Higgins, the fireman.

Cushing swam on, determined to escape, realizing that each stroke increased his chances. Behind him he could see the Confederates rowing about in small boats and picking up the men who had not followed his example. One of these boats, attracted by Higgins' dying yell, was rowed toward him. He floated, his head barely above the surface. The craft came so near he could overhear the conversation of the men in it, even recognizing his own name, but he was not discovered. As it turned back, he struck out downstream, and again headed for shore, this time toward the Plymouth side. Just then he heard a groan in the river behind him. He turned and saw a swimmer.

Approaching cautiously, Cushing recognized John Woodman. "I can't swim any longer," gasped Woodman.

Cushing knocked his cap from his head, put an arm under him, and told him to swim. For several minutes Woodman remained afloat. Finally, his strength completely gone, he sank like a stone, only a few yards from the bank where he so frequently had watched the ironclad.

Again alone in the water, Cushing swam on. At last he felt the touch of soft mud. His feet sank into it. He raised his body and made one step forward, then fell and lay there, half in the water and half out, his brain in a whirl.

Daylight revealed him still lying there. At last he stirred, crawled up the bank, and looked around. He was on the edge of a swamp extending up toward the town and only about forty yards from a fort. He crept into the rushes and hid. While he crouched only a few feet from a path, two officers passed. From their conversation he gathered that the *Albemarle* had been sunk.[33]

Later in the day he worked his way downstream until he came to a spot where seven Confederate pickets were stationed. A few yards away from them, fastened to the roots of a cypress tree on the bank of the river, was a flat-bottomed, square-ended skiff. He crept into the stream and swam silently toward the boat. Reaching it, he cast it loose and, hiding behind it, worked it out into the current.

At ten-fifteen that night, sailors on board the U.S.S. *Valley City* at the mouth of the Roanoke heard someone shouting: "Ship ahoy! Send a boat!" An armed crew was sent to investigate. In a few minutes they returned with Cushing, towing the skiff in which he had made his escape. He was in his stocking feet, wearing only shirt and pants, and he was wet, cold, tired, and hungry.[34]

Soon all hands were called to "cheer ship." Earlier in the day the cutter, with Burlingame and Peterkin, had appeared with four Confederate pickets they had taken from a schooner near the *Southfield*.

The following day the *Valley City* ran up Middle River, sailors on deck scanning the banks for signs of life. It was a rewarding effort. Shortly after noon, a bedraggled figure waved from a swamp, and a boat sent ashore brought back Edward Houghton, the only person besides Cushing to escape.

The fear of Confederate Army officers that Plymouth would quickly fall if the *Albemarle* was lost, was quickly borne out after Cushing's success.[35] Federal gunboats began shelling the town at 9:30 A.M., October 31, and after an hour or so, the Confederates evacuated their fortifications. Union forces pushed in, and in the local post office they found a letter a sailor on the *Albemarle* had addressed to a friend. It told of the sinking of the ironclad and added: "We are in an awful condition. I believe they are going to hold the place to the bitter end. Captain Warley says he intends to fight as long as there is a man left (this is all gas)." [36]

November days passed, with attention focused on complete possession of the North Carolina sounds. Now and then the conversation turned to John Woodman and Sam Higgins. Sailors said to one another: "Wonder what became of them." At eight on the morning of the 8th, the U.S.S. *Shamrock* was able to supply part of the answer. A body floating near the ship was found to be that of Woodman.[37] In the late afternoon, after the steamer *Massasoit* arrived with troops from New Bern, the rest of the answer was available. The body of Higgins was picked up as it came floating past.[38]

★ 22

The curtain begins dropping

OCTOBER-NOVEMBER 1864

The war was ending its fourth year, and all over the world invisible gates were closing on the Confederacy. In every quarter, its agents were fighting losing battles. Capitals of foreign countries once friendly were turning them away. The days when Confederate ships could roam the seas and run into the nearest port for coal and other supplies had passed. Yet the task of bringing the South to its knees, of cornering the last of its greyhounds of the sea, so devastating in their attack on Union commerce, was to be an extended affair. At Richmond, ambitious projects were drafted anew—even another try at Johnson's Island [1]—and the tenor of official departmental reports was not completely pessimistic.

Although the Confederate Congress in January had passed legislation providing stiffer control of the blockade-running business, the number of ships engaged in it was still large. President Davis reported forty-three vessels had run safely in to Charleston and Wilmington during a five-week period, that only a small number of those running out were captured, and that out of 11,796 bales of cotton shipped, only 1,272 were lost. Among the supplies that runners had brought in during the last year were 8,632,000 pounds of meat; 1,507,000 pounds of lead; 1,933,000 pounds of saltpeter; 546,000 pairs of shoes; 316,000 pairs of blankets; 520,000 pounds of coffee; 69,000 rifles; 97 packages of revolvers; 2,639 packages of medicines; and 43 cannon. In ten months, the value of cotton sent out on Government account was $5,296,000.[2]

Overseas, Confederate Agent Bulloch was still trying to wring supplies from the British. He notified Secretary Mallory that four double-screw steamers ordered for the Navy Department were "progressing rapidly" and that the builder had just given assurance they would be ready on the contract's deadline. Since April, he had sent twelve small marine engines to the Confederacy, but not without difficulty, for shipowners were becoming more and more unwilling to carry heavy freight from Europe.[3]

The die-hard attitude of the South was clearly reflected in a periodic report from John L. Porter, chief constructor of the Confederate Navy. In ten shipyards scattered from Virginia to Alabama, twenty-two vessels were in various stages of completion. Seven of these were delayed for want of iron, a deficiency that for the moment amounted to at least 4,230 tons. One of the busiest centers was at Edwards Ferry in North Carolina, in the cornfield where the Southerners had built the *Albemarle*. There a wooden gunboat was on the stocks, and a contract had just been let for the building of another ironclad. At Richmond, the C.S.S. *Virginia II* had been launched, another was on the stocks, and four torpedo boats were under construction. In South Carolina, six vessels were either ready or on their way. Five were on the stocks in Georgia; and in Alabama, two large ironclads and two double-propeller steamers could be launched as soon as their armor was added.[4]

But the most graphic evidence of continued Southern resistance was the toll of Union commerce. M. M. Jackson, the U.S. consul in Nova Scotia, reported that hundreds of persons had formed an organization "for the purpose of seizing, plundering, destroying, and, when practicable, appropriating American steamers and other vessels at different points along the Atlantic and Pacific coasts and on the upper lakes." Their base of operations was to be Havana, and vessels carrying the largest amounts of money would be the special objects of attack.[5] Meanwhile, several Confederate cruisers, including the C.S.S. *Florida,* on which John Maffitt had started his meteoric career, were still combing the seas. Within a few days of each other, the C.S.S. *Tallahassee* and the C.S.S. *Chickamauga* ran into Wilmington, leaving behind a string of scuttled vessels, some of them just off the Delaware Breakwater.

Early one evening the *Florida* ran into the Brazilian port of Bahia, Bay of San Salvador, and by 8:15 P.M. was anchored in the mouth of the harbor. There ahead of her was the U.S.S. *Wachusett.* The *Wachusett*'s Commander, Napoleon Collins, sent a boat to learn her identity. As soon as this was known, Collins got up steam, hove short, and cleared ship for action.

But there was no action that night, nor, by international agreement, was there any reason to think there might be. At the helm of the *Florida* was her third commander, Charles Manigault Morris, formerly of the U.S. Navy. Since January, he had conducted his ship over a large field of action, remembering always his original instructions: "Your position is an important one, not only with reference to the immediate results to the enemy's property, but from the fact that neutral rights may frequently arise under it. Reliance, however, is placed in your judgment and discretion for meeting and promptly disposing of such questions." [6] He was told to do the enemy's commerce "the greatest injury in the shortest time," beginning at the equator, where he was to watch for vessels on their return from California and the East Indies, and working toward the northern coasts of the Confederacy, to intercept supply steamers, and even to make a dash on the New England coast.

Morris realized that he was stepping into illustrious footsteps. Since Maffitt had run the *Florida* out of Mobile, with a crew hardly sufficient to man her and a staff of officers the oldest of whom was barely twenty-seven, she had been taken on a cruise that had meant much to the Confederacy, both in prizes and prestige. Then, in the fall of '63, Maffitt had brought her into Brest, France, for repairs, and before he could get away, his health failed, a heart condition developing from the severe strain placed upon his body by the attack of yellow fever that had come upon him at Cardenas in the summer of '62.

A London *Times* correspondent visited the *Florida* at Brest, and, not noticing Maffitt's illness, was moved to write: "Of the captain himself I may say that he is a slight, middle-sized, well-knit man of about forty-two, a merry-looking man with a ready, determined air, full of life and business—apparently the sort of man who is equally ready for a fight or a jollification and whose preference for the latter would by no means interfere with his creditable conduct of the former. His plainly furnished little stateroom looked as businesslike as a merchant's office. The round table in the center was strewn with books and innumerable manuscripts." [7]

But Maffitt knew a rest was needed, and he had no trouble convincing his superiors. To relieve him was sent Commander Joseph Nicholson Barney, an experienced officer who might have taken over the command while the ship was lying idle at Mobile late in '62 but for the timely interference of President Jefferson Davis, who acted at the request of Franklin Buchanan, naval commander at that port. Barney was to captain the cruiser but a short time, for soon his health also failed, and on January 9, '64, he turned over the command to Morris.

A short time later, Morris ran into Funchal, Madeira, for coal, and there encountered an old friend, Union Commander George Henry Preble, and the U.S. sloop of war *St. Louis*. Going ashore, the Confederate officer bluntly explained his mission: he was not out to fight, but to destroy commerce. When asked how he would pay for the coal, he showed Bank of England notes, American twenty-dollar gold pieces, and English sovereigns. Preble wrote Welles: "My crew are eager to fight the *Florida*. . . . With her steam power she can, however, laugh at my canvas, and choose to fight or run as she prefers. The men are also very desirous to cut her out with the boats, and it could be done, but that your instructions forbid such use of friendly waters." It was said the *Florida* carried a spare engine.[8]

After coaling, the *Florida* got to sea, eluding the *St. Louis*. Preble wrote Welles about it at one-thirty in the morning, adding: "I shall follow her at once, though hopeless of catching her out of port. Nelson[9] said the want of frigates in his squadron would be found impressed on his heart. I am sure the want of steam will be found engraven on mine." [10]

By July, Morris was burning ships fifty miles east by south of Cape Henry. He was next heard from off the Capes of Delaware. Ship after ship was sent on his trail, among them the *Kearsarge* that had put an end to the *Alabama*. By August he was at Santa Cruz, Teneriffe, and then he went toward Bahia. Collins of the *Wachusett* had received a false report of the Confederate's arrival at the Brazilian port, and it was because of this that he managed to get there in advance.

Before entering the harbor, Morris had the shot withdrawn from his guns. When asked by the Brazilian naval commander to anchor inshore of his squadron, an indication that trouble was feared, he did so, and then let his steam go down and hauled his fires.[11]

Scarcely had the *Florida* come to a halt in the harbor before Collins sent his small boat to learn her identity. It passed around her in the darkness, and a voice called out from it asking her name. When this was shouted in reply, the voice identified the boat as from the H.B.M.S. *Curlew*. Next morning, Morris saw the U.S.S. *Wachusett* at anchor near by, but no British steamer, so he at once concluded that the inquiry the night before had come from the Union vessel.

During the morning a Brazilian officer visited the *Florida,* and at noon Morris was notified that the President of the province was waiting to receive him. During the interview, the Confederate was granted forty-eight hours to refit and repair, unless longer time was needed, and he was urged to observe strictly during this period the laws of neutrality. Morris gathered that whatever uneasiness of this nature existed, it concerned him and not Collins of the *Wachusett*. In fact, the President told him that he had received solemn assurances from the U.S. consul, Thomas F. Wilson, that the U.S. steamer would do nothing while in port contrary to the laws of other nations or of Brazil.[12]

What the U.S. consul did not tell the President was that he and Napoleon Collins were not acting in harmony. The ship's captain later averred that he had told Wilson that he would handle his own affairs and that the consul was not authorized to speak for him. His cocksureness was based on an understanding that the U.S. minister, General J. W. Webb, had ordered Union vessels to attack Confederate cruisers in any of the ports of Brazil, promising that he "would make it all right" with that country.[13]

When Morris returned to his ship, he found a Brazilian engineer on board. This emissary had examined the vessel and was of the opinion that at least four days would be required for repairs. Morris felt at ease, and on the strength of what happened in his consultations during the day, moved his ship closer to shore. That afternoon he let the port watch take a few hours of leave. That night a boat came alongside bringing an official communication from U.S. Consul Wilson. First Lieutenant Thomas K. Porter received it, saw that it was addressed to "Captain Morris, sloop *Florida*," and handed it back as improperly addressed, explaining that his vessel was the "C.S.S. *Florida*."

Next day a Mr. L. de Videky came on board, bringing the same letter and also a written challenge. Morris refused to receive either of them, saying he had come to Bahia for a specific purpose, that he would neither seek nor avoid a contest with the *Wachusett*, that should he encounter her outside Brazilian waters, he would use his "utmost endeavors to destroy her."

During the afternoon the port watch returned from leave.

Morris immediately sent the starboard watch ashore and, with several of his officers, soon went on liberty himself.

At three-thirty next morning, Morris was awakened by the proprietor of the hotel at which he was staying and was told there was trouble on board the *Florida.* Firing and cheering had been heard in the direction of the vessel, he was informed, but because of the darkness, no one had been able to see from shore what was happening. Morris dressed and hurried to the landing. There a Brazilian officer said the *Wachusett* had rammed and captured the *Florida* and was towing her out of the harbor.

It would not be long before Morris learned firsthand what had happened. Back on the ship, he had left fifty-eight men and twelve officers. Six of these managed to escape and swim to shore.

Unknown to anyone on board the *Florida,* a small boat from the *Wachusett* again had reconnoitered the Confederate vessel during the night. At 3:00 A.M. the Federal ship got under way and, with a full head of steam, steered toward the *Florida.* Fifteen minutes later, Acting Master T. T. Hunter, Jr., in charge of the cruiser's deck, heard the sloop coming. He had time to hail, and receiving no answer, to call all hands to quarters.

When Lieutenant Porter rushed on deck, the *Wachusett* was only twenty yards off. "A moment after," he reported, "she struck us abreast the mizzenmast, broke it into three pieces, crushed in the bulwarks, knocked the quarter boat in on deck, jammed the wheel, carried away the main yard, and started the beams for about thirty feet forward. At the same time she fired about two hundred shots from her small arms and two from her great guns.[14] She then backed off about one hundred yards, and demanded our surrender. I replied to the demand that I would let them know in a few moments. The reply from the *Wachusett* was to surrender immediately, or they would blow us out of the water. As more than half our crew were ashore, and as those on board had just returned from liberty, I believed that she could run us down before we could get our guns loaded. But as I did not like to surrender the vessel without knowing what some of the other officers thought of it, I consulted Lieutenant (S. G.) Stone, the second officer in rank, and finding that he agreed with me that we could not contest against her with any hopes of success, I informed the commander of the *Wachusett* that under the circumstances I would surrender the vessel." [15]

After Porter yelled that he would surrender, armed boats shoved out from the *Wachusett*. At that moment, fifteen men leaped overboard from the *Florida* and began swimming toward shore. Nine of them were shot and killed as they swam.[16]

On shore, Lieutenant Morris was successfully stirring the Brazilians to action, but the effort was wasted. Several shots were fired from the forts, and a sailing corvette and a sidewheel war steamer fired their guns and later ran out of the harbor and gave futile chase. The *Wachusett* by dawn was headed for the West Indies, towing the *Florida*. The Confederate ship's officers were paroled, and crewmen placed in double irons.

Back at Bahia, Morris protested to anyone who would listen. His only consolation as the hours passed was a letter from Mr. De Videky, the intermediary who had come on board with the consul's challenge to battle:

"I feel bound to address you after the fatal affair of last night has happened," it stated. "When I accepted to go on board your vessel, I did so firmly believing that the mission I had to you was meant honestly and in good faith. Had I had only the slightest idea that the man who sent me to you on a mission, as I thought of honor, was at the same time meditating (as it appears now) such an infamous, blackguardly trick as he played, I certainly never should have accepted it. How could I think such villainy to be possible! Be sure that whenever I shall meet that faithless scoundrel who calls himself a consul of the United States of America, and goes by the name of Wilson, I will take my revenge, and treat him as he deserves it. . . . I am still in possession of his two letters, which I could not deliver to him, as I could not find him after I saw you. He has not got your answer at all, which proves still more that miserable and lawless trick must have been meditated before and at the same time when he pretended to offer a fair engagement outside the jurisdiction of the Government of the Brazils." [17]

Morris sent a formal protest to the President of the Province of Bahia. It drew no written answer; instead, a messenger explained orally that the Brazilian Government had not yet recognized the Confederate States of America as an independent nation.

During November the *Wachusett* arrived at Newport News with the *Florida*. Under international agreement, a prize seized in neutral waters was required to be returned to the government that controlled these waters, but there were people who said this would never happen to the Confederate vessel because the Union did not want her turned loose again to continue as a scourge of the sea. Rumors told of an interview between Union Secretary of State Seward and Admiral David Porter in Washington.

"I wish she was at the bottom of the sea!" Seward was reported to have said of the *Florida*.

"Do you mean it?" exclaimed Porter.

"I do, from my soul."

"It shall be done," said Porter.[18]

Before November was past, the Confederate cruiser was resting on the bottom in nine fathoms of water. Her acting master, Jonathan Baker, reported that she was leaking badly when he took command and that the leak had increased, following a collision with the Army transport *Alliance*. Pumps, he said, failed to keep her afloat until she could be towed into shoal water. A court of inquiry found that she had sunk "owing to the giving out of the steam or donkey pump on the night of her sinking, to the neglect of the fireman on watch to call the engineer in time, and to the fact that some of the deck pumps were out of order." [19]

It was December before a long, formal protest was received from Brazil. Union Secretary Seward replied: "You have justly expected that the President would disavow and regret the proceedings at Bahia. He will suspend Captain Collins, and direct him to appear before a court-martial. The consul at Bahia admits that he advised and incited the captain and was active in the proceedings. He will therefore be dismissed." Seward would admit no falsehood, treachery, or deception, and concluded with a report that the *Florida* had sunk as "a consequence of some unforeseen accident which cast no responsibility upon the United States."

In time, the Federal Navy Department would fire a twenty-one gun salute to the Brazilian flag at Bahia in order to make the *amende honorable* for the capture of the *Florida,* thus putting an end to a ticklish situation.[20] This encouraged a reply from the President of the province, announcing that "the honor of the nation being thus satisfied, not the slightest resentment will remain against a Government which thus solemnly shows before the civilized world that she does not avail herself of the force at her disposal against an injured power." [21]

Napoleon Collins in the meantime was smugly watching developments. A court-martial found him guilty of an unlawful attack within the territorial jurisdiction of a neutral power and sentenced him to be dismissed from the U.S. Navy. But Secretary Welles, in reporting the verdict, added: "The sentence of the court is not approved." [22]

Another Union naval officer was watching developments. He was Commodore Charles Wilkes, who earlier in the war had squeaked through the *Trent* affair that almost brought England and France into the conflict. Some weeks after the attack at Bahia, Collins wrote him: "In taking the *Florida* in port I felt convinced I was only doing what you would have done with pleasure. . . ." [23]

Butler's folly

DECEMBER 1864

A ship packed with more than two hundred tons of powder, pushed close to shore and exploded with a timing device, could put an end to Fort Fisher.[1] So assumed Union General Ben Butler, and he made it sound so simple that even Admiral David D. Porter, a man who usually took no one's advice but his own, and Gideon Welles, the small-town politician who had become Secretary of the Navy, were won over to the plan. It seemed an easy way to knock out a major Confederate fortification without getting a lot of Federal soldiers and sailors killed and ships damaged or sunk.

The Union had weighed seriously for months the idea of eliminating Fisher, the powerful bulwark guarding Washington, the great importing depot of the South. Repeated reconnaissances during the early summer were made, on the assumption that success could be gained through landing men by small boats in a surprise movement that would catch the Southerners in a state of depletion. It was well known that troops from North Carolina had been hurried off to reinforce both Lee and Beauregard.

In June, Colonel James Jourdan, commanding the Union forces stationed in the Sub-District of Beaufort, engaged in a bit of horseplay that fellow officers admitted was "a daring-looking affair," but ill-conceived because it induced the Confederates to be more vigilant. Jourdan steamed down past the fort in the U.S.S. *Niphon,* drawing the Rebel fire, but remaining out of range. Then he went on board the U.S.S. *Nereus* and talked confidently to her commander, J. C. Howell, of secretly landing fifteen hundred men on the beach between the hours of 11:00 P.M. and 1:00 A.M. Howell scoffed at the plan, estimating that all the boats available in the fleet could in three hours land no more than three hundred fifty men. He also reminded him that on dark nights the entire beach was alive with signal lights.

It was soon mentioned that Jourdan was making a diversion in another direction, "as he has every reason to believe his first plans are suspected, if not too well understood." [2]

Early in September, Gideon Welles wrote Admiral Lee, commanding the North Atlantic Blockading Squadron, for detailed information on Fort Fisher, listing fourteen specific things he would like to know. Two days later he sent off a dispatch to Admiral Farragut, only a month after his grueling battle of Mobile Bay. It told that the Navy had been trying for two years to get the Army to co-operate in a joint attack on the defenses of Cape Fear River and that now General Grant had indicated that some of his troops would be ready to co-operate by October 1. "You are selected to command the naval force, and you will endeavor to be at Port Royal by the latter part of September, when further orders will await you," the Secretary informed him. [3]

But Welles was placing his dependability in the wrong men. Lee responded in admirable fashion. He sent a letter marked "confidential," that gave much information about Fort Fisher, and then followed it up with a request for a leave of absence, under the excuse that for the last four years he had been on constant and arduous sea service. [4] On the same day Lee was asking for time off, a similar message arrived from Farragut. In it he pleaded impaired health and overtaxed energies, and asked to be excused from the Wilmington campaign. Welles calmly bowed to the wishes of these two veterans. His next choice of a leader was David Porter, a sort of runner-up to Farragut in the Mississippi River operations.

Rapidly, as fall came on, the Fort Fisher plans were pursued. During September, vessels began accumulating at Hampton Roads, and more information on the depth of water and other conditions along the Carolina coast was gathered. Some of it was not pleasing. Captain B. F. Sands, commanding the harbor at Beaufort, wrote, for instance, that "within the week ending September 9 a suspicious object in the water has been seen by three of the bar tenders, at three different times, supposed to be a torpedo boat, and which was fired upon four times on the night of the 8th instant or morning of the 9th by the *Victoria* on the other occasions it disappeared upon the turning of the wheels or propeller of the vessels from which it was seen." [5]

It was not known what to expect from the desperate Southerners, and for that reason, frequent reconnaissances were made. In October, Porter assumed his new command, and right away an air of impatience was injected into the operation. He soon announced that he was ready with a sufficient force to cover any landing the Army might make.

Welles shortly afterward complained to Abraham Lincoln about delay by the Army. He said the Navy was ready with a squadron of one hundred fifty vessels, including several ironclads—the largest fleet in American history, an immense force lying idle at Hampton Roads and Beaufort—waiting for the Army to move. Every other squadron had been reduced, he said, to make possible the attack on Fort Fisher. [6]

The frequent reconnaissances revealed that the Southerners were not idle. In command at Fort Fisher was Colonel William Lamb, a Norfolk, Virginia, newspaperman and politician married to a Northern girl, Susan Anne Chaffee, of Providence, Rhode Island. Handsome, with black wavy hair and a small mustache, he was an efficient officer who had never ceased to strengthen the work since he had taken over the assignment in the summer of '62. He set up a home in a small cottage a mile up the beach from the fort, and to this he brought his wife and children. They came to a hectic and yet happy life, one that was never without its excitements and its threats as the war drew nearer to their door.

Traffic along the Cape Fear River was Lamb's constant concern. Always alert, the signals flashed under his direction caused him to be looked upon as the blockade-runners' guardian angel. It was said of him that "many a small vessel did his skill and activity snatch from the very jaws of the blockaders." [7] Many prominent officers, war correspondents, ship masters, and others they entertained in their little home.

Fort Fisher was situated on a peninsula eighteen miles south of Wilmington, near the end of a stretch of sandy soil, partly wooded, stretching down between the Cape Fear River on the west and the Atlantic Ocean on the east and south. It had been called Federal Point before the war, but was now renamed Confederate Point. Seven miles north of the end of this peninsula stood a high hill known as "Sugar Loaf," where was intrenched a camp for the Confederate troops stationed at Wilmington. By following a road along the back of the river, troops could be moved without being seen from the sea side, a natural feature that added to the advantages of the fort.

When Lamb assumed command, Fort Fisher was comprised of several detached earthworks, with a casemated battery of sand and palmetto logs, mounting four guns.[8] From the start, he was determined to build a work of such magnitude that it could withstand the heaviest fire of any guns in the Union Navy. To this end, he employed at times more than a thousand men, whites and Negroes. They worked steadily, sometimes at night, sometimes on Sunday, yet some of the improvements that Lamb had in mind still were unfinished. The fort was laid off with two faces, a land face six hundred eighty-two yards long, mounting twenty of the heaviest seacoast guns, and a sea face one

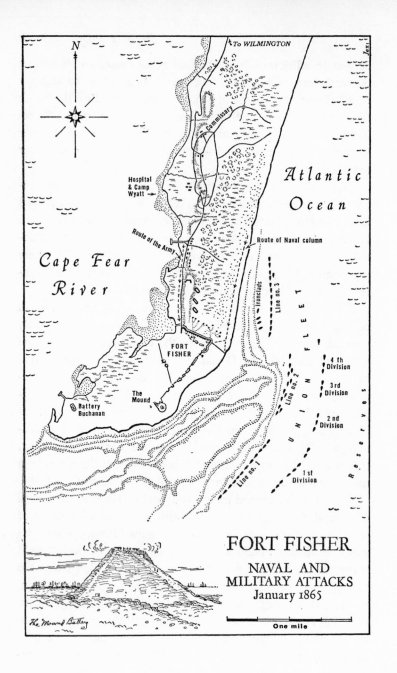

The Mound Battery

FORT FISHER

NAVAL AND
MILITARY ATTACKS
January 1865

One mile

thousand eight hundred ninety-eight yards long, with twenty-four guns.[9]

Several outlying batteries also were constructed along the peninsula, the nearest of them The Mound, the earthwork the Federals had watched with much interest as it gradually took form, a heap of earth rising sixty feet above the peninsula, from which a plunging fire could be aimed at passing ships. Two inclined railways had supplemented the labor force. This work was at the southern end of the sea face. On the point, a couple of miles away, was Battery Buchanan, a citadel at which reinforcements could be landed or to which an overpowered garrison might retreat to be transported away by boat at night. A wharf for large steamers was near by. The land between was flat and sandy, so low it sometimes was inundated.

As a defense against infantry, a line of torpedoes was buried entirely across the peninsula, five to six hundred feet from the land face. Behind these was a heavy palisade of sharpened logs nine feet high, pierced for musketry and so laid out as to have an enfilading fire on the center, where there was a redoubt.

Information that a Union fleet was building up under command of Admiral Porter reached the Wilmington area on October 24. That same day, an anonymous letter arrived at the headquarters of Generals Braxton Bragg and W. H. C. Whiting, senior Confederate officers on duty there. It told that Southern men who had lost faith in their cause were to cut telegraph wires, spike guns, and pilot the enemy to the city. This message was conveyed confidentially to Lamb, who immediately repudiated it so far as his garrison was concerned.

Lamb was writing daily in a diary in which he intended to convey an accurate account of the herculean task he faced at Fort Fisher. He wrote in it on October 28 that his guests for dinner were General Whiting, General Louis Hebert, his immediate superior, and Flag Officer Robert F. Pinckney, top-ranking Confederate naval officer in the area. They had come on an inspection visit.

By November, Butler had managed to get the Navy Department to consider seriously his plan of blowing up Fort Fisher with a boatload of powder. Made available to the Navy were copies of War Department reports on the results of powder explosions, including a recent experiment in England, and an estimate of the conditions to be overcome at Fort Fisher.[10] These were considered at a special meeting called secretly by Assistant Secretary Fox at a private residence and then sent by special messenger to Porter, along with a request for his opinion of the project. Fox stated that it was his conviction the explosion would have no useful results, and some of the engineers agreed with him.

But Porter, true to his faith in gimmicks, approved the plan promptly.[11] Soon he was writing Lieutenant Commander Pendleton G. Watmough, senior officer off New Inlet, that he proposed running a vessel drawing eight and a half feet as near Fort Fisher as possible. She was to be loaded with three hundred fifty tons of powder and exploded by running her up on the beach. "My calculations," he added, "are that the explosion will wind up Fort Fisher and the works along the beach, and that we can open fire with the vessels without damage." He asked for all the information he could get on the depth of water opposite the fort.[12]

By early December, the vessel to be exploded had been chosen and was waiting at New York. She was the U.S.S. *Louisiana,* an old iron gunboat of two hundred ninety-five tons, purchased by the Federal Government at Philadelphia in 1861. Her draft under normal load was eight and a half feet. Taken to Norfolk, her battery, masts, part of the deckhouse, and all unnecessary items were removed. On her deck then was built a framework seventy feet long and the width of the ship. This was covered with canvas. None of the powder was to be stored below the water line. It was to be stacked in this house, on the berth deck, and in the afterhold, or coal bunker. Last-minute touches were designed to make her resemble a blockade-runner.

Activity along the coast of North Carolina increased rapidly as the December days passed. A sailor wrote home: "I will give you a piece of information, which is *confidential* and not to go out of our family on any account whatever. General Grant is ready with his men and we will attack Wilmington in five days from now. Everything is ready and working smoothly. The attack will be a surprise." [13]

Preparations also were in progress in the North Carolina sounds. One day a fleet of eight vessels steamed up the Roanoke River toward Rainbow Bluff for purposes of diversion. A "reliable" source said there were no torpedoes for a distance of twelve miles upstream. At nine that night the ships came to anchor off Jamesville, in what was supposed to be water free of danger. As they drew together there was a tremendous explosion, and the U.S.S. *Otsego* went to the bottom, victim of two torpedoes. Next day the U.S.S. *Bazeley,* steaming in the vicinity, was suddenly shaken by a terrific shock and immediately sank.

Vessels began dragging North Carolina streams for torpedoes on a co-operative basis. Boats were rowed upstream at distances of twenty feet apart, a chain stretched between them. In one straightaway, eighty torpedoes were found.[14] It was back-breaking work. Ships were warped up some of the streams by hawsers fastened to trees on either bank. Sometimes they became jammed, and much effort was required to release them. Enemy sharpshooters were relentless. "Two weeks of more severe labor could scarcely be conceived than those which we have just passed through," wrote one ship's commander, "the officers and crew being almost incessantly engaged either in dragging for torpedoes, working anchors and hawsers, or fighting the guns, and sometimes all at the same time." [15]

For a week the U.S.S. *Valley City* was kept busy searching for the explosives; then her crew was given a day off. She lay at anchor in the river near the small town of Williamston, and at her rail stood Surgeon John M. Batten. Suddenly he straightened and stared out across the water at an object swimming past the vessel, unable to believe his eyes. He had been told such things did not happen, so he hastened below to write in his diary: "This was the first and only hog I ever saw swim." [16]

Excitement increased along the Virginia coast. As December came on, Union troops could be seen going on board ships in the Hampton Roads area, and it was commonly known that they were headed for North Carolina. Joseph Bloomfield Osborn, who signed his letters "Bloom," wrote Louise Landau, his fiancée, from the U.S.S. *Vanderbilt*. He had been wounded in the battle of Chancellorsville, fighting as a soldier. Returning to service, he had joined the Navy and was now starting on his first expedition. "We are not agoing to Brasille but are on our way with the rest of the fleet to Wilmington," he reported. "There is going to be a great naval engagement there, and perhaps by the time this reaches you I may witness one of the grandest struggles of this war. There is about one hundred of the best vessels in the U.S. Navy in this fleet and something is agoing to be done. I am proud that we are going along. Beside of us is a powder boat to run up near the Rebel fort and then blow it to pieces, and as the steamer is a iron one I guess it will startle the Rebels some if not blow their forts to pieces. I hope I may witness the explosion." [17]

"Bloom's" prediction of a battle within five days failed to develop. Delay set in, much of it due to bad weather, although the Army received most of the blame. On December 13, the fleet at Hampton Roads began moving southward—fifty-seven vessels with six hundred twenty-seven guns.[18] The *Sassacus* was assigned the task of towing the powder-laden *Louisiana,* which had been placed in command of Acting Master Whitman Chase of the U.S.S. *Wabash,* with specific instructions for no fire to be lighted and no cigars to be smoked on board.[19] It was packed with one hundred eighty-five tons of powder; more would be added after she reached North Carolina.

Army transports, loaded with troops, began leaving Hampton Roads about the same time. Porter was surprised to find that Ben Butler was accompanying them; he had thought Weitzel was to command the men in the field and that Butler was merely taking a hand with the preparations. At the start there was trouble between the two leaders. Porter wanted Butler to wait thirty-six hours before following, to give the slow-moving monitors time to reach North Carolina. He was also critical because the Army officer was not more careful about concealing his movements and was sloppy with preparations, taking his troops away without sufficient water or supplies, and without even trenching tools.

Porter prepared a specific order of attack for his fleet. It was to remain twelve miles off the coast until the powder boat had done its task, and then was to move up for the assault. Vessels would close in by divisions at varying distances and let loose a terrific bombardment while troops were being landed.[20]

The powder boat was to be under the command of the veteran Alexander C. Rhind, a native New Yorker, captain of several vessels at various times in the fighting along the Atlantic Coast.[21] Even Secretary Welles looked upon him as "an impulsive but brave and rash man." [22] Porter gave Rhind detailed instructions that pulled no punches: "Great risks have to be run, and there are chances that you may lose your life in this adventure; but the risk is worth the running, when the importance of the project is to be considered and the fame to be gained by this novel undertaking, which is either to prove that forts on the water are useless or that the Rebels are proof against gunpowder." [23]

Along with these instructions, Porter revealed that over the weeks he had developed certain reservations toward the powder-boat project. "I do not anticipate such a dreadful earthquake as some suppose will take place (destroying everything), nor do I think the effect will in any way be mild," he wrote. "I take a mean between the two, and think the effect of the explosion will be simply very severe, stunning men at a distance of three or four hundred yards, demoralizing them completely, and making them unable to stand for any length of time a fire from the ship. I think that the concussion will tumble magazines that are built on framework, and that the famous Mound will be among the things that were, and the guns buried beneath the ruins. I think that houses in Wilmington and Smithville will tumble to the ground and much demoralize the people, and I think if the Rebels fight after the explosion they have more in them than I gave them credit for."

By the morning of the 17th, the *Louisiana* was ready for action. On board had been carefully stowed thirty more tons of powder, some in bags, some in barrels, as much additional weight as she could take without making her draft too deep. She would have started in to New Inlet that night but for a heavy sea rolling in on the beach.

Next morning it was nearly calm at Beaufort. Seaman J. C. Gregg, on board the U.S.S. *Brooklyn,* recorded in his diary: "A rumor is afloat and credited that the powder boat that is to blow up Fort Fisher is going at twelve tonight and we are to follow at daylight. It looks quite probable as the order was given after hammocks was piped down to get up sand bags and take down all the sailings on the spar deck, which is now being done. A great deal of signaling going on." [24]

The *Louisiana* was towed away from Beaufort in the early morning. After getting outside, where it was found there was still considerable swell on, she got up steam and remained under it. A little later in the forenoon, a breeze sprang up from the eastward and continued steady but light throughout the day, freshening toward night. The vessel arrived off Fort Fisher just after dark, and plans were made to run her in that night. At nine o'clock she pulled away from the *Kansas,* which was supplying her range light, and was towed by the *Wilderness,* a swift tug having on board George F. Bowen, one of the best bar pilots available. As she approached the shore, the light on the *Kansas* disappeared. Soon the lights on The Mound were put out by the Confederates, and this caused the pilot to advise caution. He said it would be dangerous to take the vessel in, with so much swell on, without the aid of landmarks. Commander Rhind accepted his advice and gave orders to stand offshore and wait for another night. Shortly afterward the U.S.S. *A. D. Vance* ran into view and began signaling. She had a message from Porter to delay the explosion. It was sent at the request of General Butler, standing by with his troops in transports at Beaufort. Butler did not think it would be possible to land troops next morning through the heavy surf.

In perfect agreement with Butler's attitude was J. S. Bradford of the United States Coast Survey. He had left the *Wilderness* and had almost capsized trying to get close to the beach in a small boat, to reconnoiter. A sailor on board the U.S.S. *Canonicus* wrote a letter home about the weather on the 18th: "I cannot remember seeing the sky look so threatening as it did all through that night. I had scarcely a wink of sleep, and in the morning when it began to look clear and pleasant my spirits went up to a tremendous height. Every ear was strained to hear the explosion of our powder vessel, which we think will bring down the forts around their ears." [25]

Daylight next morning found conditions no better. The wind had increased to gale proportions. Throughout the day there was talk of making another attempt, but at 5:30 P.M. signal was given that Porter had issued orders "not to go in tonight." [26]

Excitement in the meantime was running high on Confederate Point and at Wilmington. It was well known the Union fleet was standing by and that an attack could be expected at any moment. Lamb was especially worried because he had at hand only half his garrison—five companies of the Thirty-sixty North Carolina Regiment—the other half having been sent to Georgia to help check Sherman's army. Orders called for every available officer and man to be hurried toward Fort Fisher.

Flag Officer Pinckney, among officers who came to assist Lamb, suggested that the guns of the heavy Union ships would drive the Confederates from the sea face with a few broadsides of grape and canister. Lamb strongly but respectfully disagreed.[27]

A detachment of three officers and twenty-five sailors from the Confederate Navy reached Lamb on the 21st, after spending the night at Battery Buchanan.[28] A strong gale was still blowing from the southward and eastward, and there was a heavy sea on, outside. In the fort the sand was blowing in all directions.

After night had settled and while a terrific wind was howling and the rain beating down in torrents, four blockade-runners ran clear of the Federal sentinels "without the loss of a rope yarn." One of them was the steamer *Owl,* laden with seven hundred eighty bales of cotton and captained by the indomitable John Maffitt.[29]

The weather was better on the 22nd, but intensely cold. On the 23rd, there was little change, except that the wind had gone down. But this was enough to cause the *Louisiana* to be signaled to go in to shore that night. She was ready and waiting, with the major worry confined to the method chosen to explode the powder. Most complicated of the detonation systems was a device built around a ship's clock and comprised of pins and tubes and fuses and weights, and even a piece of catgut. Three of these, regulated to fire simultaneously, were installed at specific points about the ship. Slow matches also were placed to backstop the clocks. As a final precaution, Porter instructed Rhind to light a fire in the stern of the vessel the last thing before leaving her. "There may be something yet unthought of that will affect the clocks and fuses, but there will be no mistake in a fire," he advised.[30]

At Fort Fisher and up at Wilmington, the Confederates were struggling with worries that increased by the minute. More reinforcements reached the fort during the day. Included were two companies of the Fortieth North Carolina, one company of the Thirteenth North Carolina, and the Seventh Battalion of Junior Reserves, the last an outfit of North Carolina boys between the ages of sixteen and eighteen. The additions brought Lamb's total force to nine hundred.[31] Whiting, trying frantically to amass more strength, wrote Richmond: "Our position here is very precarious." He expected the Federals to attack at any moment, and it was not the fleet of ships off the bar that worried him most. He had heard of the exercising of Union troops in an immense number of small boats at Norfolk, and this reminded him of what had happened at Plymouth only a few weeks back. "From various circumstances," he reported, "I fear their plan is one I have been apprehensive of ever since Cushing's memorable exploit of coming in the harbor at night in a small boat—that is, to send in barges the first smooth and dark night with troops over New Inlet Bar, land on the beach at Confederate Point, and carry the batteries." The absence on the outside of Butler's transports, then waiting at Beaufort, was to him a strong indication of such a movement.

The wind subsided as the day waned. Inside Fort Fisher men passed the hours in customary diversions. The notes of "Lorena," "My Maryland," and other songs popular at the time came from the violin and accordion, and floated through the enclosures of the earthwork. Here and there, little groups sat at cards and other games. Occasionally a serious-minded or religious individual would be found off to himself reading the Bible. Above the fort waved a hand-sewn flag proudly presented by the ladies of Wilmington.[32] Lamb gave his men his complete attention; Susan and the children had been taken to a plantation across the Cape Fear River for a few days.

Out in the ships the pattern was much the same. As darkness neared, "Bloom" got off another letter to Louise: "We have laid here at anchor now for some days, expecting every day to receive orders to move against the forts. But for several days the sea has been very high on account of the windy weather. It has also been extremely cold. The wind has now gone down and we expect to fight on the morrow. . . . You may think that we tonight are perhaps a sober set. Not so. The boys are dancing, singing, and are more noisy than I have heard them in some time." [33]

At seven that night the *Louisiana* and *Wilderness* came in from outside and lay to until 11:00 P.M. Then they started toward the shore opposite Fort Fisher, Rhind bearing in his pocket a note with these words from Porter: "I expect more good to our cause from a success in this instance than from an advance of all of the armies in the field. . . . The names of those connected with the expedition will be famous for all time to come." [34]

Half an hour after they started in, the *Louisiana* was cast off by the *Wilderness* and continued under her own power. Her trip was easy. A blockade-runner, the *Little Hattie,* making her second run from Nassau in a month, had just passed in a few minutes earlier, and signals were flashing between her and Fort Fisher.

To a point two hundred fifty to three hundred yards north of the fort, the *Louisiana* steamed before stopping.[35] Rhind would have taken her closer, possibly to within one hundred fifty yards, but the night was so clear he was afraid the Confederates would see her in time to frustrate the plan. The wind was light offshore, and he expected the powder boat would tend to the tide if anchored, so an anchor was let go. Then the detonation systems were prepared. The clocks were set to an hour and a half. It was twelve minutes to midnight at the time, which would schedule the explosion for 1:18 A.M. While tending to the clocks, Rhind noticed that the vessel would not tail inshore, so he let go another anchor, this with short scope. His last act was to light a fire under the cabin.

Shortly after midnight, Rhind and his crew returned alongside the *Wilderness* in a small boat. As soon as they reported, six rockets were sent up to warn the fleet, and then the vessel headed toward the outside. It was now only a matter of waiting.

Time passed slowly. All eyes on the ships standing off twelve miles from shore were turned toward the fort. In the distance they could see the fire that had been started on the *Louisiana*. It was small, and had been set, Rhind said, so that it would not reach the powder until after the clocks were scheduled to touch off the explosion.

At Fort Fisher the captain of the blockade-runner *Little Hattie,* happy over another successful run, sat in conversation with

Lamb and other officers. As he prepared to leave, the officer of the day reported a vessel on fire off the beach. Lamb went to the ramparts and saw what he took to be a blockade-runner aflame at its stern. The *Hattie*'s master said it might be the *Agnes Fry,* which had left Nassau for Wilmington with him. Lamb stood there watching the vessel burn for half an hour, and then returned to his quarters after cautioning the mounted pickets to watch out for small boats.[36]

The minutes ticked away. One o'clock passed, and it was easy to see that the flames were spreading on the *Louisiana.* Rhind and others thumbed their watches.

The great moment of expectancy—1:18—passed without an explosion. Rhind had no explanation, but mentally he blessed Porter for his wisdom in instructing that a fire be set. This feeling of expectancy increased as 1:30 came . . . then 1:35. At 1:40, flames shot up into the heavens in a great outburst above the point toward which they were staring. Seconds later, the sound of an explosion came to their ears, and then the repercussion. Other explosions followed, with the same effect, and the flames spread out as the powder could be seen burning over a broad area of the water's surface. Hopes plummeted. No one was knocked down or even badly shaken.

At the fort, Lamb, after returning from watching the burning ship, had stretched out on a lounge for a few hours of sleep. Scarcely had he closed his eyes before he felt a gentle rocking which he would have attributed to imagination or to vertigo. But it was instantly followed by other explosions that sounded little louder than the report of a ten-inch columbiad. He heard the sentinels shouting in every direction for the corporal of the guard. Before he could leave his couch, the officer of the day reported the vessel that had been on fire had blown up. Lamb telegraphed the news to Whiting at Wilmington and again retired to rest, mentally noting that he would record in his diary in the morning: "A blockader got aground near the fort, set fire to herself, and blew up." [37]

In the morning, the explosion was generally discussed by

Fort Fisher officers and men. Some of them had not even been awakened by the noise. A Tarheel sentinel, speaking to the man who came to relieve him, said: "Reckon one of them Yankee gunboats off thar done busted her biler." [38]

The explosion appeared to have jarred distant objects more severely than it did those in close proximity. Sixty-nine miles away at Beaufort, it was felt by men on duty in the Union storehouse and carpenter shop. The lookout on the U.S.S. *Arletta,* a schooner anchored there, reported that he saw a vivid light bearing about west.[39]

Daniel Ammen, commanding the U.S.S. *Mohican,* was among the men out in the ships who forsook sleep to watch for the explosion. He saw it, thought it resembled the flash of distant lightning, and noted that a dull sound came across the water after a lapse of time. Two hours later a dense bank of powder smoke enveloped parts of the fleet.[40]

At daylight, no part of the *Louisiana* could be seen. But Fort Fisher looked the same as ever.

The storm had ended, leaving the sea as calm as a lake. Porter waited. He assumed Butler was on his way, and he knew that six or seven hours would have to intervene before the troops arrived.

At 12:30 he decided to wait no longer. The Army should be on hand within the hour, according to his estimate, so he gave the order for the fleet to move in and open on the fort.

The *New Ironsides,* mightiest of the ironclads, was in the lead. Forty-nine other vessels followed her. The first two ships in this grand armada carried more shot and shell than was contained in all the magazines on Confederate Point.[41]

"The *Ironsides* took her position in the most beautiful and seamanlike manner," Porter reported, "got her spring out, and opened deliberate fire on the fort, which was firing at her with all its guns." [42]

The largest of the vessels pushed up in line and opened a fierce barrage. Others joined in, sending out a continuing thunder that seemed to shake the rollers turning somersaults along the beach. The air was so calm that smoke shot out of the guns and hung listlessly, blocking the view of men on both sides. It enveloped ships and it enveloped the shore, at times shutting out the fort from the fleet and the fleet from the fort.

Clarence Cary, who had come down from Wilmington to Fort Fisher with other sailors and been quartered in an old shanty, was a member of a gun crew busily fighting. His thoughts went frequently to his diary, and later in the afternoon, after a piece of shell wounded him in the left knee, he would be taken to the hospital where he would have a chance to record the opening scenes as he saw them:

"Movements of the fleet plainly visible, as they are close in. The long roll beat about 1:00 P.M. and we went to quarters and were soon all ready for action. The frigate (ironclad) *New Ironsides* and three monitors . . . led the way, the frigates coming next, and then the sloops and gunboats last. They came up two abreast until opposite the forts, when the outer line came on around the sea face and took their positions. . . . At 1:20 the Yankees fired the first gun, and then the action commenced in earnest. It is estimated that the enemy threw on an average one hundred shells a minute. The fort replied slowly, as the firing was too hot to keep the men at their guns. The quarters in the fort were soon in flames, and the flag was soon shot away. The noise of the guns and the bursting shell was deafening. Our sailors behaved with great coolness, and as we had no relief crews, they had tiresome work."

Projectiles of every description, from three-inch rifle shell to a fifteen-inch round shell, were falling along Confederate Point around and beyond Fort Fisher. Sometime after the bombardment started, the garrison flag, gift of the Wilmington ladies, was shot away and its shaft destroyed. Lamb sent word for the battle flag of The Mound to be raised. This posed a problem, for the halyards on this staff were so unreeved that they were useless. Christopher C. Bland of Company K, Thirty-sixth North Carolina Regiment, volunteered to raise the banner and, given permission, shinned up the pole and fastened it to the top.

Immediately a terrific barrage was trained on The Mound. As Bland descended, the lower corner of the flag was shot loose, and again he worked his way up and repeated his act. Not a bullet or piece of shell touched him.[43]

Out on the U.S.S. *Powhatan,* Commodore James F. Schenck sent an officer aloft with a glass to locate some guns that were annoying the ship. The officer, Acting Ensign Robley D. Evans, an eighteen-year-old, born in Floyd County, Virginia, brother of a member of Confederate General Lee's staff, had on a double-breasted coat, its pockets stuffed with hardtack. Poised in the mizzen rigging, just below the top, he put the corner of piece of hardtack in his mouth and held it between his teeth while he scanned the shore. He found the guns. Presently he saw one of them swing around until he seemed to be staring directly into its mouth. A puff of smoke burst forth, something that looked like a lamppost crossed the field of his vision, and a moment later a shell passed through the rigging four feet below him, causing him to swing into the mast. When he had recovered his composure, he felt for the hardtack. It was gone, and for the rest of his life he would wonder whether he had swallowed it.[44]

"In one hour and fifteen minutes after the first shot was fired," according to Porter, "not a shot came from the fort; two magazines had been blown up by our shells and the fort set on fire in several places, and such a torrent of missiles were falling into and bursting over it that it was impossible for anything human to stand it." [45]

Porter's casualties were light, a majority of them victims of his own guns. Five one-hundred-pounder Parrotts had exploded, one each on the *Ticonderoga, Yantic, Juniata, Mackinaw,* and *Quaker City.* Forty-five men were killed or wounded by the blasts.[46]

In late afternoon, Porter prepared a report to be telegraphed to Gideon Welles. Fort Fisher had not been heard from since before two o'clock, and he considered it well in hand. "There being no troops here to take possession," he wrote, "I am merely firing at it now to keep up practice. The forts are nearly demolished, and as soon as troops come we can take possession. We have set them on fire, blown some of them up, and all that is wanted now is the troops to land to go into them. I suppose Butler will be here in the morning." [47]

At sunset Butler showed up in his flagship, the *Ben De Ford,* along with two or three transports. The others, he said, were on the way.

Disgusted, Porter gave orders for the fleet to cease its bombardment and withdraw. The action had lasted nearly five hours. As the ships' guns were silenced, a single shot was fired from Fort Fisher. It was the last of the day.[48]

Inside the fort, Colonel Lamb prepared a report of damages. Much of the afternoon he had remained on the parapet of the sea face, and during this period, only one shell exploded near enough to endanger his life. Most of the firing seemed aimed at the garrison flagstaff, causing many of the shells to go over the fort and into the river beyond.[49] Half the quarters, including headquarters, were destroyed, and there was damage, more or less, to some of the parapets and traverses, but no part of the work was greatly injured except in front of a gun on the right of the northeast salient. Four gun carriages had been disabled and two guns dismounted. Only one of his men lay dead and but twenty-two wounded, three of them severely. "As the enemy attempted no passage of the bar and stayed out at long range, with the exception of their ironclads, I fired very slowly and deliberately," he reported. "I am unable to know what damage was done them, but I am certain the injury inflicted upon them far exceeds the injury their bombardment did us. Our Heavenly Father has protected my garrison this day, and I feel that He will sustain us in defending our homes from the invader." [50]

General Whiting had come into the fort from Wilmington in the late afternoon, just before the bombardment ended. He refused to take command, standing by as a witness, along with Flag Officer Pinckney. Guns in the fort had fired six hundred twenty-two projectiles.[51]

That night a message from Butler reached Porter's flagship. It suggested a landing about eight next morning, subject to the outcome of a consultation between the Admiral and General Weitzel, who would command the troops. This was to be carried out following a reconnaissance by a party sufficiently strong to maintain a foothold, could one be gained. If an assault on the fort were then deemed practical, it stated further, an assault would be made.

This message arrived after a query by signal from the *Ben De Ford* as to whether any of the enemy's armed vessels had been visible during the day and whether any shots had been exchanged between the fleet and the Half Moon and Flag Pond Hill Batteries[52] to the north of Fort Fisher. This served to fan a peeve that Porter had been building up against Butler since their departure from Norfolk. He replied: "There was one Rebel vessel seen today, supposed to be an armed one. She was entirely out of range and could not be brought into play even if her guns were of any account. The Flag Pond Battery has been dismantled and the guns taken away. It was a small affair anyhow, and only used to drive off our blockaders. There are no batteries along the shore, at least we saw none today, and our vessels came close along the beach."[53]

During the dark hours that night, a vessel came down the Cape Fear and headed for sea, completely unnoticed by the besieging fleet. She was the *Chameleon,* formerly the dreaded *Tallahassee,* and at her helm was John Wilkinson. Cotton, turpentine, and other valuables filled every foot of space in her hold and on her decks. She was headed for Bermuda and would be on her way back in four weeks, laden with provisions for Lee's starving army.

The next day was Christmas, a Sunday. Porter had things stirring before it was full daylight. By 10:00 A.M. he gave the order to get under way and form line of battle. Vessels moved up as they had the day before, the *New Ironsides* leading. At 10:30 they began a slow bombardment that continued until late afternoon.

All morning Porter fretted. The fort was firing slowly, apparently softened up, and he could not understand why the Army did not make its attack. It was 2:00 P.M. before he saw forty-one boats push in for the first landing, near Flag Pond Hill Battery, four miles up the beach. Five hundred men were supposed to attempt this first foothold. Porter had suggested that it would probably be better to land more, that the weather might become bad and prevent other boats following, but this got from Butler only a remark that "we had better not land any." [54]

Before the landing was attempted, several vessels steamed up to within two hundred fifty yards of shore and opened fire on the Flag Pond Hill Battery. This was kept up for two or three hours. Porter had informed Butler that the battery was deserted, so it was to his embarrassment that a white flag appeared above it within minutes after the first soldiers landed. [55] But it was the Navy and not the Army that accepted the surrender. Boats from the *Britannia, Tristram Shandy, Howquah,* and *Santiago de Cuba* headed toward it. The *Britannia's* arrived there first, planted the ship's ensign, and soon prisoners were marching down to the beach. They were boys from the North Carolina Junior Reserve. [56]

Porter kept the bombardment at a slow pace because he thought all the damage had been done to Fort Fisher that needed to be done and that all required now to bring about its capture was for the Army to move in. So well in hand did the situation seem that he ordered small boats lowered from the ships in the middle of the afternoon to sound the bar and drag for torpedoes, hoping that a channel across the bar might be found or opened. The Southerners in Battery Buchanan, including Clarence Cary, released from the hospital the evening before, after his knee wound had been bandaged, saw these boats out there and trained guns in their direction. On the fourth shot, one of the Brooke rifles in the fortification exploded, knocking

Cary and others down, wounding five or six, but killing none. Shortly afterward another exploded in the same manner, its bands separating and flying in all directions. Again there were no fatalities.[57]

Out on the water, as a result of these and other shots, a scene occurred that brought cheers from the men in the battery. Each boat engaged in sounding was commanded by an officer seated in the stern. One of these got nearer the beach than the others, and the Southerners concentrated their attention on it. First they cut away its flag. This was rescued from the water by the officer in charge. He scooped it up and waved it above his head before replacing it on the broken staff. This caused the gunmen at Battery Buchanan to take dead aim. Their next shell cut the boat in two, spilling its crew in the water and bringing other boats to their assistance. Thus ended the sounding and torpedo searching.[58] William Cushing had been in charge of one of the boats trying to locate a channel, but not even the amazing Cushing was successful in this instance.[59]

The action grew hottest after four o'clock. At 4:30 Lamb saw Union sharpshooters on the left flank of the fort. A few discharges of canister drove them back.

At 5:20, in the growing dusk of a winter's day, a message arrived at Battery Buchanan from Fort Fisher saying that the enemy was advancing and asking for reinforcements. Two-thirds of the Confederates on duty there immediately were hurried toward the fort.

While these troops were running up the peninsula, following the river side and stooping low, the bombardment was stepped up to a terrific pace—one hundred thirty shots per minute, or more than two per second. One of the shells, with a burning fuse, fell in a gun chamber of the fort. Private James Turner and J. H. Brisson of the Thirty-sixth North Carolina leaped toward it and quickly threw it outside.[60]

The firing reached its peak for the day. "Never since the foundation of the world was there such a fire," Lieutenant

Aeneas Armstrong, a voluntary defender that day, wrote in describing it. "The whole of the interior of the fort, which consists of sand, merlons, etc., was as one eleven-inch shell bursting. You can now inspect the works and walk on nothing but iron." [61]

The shells from the ships went down the palisade line of Fort Fisher. In a few minutes a line of skirmishers was seen advancing on the works. Before the bombardment ceased, an incident occurred that would bring the Congressional Medal of Honor to a Union soldier. He was Captain W. H. Walling of the One Hundred Forty-second New York Infantry, three companies of which were in the advance. He saw a flag lying behind the palisade of the fort. Telling his men to keep a watch for Confederate sharpshooters, he dashed through a hole in the palisade and captured the flag, returning unscathed.

But a Southern courier's fate was not so good. This fellow darted out of the fort on horseback, hoping to get past the advancing line. He was shot and killed and his horse captured.[62]

In the fort were nine hundred twenty-one veteran troops and four hundred fifty Junior Reserves. As soon as the fire of the fleet died away, the parapets were manned, and half the garrison was stationed outside, behind the palisades. There was no fear of an assault from the front; what the defenders were worried about was a possible landing between The Mound and Battery Buchanan, in the opposite direction.[63]

Grape and canister poured out from the heavy guns of the fort. To within seventy-five yards, the line advanced, hugging the ground behind the sand curtain. At that point it stopped and slowly fell back.

Out on his flagship, Porter was waiting for the complete victory. He estimated that three thousand men already had been landed. Signals from the *Ben De Ford* informed him General Weitzel was reconnoitering in person, to determine whether an assault was feasible. The Admiral was confident it would be.

Darkness came on. A message was flashed to Porter: "Butler's troops are re-embarking." Porter was dumfounded, and his anger began rising. This was not his style of warfare. He stormed and he ranted, and while he cursed the stupidity of certain military leaders, rain began falling, blown by a wind that made it impossible to take small boats in to shore. Stranded there without supplies or entrenching tools were seven hundred men.

Before Porter went to sleep that night, he received a medium-length report from Butler. The General revealed that both he and Weitzel were of opinion the fort could not be carried by assault, that it could be taken only by the operations of a regular siege, which did not come within his instructions. He added: "In view of the threatening aspect of the weather, wind arising from the southeast, rendering it impossible to make further landing through the surf, I caused the troops with their prisoners to re-embark, and see nothing further that can be done by the land forces. I shall therefore sail for Hampton Roads as soon as the transport fleet can be got in order." [64]

Throughout the night, musketry was heard from the stranded infantry, lying in foxholes dug by hand in the pouring rain. At 3:20 A.M. the monitors, nearest of the fleet, opened on Fort Fisher, an effort designed to keep the Confederates within its walls.

Before daylight, Porter sent a message to Captain James Alden of the U.S.S. *Brooklyn:*

"We must get those poor devils of soldiers off today, or we will lose them; they are starving for want of provisions and water. I want you to go in and see what the *Brooklyn* can do. Rig a large raft out of spars, get the end of a hawser on shore to them, and with another hawser to the raft you can get them through the surf; or lash two boats together and let them drop in. Get provisions to them (and water) at all hazards.

"I know the sailors are not all dead on board the *Brooklyn,* and you can do it. I send a tug for you to use. Anchor her securely outside the breakers and drift the raft in, and let them haul out to the tug, when the boats will take them off, and won't I be glad to get rid of them; ain't a soldier troublesome? Go at it as soon as it is light enough; we can have them all off by 12; there are seven hundred on shore." [65]

At dawn, Lamb stared with his glass through the fog along the beach extending northward from the fort. He could see a number of new graves, and scattered about were an officer's sword and some small arms and accouterments. His men had been kept at their arms all night. Once a boat party was reported advancing on The Mound, and a force sufficient to repel such an attack was hurried off in the rain, but it was a false alarm.

At 9:00 A.M. ships began shelling the stretch of woods lying next to the fort, a further effort to isolate the infantry until it could be rescued. Every attempt failed. During the late morning, the men on shore tried to launch a boat that had washed in to them. It was immediately swamped. But shortly afterward a transport managed to get a line ashore with a lifeboat, and communication was opened with the stranded troops.

All morning, Porter, burning with indignation toward Butler, stormed about the deck of his flagship. Toward noon he sent the General a message dripping with sarcasm:

"I wish some more of your gallant fellows had followed the officer who took the flag from the parapet, and the brave fellow who brought the horse out from the fort. I think they would have found it an easier conquest than is supposed.

"I do not, however, pretend to place my opinion in opposition to General Weitzel, whom I know to be an accomplished soldier and engineer, and whose opinion has great weight with me.

"I will look out that the troops are all off in safety. We will have a west wind presently, and a smooth beach about three o'clock, when sufficient boats will be sent for them." [66]

True to Porter's prediction, the wind did change and the sea became calm, but heavy breakers still rolled on the beach. It was late afternoon before the first of the troops were brought away from shore. Meanwhile, the ships continued shelling the woods along the peninsula.

Clarence Cary was looking on and wrote in his diary: "The sea being quite rough was, I suppose, the reason that the Yankees did not come up this day. We could see from the parapet, with a glass, the Yankees embarking from the beach in their small boats. I watched the heavily laden transports go off to sea and then, with great pleasure, a portion of the fleet sail. Everybody in the fort busily engaged today in repairing damage done to the works. Some few of the guns were disabled, but the fort is still in good condition. The casualties in the garrison yesterday amounted to about seventy killed and wounded. The inside of the fort is covered with pieces and whole shell."

Porter was purposely sending off the ships of the fleet gradually. He thought it best not to let the Confederates think the expedition had been abandoned entirely. The vessels were directed to a rendezvous near Beaufort, moving away one or two at a time, to look as if they were crippled.[67]

To the echo of guns firing at the woods in a desperate effort to save the soldiers still stranded on the beach, Porter wound up the 26th by sending Welles a brief report. His mood had not changed, and the innuendo was heavy. "Until further orders I shall go on and hammer away at the forts, hoping that in time the people in them will get tired and hand them over to us," he wrote. "It is a one-sided business altogether, and in the course of time we must dismount their guns, if, as General Weitzel says, we can not 'injure it as a defensive work.' The Government may also think it of sufficient importance to undertake more serious operations against these works. An army of a few thousand men investing it would soon get into it with the aid of the Navy." [68]

Another night of rain and occasional shelling was passed. At 11:37 A.M. the last boatload of stranded men left the beach. Lamb immediately wired headquarters at Wilmington: "This morning, December 27, the foiled and frightened enemy left our shore."

But Porter still stood by off the bar, sending his ships away a few at a time. On this date he dispatched a long report to Welles in which he poured out more disgust at Butler and the Army and exercised to greater degree than previously his penchant for making erroneous statements:

My dispatch of yesterday will give you an account of our operations, but will scarcely give you an idea of my disappointment at the conduct of the Army authorities in not attempting to take possession of the forts, which had been so completely silenced by our guns; they were so blown up, burst up, and torn up that the people inside had no intention of fighting any longer. Had the Army made a show of surrounding it, it would have been ours, but nothing of the kind was done. The men landed, reconnoitered, and hearing that the enemy were massing troops somewhere, the order was given to re-embark.

They went away as soon as the majority of the troops were on the transports, and it coming on to blow rather fresh, about seven hundred were left on shore. . . . To show that the Rebels have no force here, these men have been on shore two days without being molested. . . .[69]

I can't concive what the Army expected when they came here; it certainly did not need seven thousand to garrison Fort Fisher; it only required one thousand to garrison all these forts, which are entirely under the guns of Fort Fisher; that taken, the river is open. . . .

There never was a fort that invited soldiers to walk in and take possession more plainly than Fort Fisher, and an officer got on the parapet even, saw no one inside, and brought away the flag we had cut down. . . .

If General Hancock, with ten thousand men, was sent down here, we could walk right into the fort.[70]

Rain still fell on the 28th, and Porter remained in his cabin. A part of his day was taken up with interviewing some of the Confederate prisoners brought away from Confederate Point. For some reason or other, they were telling him just what he wanted to hear. They said the powder boat had created a perfect panic in Fort Fisher, had stunned and disabled the men to such a degree that they had refused to fight, notwithstanding the efforts of their officers. They also informed him that the bombardment had so completely demoralized the garrison that two hundred men could have gone in and taken possession of the works. Porter hurried this information off to Welles.[71]

Wind-whipped rains were still beating down on the morning of the 29th, creating such a fury of fog and dampness that a two-masted side-wheel blockade-runner with two smokestacks, encountering not the slightest difficulty, ran up past the fleet and headed for Wilmington shortly after 9:00 A.M.[72]

Porter arrived that day at the rendezvous point off Beaufort. Back at the mouth of the Cape Fear River was left only the normal blockading fleet.

It had been humiliating to Porter to have to leave under such circumstances, and two letters he wrote that day indicated his feelings. In one of these, addressed to Welles, he still ranted about Butler and still veered sharply from the facts:

When I started on this expedition, you may remember, I said how the place would be taken, viz, with the Navy attacking it by water and twelve thousand troops properly provided to work on the land. Well, sir, it could have been taken on Christmas with five hundred men, without losing a soldier; there were not twenty men in the forts, and those very poor, miserable, panic-stricken people, cowering there with fear, while one or two desperate men in one of the upper casemates some distance above Fort Fisher managed to fire one gun, that seldom hit anyone.

I feel ashamed that men calling themselves soldiers should have left this place so ingloriously; it was, however, nothing more than I expected when General Butler mixed himself up in this expedition, starting his troops out from Hampton Roads with only a few days' provisions, and without water, trusting to the steamers to make it, which they could not do. . . .

General Butler only came here to reap the credit of this affair, supposing that the explosion would sweep the works off from the face of the earth. Had he supposed in the first instance that there would have been difficulties he would never have joined the expedition.

. . . If this temporary failure succeeds in sending General Butler into private life, it is not to be regretted, for it cost only a certain amount of shells, which I would expend in a month's target practice anyhow.[73]

The other letter went to his friend William Tecumseh Sherman, then hammering away at Savannah, Georgia. It ridiculed Butler and added: "This is merely on your way to Richmond. Take this place and you take the *creme de la creme* of the rebellion. . . . I do hope, my dear general, that you will second me here, and let our people see the folly of employing such generals as Butler and Banks. I have tried them both, and God save me from further connection with such generals." [74]

The following day found General Grant writing Porter a letter from City Point, Virginia. It asked the Admiral to hold on where he was for a few days, "and I will endeavor to be back again with an increased force and without the former commander." Transports supplied with coal and water, he revealed, were supposed to be ready by January 2. "There is not a soul here except my chief of staff, assistant adjutant general, and myself knows of this intended renewal of our effort against Wilmington," he added. "In Washington but two persons know of it, and, I am assured, will not. The commander of the expedition will probably be Major General Terry. He will not know of it until he gets out to sea. . . . The same troops that were with the first expedition, reinforced by a brigade, will be sent now." [75]

Porter employed the last day of '64 to prepare a long tirade to Welles, imploring the Secretary not to make changes in the fleet until plans for capturing Fort Fisher could be worked out. Again he lambasted Butler, especially over the General's claim that the Army had taken the Flag Pond Hill and Half Moon Batteries. And then he bluntly stated: "I am not very particular, I am well aware, how I express myself in these cases. I have always said what I thought since the first day I took up arms to fight this rebellion, and I intend to do so (impolitic though it may be) until the war is over. . . . From beginning to end the military part of the expedition has been a failure." [76]

★ 24

Fort Fisher falls

JANUARY 1865

It was the night of January 12. Colonel Lamb stood on the ramparts of Fort Fisher and gazed seaward. Out there, like fireflies in conclave, he could see a swarm of lights becoming constantly more numerous. The sight was not new to him. In December he had witnessed a similar scene, the nerve-tingling spectacle of many hostile ships gathering for attack. As then, they bobbed up and down, weaved and rocked as they were individually affected by the roughness of the water. Earlier in the evening, his mounted couriers had informed him the fleet was on its way. He had been expecting it for days.

Lamb reacted with the precision of a man who is sure of himself. Leaving the ramparts, he sent a messenger to his wife, giving her notice that she and the children and servants must be ready to leave as soon as he could come to tell them good-by. A barge was waiting at the wharf to take them across the river.

Then he put his defensive plan in motion, setting aright the many little things necessary to prepare the fort for action. He had eight hundred men, all from the Thirty-sixth North Carolina Regiment. At least one hundred of them were unfit for duty. For days he had been trying to get reinforcements, and now off to Wilmington he sent another telegram asking for help.

At dawn, Lamb looked again from the ramparts. Ships cluttered the horizon, some the mighty men-of-war of the Union Navy, others the smaller, troop-laden transports of the Union Army. They made up the most formidable armada the nation had ever known. He could see they were more numerous than the fleet he had beaten off in December. This time, he knew, they were here for the kill. As he stared at them, through his mind must have run the date: it was Friday, the 13th.

Off along the beach, a short distance from the fort, was a reminder to Lamb of the responsibility now facing him. It was the remnants of a giant picnic arranged by the ladies of Wilmington to celebrate the December repulse. Promises had been made during this gathering, and his promises he liked to keep. He had assured them that the garrison would fight to the last sand hill to defend their homes. And fresh in his mind was a reminder from General Lee that he could not sustain his army without the supplies brought in along the Cape Fear past Fort Fisher.[1]

As Grant had promised, the army that had come to subdue Fisher was the same that had faced it three weeks earlier, except that it was augmented by two brigades of Negro troops, about five thousand men. At its head was Major General Alfred H. Terry, a thirty-seven-year-old Connecticut lawyer-soldier who had taken part in such extended campaigns as the Port Royal expedition and the siege of Fort Wagner. Grant personally recommended him, and David Porter, who was convinced that if Butler had captured Fort Fisher he would have been the next President—"the greatest calamity that could have happened to the country"—accepted him, although disappointed that he could not have Sherman. He had written Grant: "I hold it to be a good rule never to send a boy on a man's errand. . . . There is no use fretting over the past; we must endeavor to avoid mistakes in the future. . . . I hope Sherman will be allowed to carry out his plans; he will have Wilmington in less than a month, and Charleston will fall like a ripe pear." [2]

Terry arrived with his troops at Beaufort on the 8th, but a gale was in progress, and there was no thought of an attack. Porter advised the General to get his transports inside the harbor until the storm had passed.

The gale lasted two days and nights. Some of the transports lay outside and weathered the storm, riding out at their anchors, and so did the ships of war, with the exception of the U.S.S. *Colorado,* forced to go to sea because she had only one anchor. The sea was heavy from the southwest, sometimes breaking completely over the vessels.

During this period of waiting, and despite adverse conditions, the ships were loaded with ammunition and coal. On the morning of the 12th, the wind was fair and moderate, and the fleet, including the transports, steamed off for Fort Fisher. Porter and Terry had hopes of landing the troops by nine or ten that night, but the wind changed, hurling huge breakers on the beach, so they were forced to anchor the fleet for the night, with soldiers still on board, off Half Moon Battery. It was while this was in progress that Lamb stood on the ramparts of the fort and watched the enemy horde assembling.

For days the Colonel had been asking for timber and labor. He needed twelve-by-twelves and three-inch planks, some for mounting guns, some for repairing the earthworks. On the 8th, he had telegraphed: "I am ready to repel Admiral Porter, but if you give me five hundred Negroes and enough timber to mount guns, I will make him leave some of his vessels behind." [3] The two hundred Negroes he was employing at the time were feeble and worn out. Soldiers, meanwhile, were fully engaged in moving guns and ammunition and in fixing quarters.

At four on the morning of the 13th, hours before dawn, the inshore division of naval vessels stood in close to the beach to cover the landing. Behind them came the transports. The ironclads moved down to within range of the fort and opened fire on it. Another division of ships was placed to the northward of the landing place, to protect the troops from an attack in that direction. At 8:00 A.M. a swarm of boats and steam tugs gathered around the transports, and the disembarkation of men, provisions, tools, and ammunition began. The unloading point was the same as that selected in December. Soon hordes of men were spreading out over the peninsula, tents were springing up, campfires were burning, and miles of supplies began taking on the appearance of hills above the sandy terrain. The first boatload of soldiers to land soon was seen driving in a herd of cattle found somewhere in the growth of trees in that area, animals that represented beef on the hoof for the garrison of the fort.

By 3:00 P.M. nearly eight thousand men, each with three days' rations and forty rounds of ammunition, had been put on shore. With them also went six days' supply of hard bread in bulk and three hundred thousand additional rounds of ammunition. The weather had become quite pleasant, but the surf on the beach was still high, causing some of the rations and ammunition to be ruined by water.

One of Terry's first steps after landing the men was to throw a strong defensive line across the peninsula. Facing Wilmington from the Cape Fear River to the sea, this defense was to protect the rear from attack while he operated against Fort Fisher.

During the day, as men on foot went about preparations for action, the warships hammered away at the fort. Up front, only a thousand yards from Fisher, was the *New Ironsides,* and near by, the *Monadnock, Mahopac, Canonicus,* and *Saugus,* all ironclad. Next were the ships of the No. 1 battle line—the *Brooklyn, Mohican, Tacony, Kansas, Unadilla, Huron, Maumee, Pawtuxet, Seneca, Pontoosuc, Pequot, Yantic,* and *Nereus.* Two other lines were farther back. Porter had given them specific instructions about how to fire: "The object is to lodge the shell in the parapets, and tear away the traverses under which the bombproofs are located. A shell now and then exploding over a gun en barbette may have good effect, but there is nothing like lodging the shell before it explodes." [4] And the Admiral had some thoughts about firing at the flagstaff over the fort. "These are generally placed at a point to entice us to fire at them," he advised, "and no harm is done by this kind of firing. Commanders are directed to strictly enjoin their officers and men never to fire at the flag or pole, but to pick out the guns; the stray shells will knock the flagstaff down." [5]

Porter's directions were closely adhered to as the bombardment proceeded. Projectiles rained down upon the target. One sailor wrote his mother at the close of the campaign: "Nothing was to be seen of the fort, the smoke and sand mingling together, completely obscuring it from sight (just imagine the effect of three hundred shells exploding in a fort per minute)." [6]

At 7:30 A.M. the fort had opened on the nearest vessels. Porter hoped this would happen, because it would show him what guns the Southerners had and where they were located. A spirited engagement developed between the fort and the ironclads, and the *Canonicus* in particular felt the effect of it. Her commander, George Belknap, was convinced some experienced artillerists had been assigned to the fort since the December attack, because the fire from the Southerners was much more spirited and accurate than it had been before. His vessel was struck thirty-six times during the day, and everything about the deck not shotproof was cut up. Shells struck against her turret, stunning the men at the guns, and twice her flag was shot away. Now and then the bullet of a sharpshooter whistled past.

In the midst of the bombardment, General Whiting and his staff came walking into the fort from Battery Buchanan. Lamb was busy on the sea face.

Whiting said: "Lamb, my boy, I have come to share your fate. You and your garrison are to be sacrificed."

"Don't say so, General," Lamb replied. "We shall certainly whip the enemy again."

"No, I'm afraid not," Whiting replied. "When I left Wilmington, General Bragg was hastily removing his stores and ammunition and was looking for a place to fall back upon."

As in December, Lamb offered his superior the command of the fort, but Whiting once more refused.[7]

Traverses about the fort began to disappear as the day developed, and the southern angle appeared dilapidated. Eventually, Lamb's guns became silent, with the exception of one heavy gun on the southern angle. Porter kept a close watch. At times he thought his vessels fired too rapidly and made too much smoke. Several had been damaged. After dark the wooden ships withdrew, leaving the ironclads to maintain their positions and to keep up a slow fire through the night.

The close of day this Friday the 13th was a suitable subject for an artist's brush, in the opinion of some of those who saw it. Lieutenant John R. Bartlett of the U.S.S. *Susquehanna* was deeply impressed, and he wrote glowingly of it to his sisters: "At sunset it was a most beautiful sight. The sun set directly behind the fort. I think I never saw a more beautiful one. The smoke of bursting shell against the bright red sky and half the fort in full blaze made the most magnificent picture ever seen." [8]

Porter started off the 14th by preparing a long report to Secretary Welles. "The firing from the fleet," he wrote, "will commence as soon as we get breakfast, and be kept up as long as the Ordnance Department provides us with shells and guns." He was finding Terry most agreeable and efficient.[9]

One of the main jobs marked out for this second day was that of unloading field artillery pieces on the peninsula, in preparation for an all-out attack on the 15th. A galelike wind was blowing, driving sand into the eyes of the soldiers and causing them to seek shelter whenever possible. While this work was under way, Porter centered his fleet's attention on the point of the works where he and Terry had decided the assault should be made.

Early in the afternoon, Lamb saw the *Isaac Welles,* a small steamer loaded with ammunition and forage for the fort, approach a landing within the Union lines. He had guns fired at her to warn her off, but on she came, falling an easy prey to the foe. But she was not to float for long. The C.S.S. *Chickamauga,* standing farther up the Cape Fear, opened up on her and sank her. At night she could have come in to the wharf at Battery Buchanan easily. "This incident," Lamb later commented, "gave me the first information that General Bragg was shamefully ignorant and indifferent to the situation of affairs." [10] He sent Bragg a message that his garrison would co-operate with him in a night attack on the troops landing farther up the peninsula. There was no reply.

Porter's barrage this day was much heavier than on the 13th. All the small gunboats bearing eleven-inch guns were ordered to move up and to fire slowly, in an effort to dismount the heavy guns the Southerners were still bringing to bear. The ironclads and the larger vessels in the meantime were firing at a more rapid pace. By nightfall many scars could be seen along the face of the fort. The concerted attack from the fleet lasted until well after dark.

That night was far from serene. Hundreds of campfires burned in the area beyond the range of the fort, and the noise of an army in bivouac swelled out over the waters and along the wave-lapped beaches. Down the line, throughout the dark hours, the ironclads lobbed over eleven- and fifteen-inch shells, scattering shrapnel with deadly effect. Fully two hundred men, Lamb estimated, had been killed and wounded in the first two days of fighting.[11] With the continued bombardment at night, damage could not be repaired, meals could not be cooked for the garrison, and it was almost impossible to bury the dead without causing fresh casualties.

At daylight on the 15th, a clear day, the fleet redoubled its fire on the land face of the fort, and Lamb knew the assault was near. He braced for whatever might come. During the preceding day and night, seven hundred North Carolina troops, light and heavy artillery, and a detachment of fifty sailors and Marines had arrived, giving him a total of fifteen hundred men, including the sick and slightly wounded.[12]

The sea was smooth, and the fleet could fire with better accuracy. By noon, every gun on the sea face of the fort was silenced except one columbiad that was somewhat protected by the angle formed by the northeast salient. The palisade had been virtually destroyed as a defensive line. The number of Lamb's dead and wounded was increasing; he estimated the remaining men able to fight at twelve hundred.[13] He could see the enemy concentrating along the peninsula and skirmishers digging rifle pits close to his torpedo lines on the left. Sharpshooters were sending a hail of bullets at the fort, blazing away at every head that came into view along the ramparts.

Sometime after noon, a brigade of South Carolina troops, sent by Bragg in a steamer to reinforce Lamb, drew up to the wharf at Battery Buchanan. They were men from the Twenty-first and Twenty-fifth Regiments. Three hundred fifty of them went ashore before the fleet sent such a barrage at the vessel that she had to withdraw. "Never was there a more stupid blunder committed by a commanding general," charged Lamb. "If this fresh brigade had been sent to this point the night before, they could have reached the fort unobserved, could have been protected until needed, and could have easily repulsed the assault by the enemy on our left; but landed in view of the fleet, they had to double-quick over an open beach to The Mound under a heavy fire. When they reached the fort, they were out of breath, disorganized, and more or less demoralized." [14] They brought his strength to better than fifteen hundred, but the vessel beaten back from the wharf was forced to take away seven hundred fifty badly needed men.

In the plans for the land attack, Porter took steps to make sure the Navy had a part in it. Since the opening day, he had had boats kept in readiness, lowered near the water on the off side of each vessel, to take his men ashore when the moment arrived. A call for volunteers brought offers from more men than he could spare. Commander James Findlay Schenck of the U.S.S. *Powhatan* found himself with a problem in this respect: so many men clamored to participate that he had to make choices. These began with the three men who aspired to lead the shore detail. Lieutenant George M. Bache, Jr., claimed the privilege by virtue of seniority. Ensign Ira Harris maintained he had a better right because he was one of many children and not an only child as was Bache. Acting Ensign Robley D. Evans founded his claim on the fact that the other members of his family were fighting for the South. Schenck did a beautiful job of side-stepping: he let all three go, and all three were wounded.

Porter gave last-minute orders. Every man who went ashore was to be armed with revolvers and with cutlasses well sharpened. His flag lieutenant, Samuel W. Preston, the man who had helped Rhind light the fuses in the powder boat back on December 24, was to command a special detail of men with shovels. It was to advance as near the fort as possible and commence throwing up rifle pits. As soon as ditches deep enough for shelter could be dug, the Marines were to move in, in thin squads, and occupy them. Other sappers then would come in behind and dig the ditches deeper, to at least three and a half feet. In the charge, the sailors were to concentrate on the fieldpieces in the fort and kill the gunners. If, after they were in the fort and the guns on The Mound began firing at them, groups of three men were each to seize a prisoner, pitch him over the walls, and get behind the fort for protection.

Terry and Porter had a conference during the morning to discuss plans for the assault. The sailors would take the ocean side, along the beach, and the soldiers the river side, charging from the cover of woods.

At 10:00 A.M. the entire fleet began a heavy fire, with orders to continue it until everything was in readiness for the attack. Simultaneously, the flagship made signal to "arm and away all boats" and to assemble on the beach. In a few moments the water was swarming with hundreds of boats pulling for shore. Immediately upon landing, the sappers were sent toward the fort. Later, the main body was marched up to within a mile of Fisher and formed in four lines, to wait for the Army, expected to be ready at 2:00 P.M. While they stood there, the Southerners began firing, wounding several Marines in the front line and forcing everybody to drop to the sand in order to make as small a target as possible.

Preston took his sappers to within two hundred yards of the fort. They dug like mad, everyone aware that he was hungry, that he had had no food since dawn. At two o'clock it was learned the Army would not be ready to move before three. Sharpshooters were already in position, but the main body of soldiers still had to come up.

The tide was low, and the sailors were ordered to file down on the beach and march toward the fort on the double-quick. In front of them as they came the fleet dropped a barrage, setting up a dense screen of sand and smoke. When within half a mile of Fisher, they lay down on the sand, out of the line of musketry, taking advantage of a rest they needed, for they were out of breath. Some of them threw up protective banks with their hands. Most of the firing was over their heads, but now and then a bullet fell short, adding to the number of wounded.

Lamb's headquarters were in the Pulpit Battery on the sea face, one hundred yards from the northeast salient and adjoining the hospital bombproof. At 2:30, as he was returning from another battery, Private Arthur Muldoon, one of the lookouts, shouted to him: "Colonel, the enemy are about to charge!" [15]

Now, as never before, the officers in Fort Fisher, looking up the peninsula where the Federals were forming for the assault, wished that Bragg might attack in the rear, from the direction of Wilmington and Masonboro Inlet, or anywhere else that would take attention away from the Southerners in the earthwork who were outnumbered nearly ten to one. But there was no indication of forthcoming action from Bragg. His last gesture of co-operation was the steamer that had been driven away from the wharf at Battery Buchanan. Facing him on the north, along the protective line that Terry had thrown across the sandy strip on first landing, were two brigades of Negro troops, men stationed in formation without protective impedimenta in front to aid them.[16]

At Lamb's request, Whiting telegraphed Bragg: "The enemy

are about to assault; they outnumber us heavily. We are just manning our parapets. Fleets have extended down the sea front outside and are firing seven hundred yards from us. Nearly all land guns disabled. Attack! Attack! It is all I can say and all you can do." [17]

After talking with Whiting, Lamb passed hurriedly down in rear of the land face and through the galleries. Then he ordered additional sharpshooters to the gun chambers, with instructions to pick off the officers in the assaulting columns. Battery commanders were directed to form their detachments and to be ready to rush to the top of the parapets when the firing from the fleet stopped.

Lamb was on the way back to his headquarters shortly after 3:00 P.M. when the roar of artillery suddenly ceased and steam whistles of the fleet sent out in unison a mighty blast that told friend and foe alike that the crucial point in the battle was at hand. "It was a soul-stirring signal both to besiegers and besieged," Lamb remembered.[18]

Sending his aide, Lieutenant Charles H. Blocker, to double-quick the Twenty-first and Twenty-fifth South Carolina Regiments to reinforce Major James Reilly, commanding on the left, where the Army would attack, Lamb went to the northeast salient, believing this to be the point that would need the most protection. There he rallied the garrison, put three hundred men on top of the bastion and adjoining parapets, and held two hundred more in the adjoining batteries.

General Whiting left a picture of the situation as it applied to the Southerners: "Not a gun remained on the land front. The palisade was entirely swept away; the mines in advance, so deeply did the enemy's shot plow, were isolated from the wires and could not be used. Not a man could show his head in that infernal storm, and I could only keep a lookout in the safest position to inform me of the movements of the enemy. Contrary to the previous practice, the fleet kept up the fire all night. Cooking was impracticable. The men, in great part, in Fisher at the second attack were not those of the first, and were more demoralized. The casualties were greater, with but one ration for three days." [19]

Firing in the fort came from the lone columbiad and from three mortars that had been mounted during the night.

The assaulting column on the sea side—two thousand men—lay in four lines, the first made up of Marines led by Captain L. L. Dawson, the latter three comprised of sailors from the squadron and led successively by Lieutenant Commanders C. H. Cushman, James Parker, and T. O. Selfridge. In over-all command as Porter's personal respresentative on shore was Fleet Captain K. R. Breese. The Marines, with rifles, were to run ahead to the ditches dug by the sappers and from there lay down a sharpshooters' fire to protect the charging sailors, whose cutlasses and revolvers would be virtually useless until the men climbed the ramparts.

The episode that was about to take place had had other parallels in this war, the most notable at Gettysburg in July of '63 when Pickett's gallant Southerners went charging up Cemetery Ridge in the face of death. Here at Fisher the bullets singing above the heads of the sailors and Marines as they lay prone along the beach foretold the danger that was marked out for them. They were to charge along the water's edge to three sandy hillocks and then swing right, straight for the sea face of the fort. The Army, in its part, would attack on the left flank and rear of the fortification.

Lamb, at sight of the sailors and Marines, more clearly visible to him than the soldiers, misjudged what was happening. He took these men along the beach to represent the main assaulting column. Accordingly, he concentrated his garrison on the sea face, leaving a lesser part of it to face the soldiers coming in from another direction. By his order, a line of riflemen along the entire front of the fort laid down a murderous fire, and from the guns on The Mound came charge after charge of grape and canister.

Federal officers shouted their commands, and the Marines pressed forward, followed by the lines of sailors, cheering as they ran, cutlass in one hand and revolver in the other. The men in front reached the hillocks, halted momentarily, and then headed for the palisade. They ran in ragged formation, in little clusters, in singles, twos and threes, as individual men mustered their bravery and risked their lives against fate. As the seconds ticked off, dead and wounded began piling up along the beach. Some fell and lay still; others fell, stunned, and then, as they recovered from the shock of bullet or shrapnel, crawled down toward the water to escape the relentless fire. Those remaining on their feet pushed on to the palisade near the salient. A few men went beyond, but most of them dropped on the sand, under cover of the crest of the beach. Their revolvers were futile against the more powerful rifles in the hands of the Southerners.[20] Confusion set in. Lines disappeared. Sailors and Marines alike were scrambled in a frantic mass.

Robley Evans of the *Powhatan* teamed with Lieutenant Bache and Ensign Harris in urging forward that vessel's contingent. Suddenly one of the seamen, a young fellow named Flannigan, reeled to one side and dropped. Evans rushed to his side. A faint smile flickered over the fallen man's face before he died. It was with a queer feeling that Evans turned away. The night before, Flannigan had brought a small box of trinkets and asked the acting ensign to give it to his sister in Philadelphia. "Why don't you wait and give it to her yourself?" asked Evans. Flannigan answered: "Because I'm going ashore, and will be killed." "Do you know how many bullets it takes to kill a man in action?" Evans asked reassuringly. Flannigan shrugged and walked away.[21]

Running with the front column was Flag Lieutenant Sam Preston. After finishing his work with the sappers, he had volunteered for further service and had been accepted. Near the palisade, a bullet struck him in the left groin, severing the femoral artery. He fell forward. A man hurrying behind him stopped and stooped to assist, just as a bullet ripped into him. He dropped on the prostrate Preston. Someone separated them, took a quick look, and kept running.

Lieutenant Cushman was down, shot in the leg. A few feet away lay the flag captain, Lieutenant Benjamin H. Porter. He was already dead, a gaping hole in his left breast. Both he and Preston had only recently been released from the Confederate prison at Columbia, South Carolina, where they had been since the battles around Charleston in '63.

Twenty paces ahead of the unfortunate Preston, scurried Lieutenant R. H. Lamson of the U.S.S. *Gettysburg*. A bullet struck him in the left arm and shoulder, whirling him about and dropping him near the palisades. He lay there and fumbled for a bandage to stop the flow of blood. As soon as he got it tied, he began to crawl toward Preston. A wounded man lying near yelled that Preston was dead, and Lamson crawled back toward the palisades, convinced that Preston had had a premonition: a note he had left behind asked that he be interred at Annapolis.[22]

From his burrow in the sand, Lamson could observe the action around him: "The officers were doing their utmost to get the men forward, but the hopelessness of attempting to get over the palisades, ditch, and the steep parapet was apparent, and the men fell so fast that every formation was instantly broken; still I think we would have made a more desperate effort if so many of the leading officers had not been killed or wounded." [23]

Up near the palisades, Assistant Surgeon William Longshaw, Jr., of the U.S.S. *Minnesota,* running with instruments in hand, stopped to bind the wound of a sailor. As he knelt over the prostrate form, a bullet struck him in the head. After the battle they would be found there lying together, both dead, bandages and doctor's kit scattered over the sand near by. On this very day, the young doctor had been granted a leave of absence, but he had postponed his departure to take part in the assault.[24]

Selfridge, leading the fourth column, pushed his men forward into the confused mass in front. "When we finally reached the palisades," he reported, "I found the columns which had preceded me halted and lying down. Going to the front, an effort at this time was made to get the men to charge, but the fire was so heavy that the few who passed through the stockade were compelled to fall quickly back. At this moment an unexplained panic took place in the rear, which so quickly communicated itself to the whole that it became impossible to rally the men." [25] Breese was in there, shouting, waving his sword, trying to start a rally, but the severe and galling fire of the Southerners, only sixty or seventy yards away, made futile his efforts. "How he escaped death is a marvel to me," observed a fellow officer.[26]

Even Colonel Lamb was moved by what was taking place. "We witnessed what had never been seen before, a disorderly rout of American sailors and Marines," he afterward related. "Had the fleet helped their own column as they did afterward that of the Army, theirs would have been the glory of victory." [27]

Parker, heading the third column, had pushed up to within yards of the salient. He saw Southerners on the parapet of the fort waving their hats and beckoning him forward, and he gave the order to charge, rose up and ran forward, followed by officers and their men and a few Marines. "As I did so," he reported, "I turned to see if the rest of the men were following, and to my intense surprise and mortification saw that a panic had seized the force and that they were ingloriously flying along the beach away from the fort." [28]

Acting Ensign George H. Wood of the U.S.S. *Chippewa*, running with sword in hand, saw his men waver. He turned to urge them on. William McGill, his flag-bearer, was close at hand. So was Acting Ensign William H. DeGrosse, also waving his sword.

"Here is where our lines were broken," Wood reported, "and I wondered where our men were, but still kept going on parallel with the stockades, which are built from the beach up to the fort. There was an opening in the stockade which we made for, and it was here I passed Lieutenant Commander James Parker in this opening, shouting for the men to come on. . . . It was here I heard voices saying, 'They are retreating,' and turning around saw the Marines and bluejackets on the retreat, and then came out of this opening and went about fifty feet up the other side of the stockade, and when I saw no one following me, I retreated to get behind a pile of sand which was thrown up at the opening in the stockades."

Above him the parapet of the fort seemed to be lined with Southerners. He noticed one Confederate officer standing up there clapping his hands and singing out to his men: "Kill the Yankee sons of bitches!"

Wood crawled behind the stockade. There he found other officers and men throwing up sand for protection, so he commenced doing the same thing. It seemed that every handful brought ten bullets ripping down from the parapet.

As the retreat began, Auzella Savage joined in. He was an ordinary seaman from the U.S.S. *Santiago de Cuba,* serving for the moment in the exalted position of the ship's flag-bearer, a distinction in which he took much pride. But pride sometimes falters in the face of danger, and Auzella found himself keeping pace with the leaders. Suddenly the flagstaff was shot away above his hand, and the colors and the bobtailed staff fell in dishonor upon the sand. But not to stay. Auzella skidded to a stop, whirled, ran back, scooped the flag to his bosom, and continued his flight.

William Cushing was out there trying to rally the men. An acquaintance came upon him and recorded the scene: "I saw him half way back to the rifle pits. He had seen his friend Benjamin Porter shot down. He was crying and swearing at the men he had gathered together and who were being called away by their wounded friends lying near. I spoke to him, and at once he controlled himself perfectly." [29]

Another figure near Cushing was trying to rally the men and meeting with no better success. He was Carlisle P. Porter, son of the Admiral.

Lieutenant Bartlett was among those who got nearest the fort. "I shouted and waved my sword for the sailors to come back," he wrote his sisters, "but, no, off they went down the beach. About a dozen officers and twenty men remained at the palisades. I had made up my mind to go into that fort, and could not run. I could have cried when the blue jackets retreated, but it was high time for me to look out for myself. I began to dig a hole with my hands. You would have laughed to have seen me. It did not take me long to get a pile of sand in front of me high enough to screen me from fire. This was at about half past three. I kept on digging until I had a hole that I could stand up in. The sand was very soft and dry, so that it was easily thrown up. Every time I threw up a handful of sand on the edge of my pit, a dozen bullets would skip over my head. It was rather unpleasant, as it knocked the sand all down on me."

Only about sixty men were left up near the fort. The Southerners, cheering over the repulse, concentrated their fire on this group. Four men, three of them officers, were wounded in a matter of seconds. Parker steered them into the cover provided by an angle in the palisades and by nearby sand hills, and there they lay still until dark.

Bartlett was one of these sixty. "When the sailors started to run they were shot down like sheep," he related. "Over fifty lay dead at the foot of the palisades. Now and then a wounded man would raise his head; a dozen bullets would fly toward him in an instant. It was low tide when we made the charge and a few fell close to the water. Before dark the tide rose and the waves washed up on the poor fellows, some only wounded. It was hard to look on and not be able to give them any help. I wished to see if my friend Porter was still alive, so I waited till near the last. He was lying on the beach about a hundred yards from the palisades. I ran to him and dropped beside him. I found him dead, a shot having passed through his body. I took his sword, belt, and glove, and then, oh! how I did run for a little way. The Rebels fired about twenty shots at me."

Commander Parker had a new impression of war as he lay there waiting for the darkness. "It is painful to write such a record," he said in his official report, "but I feel compelled to state that I often saw the Rebels deliberately fire in squads at the wounded who were endeavoring to crawl away." [30]

As the fight raged, Lamb suddenly realized he had placed too many of his eggs in one basket. While he had been busy fighting off the Navy, the Army had poured in on Major James Reilly and the South Carolinians. "As our shouts of triumph went up," Lamb reported, "I turned to look at the western salient, and saw, to my astonishment, three Federal battle flags upon our ramparts. General Whiting saw them at the same moment and, calling on the men to pull down those flags and drive the enemy from the work, rushed toward them on the parapet."

Lamb passed through the sally port. On the outside he witnessed a savage hand-to-hand conflict between the South Carolinians and the Union Army forces for possession of the fourth gun chamber from the left bastion. He saw the Southerners, led by Whiting, drive the standard bearer from the top of the traverse and the enemy from the parapet in front. The gun chamber was recovered with great slaughter, and on the parapet and on the long traverse of the next gun chamber, the contestants were firing into each other's faces and even clubbing with their guns, being too close to load and fire. Whiting was wounded twice, in quick succession.

"I saw that the Confederates were exposed not only to the fire in front, but to a galling infantry fire from the captured salient," Lamb related. "I saw also a fresh force pouring into the left of the work, now offering no resistance. I doubt if ever before the commander of a work went outside of it and looked back upon the conflict for its possession; but from the peculiar construction of the works it was necessary to do so in order to see the exact position of affairs. I was in front of the sally port and concealed from the army by a fragment of the palisade."

While Lamb stood there, two Marines who were feigning death in front of the northeast salient spotted him. One of them rose from his place of concealment to fire on him, but before he could do so a bullet from the fort struck him in the head.[31]

Lamb returned to the fort and tried to direct the fire upon the area occupied by the enemy. Believing it could be recovered before sundown, he sent Bragg a telegram imploring him to attack.

Suddenly the fleet opened fire again, concentrating its aim on that part of the fort occupied by the Southerners. The shells came with such deadly precision that even company formation was prevented. They drove back friend and foe alike, but they did not stop the fighting that was going on inside Fisher.

"If there has ever been a longer or more stubborn hand-to-hand encounter," wrote Lamb, "I have failed to meet with it in history." It went on despite the fire of the fleet. As men fell, others took their places.

Lamb passed through the fort for the last time. The scene was indescribably horrible to him. Great cannon were broken in two. Everything seemed a mass of dirt. The dead and wounded lay over the ruins, some partly buried in graves dug by the shells which had injured or killed them.

The Colonel believed a determined bayonet assault upon the enemy's front would drive them out. He shouted for officers and men to follow him. A mighty cheer rose above the noise of the firing. Lamb gave the order, "Charge bayonets!" Then he sprang upon the breastwork, waved his sword, and yelled, "Forward! Double-quick! March!" At that moment he fell on his knees, a rifle ball through his left hip. A heavy volley, too high to be effective, was aimed in his direction by the Federals.

Someone raised Lamb. He handed his sword to Captain Daniel Munn, shouting, "Keep the enemy in check! I'll be back!"

But before Lamb reached a hospital he knew he would be unable to take further part in the battle. There he found Whiting, more concerned over not having heard from Bragg than over his own wounds. The fire in the fort was noticeably slackening.

Darkness was coming on as Major Reilly appeared at Lamb's side in the hospital. There was fire in his Irish eye. The fight would continue, he promised, as long as he had a man and a bullet left.

Soon after Reilly departed, the roar of the battle around the fort increased, but only for a short period. Around eight o'clock, Lamb's aide, Lieutenant Blocker, came into the hospital. He reported that the ammunition was giving out, that all to be found on the dead and wounded had been gathered in a blanket and distributed, that the enemy had possession of almost the entire land face, and that it would be impossible to hold out much longer. He suggested surrender.

"As long as I live I will not surrender this fort," said Lamb. "Bragg has got to come to the rescue."

Whiting spoke up from his cot: "Lamb, when you die I will assume command, and I will not surrender the fort." [32]

Within the hour there was another hot outburst of fighting as more Federal troops poured into the fort. Stretcher-bearers came and moved Whiting and Lamb off in the direction of Battery Buchanan. As the wounded men were taken away, spent balls fell like hailstones around them, and they could tell that the hand-to-hand engagement now was going on around the traverse adjoining the hospital. Some members of the garrison passed them, falling back in orderly retreat. The rear guard stopped around The Mound, making a last stand, hoping to give the officers a chance to escape.

But Battery Buchanan was no longer in the fight. When the forces from Fisher arrived, they found it deserted and still. The men who had been on duty there had spiked the guns and departed by barge. The end came at 10:00 P.M., Federal officers arriving at that hour to accept the surrender.

Noise of gunfire soon died away, and over Confederate Point came a different sound, that of a victorious horde. It seemed that each vessel tried to make the most noise. "Of all the cheering and blowing of steamer whistles, rockets, illumination, etc., on board the vessels in the harbor I don't think ever was or will be witnessed again," an officer described. "Cheer after cheer came from the fort and was answered by the ships with cheers, rockets, lights of all colors, ringing of bells, steam whistles, and all sorts of unearthly noises." [33] There was not much sleep around Fort Fisher that night. As one of the sailors wrote home: "The rockets seemed to shoot higher and sparkle more brilliantly than usual. The steam whistles (the sound of which was always disagreeable to my ear)— they, too, seemed to discourse a sweet melody." [34]

Shortly after midnight, Lieutenant Colonel Samuel M. Zent of the Thirteenth Indiana Volunteers was instructed to place guards over all of the magazines. He found thirty-one and stationed three men over each, but missed the most important of all, the main magazine, a sod-covered mound inside the fort, with its entrance toward the river.

Looting and revelry went on through the night. At daylight, soldiers, sailors, and Marines were still celebrating, some of them intoxicated and firing off their pistols. Officers closed their eyes to the scenes around them. Fort Fisher had been a hard fight.

A sailor from Porter's flagship climbed the ramparts of the fort to get a view of the peninsula along which he had charged the afternoon before. He stared out upon a stretch of sandy beach littered with dead and wounded, pieces of clothing, weapons, canteens, fragments of shell. Dark splotches marked the sand where bleeding men had fallen. Down around the sand hillocks from which the final charge was made, bodies lay several deep, twisted and swollen and in the inexplicable disarray so characteristic of an area in which many men have made their final supreme effort.[35]

Inside the fort, the scenes were even more horrible. "If hell is what it is said to be," one of the participants wrote home, "then the interior of Fort Fisher is a fair comparison. Here and there you see great heaps of human beings laying just as they fell, one upon the other. Some groaning piteously, and asking for water. Others whose mortal career is over, still grasping the weapon that they used to so good an effect in life." [36]

Union fighters who surveyed Fort Fisher during the hours immediately following its capitulation were filled with admiration for the outnumbered Southerners who had been their targets. "Just think of it," one of them observed, "three thousand men, sustaining an assault for seven hours, against ten thousand men in the front and a fleet of gunboats in the rear." [37]

Sometime after dawn, First Lieutenant George F. Quimby of the Fourth New Hampshire Volunteers was walking about the fort. He approached a group of soldiers standing around the entrance to the main magazine—the one Zent had missed. Its sod covering, now the bed for numbers of men from the One Hundred Sixty-ninth New York Regiment, looked so deceiving that he was not surprised to find its door unguarded. As he walked past, he heard one of the men say, "Have you got all out?" Another replied, "Maybe not. They got a light in there now." The officer stepped to the entrance and asked what the magazine contained. "Boxes of powder," someone on the inside replied. "Then put your lights out and don't take any more in," the lieutenant instructed, and went on with his rounds. A lucky man was he. A few minutes later a terrific explosion shook the fort, and Quimby looked back at the magazine he had just left.[38] Thirteen thousand pounds of powder had torn it to bits, killing and wounding more than two hundred men.

Smoke clouded the skies along the Carolina coast as the Southerners, realizing the meaning of the loss of Fort Fisher, destroyed property to keep it out of the hands of the advancing hordes. Fort Caswell, Smith's Island, Reeves' Point felt the effect of the torch. So did two steamers, one of them the *Chickamauga,* that had been taken up the Cape Fear. But one hundred sixty-nine guns fell to the invaders. So did nineteen hundred prisoners, including Lamb and Whiting.[39] Nearly four hundred Federal sailors were listed as killed, wounded, or missing, and to these were added hundreds of soldiers.[40]

Down from the fort came the flag presented by the ladies of Wilmington. It was sent by express to Secretary Welles.[41]

Porter waited until the 17th to send Welles a report, and in it he praised Terry in words he had used in the past only with reference to Sherman. It wound up with the announcement that Wilmington was hermetically sealed against blockade-runners, "and no *Alabamas* or *Floridas, Chicamaugas* or *Tallahassees* will ever fit out again from this port, and our merchant vessels very soon, I hope, will be enabled to pursue in safety their avocation." In the first battle, 20,271 projectiles weighing 1,275,-000 pounds had been expended; in the second, 19,682 projectiles with a weight of 1,652,638 pounds.[42]

"The success is so great that we should not complain," Porter added. "Men, it seems, must die that this Union may live, and the Constitution under which we have gained our prosperity must be maintained. We regret our companions in arms and shed a tear over their remains, but if these Rebels should succeed we would have nothing but regret left us and our lives would be spent in terror and sorrow." [43]

★ 25

Those who would not quit

JANUARY-APRIL 1865

The invisible gates closing on a dying cause swung more rapidly after the fall of Fort Fisher. All now that kept them from shutting completely was the indomitable spirit of last-ditch Southern fighters. The war was not yet over in January, '65; and, so far as the Confederate Navy was concerned, it would not end for months to come.

Over the Southland, Federal armies, aided almost always by the intrepid gunboats against which the Southerners could not compete, rapidly infiltrated, besieged, and captured strong points. And the areas so far unsurrendered were bound to fall in time.

But off at sea and at certain points on inland waters, the story was different. Each ship that floated was an empire unto herself, as strong and as indomitable as the man who commanded her. Conditions were such that her fate depended not on the progress of Lee's army, not on administrative measures at Richmond: She was her own boss, a floating island, free to come and go as the blockade and the Union ships abroad permitted.

Capture of Fort Fisher spelled doom for the blockade-runners, for it meant elimination of the last haven they could expect to enter with any degree of success. In the four days from January 12 to January 16, eight vessels left Nassau—where two and a half million pounds of bacon waited to be transported to the starving Confederacy—and headed for North Carolina. On arrival, the *Dumbarton, Charlotte, Blenheim,* and *Stag,* all British owned, were captured; the others were more fortunate and managed to escape to fight another day.

On the very night that the garrison at Fisher surrendered, John Maffitt, who had left Wilmington while the first battle for the fort was about to begin, ran the *Owl* in over the bar near Fort Caswell on the opposite side of the Cape Fear River and dropped anchor at Smithville. But as soon as he learned what had happened, he turned his vessel about and headed for Bermuda, arriving there on the 21st, in time to stop the *Maud Campbell, Old Dominion, Florence, Deer,* and *Virginia.* There he rested, thinking next of running to Charleston, but first he would have to have information. On the 20th, the *Chicora* came in with news that that port still had not fallen. Two days later the *Owl, Carolina, Dream, Chicora,* and the *Chameleon,* whose captain, John Wilkinson, had duplicated Maffitt's action in fleeing from Wilmington, sailed within a few hours of one another. Their time was running short. They found Charleston fully blockaded, and they fled in desperation.

But men like Maffitt and Wilkinson were not yet ready to quit. They ran wherever their wits told them, waiting for the end. At Nassau were gradually assembled thirty-five British runners valued at fifteen million dollars.[1] Desperate, foiled, loaded with cargoes they could not deliver, they were faced with the ever deepening knowledge that their occupation was gone. But blockade-running was a business that died slowly. In the Trans-Mississippi it continued until the last Confederate arms were laid down.

As men poured over the wreckage of Fort Fisher, and sand

was shoveled on the final body to be buried there, naval warfare broke out anew along the James River in Virginia. It was a desperate threat by the Confederates in that area, a move planned at a time when the Union had its ships concentrated along the North Carolina coast.

The Confederates seemed to keep it no secret that they planned a dash down the James. Two days before the attack occurred, Brigadier General John A. Rawlins, chief of staff at the Union base at City Point, sent notice to Commander William A. Parker, whom Porter had left in charge of the James River fleet, that the action was coming. He cited the desperation of the Southerners: "On the return of our ironclads, theirs could be permanently shut up in the upper part of the river. Even if the movement resulted in the loss of their vessels, it could be no worse than what would eventually be the case, and might inflict incalculable damage upon us." [2] Parker responded by writing Porter for more monitors.

This action by Parker was a clear indication of what he would do when the Confederate vessels appeared. Porter had left for North Carolina, confident that no danger could be expected from the Southerners on the James, placing his faith largely in the presence there of the huge *Onondaga,* a double-turreted monitor armed with two fifteen-inch Dahlgrens and two one-hundred-fifty-pounder Parrott rifles. Also in the fleet were the *Massasoit, Hunchback, Commodore Morris, Eutaw, Daylight, Miami, General Putnam, Spuyten Duyvil, Dawn,* and *Commodore Barney.* Against these, the Rebels had the *Virginia No. 2,* an ironclad from which much had been expected for a long time, and the ironclads *Richmond* and *Fredericksburg,* as well as several smaller boats.

The Southerners planned to move on the night of January 22, but were prevented by thick weather. This was only a temporary setback for Flag Officer John K. Mitchell, commanding the Confederate ships. "If we successfully pass the torpedoes, etc., as far as Trent's Reach and find there a practicable channel through the obstructions," he reported, "I hope to overcome any force the enemy can bring against us at this time, unless we have been deceived in our information." [3] Two of the officers available to him at the moment were among the South's most distinguished fighters. They were Lieutenant Charles W. Read, only a few months out of prison following his capture while raiding Union shipping along the coast of Maine, and Commander John McIntosh Kell, Raphael Semmes's executive.

The following night, when darkness permitted, Mitchell started the fleet downstream. The *Fredericksburg* took the lead, with the gunboat *Hampton* and torpedo boat *Hornet* tied alongside. Next came the *Virginia,* with the gunboat *Nansemond*; tug *Torpedo,* with torpedo boat *Scorpion* tied to her. The *Richmond* was last, aided by the gunboats *Drewry* and *Beaufort* and the torpedo boat *Wasp.* Past Fort Brady they ran, undeterred by about twenty-five shells. Near the Federal obstructions in Trent's Reach they halted long enough for Read to make a reconnaissance. When he returned with a favorable report, the *Fredericksburg* started moving and was able to get past the barrier. The Federal fleet in the meantime had been moved downstream. Even the powerful *Onondaga* was taken out of range.

But as on many other occasions, fate refused to side with the South. When the *Virginia,* anchored half a mile above the obstructions, prepared to move, it was found she was aground. The same soon was true of the *Richmond,* the *Drewry,* and the *Scorpion.*

Suddenly a powerful light from the Federal batteries flared across Trent's Reach, lighting it up so well that fire could be directed almost as accurately as by day. Guns opened from along the banks. All the vessels that could, ran back upstream, but those grounded were forced to wait for high tide. At daylight the *Onondaga* and other Union vessels steamed up and joined in the shelling. Shortly afterward, the *Drewry* was blown to pieces when a mortar shell exploded in her magazine. Her crew had just been removed. The *Scorpion,* stranded near by, was so badly damaged by the explosion that she had to be abandoned.

At eleven next morning the *Virginia,* last of the ships to get free, started back up the James. Her smokestack was peppered with holes, and her exhaust pipe had been cut in two, allowing the steam to escape on the spar and gun decks. She had been struck seventy times. Her flight followed a council of war in which it was decided that it would be futile to pursue the offensive. Only one man in the fleet had been killed. Eight had been wounded. Blame for the fiasco was placed on the pilots.

On the Federal side, the scapegoat was Commander Parker. Before the day was over, he had been removed from his command. Even General Grant heaped criticism upon him. Porter wrote: "No man ever had a better chance than you had to make yourself known to the world." [4] In his defense, Parker told Welles: "I kept the monitor *Onondaga* out of range of the enemy's batteries by direction of Rear Admiral Porter." [5]

No matter who was to blame for the timid handling of the *Onondaga,* the South's James River Squadron was still bottled up where it had been before the offensive began. In this situation, the Confederate Navy Department decided on a removal, too. During February, Commander Mitchell received orders to turn over his post to Raphael Semmes, now back from England, and a newly appointed rear admiral.[6] The lines were drawing tighter.

On February 18, Admiral Dahlgren sent a message to Admiral Porter from Charleston, the spot he and Du Pont and others had tried for four years to reach: "You will see by the date of this that the Navy's occupation has given this pride of rebeldom to the Union flag, and thus the rebellion is shut out from the ocean and foreign sympathy." [7] At 9:00 A.M. on the day prior, the Union flag had been raised again over Fort Sumter, where it had been lowered in April, '61.[8] The Southerners had evacuated as Sherman's army pushed in from the land side. Fires and explosions in and around the city indicated the mood in which it was surrendering. The day was beautiful and springlike, with a gentle breeze.[9] Until the Federals took over, the Confederate flag continued to fly over Fort Moultrie and Castle Pinckney.[10]

Dahlgren was jubilant. "To me the fall of Charleston seems scarcely less important than that of Richmond," he wrote Welles. "It is the last seaport by which it can be made sure that a bale of cotton can go abroad. Hence the Rebel loan and credit are at an end. Our own credit must improve accordingly. Then the fall of the city enables the Navy Department to reduce its force afloat to such an extent as to reduce the public expense materially." [11]

Union soldiers besieging Fort Sumter had only admiration for the determination of the Southerners. "It was simply an irregular curved pile of pulverized masonry, which had with enormous labor been industriously shoveled back into place as fast as we knocked it out of shape, and was held up on the inside by gabions and timber work," one of them reported. "So many tons of projectiles had been fired into it that the shot and shell seemed to be mixed through the mass as thick as plums in a pudding." [12]

Savannah had fallen; Wilmington fell. Mobile was left, and that, too, shut off from contact with the sea since Farragut's feat in early August, in time would become a victim of the Union's overwhelming land forces.

In the midst of the steam-roller activities by the victorious Federals, an incident occurred in the North that saddened many a Southern heart when the news finally spread. John Yates Beall, the ardent Virginian who had shifted his activities from the Eastern Shore to Canada, was given a quick trial by military commission and sentenced to be "hanged by the neck until dead." After a reprieve of six days, he was put to death.[13] Three days later, Robert Ould, Confederate Agent of Exchange at Richmond, received a letter from the doomed man in which he said: "The authorities are possessed of the facts in my case. They know that I acted under orders. I appeal to my Government to use its utmost efforts to protect me, and if unable to prevent my murder, to vindicate my reputation. I can only declare that I was no 'spy' or 'guerrilla,' and am a true Confederate." [14]

Beall's letter brought Ould the first knowledge he had of the case. He wrote President Davis: "The cruelty of the enemy was so swift that not sufficient time intervened between a knowledge of the facts and the execution to enable any proceedings to be taken." [15]

The day Beall died, Secretary Mallory, unaware that he had lost, at the end of a rope, one of his most zealous acting masters, wrote a long letter to John Maffitt, addressing it to Nassau. Loss of Savannah and Charleston, last of the deep-water ports accessible to runners, had posed a problem for the *Owl* and *Chameleon*. The department head explained that no vessel with a draft of more than six feet now would be able to reach the Confederacy. For that reason, he directed that the *Owl* be turned over to J. B. Lafitte, the Nassau agent of Fraser, Trenholm and Company, and that the *Chameleon* be sold, the proceeds to be used to buy a smaller steamer with which small arms and supplies could be brought to Columbus, Georgia, by way of Apalachicola Bay. Discretion in the matter, the letter directed, was to be left to Maffitt, who should maintain contact with John Wilkinson and with James Bulloch.

Mallory's letter represented one of the final gasps of the dying cause, a cause that was *ipso facto* hopeless, but which still had enough power left to cause trouble. Water mines, one of the trumps used by the South in its uphill fight, were sinking Federal ships at an alarming rate. Admiral Dahlgren sat in the cabin of his flagship, the *Harvest Moon,* one morning, waiting for breakfast, when an explosion suddenly separated the bulkhead next to the wardroom and drove it in toward him, sending articles in all directions. He at first thought the boiler had burst, the engineer having reported the evening before that it needed repair badly. Then he got the smell of gunpowder and supposed the magazine had exploded. Running feet soon brought him the news of what actually had happened, and he fled with others from the vessel, watching her sink in two and a half fathoms of Georgetown Bay. She went down in five minutes, leaving him with only the uniform he wore. John Hazzard, wardroom steward, was drowned.

The *Harvest Moon* was one of many. Near Fort Sumter the ironclad *Patapsco,* aiding vessels employed in removing obstructions, struck a mine and sank almost immediately, taking sixty members of the crew with her. Even the little Union survey vessel *Bibb* met her end in this manner. The transport *Thorn* was blown up in Cape Fear River; and down around Mobile, in a period of two weeks, mines destroyed the monitors *Milwaukee* and *Osage,* gunboat *Rodolph,* and the steamer *Ida.* In one day, the gunboats *Sciota* and *Itasca,* the steamer *Rose,* and a cutter from the ironclad *Cincinnati* were sunk. A steamer from New Orleans, carrying the Third Michigan Cavalry, struck a mine that killed and wounded thirteen. The vessel was destroyed.

In his report to Welles of the sinking of his flagship, Dahlgren had this observation: "So much has been said in ridicule of torpedoes that very little precautions are deemed necessary, and if resorted to are probably taken with less care than if due weight was attached to the existence of these mischievous things." [16]

With this continued show of force from a beaten South, rumors multiplied. One of the most disturbing came from the U.S. consul at Halifax, Nova Scotia, who said he had been informed "from sources believed to be reliable" that four ironclads were on their way from French and English ports to attack New York City and that five blockade-running steamers, converted into privateers with two guns each, would co-operate. The latter were to be under command of John Maffitt.[17] This was contradicted by a report from General Grant to the effect that the rams were to be directed against Mobile Harbor.

But rumor or no rumor, the crumbling of the Confederacy reached a more rapid pace in April. About four on the afternoon of the 2nd, a special messenger from Richmond found

Raphael Semmes seated at a late dinner on his flagship, the *Virginia No. 2*. He handed the Admiral a sealed package.

In later years, Semmes clearly remembered the day. About it he wrote: "The sun was shining brightly, the afternoon was calm, and Nature was just putting on her spring attire." [18]

Semmes tore open the package. In it he found a message from Stephen Mallory. The usual formalities were missing. It read: "General Lee advises the Government to withdraw from this city, and the officers will leave this evening accordingly. . . . Lee withdraws from his lines toward Danville this night; and, unless otherwise directed by General Lee, upon you is devolved the duty of destroying your ships this night, and with all the forces under your command joining General Lee. Confer with him, if practicable, before destroying them." [19]

Certain components of this message must have been impressed upon Semmes. The emphasis was on time—"this evening," "this night," and "this night." He looked out upon the waters of the James. Within his view at the moment were flag-of-truce boats still plying between Richmond and the enemy's headquarters at City Point.[20]

He adjusted himself to the situation at hand. The factor on which he was to act was represented by the message and not the military activity within his view. He dismissed the courier and ordered the signal to be given for all commanding officers in his bottled-up fleet to report on board the flagship.

A few minutes later he dispatched an officer on shore to send a message to General Lee from the signal station at Drewry's Bluff. No answer came; and after nightfall Semmes got his vessels under way and ran up toward the bluff. It was there he planned to blow up the ironclads, put his crews on board the lighter wooden gunboats, and proceed to Manchester, opposite Richmond, on his way to join Lee. But within an hour he saw the horizon above the Confederate capital aglow with fires.

After that, Semmes had no doubt about the action he should take. Arms had to be broken out, provisions brought up out of the hold and broken into such packages as the sailors could carry, hammocks had to be unlashed, and blankets taken out and rolled compactly. It was between two and three in the morning of the 3rd before this had been done and the crews transferred to the gunboats. After he was sure the ironclads were well afire, he moved off up the river. He had not gone far before an explosion "like the shock of an earthquake" took place, and the air was filled with missiles. The *Virginia No. 2,* the vessel intended, like her namesake, to be a great source of pride for the Southerners, was no more. Her shell room had been full of loaded shells.

Semmes moved on. At one bridge between Drewry's Bluff and Richmond, the draw was down, with troops passing over it, and his little fleet had to wait more than an hour. It was dawn when he was able to continue, and so light he soon was able to make out the school ship *Patrick Henry* burning in the lower part of the city. Behind it, houses in the navy yard were ablaze, and along the river front everything seemed to be on fire.

In the excitement, Semmes got his men ashore and set aflame each of the gunboats. When they were burning at a lively rate, they were shoved off from the landing. As the last of them drifted away, he directed his men toward the railroad station.

People were running along the streets, some in panic, without their possessions; some in more orderly fashion, with bundles. Semmes stopped a man and inquired about the trains.

"Trains!" was his answer. "The last train left at daylight this morning. It was filled with civil officers of the Government."

Semmes moved on to the railway station. There he found a throng of frightened men, despairing women, crying children. Military wounded were hobbling about. A few civilians had crowded into several passenger cars standing in the yards.

On land, the Admiral acted with the same precision that marked his manner on deck. He ordered the people out of the cars, and to their protests he answered that the enemy would be easier on unarmed civilians than on soldiers or sailors with arms. To some of the steam engineers in his crew he pointed out a small locomotive standing farther down the track, obviously without a fire under its boiler. While men tore down a picket fence in front of a nearby home and started a fire in the engine, the cars were pushed together. The seamen climbed into them, and then all the citizens who could find places were permitted to get aboard.

When coupled up, the little locomotive began pulling the cars along the track at a snail's pace. Semmes was beginning to feel completely frustrated, when one of his engineers ran to him with the announcement that another engine, this one with steam up, had been found. It was connected to the train, and soon it was moving at a speed of five or six miles an hour.

About midnight of the following day, Semmes reached Danville in southern Virginia. There he found Jefferson Davis and Mallory, and these officials arranged for the naval brigade to be organized as artillery and assigned to the defenses of the place. For days it would see duty there, and then go on toward Greensboro, North Carolina, where Semmes, days later, witnessed the windup ceremonies of General Joseph E. Johnston's Army of Tennessee.

On April 9, Lee's Army of Northern Virginia, a part of it the naval garrison from Drewry's Bluff under Flag Officer Tucker, serving with General Custis Lee's division of Ewell's Corps, surrendered at Appomattox. That same day the C.S.S. *Chameleon,* alias *Atlanta,* alias *Tallahassee,* alias *Olustee,* reached Liverpool under the experienced guidance of John Wilkinson. Three days later, Mobile fell.

The feeling of doom deepened, but there were still zealots. One Southerner who had not yet been stopped was Lieutenant Charles Read, who had fled southward after the Federals forced destruction of the James River fleet. Still uncaptured up the Red River, where it had fled after the battle of New Orleans, was the powerful, two-hundred-foot paddle-wheel steamer *William H. Webb,* a New York icebreaker that the Confederates had converted into a ram. She had demonstrated her might during early '63 by ramming and sinking the U.S.S. *Indianola.* Secretary Mallory imagined she would be even more dangerous if taken into open water, so he gave the assignment to Read.

When Read found her, she was eighty miles below Shreveport, totally unprepared for the service upon which she was to be taken.[21] She had not a single gun on board, little or no crew, no fuel, and no small arms except for a few cutlasses. Read took her up to Shreveport and there asked for the aid of General Kirby Smith, commanding the Trans-Mississippi Department, and this he got in unstinted degree.

Smith provided a thirty-pounder Parrott for a bow pivot, as well as two small iron twelve-pounders. Carpenters were given supplies to build a rough bulwark around her forecastle. Drawing on volunteers from the Army, Read got together sixteen officers and a crew of fifty-one.

Returning downstream, Read piled wood, most of it pine knots, in every available space on the ship, taking on enough fuel to last him five days. Then he loaded one hundred ninety bales of cotton, stacking it as a shield around the machinery. While tied up there, he heard of the assassination of President Lincoln, a tragedy that later would be employed as a part of his efforts to deceive the enemy gunboats along the course he was to follow.

Before leaving Alexandria the night of April 22, Read prepared a report on the undertaking for Mallory. "As I will have to stake everything upon speed and time," he wrote, "I will not attack any vessel in the passage unless I perceive a possibility of her arresting my progress. In this event I am prepared with five torpedoes (one hundred pounds), one of which I hold shipped on its pole on the bows." [22]

Fifteen miles below Alexandria the *Webb* drew up to take on board George Price, a special pilot from a steamboat battalion stationed at Marksville, Louisiana. From there they headed toward the mouth of the Red River. It was Read's information that he would meet at that point three ironclads, the *Tennessee, Manhattan, Lafayette,* and a plated gunboat, the *Gazelle.*[23]

Read reached the mouth of the river well after dark. He ordered the *Webb* run slowly, to reduce noise. She was displaying the lights of a Union transport; all others were concealed. The steam was high, ready to force the vessel ahead at maximum speed when necessary.

William Biggio was at the wheel, and he thought the *Webb* came within five hundred yards of the Union ships before she was discovered. But it was a night when the land was dark and the sky dimly lighted, and the line of smoke coming down the Red could be seen by the blockaders. Pilot Wiley Jones on the *Vindicator,* a vessel that Read had not known was there, saw it and called it to the attention of his captain. The wind was light from the west. "That's the *Webb* trying to escape," Jones declared. On board the U.S. monitor *Manhattan,* the officer of the deck, Acting Ensign C. H. Sinclair, saw the smoke and beat to quarters.

"In one minute from the time the gong was first struck," reported Robert B. Ely, captain of the *Manhattan,* "the crew were at their quarters, the port chain slipped, hatches closed, shackle off the starboard chain, and the ship ready for action. The smoke was now seen to be that of a vessel coming out of Red River and within five hundred yards of this vessel, off the starboard bow, and going full speed down the river. I fired the howitzer to bring her to, and at once ordered the fifteen-inch guns to be trained at the strange vessel, the guns at the time being trained on the port beam. The turret was immediately revolved, and No. 1 gun was fired, as soon as it could be brought to bear, at the stranger, then only distinguishable in the darkness by the black smoke off our starboard quarter. I am not able to state whether this shot took effect or not." [24]

The *Manhattan* made General Signal No. 570: "Strange vessel in sight, positively an enemy." Then a rocket soared from her deck.

On board the *Webb,* Read shouted, "Let her go!" Biggio rang the fast bell. The engineer opened the throttle as wide as it would go, and the vessel seemed to leap ahead.

"Keep her for the biggest opening between them!" shouted Read.[25]

Biggio described the scene: "By this time every whistle in the Federal fleet was screaming, drums were beating, rockets were going up, and it seemed as if the very devil was to pay. I kept the *Webb* straight on her course."

The shots from the *Manhattan* missed the *Webb* by hundreds of yards. The Confederate vessel was fast and she soon was clear of the Union vessels, none of which gave chase. Ahead, between her and the Gulf, stretched three hundred miles of the Mississippi. Read raced on, stopping every fifteen miles or so to cut telegraph wires along the bank in the hope that no warning would get through to New Orleans.

At daylight the *Webb* was approaching Donaldsonville, still carrying the signals of a Union transport. Federal officers at that point who saw her thought she was on her way to New Orleans under guard.[26]

It was nearly 1:00 P.M. when New Orleans came into view. About ten miles above, Read hoisted a United States flag to half-mast. As they approached the city, men on watch on the Union ships were duped more by the flag than by the disguise of the ram. They took her to be a Federal transport, duly mourning the untimely death of President Lincoln.

But one of those watching her, a sailor on the U.S.S. *Lackawanna,* had the uncanny ability of a seaman to identify a vessel he had seen before. He called out her identity, and signal flags, rockets, and guns were soon spreading the alarm. Several shots were fired at her, one of them going wild and damaging the homes of H. Eckluanand and John Garity on shore.[27] Three struck the *Webb.* One of them entered the bow about a foot above water, deranging the torpedo fixtures to such an extent that Read stopped the *Webb* for a couple of minutes to cut the explosive loose. A second shot passed through her chimney and severed a chain, one flying link of it wounding a man. The third shot was buried harmlessly in a bale of cotton.[28]

One of the last vessels they passed was the U.S. storeship

Fearnot, at the rail of which a Union officer could be seen standing at the side of a woman. Pilot George Price raised a rifle and aimed at the officer. Read, fearing he would hit the woman, told him not to shoot.

Price laid down the rifle with the remark, "That's the first time I was ever ordered not to shoot a yankee." [29]

As soon as he cleared the Union fleet, Read dropped the Union flag flying at half-mast and hoisted to the top a Confederate flag. The *Hollyhock* and *Florida* set out downstream on his trail. Already the rumor was flying that Jefferson Davis, John Wilkes Booth, and the mythical Confederate treasure were on the *Webb.*

Mile after mile the pursuit continued, with the *Webb* remaining easily in the lead. Read knew that the next danger point ahead of them was Forts Jackson and St. Philip, which he wanted to make sure not to reach until after dark.

The *Hollyhock* gradually forged well in advance of the *Florida.* Read watched the gap growing between the two vessels. He was thinking seriously of slowing up to capture the *Hollyhock,* when the lookout shouted from above and Read turned his attention in another direction. There ahead of them, anchored to repair her engine, was the U.S.S. *Richmond,* a first-class sloop with twenty-one guns.

Read debated only a moment before directing the pilot: "Make straight for the *Richmond*'s bow and ram."

"I can't reach her bow because of a shoal," the pilot replied, "but I can come in under her broadside."

"I've been under the *Richmond*'s broadside before," said Read, "and I don't wish to try it again." [30]   Read called officers and crew in front of the pilothouse.

"It's no use," he said. "The *Richmond* will drown us all, and if she doesn't, the forts below will, as they have a range of three miles each way up and down the river, and they know by this time that we are coming. Had we passed New Orleans without being discovered, I would have cut the wires below the city and we could have reached the Gulf with little trouble. As it is,

I think the only thing for us to do is to set the *Webb* on fire and blow her up." [81]

Not a word came from his listeners.

"Head for shore," he directed.

Barrels of turpentine were broken open and spread about the ship. When she struck bottom, fifty yards from shore, life lines were thrown over the bow and men began climbing down them, some remembering that when they had left Shreveport they had seen rats swimming away from the *Webb*—in the seaman's superstition, an indication that a vessel is doomed. Read touched a match in several places before going over the side himself.

Back in the bushes of a nearby plantation, the men from the *Webb* lay in hiding until they heard her magazine explode. Then they separated into groups and headed in various directions, only a few hours of freedom left to most of them.

An end to a navy

MAY-NOVEMBER 1865

Discovery of a ship captain's body preserved in a cask of whiskey was a new experience for the C.S.S. *Shenandoah,* steaming blithely through the icy waters of the Arctic Ocean in search of whalers, unaware that the cause for which she was fighting had ended weeks earlier.

Just the day before, the Confederate cruiser had come in sight of eleven whalers. She was under a head wind, and the sails spotted were all to windward. Her captain, James Iredell Waddell, knew that while the wind blew he would lose the greater part of his intended victims if he tried to capture any one of them, so he lowered his vessel's smokestack, keeping a luff and retarding her progress as much as possible so as to arouse no suspicions, and continued in their rear. Throughout the night he held to his position, and in midmorning a calm ensued. It was then Waddell raised an American flag and steamed in among them, causing all to raise the same flag.

They were in East Cape Bay. While boats on the *Shenandoah* were being armed, preparatory to taking possession of the prizes, a boat from the whaler *Brunswick* visited the steamer. The mate in charge announced as he came alongside that his ship had struck a piece of ice and needed assistance. Lieutenant William C. Whittle, Jr., to whom he spoke, replied: "We are very busy now, but in a little while we will attend to you."

Waddell smiled at the facetiousness of the reply.

"Which vessel is the *James Maury?*" he asked.

The mate pointed to a whaler anchored a short distance away.

In position to command all of the vessels with the *Shenandoah*'s guns, Waddell now raised the Confederate flag and dispatched his armed boats to take possession, each with orders to bring back the captains with their ships' papers. All of the American flags came down except one, and Waddell later learned that the crew on board that particular vessel was too drunk to attend to such matters.

"All the captains and masters were more or less under the influence of liquor," Waddell reported, "and some of them swore their sympathy for the South, while others spoke incoherently of cruiser, fire, and insurance. A drunken and brutal class of men I found the whaling captains and mates of New England." [1]

Lieutenant Francis T. Chew of the *Shenandoah* boarded the *James Maury,* a vessel Waddell had heard about at the island of Ascension. When her mate was brought back to face Waddell, he told about the efforts to preserve the captain's body until it could be taken back to shore for burial. His widow, with her two little children, was on board. Reluctant to bury her husband at sea and practical enough to want to capture as many whales as possible before leaving, she had simply preserved his remains in a barrel of whiskey.

Waddell was sympathetic. "I sent a message to the unhappy woman to cheer up," he wrote, "that no harm should come to her on the vessel; that I knew she was an owner in the vessel, and that the men of the South never made war on helpless women and children; although an example to the contrary had been set them by their Northern enemy, we preferred the nobler instincts of human nature." [2]

The *James Maury* was ransomed for $37,000, the bark *Nile* for $41,000. The other nine ships were burned.

"An occasional explosion on board of some one of the burning vessels informed me of the presence of gunpowder or other combustibles," Waddell described, "and a liquid flame now and then pursued some inflammable substance which had escaped from their sides to the water, and the heavens were illuminated with the red glare, presenting a picture of indescribable grandeur, while the water was covered with black smoke commingling with fiery sparks. Discharges on board often resembled distant artillery, and while that scene of destruction was going on the steamer turned her head northward in search of additional prey." [3]

Waddell was carrying out another stratagem adopted by the Confederacy in its final moments of desperation. The preceding August, Secretary Mallory had written Bulloch: "The enemy's distant whaling grounds have not been visited by us. His commerce constitutes one of his reliable sources of national wealth no less than one of his best schools for seamen, and we must strike it, if possible. If you can not do better, can you not send in so safe and secret a manner that your action will not be known until their blows are felt two clipper sailing ships, lightly armed, with judicious officers, against this commerce?" [4]

Bulloch did better. He soon notified Mallory of the purchase of a successor to the *Alabama,* a ship with frames and beams of iron, and planked from keel to gunwale with East Indian teak. She had a lifting screw and was a fast sailer, having made three hundred thirty miles in twenty-four hours with screw up. She had been originally named the *Sea King,* but Bulloch wrote that he planned to rename her the *Shenandoah.*[5]

Since October of '64, Waddell had been directing this newly acquired vessel. He was at home on the sea and one of the most experienced and capable ship masters in either Navy. A six-foot North Carolinian, he had black hair and thick sideburns, was stubborn, proud, hot-tempered, alert. So long had he braved the winds that his face was a deep mahogany. As he moved about deck, he limped slightly from an old dueling wound that his crew sometimes discussed but knew little about. They respected him and had faith in his integrity, and there was no resentment of the fact that he remained aloof.

Assuming command off the island of Madeira, where the raider had been brought from Liverpool, Waddell left a trail of burning vessels in the South Atlantic. Then he went around the Cape of Good Hope to stop at Australia for repairs, as well as to fill out his crew. He was next heard from in the South Pacific, and finally in the Sea of Okhotsk and the Arctic Ocean. After disposing of the little fleet in East Cape Bay, he continued northward through snow and ice until the going became so rough he turned about and headed to the south.

Newspapers taken from some of his captures indicated to Waddell that Lee's army had surrendered, and he was so informed by some of their captains. But he also learned that the seat of government had been moved from Richmond to Danville and that Jefferson Davis had urged the Confederacy to fight on, which was to him sufficient reason to continue the *Shenandoah*'s depredations. He planned to keep on southward and to devote his attention to the steamers running between Panama and San Francisco, and possibly to the city of San Francisco.

Bulloch in the meantime was trying to communicate with Waddell. At Nagasaki, Japan, and at Shanghai and the Sandwich Islands were held copies of a letter sent out from England. It announced the surrender of the Southern armies and the arrest of President Davis and his Cabinet. "President Johnson," it added, "has formally declared the war to be at an end. . . . I hereby direct you to desist from any further destruction of United States property upon the high seas and from all offensive operations against the citizens of that country." Bulloch suggested that Waddell come to Europe before going to the U.S.[6]

But Waddell visited none of these points where the letter was held and was thus ignorant of developments. On August 2, he came up with and boarded the British bark *Barracouta*, thirteen days out of San Francisco. From newspapers found on her, Waddell gained the information that Bulloch was trying to supply by letter.

"My life had been checkered," Waddell wrote, "and I was tutored to disappointment; the intelligence of the issue of the fearful struggle cast a deep stillness over the ship's company and would have occupied all my reflection had not a responsibility of the highest order rested upon me in the course I should pursue, which involved not only my personal honor, but the honor of that flag intrusted to me, which had been thus far triumphant." [7]

He thought at first of running to a South Atlantic port, but finally decided instead to head for Europe, seventeen thousand miles away. The distance was covered without mishap, and on the morning of November 5, the *Shenandoah* entered St. George's Channel on the coast of England.

Much news awaited Waddell and his crew, for much had happened since they last had been in touch with happenings over the world. Back home, the windup of the war had not been without its tragedies, large and small. Near Memphis, the passenger and freight steamer *Sultana*'s boilers had exploded. Her legal load was three hundred seventy-six persons, but at the time, she was trying to make her way upstream with two thousand four hundred Ohio, Indiana, Michigan, Tennessee, Kentucky, and West Virginia soldiers from prison camps in the South, as well as one hundred civilians and a crew of about eighty. The death toll was estimated at one thousand five hundred eighty-five, a marine disaster that would go down in the records as the greatest in history.

Concern in the North after the surrender of Lee's army was

over the Confederate vessels still at sea. Gradually these came in, or were reported out of action. Newest of them was the ironclad C.S.S. *Stonewall*. She had been built in France for the Confederacy, and on January 6, '65, she sailed under command of Captain Thomas Jefferson Page, a fifty-three-year-old Virginian, formerly in the U.S. Navy, who had spent much of his career as a naval explorer. The *Stonewall,* damaged by a storm, was forced to go into Ferrol, Spain, for repairs, and while there the U.S.S. *Niagara* and the U.S.S. *Sacramento* arrived and stood by, watching her. On March 24, she came out and tried to start a battle, but neither of the Union vessels would take her on, so she headed for Lisbon, Page planning to cross the Atlantic and strike at General Sherman's base at Port Royal. He reached Nassau on May 6, and went next to Havana, but there he learned that the war had ended. On May 19, he delivered the *Stonewall* into the hands of the captain-general of the island, to be held under the protection of the Spanish flag until her final disposition could be decided.[8]

Confederate forces in the Trans-Mississippi surrendered on June 2, and the following day the C.S.S. *Missouri,* an ironclad built and operated along the Red River, was given up at Alexandria, Louisiana. But still unaccounted for was the C.S.S. *Shenandoah,* known to be off somewhere raiding Union commerce. There was fear she would come back and attack along the American coast. So concerned was Secretary Welles that he dispatched warnings to Union ships in ports all the way from Maine to Texas.

In June the veteran Admiral Samuel F. du Pont, who had tried so diligently but unsuccessfully to take Charleston earlier in the war, went to Philadelphia, accompanied by his wife. The following night he was stricken with acute illness, and by morning he was dead.[9]

Early August brought further reports of the *Shenandoah,* said to be in the North Pacific, and the Pacific Squadron was directed to track her down. "Being an erratic ship, without country or destination, no definite instructions can be given you," Welles wrote the commanding officer, Acting Rear Admiral George F. Pearson.[10] Before the month was out, it was known that she was burning whalers in the Arctic. During September and October, Union ships searched for her in many parts of the globe. And then came word that she had been surrendered to the British.

After reaching St. George's Channel, Waddell dropped anchor to wait for a pilot. It had been one hundred twenty-two days and twenty-three thousand miles since his crew had seen land, the last the Aleutian Islands.

When the pilot arrived that night, he was informed of the character of the steamer, and he commented in surprise: "I was reading but a few days ago of her being in the Arctic Ocean."

Waddell asked for American news, and it was then he learned the most important developments since he last had been in contact with affairs at home. Before going to bed, he worked diligently over a letter to Earl Russell, the British Secretary of State for Foreign Affairs.

Next morning the *Shenandoah* steamed up the Mersey in a thick fog. Overhead waved the Confederate flag. As she came to anchor at Liverpool, near the British ship of the line *Donegal,* commanded by Captain James A. Paynter, some of those on board remembered that it had been thirteen months since she had set out from this port. The last gun in defense of the South had been fired from her deck in the Arctic Ocean on June 22. She had been around the world, traveled fifty-eight thousand statute miles, sailed for eight months without lowering her anchors, and had visited every ocean except the Antarctic. Only the *Alabama* had exceeded her record of captures. Thirty-eight ships and one thousand fifty-three prisoners she had taken. Thirty-two of the captured vessels had gone up in flames. Total damage inflicted by her upon Union commerce was estimated at $1,361,983.

Shortly after she anchored, a lieutenant arrived from the *Donegal,* bringing official intelligence of the termination of the American Civil War. He was polite to Waddell, and obviously sympathetic.

At ten o'clock that morning of November 6, the Confederate flag was officially lowered for the last time. Then Waddell sent off the letter to Earl Russell.

A gunboat came alongside the *Shenandoah* the following day and made fast to her. Customs officials soon took possession, and Waddell relieved his officers and crew of all duty. But they were not yet to go ashore. Charles Francis Adams, the U.S. minister to Great Britain, had acted in an effort to keep the ship from getting to sea again, and his complaints would delay the sailing temporarily.

On November 8, the men on the *Shenandoah* were unconditionally released, after their baggage had been inspected by customs officials, "more in hunt of tobacco than treasure," Waddell suspected. The captain presented his tumblers, decanters, bedding, and a few trophies from the islands to the wife of the lieutenant commanding, in whose direct custody he had been and whom he praised for his faithfulness to duty.

After nightfall the Confederates were taken to the Great George Landing at Liverpool and there set ashore. Waddell walked away with a great feeling of relief and satisfaction, feeling there could be no complaint about the way he had handled the *Shenandoah*. "I claim for her officers and men a triumph over their enemies and over every obstacle, and for myself I claim having done my duty," he wrote later.[11]

So ended the Confederate Navy, a mythical force in '61, but a definite threat from that year until Waddell furled the *Shenandoah*'s flag. From start to finish, an uphill fight had been the lot of Southern naval men. But out of their tribulations, in the face of what seemed impossible odds, had come inventions and new ideas that would set a fast pace for the North and leave their marks upon the wars of future generations—the water mine, the ironclad ship, the torpedo boat, the submarine, explosive coal. And its examples of heroism, with no parallels in history, would cause a requiem of memories down through the ages—men like those on the C.S.S. *Tennessee*, battling an entire fleet with a single ship, and men like those on the C.S.S.

Hunley, struggling into their cramped quarters on board the tiny craft with the knowledge that almost every man who had preceded them had gone to his death.

The North's Navy also had its brand of heroism, and it also set a record of achievements which would be inspiring to future generations. It had grown from ninety-odd ships in '61 to more than six hundred in '65. It was this rapid buildup in strength that startled the rest of the world. And no doubt a strong reason for the two global leaders, England and France, to keep out of the war was the speed with which the Federal Government built ironclads and tinclads and monitors and gunboats.

No matter what their contrast in strength, and putting aside all comparisons of bravery in their men, the two navies could join hands in a mutual complaint: their role in the war would be underrated and in many instances ignored. Thirty years would pass before President Grover Cleveland's Navy Secretary, Hilary A. Herbert, a Southerner who had fought in the Alabama Infantry, declared:

"I do not think anybody knows better than I . . . the value of the service of the Navy of the United States during the Civil War. Basing my opinion upon personal experience, I have often said that the Navy has never had justice done it . . . for the simple reason that Army officers and their friends have written the history of that great struggle. . . . It was the Navy that cut the Confederacy into separate fragments, not only along the line of the Tennessee but up the Red River and the White River and the Yellow River, and wherever a gunboat could go there was the Navy of the U.S. cutting the communication between the different parts of the Confederate Army and destroying their supplies and their munitions of war." [12]

Mr. Herbert's words, in effect, focused a spotlight on the factor in the Union's military machinery that ultimately provided the advantage needed to win a war. Southerners on land knew by tradition how to march and how to shoot. It was the pastime for many a community, where the major excitement of ordinarily dull weeks came when the local militia marched in the cool of the evening to the village green for drill. As war enveloped the nation and hostile forces arrived in hordes from the North, the men of the South shouldered their weapons and went forth, putting into practice training which had been theirs since boyhood.

But their confidence on foot and horseback did not accompany them on water. There they were at a loss. When the Union's fierce fighting ships stormed along the Atlantic Coast and nosed up into Southern rivers, the resistance the Confederates were able to offer came largely from peacetime vessels made warlike only by the all too few guns fastened to their decks.

There were times when the South could boast important and complete victories on land, as attested by Northern armies fleeing in panic from the field. Reacting to these setbacks, Lincoln replaced generals, realigned departments, and sought new offensive plans. But the tide of war never brought him the same worry with reference to the Navy. If a fleet of one size failed, a more numerous fleet was sent to finish the task. The odds at sea were always on the side of the North. Southern leaders proved this with their strategy, for invariably in planning major battles they steered their armies away from the huge floating fortresses the Union was able to place on patrol along the coast.

Notes

[1] General David Hunter, commanding the Union army besieging Charleston in the early summer of '63, was convinced that Fort Sumter could be made untenable in two days after Morris Island was taken. See his report in *Official Records of the Union and Confederate Navies,* Series 1, XIV, 33, referred to hereafter as *O.R.N.*

[2] In his annual report for 1865, Gideon Welles, Secretary of the Union Navy, said of Charleston that it was "the most invulnerable and best-protected city on the coast, whose defense had cost immense treasure and labor."

[3] Union General Quincy A. Gillmore, who succeeded Hunter in the Charleston command, thought the Confederates made a mistake in locating Battery Wagner. In his opinion, it would have been more effective if placed near Lighthouse Inlet. See *Official Records of the Rebellion,* Series 1, XXVIII, 33, referred to hereafter as *O.R.*

[4] Robert C. Gilchrist, in his *The Confederate Defense of Morris Island* (Charleston, The News and Courier Book Presses, 1884), p. 5, referred to hereafter as Gilchrist, says: "At West Point there

are only two models of fortifications used for purposes of instruction to the cadets in the art of attack and defense; one of these is Fort Wagner, the other Sebastopol."

Wagner was named after Lieutenant Colonel Thomas M. Wagner of the First South Carolina Artillery, killed by a bursting gun in July, '62; and Gregg, after Brigadier General Maxcy Gregg, killed at Fredericksburg, Virginia, the following December. The encroaching sea, during the century since the war, has submerged the tip of the island on which they stood, wiping away all vestiges of both.

⁵ *O.R.N.,* Series 1, XIV, 32.

⁶ Du Pont never ceased to maintain that he was right in his stand regarding the futility of an attack at Charleston, and experience later bore him out. On April 16,1863, nine days after the failure of the attack on the 7th, he wrote Welles a long letter in which he reviewed the situation, and concluded: "I have to request that the Department will not hesitate to relieve me by any officer who, in its opinion, is more able to execute that service in which I have had the misfortune to fail—the capture of Charleston. No consideration for an individual officer, whatever his loyalty and length of service, should weigh an instant if the cause of his country can be advanced by his removal." *O.R.N.,* Series 1, XIV, 140.

⁷ Secretary Welles, during the fall of '62, had opposed the promotion. In his diary he wrote: "Dahlgren is grieved with my action in his case. He desires, beyond almost anyone, the high honors of his profession, and has his appetite stimulated by the partiality of the President, who does not hesitate to say to him and to me that he will give him the highest grade if I will send him a letter to that effect, or a letter of appointment. Title irregularly obtained cannot add to Dahlgren's reputation, yet he cannot be reasoned with. He has yet rendered no service afloat during the war—has not been under fire—and is not on the direct road for professional advancement. But he is a favorite with the President and knows it." And later, after the promotion was conferred: "It has gained him no friends in the profession, for the officers feel and know he has attained naval honors without naval claims or experience." See *Diary of Gideon Welles* (New York, W. W. Norton & Company, Inc., 1960), referred to hereafter as Welles.

⁸ Report of this rumor was made by Rear Admiral Oscar W. Farenholt in an address before the California Commandery, Military Order of the Loyal Legion, at San Francisco, in 1912.

⁹ *History of the Navy During the Rebellion,* by Charles B. Boynton (New York, D. Appleton and Company, 1867), p. 206, referred to hereafter as Boynton.

¹⁰ John Johnson, in his *The Defense of Charleston Harbor* (Charleston, Walker Evans & Cogswell Company, 1890), p.84, referred to hereafter as Johnson, says there was no discovery of the Federal plans at this stage, and quotes from a report of Confederate General R. S. Ripley that "up to the 8th or 9th of July the enemy, so far as ascertained, had constructed no works on Folly except to shelter his pickets from our shells."

On the other hand, General Ripley, who commanded the First Military District, C.S.A., with headquarters at Charleston, said in a report dated August 29, 1863, that the presence of the Federals on Folly and Little Folly Islands was known even before the April 7 attack, that their movements were watched from points of observation on Long, Battery, Black, and Morris Islands. "They consisted for some weeks," he reported, "in throwing up defensive works on Folly. The force was variously estimated at from three to six regiments, and, as his defensive operations progressed, his works across the neck of Folly were plainly observed and reported upon." *O.R.,* Series 1, XXVIII, 96.

¹¹ Records would indicate that these bombardments were made blindly. The Confederates had lookout stations on the ruins of the old lighthouse on Morris Island, on the masthead of the wrecked blockade runner *Ruby,* and at Secessionville on James Island, but the work going on in the undergrowth could not be seen from these points. Johnson, p. 84.

Gillmore seems to have thought the Confederates were informed of what he was doing. In a report dated July 6, Dahlgren states: "On a personal conference with General Gillmore, he further informed me that the enemy appeared to be aware of his design, and were working on Morris Island with great activity to defeat it. . . ." *O.R.N.,* Series 1, XIV, 311.

¹² *O.R.,* Series 1, XVIII, 97.

¹³ Johnson, p. 87. This is one of the best accounts available of the Union offensive against Charleston. Johnson was a member of a five-man board appointed by General Beauregard in April, 1864, to compile a military history of the siege of the city. He wrote from private notes, sketches, diaries, and the engineers' journals.

¹⁴ Beauregard later wrote in a report to Richmond: "According to my conception, it was not the want of infantry force at the command of that department, but, as I had before supposed was universally admitted, the want of adequate work of defense at

the lower end of the island, known long to be the external gate of the city, and the establishment by the enemy (without the knowledge of the military authorities) of powerful land batteries on Folly Island, screened and concealed, until fully prepared to open upon us with all the effect of a surprise, by the woods which had been allowed to remain unfelled on that island." *O.R.,* XVIII, I, 63.

In this opinion, as other officers pointed out, he was in error. The trees were an advantage, but they were not indispensable, for the sand hills on the north end of Folly Island would have concealed the Union batteries.

[15] Gilchrist, p. 13.

[16] General Stewart L. Woodford, in an address delivered in 1891 before the New York Commandery, Military Order of the Loyal Legion, said: "The assault upon Fort Wagner July 10, 1863, was the first occasion when Negro troops were prominently employed upon the Atlantic Coast." They had been used earlier, but not in large numbers. The Fifty-fourth Massachusetts was a regiment made up of Northern Negroes.

[17] Johnson, p. 90.

[18] *O.R.,* Series 1, XXVIII, 73.

[19] *Ibid.*

[20] Gillmore, in this instance, had been misled. Confederate reinforcements already were in the fort, arriving before midnight. See Boynton, p. 209. These consisted of two hundred sixty men from the Seventh South Carolina Volunteers, five hundred thirty-four from the First, Twelfth, Eighteenth, and Sixty-third Georgia Regiments, twenty from the First South Carolina Infantry, seventy from the First South Carolina Artillery, and two hundred from the Twenty-first South Carolina Volunteers. Gilchrist, p. 15.

[21] *O.R.N.,* Series 1, XIV, 321.

[22] Gilchrist, p. 17.

[23] *O.R.,* Series 1, XXVIII, 76.

[24] *O.R.N.,* Series 1, XIV, 366.

[25] *The Siege of Charleston,* by Major General Samuel Jones (New York, The Neale Company, 1911), p. 229, referred to hereafter as Jones.

[26] Report of General William B. Taliaferro. *O.R.N.,* Series 1, XIV, 368.

[27] Gilchrist, p. 20.

[28] *O.R.,* Series 1, XXVIII, 92.

[29] Robert C. Gilchrist, one of the Confederate officers who re-

pulsed the attack, said eight hundred bodies were buried the following day. Gilchrist, p. 23.

30 Another participant, Major Lewis Butler of the Sixty-seventh Ohio Regiment, later wrote: "It is but just that I notice a special order of General Beauregard, under date of July 27, 1863, directing that special care be taken of the wounded captured at Wagner, as men who were brave enough to go in there deserved the respect of their enemy. Another act of courtesy: the effects, money and papers belonging to members of the Sixty-seventh Ohio Volunteer Infantry, who died in Charleston Hospital, were sent through the lines by flag of truce." Gilchrist, p. 23.

31 *O.R.N.,* Series 1, XIV, 373.

32 *Battles and Leaders of the Civil War* (New York, The Century Company, 1887), IV, 47, referred to hereafter as *B. & L.*

33 *O.R.,* Series 1, XXVIII, 77.

34 Boynton, p. 214.

35 Gillmore to Dahlgren. *O.R.N.,* Series 1, XIV, 381.

36 *O.R.,* Series 1, XXVIII, 78.

37 Gilchrist, p. 27.

38 *O.R.,* Series 1, XVIII, 80.

39 Gilchrist, p. 29.

40 *O.R.N.,* Series 1, XIV, 445.

41 *Ibid.,* p. 515.

42 Some years later, Oscar Walter Farenholt, one of the men on the *Catskill* that day and the first man in the U.S. Navy's history to rise from seaman to admiral, presented the piece of metal that had killed Rodgers, to his brother, C. R. P. Rodgers, also a naval officer. Military Order of the Loyal Legion Papers, San Francisco, 1912, referred to hereafter as *M.O.L.L. Papers.*

43 *Ibid.,* New York, 1891.

44 *History of the Confederate States Navy,* by J. Thomas Scharf (New York, Rogers and Sherwood, 1887), p. 756, referred to hereafter as Scharf.

45 Jones, p. 254.

46 *Cities and Camps of the Confederate States,* edited by Richard Barksdale Harwell (Urbana, University of Illinois Press, 1958), p. 98.

47 Description by H. Henry Kloeppel in his unpublished manuscript in the Manuscript Division, Library of Congress.

48 *O.R.N.,* Series 1, XIV, 498.

49 Carlin is cited in *Foreigners in the Confederacy,* by Ella Lonn (Chapel Hill, University of North Carolina Press, 1940), p.

280, as one of the men from other nations who took part in the American Civil War.

50 Report made to General Beauregard. *O.R.N.*, Series 1, XIV, 499.

51 *Ibid.*, p. 500.

52 These figures were supplied by Confederate General R. S. Ripley, *ibid.*, p. 750.

53 The disposition of the comunication was explained by Beauregard as follows: "It being at night, with no proper light at hand, the communications were sent unsealed by the same messenger to my headquarters."

54 After the war, the "Swamp Angel" was bought by Charles Carr and taken, with other condemned cannon, to his foundry at Trenton, New Jersey. But it has never been melted down and is still on display in that state as a curiosity.

55 Statistics reported by Beauregard. *O.R.*, Series 1, XXVIII, 84.

56 *The New York Times,* August 28, 1863.

57 *O.R.N.*, Series 1, XIV, 213.

58 *O.R.*, Series 1, XXVIII, 24.

59 *Ibid.*, p. 25.

60 Incident related by John Harleston in the quarterly magazine of the South Carolina Historical Society at Charleston, LVII, 1 (January, 1956).

61 Johnson, p. 284.

62 *O.R.N.*, Series 1, XIV, 26.

63 John Harleston, South Carolina Historical Society magazine.

64 *O.R.*, Series 1, XXVIII, 89.

65 One of the men on duty in Fort Wagner, John B. Patrick, an Irishman captured by the Federals in the summer of '64, related: "The wires were cut by the man who invented the torpedo. I don't know why, except he had not been treated right." He also reported that a Confederate officer, Lieutenant Joseph Davidson Blake, had been arrested and tried for saying he hoped the mine would never explode, "as it was too bad to blow people up in that way; it was not Christian." *O.R.*, Series 1, IX, 770.

66 In his report of the fall of Wagner, Gillmore listed the number captured in this instance as seventy, but in a report to Richmond, dated September 30, Beauregard denied that the number was more than forty-six. *Ibid.*, XXVIII, 62.

67 Beauregard reported that only nine hundred men were on Morris Island at the time of the evacuation. He put his losses from July 10 at six hundred forty-one. *Ibid.*, XXVIII, 62.

68 *O.R.N.*, Series 1, XIV, 27.

69 *O.R.*, Series 1, XXVIII, 87.

[70] Johnson, p. 264.
[71] *Ibid.*, p. 160.
[72] *O.R.N.*, Series 1, XIV, 617.
[73] *Ibid.*, p. 635.
[74] *Ibid.*, p. 636.
[75] *Ibid.*, p. 640.

CHAPTER TWO

[1] See the unpublished journal of Edward B. Latch at National Archives.
[2] *Confederate Veteran*, XXXVI, 454.
[3] "The Story of a Hero," by Edward A. Pollard, *Galaxy* magazine, VI, 598.
[4] *O.R.N.*, Series 1, XX, 518.
[5] *Ibid.*, p. 544.
[6] Scharf, p. 525.
[7] *O.R.N.*, Series 1, XX, 521.
[8] *Ibid.*, p. 525.
[9] *Ibid.*, p. 526.
[10] *Ibid.*, p. 561.
[11] Crocker estimated the number of shots fired before the *Sachem* was disabled at thirty, but Captain F. G. Odlum, commanding the Confederate artillery at Sabine Pass, said the fifth shell struck the vessel.
[12] Report of Lieutenant Crocker. *O.R.N.*, Series 1, XX, 547.
[13] *Ibid.*, p. 526.
[14] *Ibid.*, p. 528.
[15] *Ibid.*, p. 549.
[16] *Ibid.*, p. 561.
[17] Scharf, p. 526.

CHAPTER THREE

[1] *O.R.N.*, Series 1, XV, 11.
[2] Source of the name is disputed. David C. Ebaugh, one of the builders, claimed it was named for him. Other references say the boat was called "David" by Mrs. St. Julien Ravenel, of Charleston, wife of the designer, after the Biblical character who marched out before the armies of the Philistines to slay Goliath.
[3] Sources also vary as to size. Some describe the boat as only

thirty feet long; some give the width as eight feet amidships.

4 *O.R.N.*, Series 1, XIII, 808.

5 The author's friend, Daniel Ravenel, of Charleston, has been of great help in compiling information on his kinsman, Dr. St. Julien Ravenel. The doctor was born in 1819 and had considerable reputation as a scientist. He was educated as a physician and was recognized for his skill as a diagnostician. Somehow or other the practice of medicine was distasteful to him and he turned his attention to agricultural chemistry. But he never completely forsook medicine. In 1855, during an outbreak of yellow fever, he went to the assistance of the people in Norfolk, Virginia. During the war, he served as surgeon of the Twenty-fifth Regiment, South Carolina Volunteers, and later as surgeon in charge of the Confederate hospital at Columbia, South Carolina. During the last two years of the war, he was in charge of the laboratory at Columbia where most of the medicines needed for the Southern army were made.

But, except for the David, his greatest contribution perhaps was in the field of agricultural chemistry. Even before the war, he established the first lime plant in his native section. After the war, he discovered the presence of phosphate of lime along the Ashley and Cooper rivers, the start of an industry that over the years brought much wealth to the area.

6 Scharf, p. 758, says the first David was built at private expense by Theodore Stoney. But there are conflicting reports. Beauregard indicated that South Carolina bore the brunt of the expense, while James Lachlison, of Ridgeville, Georgia, writing in the *Confederate Veteran*, XVI, 78, says the merchants of Charleston contributed the funds.

Samuel Gaillard Stoney, of Charleston, a grand-nephew of Theodore Stoney, said his kinsman got the idea of the David while watching the ineffectual fire on the *New Ironsides* from one of the batteries on Morris Island, and approached Dr. Ravenel with the idea, promising financial support.

7 Samuel Gaillard Stoney, in a letter to the author, spelled the name of the landing "Stony," and said it was not taken from the family name.

8 *South Carolina Waters*, by Maxwell Clayton Orvin (Charleston, Southern Printing and Publishing Company, 1961), p. 23.

9 Ebaugh received $1,500 from the Confederate Government for his work. In subsequent correspondence, reproduced in the South Carolina Historical magazine of January, 1935, he claims credit for the conception, design, and construction of the David.

10 *O.R.N.,* Series 1, XIII, 824.

11 Memoirs of Chief Engineer James H. Tomb, Manuscript Division, University of North Carolina Library.

12 *O.R.N.,* Series 1, XV, 12.

13 "We felt that a torpedo attack was an innovation in naval warfare," Tomb explained in his memoirs, "and that if we did not give warning of our approach we might, if captured, get a short shrift. We thought best to fire not with the particular intention of killing someone, but for our own benefit."

14 *O.R.N.,* Series 1, XV, 18.

15 Dahlgren to Welles, Oct. 7, 1863. *Ibid.,* p. 10.

CHAPTER FOUR

1 *O.R.N.,* Series 1, V, 232.

2 New York *Herald,* April 24, 1864.

3 *Deck and Field,* by Frank Warren Hackett, a compilation of addresses delivered before the United States Naval War College (Washington, W. H. Lowdermilk and Company, 1909), p. 116, referred to hereafter as Hackett.

4 *O.R.N.,* Series 1, IX, 66.

5 *Ibid.,* p. 136.

6 During the Civil War, the name of this town was spelled Newberne and New Berne.

7 *O.R.N.,* Series 1, IX, 164.

8 *Ibid.,* p. 194.

9 *Ibid.,* p. 181.

10 *Ibid.,* p. 211.

11 Hackett, p. 121.

12 *Down Home in North Carolina,* state magazine, 24, VI, 13 (Raleigh, North Carolina, 1956).

13 For this bit of information, as well as other details, the author is indebted to Gilbert Elliott, of New York City, a grandson of the shipbuilder.

14 Peter Evans Smith Papers, Manuscript Division, University of North Carolina Library.

15 *O.R.N.,* Series 2, II, 297.

16 Violet G. Alexander Papers, Manuscript Division, University of North Carolina Library.

17 Peter Evans Smith Papers.

18 According to the Peter Evans Smith Papers, Smith invented the first electric buoy two years before Edison invented the in-

candescent lamp. He surveyed and helped build the railroad from Halifax to Hobgood, North Carolina, and later was employed by the Atlantic Coast Line Railroad to lay out the railway line to Plymouth, Greenville, Washington, and Hinton in that state.

[19] Peter Evans Smith Papers.

[20] This description of the *Albemarle* is taken from the statistical data on ships supplied in the *Official Navy Records,* Series 2, I, 247.

[21] *O.R.N.,* Series 1, X, 201.

[22] *Ibid.,* p. 230.

[23] *Ibid.,* IX, 309.

CHAPTER FIVE

[1] *O.R.N.,* Series 1, IX, 120.

[2] *Ibid.,* p. 123.

[3] Not to be confused with the frigate *Merrimack* that fought the *Monitor,* the only vessel of this name spelled with a "k." There were several steamers with the name *Merrimac.*

[4] *O.R.N.,* Series 1, 463.

[5] *Ibid.,* II, 11.

[6] *Ibid.,* IX, 495.

[7] *Ibid.,* p. 497.

[8] *Ibid.,* VIII, 895.

[9] *Ibid.,* IX, 133.

[10] The Confederacy's agent in Europe, James Bulloch, had long encouraged the Government to take this step. "If the Navy Department would take the blockade-running business into its own hands," he wrote Mallory, "it might soon have a fleet of formidable, swift, light-draft screw and paddle steamers at work, so constructed as to have their engines and boilers well protected either by coal when the bunkers were full or cotton when they were empty. The beams and decks of these steamers could be made of sufficient strength to bear heavy deck loads without exciting suspicion, and then if registered in the name of private individuals and sailed purely as commercial ships they could trade without interruption or violation of neutrality between our coasts and the Bermudas, Bahamas, and West Indies." *Ibid.,* Series 2, II, 590.

[11] Charles Cowley, judge advocate of the South Atlantic Blockading Squadron, wrote after the war: "We have been accustomed

to berate the commercial classes of Great Britain for exporting goods to the Confederate States, in violation of our blockade. But probably more goods were carried into the Confederate States through the instrumentality of merchants in the United States than by all the merchants of Europe." Scharf, p. 475.

[12] Admiral David D. Porter, writing in his *The Naval History of the Civil War* (New York, The Sherman Publishing Company, 1886), p. 35, stated: "The advantage was all on the side of the runners. They could choose their own time. If the gunboats fired, they were liable to hit one another; if they made the flash signal agreed upon, the runner would make a similar one and, in the confusion, the latter going at the rate of fifteen miles an hour, would soon pass out of sight. If the Federal vessels laid close in to the bar, they ran a risk of being carried into the breakers by the current, in which case their destruction was certain. The display of a twinkling light on board one of the gunboats, near the bar, was the signal for a general discharge from the guns of nearby forts and, although these shots were more noisy than damaging, yet a stray shell striking one of the Federal boats would have knocked it to pieces."

[13] Scharf, p. 475.

[14] *O.R.N.*, Series 1, IX, 235.

[15] New York *Herald,* November 9, 1863.

[16] *O.R.N.*, Series 1, II, 221.

[17] *Ibid.*, IX, 80.

[18] *Blockade Running During the Civil War,* by Francis B. C. Bradlee (Salem, Massachusetts, The Essex Institute, 1925), p. 143.

[19] Statement made by M. P. Usina, of Charleston, in an address before the Confederate Veterans' Association at Savannah, Georgia, July 4, 1893. *Chronicles of the Cape Fear River,* by James Sprunt (Raleigh, North Carolina, Edwards and Broughton Printing Company, 1914), p. 387.

[20] *O.R.N.*, Series 1, XIV, 643.

[21] According to *Confederate Blockade Running Through Bermuda 1861-1865,* edited by Frank Vandiver (Austin, University of Texas Press, 1947): "Blockade running supplied more than three times the number of arms produced by home manufacture." P. 62.

[22] *Sketches of Nassau,* by Frank I. Wilson (Raleigh, North Carolina, 1864), referred to in the John W. Grattan Papers, Manuscript Division, Library of Congress.

[23] *O.R.N.*, Series 1, XIII, 781.

[24] Scharf, p. 479.

[25] Scharf, p. 473.

[26] *Confederate Blockade Running Through Bermuda 1861-1865,* p. 85.

[27] *O.R.N.,* Series 1, IX, 275.

[28] *Ibid.,* p. 276.

[29] *Ibid.,* p. 277.

[30] *The Navy in the Civil War,* by James Russell Soley (New York, Charles Scribner's Sons, 1883), p. 156, referred to hereafter as Soley.

[31] *Sea Dogs of the Sixties,* by Jim Dan Hill (Minneapolis, The University of Minnesota Press, 1935), p. 149, referred to hereafter as Hill.

[32] When the helmsman of the *Robert E. Lee* next met John Wilkinson, he said to him: "She would have gone in by herself if they had only let her alone, for indeed it was evident to all on board the morning of her capture that she had been close in to the shore within a few miles of New Inlet bar. She had not reached the bar, however, so that the pilot's course in refusing to take charge was justifiable; but the fatal error was committed by not making a good offing before daylight. At the time of her capture, she was not more than twenty miles from land, and in the deep bays formed by the coast between Masonborough Inlet and the Cape Lookout Shoals." *The Narrative of a Blockade Runner,* by John Wilkinson (New York, Sheldon and Company, 1877), p. 174.

[33] The *Ella and Annie* was refitted and added to the Union's fighting fleet as the flagship of Admiral David D. Porter. *O.R.N.,* Series 2, I, 133.

[34] *O.R.,* Series 4, III, 78.

CHAPTER SIX

[1] *The Confederate Privateers,* by William Morrison Robinson, Jr. (New Haven, Yale University Press, 1928), p. 221.

[2] *O.R.N.,* Series 1, IX, 204.

[3] *Ibid.,* V, 353.

[4] Isaac J. Wister, commanding U.S. forces at Yorktown, Virginia.

[5] *O.R.N.,* Series 1, IX, 204.

[6] *O.R.,* Series 1, XXIX, Pt. 1, 138.

[7] *O.R.N.,* Series 1, IX, 206.

[8] *Ibid.,* p. 208.

[9] *Ibid.*

[10] *Ibid.,* p. 306.

[11] *Ibid.,* p. 318.
[12] *O.R.,* Series 2, VI, 705.

CHAPTER SEVEN

[1] See letter of Hunter Davidson to Catesby Jones, October 25, 1862. *O.R.N.,* Series 1, VII, 61.

[2] In urging Murdaugh's promotion to command, Flag Officer Samuel Barron, under whom he served, wrote: "I am the more emboldened to make this recommendation of Lieutenant Murdaugh for the reason that Lieutenant Murdaugh is, I believe, the only officer in the naval service who during this war has been deprived of the use of a limb by the enemy's shot and shell." *Ibid.,* VI, 138.

[3] For this, see *ibid.,* II, 8.

[4] Quoted from Minor's account in *ibid.,* p. 822.

[5] Specific identification of the author of this letter seems to have been lost. The idea of an attack on Lake Erie had by this time occurred to other individuals, and some had written to Mallory. One of these was George W. Gift, stationed, since his days on the C.S.S. *Arkansas,* as first lieutenant of the C.S.S. *Chattahoochee* in Florida. It was from there, on May 11, 1863, that he wrote his sweetheart, Ellen Augusta Shackelford, of Bainbridge, Georgia, whom he later married, the following letter proposing a raid, but making no mention of freeing the prisoners:

"Last night a brilliant idea overtook me in an argument with some of the officers around the capstan. It was this: To proceed to Canada with a proper number of officers and there purchase and fit out a swift light draft propeller to cruise against the commerce of the enemy upon Lake Erie. The idea alone barely mentioned is sufficient to startle one, and when it is considered calmly the more feasible it appears. The vast shipping at Buffalo, engaged in the transportation of grain from the West towards the New York market, could be pounced upon and burned in a single night. The splendid lake steamers could be destroyed and trade suspended (by destroying the railroad along the south shore of Lake Erie) with the West. Millions upon millions of damage could be inflicted in a single month, maybe in a week. It is entirely feasible and easy of accomplishment. Oh for an opportunity. It struck me so forcibly that I at once communicated with the Secretary of the Navy upon the subject, and begged to be allowed to try the experiment. But $100,000 would be required to make the entire outfit. Is this not a small sum to stand in the way of so great an undertaking? And it is so safe. If the enemy should fit out a superior force you could throw your guns overboard and take refuge in any Canadian port. From Buffalo I would go to Chicago and lay the infamous abolition hotbed under contribution. Wouldn't it be glorious? I am all of a fever to hear from 'Old Slow Coach' at Richmond. Every one on board has volunteered to go with me except Brook and Guthrie. . . . In one week I would throw Semmes and Maffitt in the shade forever. I could burn fifty vessels to their one. . . . Besides this, it would complicate the relations of the two governments of Great Britain and the United States. It's a great scheme."

By "Old Slow Coach," Gift was obviously referring to Mallory. The following month he wrote his sweetheart again: "I have heard nothing of the Lake Erie plan. The Secretary of the Navy voted me crazy and forgot the affair." See the George W. Gift Papers, Manuscript Division, University of North Carolina Library.

[6] *O.R.N.*, Series 1, II, 823.

[7] In a letter that Minor later wrote Admiral Franklin Buchanan of the Confederate Navy, he stated that Wilkinson was in a manner somewhat committed to the plan by the message sent to him by Secretary Seddon. *Ibid.*

[8] *Ibid.*

[9] Gift obviously had gained a role in the expedition through his letter to Secretary Mallory.

[10] John B. Tabb had been captain's clerk on the *Robert E. Lee*. He later gained renown as a Virginia poet and Catholic priest. This was called to the author's attention by letter from another distinguished Virginian, Gordon Blair, born at Richmond in 1868 and well acquainted with many prominent Confederates; and by Admiral John D. Hayes.

[11] *O.R.N.*, Series 1, II, 824.

[12] Reports vary as to the size of the party. Minor (*ibid.*, p. 824) gives the total as twenty-two, but others, including Wilkinson (*The Narrative of a Blockade Runner*, p. 161) place it as twenty-six.

[13] *O.R.N.*, Series 1, IX, 461.

[14] *Ibid.*, II, 825.

[15] *Ibid.*, p. 826.

[16] *Ibid.*, p. 478.

[17] *Ibid.*, p. 496.

[18] *Ibid.*, p. 826.
[19] Quoted words are from Minor's letter to Buchanan. *Ibid.*
[20] *Ibid.*

CHAPTER EIGHT

[1] *O.R.N.*, Series 1, V, 395.
[2] George W. Gift Papers, University of North Carolina Library.
[3] Wood, aide-de-camp to President Jefferson Davis, held the ranks of colonel in the Army and commander in the Navy.
[4] *O.R.*, Series 1, XXXIII, 92.
[5] *O.R.N.*, Series 1, IX, 450.
[6] George W. Gift Papers, University of North Carolina Library.
[7] "Burning of the Gunboat Underwriter," by D. B. Conrad, an article published in *Under Both Flags,* edited by George Morley Vickers (Philadelphia, People's Publishing Company, 1896), p. 120.
[8] *Ibid.*
[9] *Ibid.*, p. 124.
[10] Lieutenant B. P. Loyall, C.S.N.
[11] A marker, telling that on February 2, 1864, "Captain John Taylor Wood, of the Confederates Navy, captured and burned the powerful gunboat *Underwriter* in a terrific hand-to-hand fight," has been erected in recent years by the New Bern Historical Society at the foot of the city's Johnson Street, where it ends on the south bank of the Neuse River.
[12] *O.R.N.*, Series 1, IX, 453.
[13] *Under Both Flags,* p. 122.
[14] *O.R.N.*, Series 1, IX, 440.

CHAPTER NINE

[1] *O.R.N.*, Series 1, XV, 28.
[2] *Ibid.*, p. 29.
[3] *Ibid.*, p. 227.
[4] Rear Admiral R. Bentham Simons, U.S.N. (Ret.), a native of Charleston, wrote this author on November 13, 1961: "My father, T. Grange Simons, a Confederate soldier, was waiting on the Fort Johnson dock for a boat to take him to Fort Sumter. The *H. L. Hunley* had been raised and was alongside the dock.

The dead crew was lying in their coffins on the dock when the relief crew marched past them and boarded the *H. L. Hunley* to go to their deaths."

5 Little is known of either of these two men. McClintock was born at Cincinnati, Ohio, in 1829, and at one time ran a steamboat out of New Orleans as the youngest captain on the river. In 1879 he was killed in Boston Harbor while experimenting with a submarine mine he had invented.

6 Under the firm name of Watson & McClintock, they operated a shop for the manufacture of steam gauges and Minié balls at 31 Front Levee, New Orleans. But local legend says the submarine they developed was built at Leeds Foundry, on the corner of Fourcher and Delord Streets. See *The Confederate Privateers,* by William Morrison Robinson, Jr. (New Haven, Yale University Press, 1928), p. 166.

7 Accounts vary as to the ultimate fate of the *Pioneer,* some saying she was scuttled, some that she was sunk in an attack on Farragut's fleet, and others that she sank accidentally. But William Morrison Robinson, Jr., in his well-researched *The Confederate Privateers,* p. 171, cites a letter written by James R. McClintock, one of her builders, to Matthew Fontaine Maury (Maury Papers, Manuscript Division, Library of Congress, XL51, Items 9087 and 9094), in which he stated: "The evacuation of New Orleans lost this boat before our experiments were completed." Years later a channel dredge accidentally brought her to the surface. She remained on the bank of the Mississippi for about thirty years and then was removed to Camp Nicholas, the Louisiana Home for Confederate Soldiers, and there remained on a concrete base. The boat is now on display in the Louisiana State Museum.

8 Some followers of the *H. L. Hunley* doubt that any of her drownings took place at Mobile, even though the mechanic Belton said she had drowned one crew there before going to Charleston. He may have confused her sinking with that of her predecessor, in which no lives were lost. He also, in talking to the Federals in January, 1864, spoke of two sinkings at Charleston, which he reached October 26, 1863. These he could not have witnessed, for they occurred before his arrival.

9 On file in the Virginia Historical Society Papers at Richmond, Virginia.

10 Apparently there were only eight men in this crew, including Hunley. A few weeks later, the Union gunboat *Signal* captured some Rebel mail on its way across the river at Alexandria, Lou-

isiana. In it was a letter from a machinist, J. D. Breaman, who had helped build the *Hunley,* to his wife. He told in it that he and another man named Whitney had bought one-fifth interest in the submarine for $3,000, and added: "We took her to Charleston for the purpose of operating there, and a few days after her arrival there, she sunk through carelessness and her crew of five men were drowned. Another crew of eight men went on from here, raised her, and while experimenting with her in the harbor, sunk her and all eight were drowned." He also related that he and a machinist named E. C. Singer had made the torpedoes for her. *O.R.N.,* Series 1, XXVI, 185.

[11] *O.R.N.,* Series 1, XV, 335.

[12] William A. Alexander, writing in *Munsey* magazine in August, 1903, stated: "Until the day the crew left Mobile, it was understood that I was to be one of them, but at the last moment Mr. Park prevailed on me to let him take my place."

Hunley and the men who died with him were buried together in Magnolia Cemetery in Charleston. There in an area known as "Hunley Circle," small, inconspicuous stones mark the individual graves, but give no hint of the tragedy involved.

[13] *O.R.N.,* Series 1, XV, 26 and 65.

[14] *Ibid.,* p. 65.

[15] *Ibid.,* p. 91.

[16] Beauregard's description was reported in "Torpedo Service in the Harbor and Water Defenses of Charleston," published in *S.H.S.P.* of April, 1878, V, 152-154.

[17] *O.R.,* Series 1, XXVIII, 553. This is a special order for one mission. Another of identical wording has been found, dated January 20, 1865, as well as requisitions signed by Dixon as commander of the submarine, dated as early as November 17, 1863.

[18] *O.R.N.,* Series 1, XV, 335.

[19] On Breach Inlet of Sullivan's Island.

[20] *Munsey* magazine, August, 1903. Article by W. A. Alexander.

[21] *Ibid.*

[22] In his report dated January 18, 1865, Tomb states that exactly a year prior to the day, he stood on the wharf at Charleston with Dixon and James A. Eason and watched the *Hunley* move out for a dive. She went down as she had done many times, he related, but did not rise again, drowning her crew. He obviously was mistaken in his date and referred to the sinking of October 15, 1863. On file is an order dated January 20, 1864, identical with the Beauregard order of December 14, 1863, urging Army

and Navy personnel to co-operate with the submariners, which would indicate the *Hunley* was ready for action on that day.

²³ *O.R.N.,* Series 1, XV, 226.

²⁴ *Ibid.,* p. 238.

²⁵ *Ibid.,* p. 239.

²⁶ Testimony of Acting Master Crosby at a court of inquiry convened on board the U.S.S. *Wabash,* February 26, 1864.

²⁷ *Rebellion Records,* III, 86.

²⁸ *O.R.N.,* Series 1, XV, 328 and 332.

²⁹ Findings of a court of inquiry held on board the frigate *Wabash,* February 26, 1864.

³⁰ *O.R.N.,* Series 1, XV, 328.

³¹ *Ibid.,* p. 327.

³² *Ibid.,* p. 335.

³³ *Ibid.,* p. 336.

³⁴ Captain M. M. Gray, in charge of torpedoes, to Major General Dabney H. Maury. *Ibid.,* p. 337.

³⁵ C. L. Stanton, one of Payne's shipmates, wrote that he often had heard the Alabamian discuss the possibility that the *Hunley* would trap herself. See the *Confederate Veteran* of September, 1914, XX, 398, in which he stated: "If my memory is not at fault, she sank in Charleston Harbor only three times."

³⁶ *O.R.N.,* Series 1, XV, 329.

³⁷ *Ibid.,* p. 394.

³⁸ In later years, it was written of her: "In all the history of any war there will be found no such record of continuous daring and almost certain death as is to be found in the story of the *H. L. Hunley,* the first submarine boat." *The Photographic History of the Civil War* (New York, the Review of Reviews Company, 1911), VI, 274. Not for half a century, until the outbreak of World War I in 1914, would another ship be sunk by a submarine.

The names of all who died on the *H. L. Hunley* will perhaps never be known. Some are memorialized in bronze on South Battery, at the foot of Meeting Street in Charleston, and some in stone in the little burial plot there, known as "Hunley Circle."

The total membership in this suicide club is another unknown. First-hand accounts by McClintock, Beauregard, and others all say there were only three instances in which there was loss of life. The reports of these men differ somewhat in regard to the number of lives lost and the causes of the loss of life.

³⁹ *O.R.N.,* Series 1, XV, 334. The *Confederate Veteran,* XXXII, 140, tells of an investigation conducted by the Boston *Globe,*

in which information concerning the raising of the *Housatonic* and *Hunley* was uncovered. According to this source, a contractor named Maillefert raised the *Housatonic* and found the submarine hanging to her chains.

But residents of Charleston do not believe the *Hunley* was ever found. Their forefathers told them, they say, that she was never brought to the surface. And if she had been, they ask, what happened to her? Such an historic ship, they point out, would most likely have been preserved. And what happened to the bodies of the last crew to die in her? Where are they buried, and why are there no suitable markers over their graves?

They also say the *Housatonic* was never raised, that in the years after the war she was dragged clear of the North Channel and left to go to pieces.

CHAPTER TEN

[1] Quoted from the report of Acting Master R. O. Patterson of the U.S.S. *Memphis,* to Commodore S. C. Rowan, commanding the South Atlantic Blockading Squadron, dated March 6, 1864.

[2] *O.R.N.,* Series 1, XV, 356.

[3] Memoirs of Chief Engineer James H. Tomb, Manuscript Division, University of North Carolina Library.

[4] *O.R.,* Series 1, XXXV, Pt. 2, 345.

[5] Memoirs of James H. Tomb.

[6] *O.R.N.,* Series 1, XV, 405.

[7] *Ibid.,* p. 356.

[8] *Ibid.,* p. 537.

[9] *Ibid.,* p. 733.

[10] Scharf, p. 763.

[11] *Reminiscences of Two Years in the United States Navy,* by John M. Batten (Lancaster, Pennsylvania, Inquirer Printing and Publishing Company, 1881), p. 14.

[12] Southern Historical Collections, University of North Carolina Library.

[13] *O.R.N.,* Series 1, IX, 594.

[14] See Report of the inquiry into the *Minnesota* affair, *O.R.N.,* Series 1, IX, 597. Also U.S. Naval Institute Proceedings, May, 1960, pp. 154-5.

[15] *Ibid.,* p. 596.

[16] *Ibid.,* p. 600.

[17] *Ibid.,* p. 603.

[18] John W. Grattan Papers, Manuscript Division, Library of Congress.

[19] *O.R.N.*, Series 1, V, 398-402, 414, 415; IX, 527.

[20] *O.R.N.*, Series 1, XXVI, 14.

[21] *Ibid.*, p. 255.

[22] *O.R.N.*, Series 2, II, 625.

CHAPTER ELEVEN

[1] *O.R.N.*, Series 1, IX, 324.

[2] *Ibid.*, p. 327.

[3] *Ibid.*, p. 384.

[4] *Ibid.*, p. 487.

[5] This vessel was never completed. After the loss of the *Albemarle*, it was destroyed.

[6] *O.R.N.*, Series 1, IX, 509.

[7] *Ibid.*, p. 555.

[8] *Ibid.*, pp. 559, 560, 584.

[9] *Ibid.*, p. 562.

[10] *Ibid.*, p. 570.

[11] *Ibid.*, p. 585.

[12] *O.R.*, Series 1, XXXIII, 297.

[13] *O.R.N.*, Series 1, IX, 609.

[14] Hackett, p. 130.

[15] *Ibid.*, p. 121.

[16] *O.R.*, Series 1, LI, Pt. 2, 857.

[17] *O.R.N.*, Series 1, IX, 628.

[18] *Ibid.*, p. 630.

[19] *Ibid.*, p. 643.

[20] This detail was revealed in the report of Commander Cooke (*ibid.*, p. 656) and in an account of the *Albemarle* written by Captain Gilbert Elliott and published in the St. Louis *Republican* of April 16, 1887. See *A Record of Events in Norfolk County, Virginia*, by John W. H. Porter (Portsmouth, W. A. Fiske, 1892), p. 222.

[21] *O.R.N.*, Series 1, IX, 634.

[22] Hackett, p. 131.

[23] *B. & L.*, IV, 626.

[24] The exact hour of the ram's arrival for battle is as confused by individual accounts as many other details concerning the attack on Plymouth. Some place her passage of the obstructions at least two hours before Cooke does.

[25] *O.R.N.*, Series 1, IX, 650.
[26] *Ibid.*, p. 641.
[27] Hackett, p. 137.
[28] *O.R.N.*, Series 1, IX, 658.
[29] *Ibid.*, p. 649.
[30] *Ibid.*, p. 669.
[31] *Ibid.*, p. 682.
[32] *Ibid.*, p. 683.
[33] *Ibid.*, p. 684.
[34] *Ibid.*, p. 688.
[35] *Ibid.*, p. 715.
[36] *Ibid.*, p. 732.
[37] *Ibid.*, p. 772.
[38] *Ibid.*, p. 765.
[39] *Ibid.*, p. 769.
[40] *Ibid.*, p. 739.
[41] *Ibid.*, p. 753.
[42] *Ibid.*, p. 748.
[43] John B. Patrick, *ibid.*, p. 769.
[44] Cooke to Commander J. M. Brooke, May 16, 1864. *O.R.N.*, Series 1, X, 641.
[45] *Ibid.*, p. 763.

CHAPTER TWELVE

[1] *O.R.N.*, Series 1, XXIII, 541.
[2] *B. & L.*, III, 571.
[3] *Personal Recollections of the War of the Rebellion,* addresses delivered before the New York Commandery, Military Order of the Loyal Legion, 1883-1891 (published by the Commandery, New York, 1891), "The Red River Dam," by General James Grant Wilson, p. 78. Origin of the idea for the Red River campaign is attributed to Halleck. Grant reveals this in his *Memoirs.*
[4] *O.R.N.*, Series 1, XXVI, 24.
[5] *Memoirs of Thomas O. Selfridge, Jr.* (New York, G. P. Putnam's Sons, The Knickerbocker Press, 1924), p. 89.
[6] Diary of William R. Stewart, Manuscript Division, University of North Carolina Library.
[7] *Ibid.*
[8] *B. & L.*, IV, 370.
[9] Porter was lavish in his praise of A. J. Smith. He wrote Welles: "I beg leave to mention as proof of the rapidity with which this

portion of General Sherman's command, under Brigadier General A. J. Smith, did their work, they marched twenty-eight miles, starting at daylight, built a bridge, which cost them over two hours' hard work, had sharp skirmishing, an artillery attack of two hours, and had possession of the forts (all intact) before sunset. It is one of the best military moves made this war." *O.R.N.*, Series 1, XXVI, 30.

¹⁰ Porter wrote of Fort De Russy: "The Rebels had depended on that point to stop any advance of Army or Navy into this part of rebeldom. Large quantities of ammunition, best engineers, and best troops were sent there, and in two or three months it would have been a most formidable place." *Ibid.*, p. 29.

¹¹ *Ibid.*, p. 29.

¹² *Ibid.*

¹³ Diary of William R. Stewart.

¹⁴ *B. & L.*, IV, 369.

¹⁵ *O.R.N.*, Series 1, XXVI, 164.

¹⁶ *Ibid.*, p. 37.

¹⁷ The presence of these speculators added an unsavory odor to the Red River campaign. It gave rise to a charge that unscrupulous Northerners and Southerners were plotting to dispose of the South's cotton through civilian dealers in the North.

¹⁸ *B. & L.*, IV, 350.

¹⁹ *O.R.N.*, Series 1, XXVI, 39.

²⁰ *B. & L.*, IV, 351.

²¹ *O.R.N.*, Series 1, XXVI, 57.

²² *Ibid.*, p. 58.

²³ *Ibid.*, p. 59.

²⁴ Kirby Smith wrote: "Our repulse at Pleasant Hill was so complete and our command was so disorganized that had Banks followed up his success vigorously he would have met but feeble opposition to his advance on Shreveport." *B. & L.*, IV, 372.

²⁵ *O.R.N.*, Series 1, XXVI, 58.

²⁶ See Porter's unpublished journal in the Manuscript Division, Library of Congress.

²⁷ *B. & L.*, IV, 363.

²⁸ *O.R.N.*, Series 1, XXVI, 60.

²⁹ *Ibid.*, p. 52.

³⁰ *Diary of an Enlisted Man*, by Lawrence Van Alstyne (New Haven, Connecticut, The Tuttle, Morehouse and Taylor Company, 1910), p. 306.

³¹ *O.R.N.*, Series 1, XXVI, 53.

³² *Ibid.*, p. 56.

[33] *Ibid.,* p. 62.

[34] Porter recorded that he opposed the departure of Smith for several reasons. To begin with, it would be construed as a victory for the Rebels. Most importantly, however, it might induce the Confederates to turn upon Steele and crush him. "I wrote to General Sherman, explaining the reasons of retaining his men," Porter informed Welles (*ibid.,* p. 46), "which deficiency he can easily make up by taking from the large force in Arkansas (now not wanted) an equal number of men." But Porter admitted he was influenced in his opinion by a desire to save his stranded fleet, something he assumed he could not do without a land force.

In his letter to Sherman (*ibid.,* p. 56), he wrote: "The Army has been shamefully beaten by the Rebels. There is no disguising the fact, notwithstanding the general commanding and his staff try to make a victory. Armies victorious don't often go back as this one has done!"

[35] *Ibid.,* p. 53.

[36] *Ibid.,* p. 79.

[37] *Ibid.,* p. 74.

[38] *Ibid.,* p. 69.

[39] *Ibid.,* p. 75. Tom Green County, Texas, was named for this general.

[40] *B. & L.,* IV, 365.

[41] *O.R.N.,* Series 1, XXVI, 76.

[42] *B. & L.,* IV, 372.

[43] *O.R.N.,* Series 1, XXVI, 95.

[44] *Ibid.*

[45] *Diary of an Enlisted Man,* p. 292.

[46] *Ibid.,* p. 314.

[47] *Ibid.,* p. 309.

[48] *Personal Recollections of the War of the Rebellion,* "The Red River Dam," by General James Grant Wilson, p. 90.

[49] *O.R.N.,* Series 1, XXVI, 95.

[50] *Personal Recollections of the War of the Rebellion,* p. 80.

[51] In his unpublished journal, Porter, relying heavily upon memory, which caused him to confuse dates by inserting May for March, charges that Banks delayed three days before agreeing for Bailey to try his plan. This conflicts with a statement he made in a report prepared for Welles under date of May 16, 1864: "This proposition looked like madness, and the best engineers ridiculed it. Colonel Bailey was so sanguine of success that I requested General Banks to have it done, and he entered heartily in the work." *O.R.N.,* Series 1, XXVI, 130.

⁵² *Ibid.*

⁵³ See the account of Lieutenant Colonel Richard B. Irwin of the U.S. Army in *B. & L.*, IV, 345.

⁵⁴ The regiments involved were the Twenty-ninth Maine, One Hundred Sixteenth, One Hundred Thirty-third, and One Hundred Sixty-first New York.

⁵⁵ *O.R.N.*, Series 1, XXVI, 130.

⁵⁶ General James Grant Wilson in the Military Order of the Loyal Legion Papers.

⁵⁷ *Ibid.*

⁵⁸ *B. & L.*, IV, 359.

⁵⁹ In testimony before the Congressional Committee on the Conduct of the War, General Banks said: "Only one of the vessels above the falls—the *Lexington*—was ready to move when the dam gave way, and that came down after the break and passed the dam in safety. . . . Had the others been ready to move, all would have passed the rapids and the dam safely on Monday."

⁶⁰ *O.R.N.*, Series 1, XXVI, 131.

⁶¹ *Ibid.*, p. 141.

⁶² See General Kirby Smith's account in *B. & L.*, IV, 373.

⁶³ After the war, Bailey settled as a farmer in Newton County, Missouri, and soon was elected sheriff. He was especially tough on border ruffians, and was shot and killed with a concealed pistol while trying to arrest two brothers near Nevada, Missouri, March 21, 1867. *Personal Recollections of the War of the Rebellion*, p. 92.

⁶⁴ Porter's unpublished journal.

⁶⁵ *O.R.N.*, Series 1, XXVI, 132.

⁶⁶ *Ibid.*

CHAPTER THIRTEEN

¹ *B. & L.*, IV, 206, 706.

² Grattan Papers, National Archives.

³ See the unpublished log of the *Aroostook* on file at National Archives.

⁴ *O.R.N.*, Series 2, II, 624.

⁵ *Ibid.*, Series 1, X, 9.

⁶ *Our Navy in Time of War*, by Franklin Matthews (New York, D. Appleton and Company, 1899), p. 198.

⁷ *O.R.N.*, Series 1, X, 10.

⁸ Log of the *Aroostook*.

[9] *O.R.N.*, Series 1, X, 9.
[10] *Ibid.*, p. 27.

CHAPTER FOURTEEN

[1] *O.R.N.*, Series 1, X, 20.
[2] *Ibid.*, p. 24.
[3] *Ibid.*, p. 39.
[4] *Ibid.*, p. 77.
[5] *Ibid.*, p. 57.
[6] *Ibid.*, p. 128.
[7] *Ibid.*, p. 202.
[8] *Ibid.*, p. 302.
[9] *O.R.*, Series 1, XXVII, 687.
[10] *O.R.N.*, Series 1, X, 42.

CHAPTER FIFTEEN

[1] *O.R.N.*, Series 1, XV, 479.
[2] *Ibid.*, p. 478.
[3] *Ibid.*, p. 490. A court of inquiry held to investigate the capture of the *Water Witch* reported: "The conduct of Acting Third Assistant Engineer Isaac A. Conover during the contest which resulted in the capture is to be deduced from his own testimony."
[4] *Ibid.*, p. 480.
[5] *Ibid.*, p. 478.
[6] *Ibid.*, p. 481.
[7] *Ibid.*, p. 482.
[8] *Ibid.*, p. 481. In his report, Surgeon Pierson stated: "Some think that the engine room was given up without proper assistance. The engineers, on their part, allege that they were unarmed, and that they understood the ship to have been surrendered before the demand to surrender the engine was made of them." But a court of inquiry cleared them.
[9] *Ibid.*, p. 469.
[10] Report of Secretary Mallory, *O.R.N.*, Series 2, II, 632.
[11] The men who took part in the venture seemed to one Federal officer to be ideally suited for their roles. Surgeon Pierson reported: "I should judge from the excellent appearance of the men that they were carefully selected for the enterprise." *O.R.N.*, Series 1, XV, 481.

12 *Ibid.,* p. 480.
13 *Ibid.,* p. 741.
14 *Ibid.,* p. 471.
15 *Ibid.,* p. 475.
16 *Ibid.,* p. 475.
17 *Ibid.,* p. 485.

CHAPTER SIXTEEN

1 *The Life of John Ancrum Winslow,* by John M. Ellicott (New York, G. P. Putnam's Sons, 1902), p. 180.
2 *O.R.N.,* Series 1, I, 814.
3 *Ibid.,* II, 764.
4 *Ibid.,* I, 816.
5 *Ibid.,* II, 764.
6 *Ibid.,* III, 647.
7 *Ibid.*
8 *Ibid.,* p. 64.
9 *Ibid.,* p. 677.
10 *Ibid.,* p. 651.
11 *Farragut and Our Naval Commanders,* by J. T. Headley (New York, E. B. Treat and Company, 1867), p. 299.
12 *O.R.N.,* Series 1, III, 677.
13 Efforts were made by some men to dissuade Semmes from fighting the *Kearsarge,* but he shook them off, having as supporters both John Slidell, the Confederate commissioner in Paris, and Barron. When urged by Ad. Bonfils of Cherbourg to advise against the battle, Slidell replied: "I cannot give to Captain Semmes the advice which you recommend. I have the most entire confidence in his judgment, his skill, and his cool courage. I believe that he would not proceed to the encounter of the *Kearsarge* unless he thought that he had a reasonable chance of capturing her. It has not been the habit of our people during this war to scan too closely the number and position of their adversaries." *Ibid.,* p. 662.
14 *Ibid.,* p. 73.
15 In discussing the comparison of ships in his *Service Afloat* (New York, P. J. Kenedy, 1903), p. 753, Semmes wrote: "Still the disparity was not so great but that I might hope to beat my enemy in a fair fight. But he did not show me a fair fight, for, as it afterward turned out, his ship was ironclad. It was the same thing as if two men were to go out to fight a duel, and one of

them, unknown to the other, were to put a shirt of mail under his outer garment. The days of chivalry being past, perhaps it would be unfair to charge Captain Winslow with deceit in withholding from me the fact that he meant to wear armor in the fight."

16 *O.R.N.*, Series 1, III, 663.

17 *Ibid.*, p. 79.

18 *Ibid.*, p. 650.

19 The excursion train was mentioned by Rear Admiral Joseph Adams Smith, last surviving commissioned officer of the *Kearsarge*, in an address before the Union League of Philadelphia, January 20, 1906.

20 *O.R.N.*, Series 1, III, 650.

21 *Ibid.*

22 *Service Afloat*, p. 763.

23 *Recollections of a Naval Life*, by John McIntosh Kell (Washington, The Neale Company, 1900), p. 248.

24 In his report, Semmes said no boat appeared from the *Kearsarge* until after the *Alabama* had gone down (*O.R.N.*, Series 1, III, 650). Second Lieutenant R. F. Armstrong of the *Alabama* also had complaints against the boats from the *Kearsarge*. Badly wounded in the side, he fought to stay afloat near one of them, but "it laid on its oars and made no exertion whatever that I could see to save me." *Ibid.*, p. 653.

25 *Service Afloat*, p. 765.

26 *O.R.N.*, Series 1, III, 61.

27 *Ibid.*, p. 666.

28 *Ibid.*, p. 650. James Magee, of Marblehead, Massachusetts, who had been a seaman on the *Kearsarge*, told Francis B. C. Bradlee in later years that it had taken three days to arrange the chains. He said they were covered with inch deal boards, forming a box that stood out at right angles to the vessel's side. He also maintained there was no mystery about the chains, that wounded *Alabama* crewmen in the hospital at Cherbourg told him the Confederate captain had mentioned them in conversation several days before June 19. See *The Kearsarge-Alabama Battle*, by Francis B. C. Bradlee (Salem, Massachusetts, The Essex Institute, 1921), p. 14.

Semmes always denied previous knowledge of the chains. In his report to Secretary Mallory, he stated: "The enemy was heavier than myself in ship, battery, and crew, and I did not know until the action was over that the *Kearsarge* was ironclad." Of the box that Magee claimed was clearly visible, Semmes wrote in his *Service Afloat*, p. 654: "Unfortunately for the *Alabama* the right angles were not there. The forward and after ends of the boxing went off at so fine a point, in accordance with the lines of the ship, that the telescope failed to detect the cheat. Besides, when a ship is preparing for a fight, she does not care much about show."

Kell, the first officer of the Confederate ship, also denied that they knew about the chains. "Had we been in possession of this knowledge, the unequal battle between the *Alabama* and *Kearsarge* would never have been fought." See his *Recollections of a Naval Life,* p. 251.

[29] *O.R.N.,* Series 1, III, 80.

[30] *Ibid.,* p. 70.

[31] *The Secret Service of the Confederate States in Europe,* by James D. Bulloch (New York, G. P. Putnam's Sons, 1884), p. 284.

[32] *O.R.N.,* Series 1, III, 81.

[33] *Ibid.,* p. 69.

[34] *Ibid.,* p. 73.

[35] *Ibid.,* p. 74.

[36] *Ibid.,* p. 667.

[37] Semmes estimated that his powder had deteriorated to the extent of one-third its maximum strength. *Ibid.,* p. 664.

CHAPTER SEVENTEEN

[1] First Lieutenant John C. Kinney, signal officer on board Farragut's flagship, writing in *Battles and Leaders,* IV, 379, published in 1887, said: "It is easy to see now the wisdom of his plan. Had the operation against Mobile been undertaken promptly, as he desired, the entrance into the bay would have been effected with much less cost of men and materials, Mobile would have been captured a year earlier than it was, and the Union cause would have been saved the disaster of the Red River campaign of 1864. At this late date it is but justice to Farragut to admit the truth."

[2] Selma was an ideal location for a shipyard for ironclads. It was near enough to the iron mines in the vicinity of Birmingham to make long haulage unnecessary, and far enough down the Alabama River to enable vessels to be floated to the sea.

[3] *O.R.,* Series 1, I, 891. Actually, the *Tennessee* was two hundred nine feet long, with a forty-eight-foot beam. She was a casemated ironclad powered by two engines and four boilers.

[4] *O.R.N.,* Series 1, XXI, 4.

[5] *Ibid.*

6 *Ibid.*, pp. 30, 31.

7 *Ibid.*, p. 35. Scharf, p. 556, says the Confederates planted one hundred eighty mines in the bay prior to the battle. This number is corroborated by Franklin Matthews in his *Our Navy in Time of War* (New York, D. Appleton and Company, 1899), p. 101.

The mines were of two types, one made of kegs equipped with sensitive primers; and the other, of tin in the form of cones fitted with cap and trigger. The former type proved more dependable because the caps of the latter were damaged by long exposure to water, and some had been planted prior to May 25, 1863. See *O.R.N.*, Series 1, XX, 828.

Matthews says that forty-six of the mines were made of kegs; one hundred thirty-four of tin.

8 *Ibid.*, XXI, 39.

9 *Ibid.*

10 The Dog River runs through what is now a residential section of Mobile. Although it is not shown on some maps, it is still known by that name.

11 Scharf, p. 553, says the *"Tennessee,* with the exception of the *Arkansas* . . . was the most formidable vessel of her class that ever carried the Confederate flag."

12 *O.R.N.*, Series 1, XXI, 52.

13 *Ibid.*, p. 870.

14 Major General Dabney H. Maury to Lieutenant General Leonidas Polk, *ibid.*, p. 872.

15 *Ibid.*, p. 91.

16 *Ibid.*, p. 879.

17 *Ibid.*, p. 112.

18 *Ibid.*, p. 102.

19 Scharf, p. 556.

20 *O.R.N.*, Series 1, XXI, 97.

21 *Ibid.*, pp. 121, 122.

22 *Ibid.*, p. 130.

23 *Ibid.*, p. 881.

24 Confederate Fleet Surgeon D. B. Conrad, writing in *Hero Tales of the American Soldier and Sailor* (Philadelphia, Century Manufacturing Company, 1899), p. 404, said of the incident: "They were burned by Federal emissaries, who were paid well for their daring deed." He added: "The secret service fund was well spent by Admiral Farragut, for we were delayed several months in building two more camels, and by that time his ironclads were finished and on their way to him. I must mention the desertion of five men the day after the destruction of the camels; they had

been working on our ironclad and furnished him with all details of her construction, all her weak points, of the character of her engines, the caliber of her armament, of all of which information he availed himself when the eventful day of action came. In addition to this, they were to be received into the Federal service if they destroyed these camels. These large bribes were offered for the reason that the fleet lying outside of Fort Morgan were solely wooden ships, and could not cope with nor resist the attack of our ironclad, and the Federal ironclads had not yet arrived."

In making this charge, Surgeon Conrad ignores the fact that nearly three months passed from the time the *Tennessee* crossed Dog River Bar until the time the battle took place.

[25] *The Life of David Glasgow Farragut,* by Loyall Farragut (New York, D. Appleton and Company, 1879), p. 394, referred to hereafter as Farragut.

[26] *Ibid.,* p. 395.

[27] George W. Gift to Ellen Augusta Shackelford, Gift Papers, University of North Carolina Library.

[28] *O.R.N.,* Series 1, XXI, 267.

[29] Farragut, p. 400.

[30] *O.R.N.,* Series 1, XXI, 270.

[31] Diary of J. C. Gregg, on file at National Archives.

[32] Scharf, p. 555.

[33] From the log of the *Tennessee, O.R.N.,* Series 1, XXI, 934.

[34] *Ibid.,* XX, 828.

[35] *Ibid.,* XXI, 298.

[36] *Ibid.,* p. 299.

[37] Farragut, p. 402.

[38] *O.R.N.,* Series 1, XXI, 904.

[39] *B. & L.,* IV, 387.

[40] *Ibid.,* p. 397.

[41] *Ibid.,* p. 376.

[42] J. Crittenden Watson, flag lieutenant on the *Hartford,* wrote in later years: "I used to help him maneuver the little blocks so as to concentrate and maintain as heavy a fire as possible upon Fort Morgan when we should be going in, and also, after the general orders were issued, we played with the blocks preparatory to practicing the ships in keeping close order when under way at varying speeds." Military Order of the Loyal Legion Papers, War Paper No. 98, read before the Commandery of the District of Columbia, December 16, 1916.

[43] *Ibid.*

[44] Log of the U.S.S. *Sebago, O.R.N.,* Series 1, XXI, 849.

[45] *Ibid.,* p. 386.

[46] Log of the U.S.S. *Hartford.*

[47] Log of the C.S.S. *Tennessee.*

[48] Drayton to Captain T. A. Jenkins, *O.R.N.,* Series 1, XXI, 395.

[49] Log of the U.S.S. *Hartford.*

[50] *Ibid.*

[51] Rear Admiral C. M. Chester, Military Order of the Loyal Legion, War Paper No. 98.

[52] Log of the U.S.S. *Hartford.*

[53] Dr. Daniel B. Conrad, fleet surgeon, C. S. Navy, *Southern Historical Society Papers,* XIX, 1891, 72, referred to hereafter as *S.H.S.P.*

[54] Log of the U.S.S. *Hartford.*

[55] *O.R.N.,* Series 1, XXI, 399.

[56] Diary of J. C. Gregg.

[57] Log of the U.S.S. *Hartford.*

[58] Logs of the U.S.S. *Hartford* and U.S.S. *Sebago.*

Farragut, in his report of the Battle of Mobile Bay (*O.R.N.,* Series 1, XXI, 417), mentions these nightly reconnaissances, but says Watson was unable to discover the torpedoes. He repeats the statement in his thanks to the ships' crews (*ibid.,* p. 438): ". . . there was no evidences of hesitation in following their commander in chief through the line of torpedoes and obstructions, of which we knew nothing except from the exaggerations of the enemy, who had given out that we should all be blown up as certainly as we attempted to enter."

But other eyewitnesses, among them Rear Admiral C. M. Chester, a young sailor fresh from the Naval Academy at the time, say mines were sunk or removed. This seems likely in view of later developments, for many of the mines were found, and removed or sunk after the battle. Five were taken out on the first day of these subsequent operations, and four of the five were found to be harmless. By August 25 the men had become so careless in handling the deadly obstructions that one of them exploded, killing five members of a crew and wounding nine others (*O.R.N.,* Series 1, XXI, 616). Among the wounded was Pilot Martin Freeman.

Moreover, the pattern followed in these later operations was similar to that employed before the battle. According to the log of the U.S.S. *Hartford,* the U.S.S. *Cowslip* continued to be used to tow the crews engaged in removing the mines.

[59] When the Drayton descendants on November 7, 1961, unveiled

a marker to the memory of the two brothers on the site of Fort Walker at Hilton Head, South Carolina, where they had opposed each other in battle, the author was present as a representative of the National Civil War Centennial Commission.

60 Lieutenant John C. Kinney, *B. & L.,* IV, 381.

61 *Ibid.*

62 *O.R.N.,* Series 1, XXI, 403. This attachment, called a "devil" by the sailors, was made up of a number of long hooks fastened to a spar slung from the bowsprit on a level with the ship's keel. See *Personal Memoirs,* by William F. Hutchinson, Rhode Island Soldiers and Sailors Historical Society, No. 8 (Providence, Rhode Island, Sidney S. Rider, 1879), p. 12.

63 *O.R.N.,* Series 1, XXI, 417.

64 Farragut, p. 405.

65 Commander James D. Johnston, captain of the C.S.S. *Tennessee,* in *B. & L.,* IV, 402.

66 Log of the U.S.S. *Manhattan. O.R.N.,* Series 1, XXI, 824.

67 Diary of J. C. Gregg.

68 Chief Engineer M. D. Alexter of the U.S. Army wrote: "Many a heart on our side sent up a prayer of thanksgiving for that breeze, and doubtless many a Rebel heart was filled with curses upon it." *O.R.N.,* Series 1, XXI, 532.

69 Scharf, p. 555.

70 Log of the U.S.S. *Hartford.*

71 "The Bay Fight," by William F. Hutchinson, Rhode Island Soldiers and Sailors Historical Society, Personal Narrative No. 8 (Providence, Sidney S. Rider, 1879), p. 13.

72 Lieutenant F. S. Barrett, officer in charge of torpedoes placed in Mobile Bay, reported: "By the course they took running in it is evident they were well informed as to the location of the torpedoes we had planted." *O.R.N.,* Series 1, XXI, 569.

By order of Lieutenant Colonel Victor von Schelia, chief of the Engineer Department, a channel of about five hundred yards had been left open, and it was thought the Federals had gained knowledge of this by watching blockade-runners steer through it, one having gone in that morning before the fleet started moving. When he heard of the battle, the Confederacy's mine expert, Brigadier General G. J. Rains, wrote Secretary of War Seddon that he had planned to block the main channel, "but my instructions and wishes were frustrated after I left, the place left open, and the enemy made use of it." *Ibid.,* p. 567.

In an endorsement to Barrett's report, Major General Dabney H. Maury, commanding the military forces at Mobile, took credit for leaving a space in the line of torpedoes, explaining that it was marked by a buoy one hundred and sixty yards from the Fort Morgan shore. Any ship passing through that space, he said, would be exposed to the fire at short range of seven ten-inch columbiads, three eight-inch guns, two eight-inch Blakely rifles, two seven-inch Brooke rifles, some 6.4-inch rifles, several thirty-two-pounders, and the rifle fire of sharpshooters. "No vessel yet built could pass through that channel in daylight," he wrote. "The enemy gave it a wide berth on the 5th of August. From the best information I can procure none of their ships passed within eight hundred yards of Fort Morgan." All of them, he said, passed over the line of torpedoes, explaining that it was probable that the rapid and changing currents and other conditions had carried away the mines. This would indicate he was not aware of the night operations of boat crews under command of Farragut's flag lieutenant.

Testimony of various eyewitnesses on the Confederate side, familiar with the channel and the lines of torpedoes, would imply that Farragut changed his original plan of going in east of the red buoy, and chose a course farther west, after the boat crews had removed the torpedoes. Major Henry St. Paul of the Confederate Army said the fleet passed so far from shore the howitzers in the tops of ships could not reach land with their projectiles. *Ibid.,* p. 570. Captain J. W. Whiting of the first Alabama Artillery Battalion informed General Maury: "There was a short space of the channel nearest the fort shore, and under the concentrated fire of all the batteries, marked by a buoy and left open for the use of our fleet. No ships of the enemy, wooden or iron, passed through this gap, however, nor according to my judgment within three hundred yards of it." *Ibid.,* p. 598.

Percival Drayton wrote Admiral Samuel F. du Pont on September 8, 1864: "We have dragged up a good many torpedoes and lost several men in doing so. By far the majority were however more or less injured as you may judge from the fact that we know of about one hundred and eighty having been laid down in the third of a mile over which our ships passed, and the only one hurt was the *Tecumseh,* and she must have been struck by the very inner one. There was a clear passage for blockade-runners, perhaps a little over a hundred yards wide, beginning at the beach and under the heaviest batteries. We almost knew that this was clear, and the order was for all vessels to pass inside. None did so, but the *Tecumseh* was within a few feet of doing so, when nothing could have hurt her. A turn on the helm would have been enough, but fate was adverse. The shore looks very close, and I believe Craven was afraid of striking it." (This letter is among the Du Pont letters now being edited by Rear Admiral John D. Hayes, U.S.N. (Ret.), Annapolis, Maryland.)

73 Scharf, p. 560.

74 *O.R.N.*, Series 1, XXI, 508.

75 *B. & L.*, IV, 387.

76 *O.R.N.*, Series 1, XXI, 425.

77 *Ibid.* J. D. Johnston pointed out in later years: "There has always been some doubt as to whether that torpedo was one of those planted by the Rebels, or was attached to a spar rigged out from the bow of the *Tecumseh*, and whose explosion was caused by her coming in contact with a large iron buoy anchored near Fort Morgan to indicate the channel to blockade-runners." *S.H.S.P.*, IX, 472.

78 The following note concerning the *Tecumseh* appears in Scharf, p. 561: "A week later when divers went down to examine the wreck they found nearly all the crew at their posts, as they sank. The chief engineer, who had been married in New York only two weeks before, and who had received from the flagship's mail his letters while the line was forming, stood with one hand upon the revolving bar of the turret engine, and in the other an open letter from his bride, which his dead eyes still seemed to be reading."

79 Craven apparently had gone below after the explosion. Gardner Cottrell, acting master of the *Tecumseh* and one of two officers to survive, reported that he saw the captain, wearing a life-preserver vest, on the turret of the vessel just before she went down. *O.R.N.*, Series 1, XXI, 490.

80 While it was generally agreed that the *Tecumseh* sank quickly, estimates as to actual time range from seconds to minutes. Farragut said she went down "almost instantaneously."

Eyewitnesses agreed that she went down bow first, that her stern raised up in the air, and that her propeller could be seen revolving as she sank.

81 Loyall Farragut, son of the Admiral, in going through his father's papers after his death, found a memorandum that stated: "General orders required the vessels to pass inside the buoys next to Fort Morgan. When the *Tecumseh* reached that point, it looked so close that poor Craven said to the pilot, 'The Admiral ordered me to go inside that buoy, but it must be a mistake.' He ran just his breadth of beam too far westward, struck a

torpedo, and went down in two minutes." Farragut, p. 422.

Acting Masters C. F. Langley and Gardner Cottrell, the only surviving officers of the *Tecumseh,* stated in a report: "When nearly abreast of Fort Morgan, and about one hundred and fifty yards from the beach, a row of buoys was discovered stretching from the shore a distance from one to two hundred yards. It being reported to Captain Craven, he immediately gave the vessel full speed and attempted to pass between two of them. When in their range, a torpedo was exploded directly under the turret, blowing a large hole through the bottom of the vessel with great rapidity." *O.R.N., Series* 1, XXI, 490.

Captain J. W. Whiting of the Confederate Artillery said the *Tecumseh* was sunk five hundred or six hundred yards from the fort, while the wooden ships passed from twelve hundred to eighteen hundred yards from it. *Ibid.,* p. 598.

82 *Ibid.,* p. 445.

83 Freeman held Farragut's complete confidence. Captured early in the war in a fine fishing smack which he owned, he pleaded no interest in the war and asked to be permitted to pursue his profession as a fisherman, but the Union demanded his services and made him a pilot first class.

84 In his personal reminiscences (Military Order of the Loyal Legion War Paper No. 98), John Crittenden Watson says: "By this movement we all knew that Farragut had decided suddenly to cross the torpedo field, which he had forbidden any of the ships to do. Some of us expected every moment to feel the shock of an explosion under the *Hartford* and to find ourselves in the water. In fact, we imagined that we heard some caps explode." In a memorandum found among his papers after his death, Farragut wrote: "Allowing the *Brooklyn* to go ahead was a great error. It lost not only the *Tecumseh* but many valuable lives, by keeping us under the fire of the forts for thirty minutes; whereas, had I led, as I intended to do, I would have gone inside the buoys, and all would have followed me." Farragut, p. 422.

85 Watson later recalled: "Although this action of Farragut's seemed instantaneous, we learn from letters to his family that he had found time to ask God for guidance, and he believed he heard a voice say, 'Go on!' "

A story current in the 1880's related that someone on the *Brooklyn* warned Farragut of the torpedoes when he passed. This is discounted by Lieutenant Kinney, the *Hartford*'s signal officer, who said: "There was never a moment when the din of the battle would not have drowned any attempt at conversation between the two ships, and while it is quite probable that the admiral made the remark it is doubtful if he shouted it to the *Brooklyn*."

86 *B. & L.*, IV, 403.

87 The *Selma*'s captain, Lieutenant P. U. Murphy, disabled by a shot, gave this report of his situation: "My wound was bleeding fast, and I knew if I left the deck for one moment the vessel might be sunk. I had eight killed and seven wounded; my deck was a perfect slaughter pen when I surrendered." *O.R.N.*, Series 1, XXI, 588.

88 *P.H.*, VI, 250. In his own mind, Buchanan seems to have had no choice about renewing the fight with Farragut. Public reaction appears to have been his motivating factor. The previous March 13, in a letter to J. K. Mitchell, now on file in the Virginia Historical Society Library at Richmond, Virginia, he wrote: "I hope Farragut will not get here before I am ready. If he does, the *Tennessee* must meet him when she is ready. Everybody has taken it into their heads that one ship can whip a dozen, and if the trial is not made, we who are in her are damned for life, consequently the trial must be made. So goes the world."

89 *B. & L.*, IV, 406.

90 Copied from the original, now in the possession of Mrs. Ted Trigg, Savannah, Georgia, formerly of Mobile. Her grandfather, John Lawrence Rapier, was captured when Fort Gaines surrendered (*O.R.N.*, Series 1, XXI, 610). He later became owner and publisher of the Mobile *Register* and in 1894 was appointed postmaster of Mobile by President Cleveland.

91 The *Tennessee*'s opposition was from the wooden ships. Percival Drayton, in a letter to Admiral Du Pont, dated September 8, 1864, wrote of Buchanan: "How he came to be so completely let alone by our own iron vessels has never been explained. The Rebs say they were afraid to approach the *Tennessee*."

A copy of this correspondence was made available to the author through the kindness of Rear Admiral John D. Hayes, U.S.N. (Ret.), of Annapolis, Maryland, who is compiling and editing the Du Pont letters.

92 Lieutenant Kinney. *B. & L.*, IV, 396.

93 *S.H.S.P.*, XIX, 76.

94 *O.R.N.*, Series 1, XXI, 429.

95 *B. & L.*, IV, 397.

96 *Ibid.*, p. 401.

97 *O.R.N.*, Series 1, XXI, 418.

98 *Ibid.*, p. 580. In his report of the battle, prepared in the U.S.

the official records under date of July 9, 1864, Admiral Lee informed Secretary Welles: "He (Cushing) at first proposed an attack on the ram with our gunboats at Plymouth, or a boat expedition, led by himself, with eighty men. I concur in Captain Smith's opinion that it would be inexpedient to fight the ram with our long double-enders in that narrow river. I proposed . . . a torpedo attack, either by means of the India-rubber boat heretofore applied for, which could be transported across the swamp opposite Plymouth, or a light-draft, rifle-proof, swift steam barge, fitted with a torpedo." *Ibid.*

13 *B. & L.*, IV, 634.

14 *O.R.N.*, Series 1, X, 386.

15 *Ibid.*, p. 339.

16 *Ibid.*, p. 341.

17 *Reminiscences of Two Years in the United States Navy*, by Dr. John M. Batten (Lancaster, Pennsylvania, Inquirer Printing and Publishing Company, 1881), p. 25, referred to hereafter as Batten.

18 *Ibid.*, p. 27.

19 These words were used by Union General I. N. Palmer, commanding the District of North Carolina, in a message to Major R. S. Davis, Assistant Adjutant General, July 19, 1864. See *O.R.*, Series 1, XL, Pt. 3, 342.

20 Maffitt, p. 339.

21 Batten, p. 33.

22 *Ibid.*, p. 40.

23 *O.R.N.*, Series 1, XI, 43.

24 *Ibid.*, X, 594.

25 Log of the *Shamrock. Ibid.*, p. 620.

26 *Ibid.*, p. 611.

27 See an article by Alexander Warley in *B. & L.*, IV, 641.

28 *O.R.N.*, Series 1, X, 611.

29 *B. & L.*, IV, 634.

30 Report of Acting Ensign Thomas S. Gay. *O.R.N.*, Series 1, X, 613.

31 *Ibid.*, p. 624.

32 *Ibid.*, p. 611. The "vigorous pull" described by Cushing would be explained to the public by the editors of *Battles and Leaders* (IV, 634) years afterward. In a footnote they pointed out: "In considering the merits of Cushing's success with this exceedingly complicated instrument, it must be remembered that nothing short of the utmost care in preparation could keep its mechanism in working order; that in making ready to use it, it was necessary

Naval Hospital at Pensacola on August 25, 1864, Buchanan blamed his defeat partly on the enemy's superior speed in avoiding the *Tennessee* and partly on his own want of experienced officers. "All were young and inexperienced, and many had but little familiarity with naval duties, having been appointed from civil life within the year," he explained. *Ibid.*, p. 577.

99 *Ibid.*, p. 581.

100 Diary of J. C. Gregg.

101 *B. & L.*, IV, 405, and *S.H.S.P.*, IX, 475.

102 In his report, Farragut, oddly enough, said: "Admiral Buchanan sent me his sword, being himself badly wounded with a compound fracture of the leg." This was corrected by Buchanan in a report to Navy Secretary Mallory, in which he said: "After the surrender of the *Tennessee*, Captain (Pierre) Giraud, the officer who was sent on board to take charge of her, said to me that he was directed by Admiral Farragut to ask for my sword, which was brought from the cabin and delivered to him by one of my aids." *O.R.N.*, Series 1, XXI, 578.

103 In reporting this incident, taken from the surgeon's own account, J. Thomas Scharf, p. 572, appended this note: "Dr. Conrad evidently writes with a strong prejudice against Admiral Buchanan, who may have spoken just as the surgeon reported him without warranting the supposition at which Conrad hints, that he was bent upon saying unpleasant things to Farragut or any other Federal officers with whom he might be brought in contact. No man cherished a more punctilious sense of the proprieties than Buchanan, and it was absurd to think of him railing at the enemy to whom fate had given victory like a disappointed beldame."

No matter what liberties he may have taken in reporting this incident of the battle, Conrad is given credit for saving Buchanan's leg. When other surgeons proposed amputation, he successfully argued against it. In later life he received grateful acknowledgment of this from Buchanan himself.

104 *O.R.N.*, Series 2, II, 632.

105 Diary of J. C. Gregg.

106 Scharf, p. 573.

107 *O.R.N.*, Series 2, II, 632.

108 Farragut, p. 422.

109 *O.R.N.*, Series 1, XXI, 563.

110 Description used by Granger in a message to Canby.

CHAPTER EIGHTEEN

[1] The *Tallahassee* played a part, in the dying moments of the Confederacy, in a concerted drive by the South to further cripple the sea commerce of the Union. Cruisers were sent out to burn and scuttle the enemy's ships. Agents were delegated to overpower crews of steamers and to bring them into port. Fires were set. Bombs were planted. Spies infiltrated. Political intrigue spread. All could be traced to desperation, and opinion as to the value of such tactics was divided. Some officials bitterly opposed the efforts. See *O.R.N.*, Series 1, X, 774.

[2] George W. Gift Papers, University of North Carolina Library.

[3] Report of John Taylor Wood. *O.R.N.*, Series 1, III, 701.

[4] *Ibid.*, p. 137.

[5] *Ibid.*

[6] *Ibid.*, X, 375.

[7] *Ibid.*, p. 386.

[8] *Ibid.*, p. 400.

[9] *Ibid.*, Series 2, II, 633.

CHAPTER NINETEEN

[1] Words used in the December 3, 1864, report of Jacob Thompson, Confederate agent in Canada. See *O.R.N.*, Series 1, III, 714.

[2] *Ibid.*, p. 719.

[3] Details of what happened in Sandusky are taken from an account written in 1926 by D. K. Huntington, member of Company K, One Hundred Thirtieth Regiment, Ohio Volunteer Infantry, who happened to be on the scene at the time and kept a diary. He noted that the part taken by Sullivan was told to him by Sullivan himself shortly before his death in the early 1900's.

Huntington's account is on record with the Western Reserve Historical Society, Cleveland, Ohio.

[4] *O.R.N.*, Series 1, III, 718.

CHAPTER TWENTY

[1] This description of Wilmington is taken from an account given in *Hope Bids Me Onward*, by Harriet Gift Castlen, a compilation of letters written by her father, George Gift, while he was

in the service (Savannah, Georgia, Chatham Printing Company 1945), p. 188.

[2] *O.R.N.*, Series 1, X, 504.

[3] *Ibid.*, p. 509.

[4] Major General W. H. C. Whiting to Mallory, October 6, 1864 *Ibid.*, p. 774.

[5] Journal of Midshipman Clarence Cary, National Archives.

[6] *O.R.N.*, Series 1, X, 438.

[7] *Ibid.*, p. 484.

[8] Bulloch wrote Secretary of State Judah P. Benjamin on Januar 25, 1864: "Mrs. Rose Greenhow has had an interview with th Emperor."

[9] *O.R.N.*, Series 2, III, 1258.

CHAPTER TWENTY-ONE

[1] *O.R.N.*, Series 1, X, 627.

[2] *Ibid.*, p. 55.

[3] *Ibid.*, p.73.

[4] *Ibid.*, p. 86.

[5] *The Life and Services of John Newland Maffitt,* by Emma Mar Maffitt (New York, The Neale Publishing Company, 1906), 339, referred to hereafter as Maffitt.

[6] *O.R.N.*, Series 1, X, 210.

[7] *O.R.*, Series 1, XL, Pt. 3, 751.

[8] Colonel George Wortham, commanding the post at Plymou *Ibid.*

[9] *Ibid.*, p. 752. Scharf, in his fine book on the Confederate Na p. 412, says: "From the 24th of May to the 27th of Octol the *Albemarle* lay in inglorious inactivity at Plymouth. . . . T long period of inactivity is unexplained either in contempo neous accounts or in any extant official records." In these sta ments he ignores the realization by the Confederates of the gr gamble they would take in bringing the ram out into Albema Sound, as is so well pointed out in the protests from Ar officers in the area. The impasse that developed—the ironc up the Roanoke and the Union fleet waiting for her in Al marle Sound—could be blamed on both sides.

[10] *O.R.N.*, Series 1, X, 239.

[11] *Ibid.*, p. 247.

[12] *B. & L.*, IV, 634. Just who first proposed the plan of att seems to be in dispute. In a "Confidential" dispatch appearing

to keep the end of the spar elevated until the boat had sur-
mounted the boom of logs, and to judge accurately the distance
in order to stop the boat's headway at the right point; that the
spar had then to be lowered with the same precision of judgment; that the detaching lanyard had then to be pulled firmly,
but without a jerk; that, finally, the position of the torpedo under
the knuckle of the ram had to be calculated to a nicety, and that
by a very gentle strain on a line some twenty-five or thirty feet
long the trigger pin had to be withdrawn."

[33] *Ibid.*

[34] Batten, p. 40.

[35] In his report, Warley gave no clean bill to the soldiers who had
arrived at Plymouth on October 27 to take over defense of the
town. "In justice to myself," he wrote, "I must say the pickets
below gave no notice of her approach, and the artillery which
was stationed by the vessel for protection gave us no assistance,
manning only one piece at too late a time to be of any service."
O.R.N., Series 1, X, 624.

[36] *Ibid.*, p. 615.

[37] Log of the *Shamrock. Ibid.*, p. 620.

[38] The Peter Evans Smith Papers at the University of North Carolina Library give the epitaph of the *Albemarle*. She was raised and
towed to the Norfolk Navy Yard, and after being stripped of
her armament and machinery, was sold October 15, 1867 to J. N.
Lenard and Company for $3,200. Before she was broken up, the
commander of the Navy Yard had a picture taken of her. It
was framed in oak from her hull and was presented to Mrs.
Cooke, widow of Captain Cooke, then living in Portsmouth,
Virginia. Some of her oak timber also was used to make the
chancel furniture for the Calvary Church at Tarboro, North
Carolina. Her smokestack, riddled with holes, was placed on ex-
hibition at the St. Louis Exposition of 1904. It is now in the Hall
of History at Raleigh, North Carolina. The flag taken from her is
preserved in the North Carolina Room of the Confederate Museum at Richmond.

CHAPTER TWENTY-TWO

[1] *O.R.N.*, Series 1, III, 721; Series 2, Pt. 2, 721.

[2] Scharf, p. 487.

[3] *O.R.N.*, Series 2, Pt. 2, 274.

[4] *Ibid.*, p. 750.

⁵ *Ibid.*, Series 1, III, 393.

⁶ These were the words used by Flag Officer Samuel Barron, Confederate naval commander in Europe, in a letter to Morris from Paris, France, January 25, 1864.

⁷ *O.R.N.*, Series 1, II, 354.

⁸ *Ibid.*, p. 614.

⁹ The reference is to Lord Horatio Nelson, the celebrated British admiral.

¹⁰ *O.R.N.*, Series 1, II, 622.

¹¹ See the report of Lieutenant Thomas K. Porter. *Ibid.*, III, 637.

¹² *Ibid.*, p. 631. Collins, in an official message to Secretary Welles (*ibid.*, p. 266), denied that he knew of any such promise by Wilson.

¹³ *Ibid.*

¹⁴ In his report (*ibid.*, p. 255), Collins is not clear about who fired the first shots. He said: "In backing clear we received a few pistol shots from the *Florida,* which were returned with a volley, and, contrary to my orders, two of my broadside guns were fired." Afterward, in a letter to Commodore Charles Wilkes (*ibid.*, p. 264), he stated: "The *Florida* fired first." He also revealed that it was his intention to sink her and then to go quietly to sea. If this failed, he would board her with revolvers, drive her crew below, attach a hawser, and tow her out of the harbor.

He officially reported that an "unforeseen circumstance" had prevented the *Wachusett* from striking the *Alabama* as intended. This "circumstance" he later identified as the failure of Lieutenant Commander L. A. Beardslee to carry out an order involving preliminary preparations of the Union ship, something that this officer vehemently denied.

¹⁵ *Ibid.*, p. 637.

¹⁶ *Ibid.*, p. 633.

¹⁷ *Ibid.*

¹⁸ Maffitt, p. 387.

¹⁹ *O.R.N.*, Series 1, III, 280. John Maffitt, in his reminiscences prepared after the war, reported that after the interview with Seward, Porter put an engineer on the *Florida* and told him: "Before midnight open the sea cock, and do not leave that engine room until the water is up to your chin. At sunrise the Rebel craft must be a thing of the past, resting on the bottom of the sea." To these writings he added a note: "Admiral Porter in 1872 thus explained to me the strange disappearance of the *Florida* and his participation in the plot, by which the United States Government was relieved from the necessity of restoring,

intact, the *Florida* to her anchorage in Bahia." Maffitt, p. 388.

20 The *amende honorable* did not take place until July 23, 1866.

21 *O.R.N.,* Series 1, III, 294.

22 *Ibid.,* p. 269.

23 *Ibid.,* p. 264.

CHAPTER TWENTY-THREE

1 Fort Fisher was named for Colonel Charles G. Fisher, who came from near Salisbury, North Carolina, and who was killed in the first battle of Manassas while in command of the Sixth North Carolina Regiment.

2 *O.R.N.,* Series 1, X, 146.

3 *Ibid.,* p. 430.

4 *Ibid.,* p. 513.

5 *Ibid.,* p. 460.

6 *Ibid.,* XI, 3.

7 *Blockade Running During the Civil War,* by Francis B. C. Bradlee (Salem, Massachusetts, The Essex Institute, 1925), p. 42.

8 *B. & L.,* IV, 643.

9 Papers of the Military Historical Society of Massachusetts, IXM, 350.

10 *O.R.N.,* Series 1, XI, 207.

11 Porter thus explained his action: "I was not opposed, myself, to the experiment (for I think everything worth trying)." *Ibid.,* p. 268.

12 *Ibid.,* p. 217.

13 John W. Grattan Papers, Manuscript Division, Library of Congress.

14 Batten, p. 67.

15 Commander A. D. Harrell of the U.S.S. *Chicopee* to Commander Macomb. *O.R.N.,* Series 1, XI, 173.

16 Batten, p. 70.

17 Papers of Joseph Bloomfield Osborn, Manuscript Division, Library of Congress.

18 Diary of J. C. Gregg, National Archives, and *P.H.,* VI, 240.

19 *O.R.N.,* Series 1, XI, 219.

20 *Ibid.,* p. 245.

21 *The Records of Living Officers of the U.S. Navy and Marine Corps,* by Lewis Randolph Hamersly (Philadelphia, J. B. Lippincott Company, 1870).

22 Welles, I, 268.

[23] *O.R.N.*, Series 1, XI, 222.

[24] Diary of J. C. Gregg, National Archives.

[25] Roderick S. McCook to his wife, December 20, 1864. This letter is in the Katherine McCook Knox Papers in the Manuscript Division, Library of Congress.

[26] *O.R.N.*, Series 1, XI, 243.

[27] Military Historical Society of Massachusetts Papers, IX, 359.

[28] Diary of Midshipman Clarence Cary.

[29] Maffitt, p. 347.

[30] *O.R.N.*, Series 1, XI, 223.

[31] Military Historical Society of Massachusetts Papers, XI, 359.

[32] *Stories Old and New of the Cape Fear Region,* by Louis T. Moore.

[33] Papers of Joseph Bloomfield Osborn, Manuscript Division, Library of Congress.

[34] *O.R.N.*, Series 1, XI, 223.

[35] The distance given here is taken from the report of Commander Rhind. Coast Survey maps give the position of the *Louisiana* after she anchored as two hundred fifty yards from the fort and seventy-five yards from the beach, while an Army War records map places it at eight hundred thirty yards from the fort and one hundred forty yards from shore.

[36] Lamb later wrote: "I had a good opportunity to note the position of the vessel and considered her a mile from the fort. General Butler, some years after the war, informed me that the wreck was found and her exact position known, but I think the remains of the *Modern Greece* were mistaken for her and that nothing was left of this vessel." Military Historical Society of Massachusetts Papers, IX, 360.

[37] *O.R.N.*, Series 1, XI, 371.

[38] From an article by Lieutenant James Parker in *Personal Recollections of the War of the Rebellion,* Military Order of the Loyal Legion Papers (New York, G. P. Putnam's Sons, 1897), p. 107.

[39] *O.R.N.*, Series 1, XI, 249.

[40] *The Old Navy and the New,* by Rear Admiral Daniel Ammen (Philadelphia, J. B. Lippincott Company, 1891), p. 403.

[41] Military Historical Society of Massachusetts Papers, IX, 362.

[42] *O.R.N.*, Series 1, XI, 225.

[43] *Ibid.,* p. 368.

[44] *A Sailor's Log,* by Robley D. Evans (New York, D. Appleton Company, 1901), p. 80.

[45] Porter obviously was writing in the excitement of battle, and with his usual wildness of claim, for Confederate records indi-

cate no magazines were damaged or exploded. As for the rate of firing, Lamb said that because of his limited supply of ammunition, he ordered each gun that bore on a ship to fire every thirty minutes, unless the fleet made an attempt to run past, when every gun should be fired as rapidly as accuracy would permit. Military Historical Society of Massachusetts Papers, IX, 362. His ammunition consisted of three thousand six hundred shot and shell for his forty-four heavy guns. For a one-hundred-and-fifty-pounder Armstrong, looked upon as the most effective of his pieces, he had only thirteen shells. *B. & L.,* IV, 647.

46 *O.R.N.,* Series 1, XI, 360.

47 *Ibid.,* p. 253.

48 *B. & L.,* IV, 657, and *O.R.N.,* Series 1, XI, 368.

49 Military Historical Society of Massachusetts Papers, IX, 365.

50 *O.R.N.,* Series 1, XI, 363.

51 Military Historical Society of Massachusetts Papers, IX, 364.

52 Flag Pond Hill Battery was called Battery Anderson by the Southerners.

53 *O.R.N.,* Series 1, XI, 250.

54 *Ibid.,* p. 333.

55 Lamb criticized General Bragg for permitting this landing without opposition. He afterward reported that Whiting had ridden over the ground with him often and had helped him select sites for batteries and covered ways, and had pointed out to him where the enemy would land on the beach beyond the range of the fort's guns, a prediction that proved correct. "It seems incomprehensible," Lamb commented, "that General Bragg should have allowed the Federal troops . . . to have made a frolic of their landing on the soil of North Carolina." *S.H.S.P.,* XXI, 266.

56 Colonel Lamb said of these boys: "They should never have been called out; it was robbing the cradle." *Ibid.,* p. 268.

57 Diary of Clarence Cary, National Archives.

58 Scharf, p. 419, and *O.R.N.,* Series 1, XI, 373.

59 *Ibid.,* p. 258.

60 *Ibid.,* p. 368.

61 *Ibid.,* p. 274.

62 The flag and courier incidents received mention in a report Porter prepared that night: "General Weitzel advanced his skirmish line within fifty yards of the fort, while the garrison was kept in their bombproofs by the fire of the Navy, and so closely that three or four men of the picket line ventured upon the parapet and through the sally port of the work, capturing a horse, which they brought off, killing the orderly, who was the bearer of a dis-

patch from the chief of artillery of General Whiting to bring a light battery within the fort, and also brought away from the parapet the flag of the fort."

Colonel Lamb, writing in *B. & L.*, IV, 646, made the following comment on Porter's report: "This piece of romance was sent North, and has gotten a lodgment in current history, and is actually repeated by General Grant in his *Memoirs,* though General Butler corrected the error in his official report of January 3, 1865. No Federal soldier entered Fort Fisher Christmas day except as a prisoner. The courier was sent out of the fort without my knowledge, and was killed and his horse captured within the enemy's lines. The flag captured was a small company flag, placed on the extreme left of the work, and which was carried away and thrown off the parapet by an enfilading shot from the Navy. It was during a terrific bombardment of the land face, when I had ordered my men to cover themselves behind parapet and traverses, as well as in the bombproofs."

[63] *Ibid.,* p. 643.

[64] *O.R.N.,* Series 1, XI, 251.

[65] *Ibid.,* p. 318.

[66] *Ibid.,* p. 252.

[67] *Ibid.,* p. 263.

[68] *Ibid.,* p. 259.

[69] Colonel Lamb blamed General Bragg for the escape of the men left on the peninsula. In an address delivered at Wilmington in 1893, he said: "It is incomprehensible why he should have allowed the seven hundred demoralized troops who were forced to remain on the beach on the night of December 26 to escape unmolested." *S.H.S.P.,* XXI, 267.

[70] *O.R.N.,* Series 1, XI, 261.

[71] *Ibid.,* p. 263.

[72] Log of the U.S.S. *Britannia. Ibid.,* p. 353.

[73] *Ibid.,* p. 263.

[74] *Ibid.,* p. 388.

[75] *Ibid.,* p. 394.

[76] *Ibid.,* p. 265.

CHAPTER TWENTY-FOUR

[1] Military Historical Society of Massachusetts Papers, IX, 287.

[2] *O.R.N.,* Series 1, XI, 405.

[3] *Ibid.,* p. 505.

4 *Ibid.,* p. 246.

5 *Ibid.*

6 This seaman was John T. Smith, assistant engineer of the U.S.S. *Wabash.* A copy of his letter to his mother, dated January 16, 1865, was furnished the author by Miss Cornelia B. Rose, Jr., secretary of the Arlington County, Virginia, Historical Society.

7 Military Historical Society of Massachusetts Papers, IX, 371.

8 *O.R.N.,* Series 1, XI, 526.

9 *Ibid.,* p. 433.

10 Military Historical Society of Massachusetts Papers, IX, 372.

11 *Ibid.,* p. 278.

12 *Ibid.,* p. 371.

13 *B. & L.,* IV, 649.

14 Military Historical Society of Massachusetts Papers, IX, 279.

15 *B. & L.,* IV, 649.

16 Whiting later would hurl grave charges against Bragg and ask for an investigation. In a letter to General Lee, he said of his fellow officer: "In all of his career of failure and defeat from Pensacola out, there has been no such chance missed and no such stupendous disaster." *O.R.N.,* Series 1, XI, 594.

17 Military Historical Society of Massachusetts Papers, IX, 374.

18 *B. & L.,* IV, 650.

19 *O.R.N.,* Series 1, XI, 593.

20 Commander Zera L. Turner, writing of the battle, said: "From the manner in which the seamen were armed, it is clear to my mind that the admiral intended the movement as a feint to draw off the major portion of the garrison under the mistaken idea that it was a combined naval and military attack. As such it was an entire success and enabled the Army to get possession of seven traverses before they encountered serious opposition." Military Order of Loyal Legion Papers, War Paper No. 25.

21 *A Sailor's Log,* by Robley D. Evans (New York, D. Appleton Company, 1901), p. 86.

22 *O.R.N.,* Series 1, XI, 451.

23 Lamb later wrote: "There was no ditch, merely a dry depression in front of the berme where sand had been dug out to repair work." See footnote, *B. & L.,* IV, 660.

24 *Ibid.,* p. 661.

25 *O.R.N.,* Series 1, XI, 477.

26 Lieutenant Commander James Parker. *Ibid.,* p. 499.

27 *B. & L.,* IV, 650.

28 *O.R.N.,* Series 1, XI, 499

29 Edward J. Harkness in *Military Essays and Recollections,* Mili-

tary Order of the Loyal Legion Papers (Chicago, A. C. McClurg and Company, 1894), II, 173.

[30] *O.R.N.*, Series 1, XI, 500.

[31] *B. & L.*, IV, 631.

[32] *B. & L.*, IV, 653.

[33] Letters of Asa Beetham, Manuscript Division, Library of Congress.

[34] Assistant Engineer John T. Smith of the U.S.S. *Wabash* to his mother, Manuscript Division, Library of Congress.

[35] John W. Grattan Papers, Manuscript Division, Library of Congress.

[36] Assistant Engineer John T. Smith to his mother.

[37] *Ibid.*

[38] From testimony given at the Army investigation of the magazine explosion. See *O.R.*, Series 1, XLVI, Pt. 1, 430.

[39] His wounds and his capture meant the end for General Whiting. He died while a prisoner at Fort Columbus in New York Harbor, March 10, 1865.

[40] *O.R.N.*, Series 1, XI, 444. Lamb, in a public address in 1893, said the Federals lost "by their own statement" 1,445 killed, wounded, and missing. See Military Historical Society of Massachusetts Papers, IX, 290.

[41] On January 19, 1933, this flag was formally returned to the people of Wilmington by Alexander D. Lathrop, of Stockport, New York, into whose possession it had come many years earlier. *Stories Old and New of the Cape Fear Region*, by Louis T. Moore, chairman of the New Hanover Historical Commission, Wilmington, North Carolina.

[42] *O.R.N.*, Series 1, XI, 441.

[43] *Ibid.*

CHAPTER TWENTY-FIVE

[1] Scharf, p. 489.

[2] *O.R.N.*, Series 1, XI, 632.

[3] *Ibid.*, p. 663.

[4] *Ibid.*, p. 658.

[5] *Ibid.*, p. 645.

[6] *Ibid.*, XII, 183.

[7] *Ibid.*, XVI, 250.

[8] Military Order of the Loyal Legion Papers (New York, privately printed, 1891), p. 280.

9 Diary of Admiral Dahlgren. *O.R.N.*, Series 1, XVI, 369.

10 *Ibid.*, p. 258.

11 *Ibid.*, p. 265.

12 Horatio L. Wait in *Military Essays and Recollections* (Chicago, A. C. McClurg and Company, 1891), I, 208.

13 These words were used by Beall himself in a letter he wrote shortly before his death. See *O.R.*, Series 2, VIII, 398.

14 *Ibid.*

15 *Ibid.*

16 *Ibid.*, XVI, 282.

17 *Ibid.*, III, 444.

18 *The Naval History of the Civil War*, by David D. Porter (New York, The Sherman Publishing Company, 1886), p. 797.

19 *O.R.N.*, Series 1, XII, 191.

20 *Service Afloat*, by Raphael Semmes (New York, P. J. Kenedy, 1903), p. 809.

21 See the report of Lieutenant Read, dated April 22, 1865, in *O.R.N.*, Series 1, XXII, 168.

22 *Ibid.*, p. 169.

23 *Ibid.*

24 *Ibid.*, p. 161.

25 Narrative of William Biggio, found in *Blockade Running During the Civil War*, by Francis B. C. Bradlee (Salem, Massachusetts, The Essex Institute, 1925), p. 153.

26 *O.R.N.*, Series 1, XXII, 158.

27 *Ibid.*, p. 165.

28 Report of Detective Allan Pinkerton. *Ibid.*, p. 152.

29 Narrative of William Biggio, *Blockade Running During the Civil War*, p. 153.

30 "The Cruise of the Clarence-Tacony-Archer," by Paymaster Robert H. Woods, an article published in the Richmond *Dispatch* of November 24, 1895.

31 Narrative of William Biggio, *Blockade Running During the Civil War*, p. 153.

CHAPTER TWENTY-SIX

1 *O.R.N.*, Series 1, III, 829.

2 *Ibid.*

3 *Ibid.*

4 *Ibid.*, Series 2, II, 701.

5 *Ibid.*

6 *Ibid.,* Series 1, III, 775.

7 *Ibid.,* p. 832.

8 *Ibid.,* p. 747.

9 *Rear Admiral Samuel Francis du Pont,* by H. A. du Pont (New York, National Americana Society, 1926), p. 293.

10 *O.R.N.,* Series 1, III, 576.

11 *Ibid.,* p. 836. Despite charges of piracy from Gideon Welles (*ibid.,* p. 602), the *Shenandoah* finally was permitted to become a ship of peace. She later was sold by the United States to the Sultan of Zanzibar, and in 1879 was lost in a storm in the Indian Ocean. Scharf, p. 812.

12 This quotation is from an article by Charles W. Stewart, copyrighted by the United Service, and now on file in the Navy Department Library, Washington, D.C.

Bibliography

GENERAL HISTORICAL WORKS

Abbot, Willis J., *The Blue Jackets of '61* (New York, Dodd, Mead and Company, 1886).

Abbott, John S. C., *The History of the Civil War in America* (New York, Henry Bill, 1866).

Albion, Robert G., and Pope, Jennie Barres, *Sea Lanes in Wartime* (New York, W. W. Norton & Company, Inc., 1942).

Alden, Carroll Stors, and Earle, Ralph, *Makers of Naval Tradition* (Boston, Ginn and Company, 1925).

Ammen, Daniel, *The Old Navy and the New* (Philadelphia, J. B. Lippincott Company, 1891).

Battles and Leaders of the Civil War (New York, The Century Company, 1887).

Bigelow, John, *France and the Confederate Navy* (New York, Harper and Brothers, 1888).

Boynton, Dr. Charles B., *The History of the Navy During the Rebellion* (New York, D. Appleton and Company, 1867).

Bradlee, Francis B. C., *Blockade Running During the Civil War* (Salem, Massachusetts, The Essex Institute, 1925).

———*The Kearsarge-Alabama Battle* (Salem, Massachusetts, The Essex Institute, 1921).

439

Brockett, Dr. Linus Pierpont, *The Camp, the Battlefield, and the Hospital* (Philadelphia, The National Publishing Company, 1866).

Bulloch, James D., *The Secret Service of the Confederate States in Europe* (New York, G. P. Putnam's Sons, 1884).

Carse, Robert, *Blockade* (New York, Rinehart & Company, Inc., 1958).

Church, W. C., *The Life of John Ericcson* (New York, Charles Scribner's Sons, 1891).

Coffin, Charles Carlton, *Four Years of Fighting* (Boston, Ticknor and Fields, 1866).

Confederate Blockade Running Through Bermuda 1861-1865, edited by Frank E. Vandiver (Austin, University of Texas Press, 1947).

Confidential Correspondence of Gustavus Vasa Fox, edited by Robert Means Thompson (New York, De Vinne Press, 1920).

Cranwell, John Phillips, *Spoilers of the Sea* (New York, W. W. Norton & Company, Inc., 1941).

Daly, Robert Walter, *How the Merrimac Won* (New York, Thomas Y. Crowell Company, 1957).

Deeds of Valor—How America's Heroes Won the Medal of Honor (Detroit, Michigan, The Perrien-Keydel Company, 1905).

Dudley, Dean, *Officers of the Union Army and Navy* (Boston, L. Prang and Company, 1862).

Dufour, Charles L., *The Night the War Was Lost* (New York, Doubleday & Company, Inc., 1960).

Du Pont, H. A., *Rear Admiral Samuel Francis du Pont* (New York, National Americana Society, 1926).

Frothingham, Jessie Peabody, *Seafighters from Drake to Farragut* (New York, Charles Scribner's Sons, 1902).

Fullam, George Townley, *The Cruise of the Alabama* (Liverpool, England, Lee and Nightingale, 1863).

Gilchrist, Robert C., *The Confederate Defense of Morris Island* (Charleston, South Carolina, The News and Courier Book Presses, 1884).

Gosnell, Harpur Allen, *Guns of the Western Waters* (Baton Rouge, Louisiana State University Press, 1949).

Hackett, Frank Warren, *Deck and Field* (Washington, W. H. Lowdermilk and Company, 1909).

Hamersly, Lewis Randolph, *The Records of Living Officers* (Philadelphia, J. B. Lippincott Company, 1870).

Hanks, Charles C., *Blockaders off the American Coast,* U. S. Naval Institute Proceedings (Menasha, Wisconsin, 1941).

Haywood, Philip D., *The Cruise of the Alabama* (Boston, Houghton Mifflin Company, 1886).

Headley, Joel Tyler, *Farragut and Our Naval Commanders* (New York, E. B. Treat and Company, 1867).

Hero Tales of the American Soldier and Sailor (Philadelphia, Century Manufacturing Company, 1899).

Hill, Frederic Stanhope, *Twenty Historic Ships* (New York, G. P. Putnam's Sons, The Knickerbocker Press, 1902).

Hill, Jim Dan, *Sea Dogs of the Sixties* (Minneapolis, The University of Minnesota Press, 1935).

History of the Ram Fleet and the Mississippi Marine Brigade in the War for the Union on the Mississippi and Its Tributaries (St. Louis, Society of Survivors, 1907).

Hubbell, Raynor, *Confederate Stamps, Old Letters, and History* (published at Griffin, Georgia).

Humphrey, Willis C., *Military and Naval Operations During the Civil War* (Detroit, C. H. Smith and Company, 1886).

Johnson, John, *The Defense of Charleston Harbor* (Charleston, Walker Evans & Cogswell Company, 1890).

Jones, Katherine M., *Heroines of Dixie* (Indianapolis, The Bobbs-Merrill Company, Inc., 1955).

Jones, Samuel, *The Siege of Charleston* (New York, The Neale Company, 1911).

Lewis, Charles L., *David Glasgow Farragut, Our First Admiral* (Annapolis, U. S. Naval Institute, 1943).

Lonn, Ella, *Foreigners in the Confederacy* (Chapel Hill, University of North Carolina Press, 1940).

MacNeill, Ben Dixon, *The Hatterasman* (Winston-Salem, North Carolina, John F. Blair, 1958).

Mahan, Alfred T., *The Navy in the Civil War* (New York, Charles Scribner's Sons, 1895).

Matthews, Franklin, *Our Navy in Time of War* (New York, D. Appleton and Company, 1899).

Merrill, James M., *The Rebel Shore* (Boston, Little, Brown & Company, 1957).

Murphy, D. F., *Full Report of the Trial of William Smith for Piracy* (Philadelphia, King and Baird, 1861).

Ninety Years of Marine Insurance (New York, Triggs Color Printing Corporation, 1932).

Olmstead, Frederic Law, *Hospital Transports* (Boston, Ticknor and Fields, 1863).

Orvin, Maxwell Clayton, *South Carolina Waters* (Charleston, Southern Printing and Publishing Company, 1961).

Parker, Foxhall A., *The Battle of Mobile Bay and the Capture of Forts Powell, Gaines, and Morgan* (Boston, A. Williams and Company, 1878).

Parrott, Enoch G., *Description and Cruise of the U.S.S. Augusta* (New York, Francis McCarten, 1876).

Photographic History of the Civil War, The (New York, The Review of Reviews Company, 1911).

Porter, David D., *The Naval History of the Civil War* (New York, The Sherman Publishing Company, 1886).

Porter, John W. H., *A Record of Events in Norfolk County, Virginia* (Portsmouth, Virginia, W. A. Fisher, 1892).

Pratt, Fletcher, *Civil War on Western Waters* (New York, Henry Holt and Company, 1956).

Quad, M., *Field, Fort, and Fleet* (Detroit, Detroit Free Press Publishing Company, 1885).

Robinson, William Morrison, Jr., *The Confederate Privateers* (New Haven, Yale University Press, 1928).

Ross, FitzGerald, *Cities and Camps of the United States* (Urbana, University of Illinois Press, 1958).

Sands, Benjamin Franklin, *From Reefer to Rear Admiral* (New York, Frederick A. Stokes Company, 1899).

Scharf, J. Thomas, *History of the Confederate States Navy* (New York, Rogers and Sherwood, 1887).

Semmes, Raphael, *Service Afloat* (New York, P. J. Kenedy, 1903).

———*The Cruise of the Alabama and Sumter* (London, Saunders, Otley and Company, 1864).

Sinclair, Arthur, *Two Years on the Alabama* (Boston, Lee and Shepard, 1895).

Soley, James Russell, *The Blockade and the Cruisers* (New York, Charles Scribner's Sons, 1890).

Sprunt, James, *Chronicles of the Cape Fear River* (Raleigh, North Carolina, Edwards and Broughton Printing Company, 1914).

———*Derelicts* (Wilmington, North Carolina, 1920).

Starr, Louis M., *Bohemian Brigade* (New York, Alfred A. Knopf, Inc., 1954).

Stern, Philip Van Doren, *Secret Missions of the Civil War* (Chicago, Rand, McNally & Company, 1959).

Trial of the Officers and Crew of the Privateer Savannah, as reported by A. F. Warburton (New York, Baker and Godwin, 1862).

Vail, I. E., *Three Years on the Blockade* (New York, The Abbey Press, 1902).

Van Alstyne, Lawrence, *Diary of an Enlisted Man* (New Haven,

Connecticut, The Tuttle, Morehouse and Taylor Company, 1910).

West, R. S., Jr., *Gideon Welles: Lincoln's Navy Department* (Indianapolis, The Bobbs-Merrill Company, Inc., 1943).

———*Mr. Lincoln's Navy* (New York, Longmans, Green & Co., Inc., 1957).

———*The Second Admiral: A Life of David Dixon Porter* (New York, Coward-McCann, Inc., 1937).

White, E. V., *The First Iron-clad Engagement in the World* (New York, J. S. Ogilvie Publishing Company, 1906).

White, William Chapman and Ruth, *Tin Can on a Shingle* (New York, E. P. Dutton & Company, Inc., 1957).

Wilson, Frank I., *Sketches of Nassau* (Raleigh, North Carolina, 1864).

LETTERS, MANUSCRIPTS, AND PAMPHLETS

Abstract of U.S.S. *Tioga's* log, on file at National Archives.

Address by Joseph Adams Smith on the *Alabama* and *Kearsarge,* delivered before the Union League of Philadelphia in 1906.

Anonymous journal kept on the U.S.S. *Carondelet,* Manuscript Division, Library of Congress.

Augustus C. Evans Papers, Manuscript Division, University of North Carolina Library.

Buchanan-Screven Papers, Manuscript Division, University of North Carolina Library.

Court-martial of Commodore Charles Wilkes, House of Representatives Executive Document No. 102, Thirty-eighth Congress, First Session.

David D. Porter's Private Journal, Manuscript Division, Library of Congress.

Edmund Rose Calhoun Papers, Manuscript Division, Library of Congress.

E. N. Kellogg Letters, Manuscript Division, Library of Congress.

F. A. Roe Papers, Manuscript Division, Library of Congress.

Frederick Milnes Edge letter on destruction of United States carrying trade, National Archives.

George W. Gift Papers, Manuscript Division, University of North Carolina Library.

Hayes, Rear Admiral John B., "Lee Against the Sea," paper read before the District of Columbia Civil War Round Table.

Insurgent Privateers in Foreign Ports, House of Representatives

Executive Document No. 103, Thirty-seventh Congress, Second Session.

"Ironclads of the Sixties," papers prepared by Thomas W. Green, and read before the Confederate Research Club, London, England, in 1959.

James B. Jones letter, Manuscript Division, University of North Carolina Library.

James Rider Randall Papers, Manuscript Division, University of North Carolina Library.

John Mercer Brooke Papers, Manuscript Division, University of North Carolina Library.

John Rapier Letters, copied from originals in possession of Mrs. Ted Trigg, Mobile, Alabama.

John W. Grattan Papers, Manuscript Division, Library of Congress.

Journal of Edward B. Latch, National Archives.

Journal of George F. Emmons, National Archives.

Journal of the *Oneida,* Manuscript Division, University of North Carolina Library.

Journals of Carpenter's Mate William M. C. Philbrick, National Archives.

Journals of Levi Hayden, Manuscript Division, Library of Congress.

Katherine McCook Knox Papers, Manuscript Division, Library of Congress.

Letter of G. J. Van Brunt, furnished the author through the kindness of W. Norman FitzGerald, Jr., Milwaukee, Wisconsin.

Letter of S. D. Greene, National Historical Foundation.

Letters of Asa Beetham, Manuscript Division, Library of Congress.

Letters of George Hamilton Perkins (Concord, New Hampshire, The Rumford Press, 1901).

Letters of Henry L. Graves, Manuscript Division, University of North Carolina Library.

Letters of Samuel F. du Pont, furnished the author through the kindness of Rear Admiral John B. Hayes, of Annapolis, Maryland.

Letters of S. P. Gillett, Manuscript Division, University of North Carolina Library.

Lloyd Phoenix Biography, Manuscript Division, Library of Congress.

Log of the U.S. ram *Lancaster,* National Archives.

Log of the U.S.S. *Aroostook,* National Archives.

Log of the U.S.S. *Hartford,* National Archives.

Log of the U.S.S. *Santee,* National Archives.

Maffitt Papers, Manuscript Division, University of North Carolina Library.

Marke de Wolf Stevenson Papers, Manuscript Division, University of North Carolina Library.
Matthew Fontaine Maury Papers, Manuscript Division, Library of Congress.
Messages and Papers of the Confederacy (Nashville, United States Publishing Company, 1905).
Military Historical Society of Massachusetts Papers.
Military Order of the Loyal Legion Papers.
Napoleon Smith Papers, Manuscript Division, University of North Carolina Library.
"Naval Lieutenant Matthew Fontaine Maury," by Catherine Cate Coblentz, Manuscript Division, Library of Congress.
Official Records of the Union and Confederate Navies in the War of the Rebellion (Washington, Government Printing Office, 1894).
Papers of Joseph Bloomfield Osborn, Manuscript Division, Library of Congress.
Peter Evans Smith Papers, Manuscript Division, University of North Carolina Library.
"President Lincoln's Campaign Against the Merrimac," pamphlet prepared by Dr. Chester D. Bradley, curator of the Casemate Museum, Fort Monroe, Virginia.
Radford Papers, abstract from log book of *Battery Brooke,* National Archives.
Rhode Island Soldiers and Sailors Historical Society Papers.
Ruffin Thompson Papers, Manuscript Division, University of North Carolina Library.
Rupert C. Jarvis, "The Alabama and the Law," paper read before the Confederate Research Club, London, England, in 1959.
"The Merrimack," a manuscript by Colonel George M. Brooke, Jr., grandson of John Mercer Brooke.
"The Virginia or Merrimac; Her Real Projector," by John Mercer Brooke.
T. O. Selfridge Papers, Manuscript Division, Library of Congress.
Violet G. Alexander Papers, Manuscript Division, University of North Carolina Library.
War Papers (Portland, Maine, The Thurston Print, 1898).
William Calder Papers, Manuscript Division, Library of Congress.

BIOGRAPHIES, DIARIES, MEMOIRS, ETC.

Alden, Carroll Storrs, *George Hamilton Perkins* (Boston, Houghton Mifflin Company, 1914).

Autobiography of George Dewey (New York, Charles Scribner's Sons, 1913).

Barr, James W., *Diaries, Letters, and Recollections of the War Between the States,* Vol. 3 of the Winchester-Frederick County Historical Society Papers, privately published by the Society, Winchester, Virginia, 1955.

Batten, Dr. John M., *Reminiscences of Two Years in the United States Navy* (Lancaster, Pennsylvania, Inquirer Printing and Publishing Company, 1881).

Butts, Frank B., *The First Cruise at Sea and the Loss of the Ironclad Monitor* (Providence, Rhode Island, Sidney S. Rider, 1878).

Castlen, Harriet Gift, *Hope Bids Me Onward* (Savannah, Georgia, Chatham Printing Company, 1945).

Davis, C. H., *Life of Henry Davis* (Boston, Houghton Mifflin Company, 1899).

Diary of A. L. Drayton, Manuscript Division, Library of Congress.

Diary of Current Events, by I. T. Gordon, National Archives.

Diary of Edwin F. Ludwig, Manuscript Division, Library of Congress.

Diary of Gideon Welles, edited by Howard K. Beale, assisted by Alan W. Brownsword (New York, W. W. Norton & Company, Inc., 1960).

Diary of H. Henry Kloeppel, Manuscript Division, Library of Congress.

Diary of Isaac DeGraff, National Archives.

Diary of J. C. Gregg, National Archives.

Diary of John A. Wilson, National Archives.

Diary of Oscar Smith, Manuscript Division, Library of Congress.

Diary of Thomas F. Galway, in possession of family.

Diary of William B. Cushing, National Archives.

Diary of William R. Stewart, Manuscript Division, University of North Carolina Library.

Ellicott, John M., *The Life of John Ancrum Winslow* (New York, G. P. Putnam's Sons, 1902).

Evans, Robley D., *A Sailor's Log* (New York, D. Appleton and Company, 1901).

Farenholt, Oscar Walter, *The Monitor Catskill, a Year's Reminiscences, 1863-1864* (San Francisco, Shannon-Conney Printing Company, 1912).

Farragut, Loyall, *The Life of David Glasgow Farragut* (New York, D. Appleton and Company, 1879).

Franklin, S. R., *Memoirs of a Rear Admiral* (New York, Harper and Brothers, 1898).

Gordon, I. T., *Diary of Current Events*, National Archives.

Hill, Frederick Stanhope, *Twenty Years at Sea* (Boston, Houghton Mifflin Company, 1891).

Hoppin, James Mason, *Life of Andrew Hull Foote* (New York, Harper and Brothers, 1874).

John Taylor Wood Diary, Manuscript Division, University of North Carolina Library.

Jones, John Beauchamp, *A Rebel War Clerk's Diary* (New York, Old Hickory Bookshop, 1935).

Journal of Midshipman Clarence Cary, National Archives.

Kell, John McIntosh, *Recollections of a Naval Life* (Washington, The Neale Company, 1900).

Letterbook of Commander J. N. Barney, National Archives.

Life of Charles Henry Davis, by Charles H. Davis, (Boston, Houghton Mifflin Company, 1899).

McGuire, Judith White, *Diary of a Southern Refugee* (New York, E. J. Hale and Son, 1868).

Maffitt, Emma Martin, *The Life and Services of John Newland Maffitt* (New York, The Neale Publishing Company, 1906).

Meade, Rebecca Paulding, *Life of Hiram Paulding* (New York, The Baker and Taylor Company, 1910).

Memoir and Correspondence of Charles Steedman (Cambridge, Massachusetts, privately printed at The Riverside Press, 1912).

Memoirs of James H. Tomb, Manuscript Division, University of North Carolina Library.

Memoirs of Thomas O. Selfridge, Jr. (New York, G. P. Putnam's Sons, The Knickerbocker Press, 1924).

Moore, Louis T., *Stories Old and New of the Cape Fear Region.*

Morgan, James Morris, *Recollections of a Rebel Reefer* (Boston, Houghton Mifflin Company, 1917).

Paine, Albert Bigelow, *A Sailor of Fortune,* memoirs of B. S. Osbon, Manuscript Division, Library of Congress.

Pasha, Hobart, *Sketches from My Life* (New York, D. Appleton and Company, 1887).

Reminiscences of George C. Remey, Manuscript Division, Library of Congress.

Reminiscences of the Old Navy, by Edgar Stanton Maclay (New York, G. P. Putnam's Sons, 1898).

Rochelle, Captain James Henry, *Life of Rear Admiral John Randolph Tucker* (Washington, The Neale Publishing Company, 1903).

Scales, Cordelia Lewis, *Dear Darling Loulie* (Boulder, Colorado, Ben Gray Lumpkin, 1955).

Smith, H. D., and others, *Under Both Flags* (Philadelphia, Peoples' Publishing Company, 1896).

Stewart, William H., *A Pair of Blankets* (New York, Broadway Publishing Company, 1911).

The Story of American Heroism (New York, The Werner Company, 1896).

Walke, Rear Admiral Henry, *Naval Scenes and Reminiscences of the Civil War in the United States* (New York, F. R. Reed and Company, 1877).

Watson, William, *The Adventures of a Blockade Runner* (New York, The Macmillan Company, 1892).

Wells, Charles W., *Army Life of an Illinois Soldier* (Washington, Globe Printing Company, 1906).

Wilkinson, John, *The Narrative of a Blockade Runner* (New York, Sheldon and Company, 1877).

Worden, J. L., and others, *The Monitor and the Merrimac* (New York, Harper and Brothers, 1912).

Wyeth, John Allen, *Life of Lieutenant General Nathan Bedford Forrest* (New York, Harper and Brothers, 1899).

NEWSPAPERS AND PERIODICAL PUBLICATIONS

All Hands, Bureau of Personnel Information Bulletin, U.S. Navy.

Atlanta *Constitution.*

Baltimore *Sun.*

The Bellman.

"Burning of the Gunboat Underwriter," by D. B. Conrad, article published in *Under Both Flags* (Philadelphia, People's Publishing Company, 1896).

Century magazine.

Civil War History.

Civil War Times.

The Confederacy magazine

Confederate Veteran.

Confederate War Journal (New York, War Journal Publishing Company, 1893).

Down Home in North Carolina, state magazine, 24, VI, 13 (Raleigh, North Carolina, 1956).

The Galaxy magazine.

Harper's magazine.

The Independent magazine.

The Journal of American History.

McClure's magazine.
Maryland Historical Society magazine.
Mobile *Daily Herald.*
Montgomery (Alabama) *Weekly Mail.*
Munsey magazine.
New Orleans *Daily Picayune.*
New Orleans *Daily True Delta.*
New York *Evening Post.*
New York *Herald.*
New York *Tribune.*
The New York Times.
Putnam's Monthly.
Richmond *Dispatch.*
Savannah *Republican.*
Scribner's magazine.
South Carolina Historical Magazine.
Southern Historical Society Papers.
The State magazine.
Washington *Evening Star.*
Washington *Intelligencer.*

Index

451